S

More Women in Literature:

Criticism of the Seventies

by

CAROL FAIRBANKS

The Scarecrow Press, Inc.
Metuchen, N.J. & London
1979

Library of Congress Cataloging in Publication Data

Fairbanks, Carol, 1935-
    More women in literature.

    Continues Women in literature.
    "General bibliography" : p.
    1. Women in literature--Bibliography. 2. Women
authors--Bibliography. I. Title.
Z6514. C5W644   [PN56. 5. W64]   809'. 933'52
ISBN 0-8108-1193-6   78-26405

For Mary Jordan Meiser and Eric Moon

who have provided, respectively,

personal and professional support.

803375

CONTENTS

ACKNOWLEDGMENTS

I would like to thank my typist, Caryl M. Laubach, who has once again made sacrifices in order to meet deadlines and has coerced commas, colons, semi-colons and parentheses into appropriate formation.

I would also like to express my gratitude 1) to the English Department Personnel Committee and especially my chairperson, Douglas A. Pearson, Jr., for continuing to hire me although I no longer speak with nouns and verbs but with authors, titles, and volume numbers; 2) to Dawn E. Whited, a graduate assistant who received a fall semester 1977 assignment to work with me on a portion of the bibliography; 3) to Richard A. Bell, Eugene A. Engeldinger, and Frada L. Mozenter of the University of Wisconsin-Eau Claire Reference Department, and Esther F. Stineman, Women's Studies Librarian for the University of Wisconsin System, who helped search, in some cases, for the unsearchable; and 4) to my sons, Ted Fairbanks Myers, Lee Fairbanks Myers, and Timothy Edward Myers, who have saved the house from being condemned by the City Health Department and have made no overt moves to have me replaced as Head of Household.

NOTE TO THE READER

Women in Literature: Criticism of the Seventies (published by Scarecrow Press in 1976) included critical and biographical books and articles on approximately 300 writers. The present bibliography, More Women in Literature, significantly extends that work, including citations for over 1000 writers ranging from Sappho--the Greek lyric poet of the sixth century B. C. --to writers publishing in 1977.

While the MLA Bibliography, Abstracts of English Studies, Women's Studies Abstracts, and the Women & Literature annual bibliographies continue to be essential bibliographical resources for students, teachers, and scholars, Women in Literature: Criticism of the Seventies and More Women in Literature, provide a focused and more extensive coverage of recent secondary materials for the analysis of women as characters and writers.

More Women in Literature includes materials published from 1970 through 1977. As in the 1976 edition, the following criteria were applied in selecting citations:

1) Literary criticism examining women characters in relation to other women, to men, to family, to work, to community, to the times and cultures in which they live.

2) Literary criticism examining women characters as myth and symbol.

3) Essays appraising feminist criticism as an approach to literature.

4) Biographical studies of women writers; also biographical studies of men writers if such study is appropriate to the interpretation of their works in relation to women characters.

vii

5) Interviews with women writers.

6) Selected book reviews.

The "General Bibliography" includes works which are comprehensive in nature, providing insights into the literature of a particular period or genre, or providing historical, sociological, psychological and philosophical backgrounds for the study of women in literature.

ACHEBE, CHINUA

Brown, Lloyd W. "The African Woman as Writer."
Canadian Journal of African Studies 9 no. 3 (1975):
493-502.

Sarvan, Ponnuthurai. "The Mirror and the Image:
Achebe's 'Girls at War.'" Studies in Short Fiction
14 (Summer 1977): 277-279.

ADAMS, ALICE

Bernays, Anne. "A Sneaky Novel About Love? Sex?
Growth and Change?" Harvard Magazine, February
1975, p. 59.

Casey, Constance. "Interview with Alice Adams." San
Francisco Review of Books 2 (May 1976): 7-10.

Prescott, Peter S. "Edgy Woman." Newsweek, 3 February 1975, p. 64. (Review of Families and Survivors.)

Robinson, Jill. "A New Place, a Chillier Season."
Book World, 23 February 1975, p. 3.

ADAMS, GLENDA

Schwartz, Lynne Sharon. "In Short: Lies and Stories."
Ms. 5 (January 1977): 41. (Review of Lies and
Stories.)

ADAMS, HENRY

Banta, Martha. "They Shall Have Faces, Minds, and
(One Day) Flesh: Women in Late Nineteenth-century
and Early Twentieth-century American Literature."

In What Manner of Woman: Essays on English and American Life and Literature, pp. 235-270. Edited by Marlene Springer. New York: New York University Press, 1977.

Barber, David S. "Henry Adams' Esther: The Nature of Individuality and Immortality." New England Quarterly 45 (June 1972): 477-484.

Bromberger, Eric Aldridge. "An Odour of Old Maid Boston as Literary Symbol." Ph.D. Dissertation, University of California, Los Angeles, 1976.

Chapin, Helen Geracimos. "Mythology and American Realism: Studies in Fiction by Henry Adams, Henry James, and Kate Chopin." Ph.D. Dissertation, The Ohio State University, 1975.

Wasser, Henry. "Science and Religion in Henry Adams's Esther." Markham Review 2 (May 1970).

Wolfe, Patrick. "The Revealing Fiction of Henry Adams." New England Quarterly 49 (September 1976): 399-426.

Wright, Dorothea Curtis. "Visions and Revisions of the 'New Woman' in American Realistic Fiction from 1880 to 1920: A Study in Authorial Attitudes." Ph.D. Dissertation, University of North Carolina at Chapel Hill, 1971.

AESCHYLUS

Dreyfuss, Cecilia Anne Stiborik. "Femina Sapiens in Drama: Aeschylus to Grillparzer." Ph.D. Dissertation, The University of Michigan, 1975.

Gelderman, Carol W. "The Male Nature of Tragedy." Prairie Schooner 49 (Fall 1975): 220-227.

Millett, Kate. Sexual Politics. New York: Avon, 1971.

Pomeroy, Sarah B. Goddesses, Whores, Wives, and Slaves: Women in Classical Antiquity. New York: Schocken Books, 1975.

AI (Florence Anthony)

French, Gary. Epoch 23 (Spring 1974): 338-340. (Review of Cruelty.)

Ostricker, Alicia. New York Times Book Review, 17 February 1974, p. 7. (Review of Cruelty.)

Redmond, Eugene. "Five Black Poets: History, Consciousness, Love, and Harshness. " Parnassus: Poetry in Review 3 (Spring/Summer 1975): 153-172.

Walker, Alice. Ms. 2 (June 1974): 41-42. (Review of Cruelty.)

AIDOO, AMA ATA

Adelugba, Dapo. "Language and Drama: Ama Ata Aidoo. " In African Literature Today No. 8: Drama in Africa, pp. 72-84. Edited by E. D. Jones. New York: Africana, 1976.

Brown, Lloyd W. "The African Woman as Writer. " Canadian Journal of African Studies 9 no. 3 (1975): 494-502.

Graham-White, Anthony. In Contemporary Dramatists, pp. 21-23. Edited by James Vinson. New York: St. Martin's Press, 1973.

Kilson, Marion. "Women and African Literature. " Journal of African Studies 4 (Summer 1977): 161-166.

AINSWORTH, WILLIAM

Garrison, Dee. "Immoral Fiction in the Late Victorian Library. " American Quarterly 28 (Spring 1976): 71-89.

AKHMATOVA, ANNA

Bayley, John. Times Literary Supplement, 16 April 1976, p. 450. (Review of Requiem and Poem Without a Hero.)

Dessaix, Robert. "Akhmatova. " Quadrant 22 (June 1977): 75-77.

Feinberg, Lawrence E. "Measure and Complementarity in Achmatova." Russian Literature 4 (October 1977): 303-314.

Haight, Amanda. Anna Akhmatova: A Poetic Pilgrimage. New York: Oxford University Press, 1976.

Leider, Emily. "Anna Akhmatova: A Clear and Elegant Howl." San Francisco Review of Books 3 (September 1977): 26-28. (Review essay.)

Punin, Nikolai. "In Love with Akhmatova: The Diary of Nikolai Punin." Denver Quarterly 12 (Summer 1977): 257-266.

AKINS, ZOE

Mielech, Ronald Albert. "The Plays of Zoe Akins Rumbold." Ph. D. Dissertation, The Ohio State University, 1974.

Zastrow, Sylvia Virginia Horning. "The Structure of Selected Plays by American Women Playwrights: 1920-1970." Ph. D. Dissertation, Northwestern University, 1975.

ALAS, LEOPOLDO

Hamblin, Ellen N. "Adulterous Heroines in Nineteenth Century Literature: A Comparative Literature Study." Ph. D. Dissertation, The Florida State University, 1977.

Ibarra, Fernando. "Clarín y Azorín: El matrimonio y el papel de la mujer española." Hispania 55 (March 1972): 45-54.

ALBEE, EDWARD

Byars, John A. "Taming of the Shrew and Who's Afraid of Virginia Woolf?" Cimarron Review 21 (1972): 41-48.

Duplessis, Rachel Blau. "In the Bosom of the Family: Contradiction and Resolution in Edward Albee." Minnesota Review 8 (Spring 1977): 133-145.

Fedor, Joan Roberta. "The Importance of the Female
in the Plays of Samuel Beckett, Harold Pinter, and
Edward Albee." Ph.D. Dissertation, University of
Washington, 1976.

ALCOTT, LOUISA MAE

Auerbach, Nina. "Austen and Alcott on Matriarchy:
New Women or New Wives?" Novel 10 (Fall 1976):
6-26.

Gay, Carol. "The Philosopher and His Daughter: Amos
Bronson Alcott and Louisa." Essays in Literature
2 (Fall 1975): 181-191.

Johnson, Diane. New York Times Book Review, 25
July 1976, p. 7. (Review of Plots and Counter-
plots.)

Moers, Ellen. Literary Women. Garden City, N.Y.:
Doubleday, 1976.

Pauly, Thomas H. "Ragged Dick and Little Women:
Idealized Homes and Unwanted Marriages." Journal
of Popular Culture 9, no. 3 (1975): 583-592.

Silver, Nancy. "To Be a Woman: Scarlett O'Hara Revisited: Looking Back at the Books That Taught Me
to Be a Woman." Redbook 146 (December 1975):
52, 54, 56, 59.

Stern, Madeleine, ed. Behind a Mask: The Unknown
Thrillers of Louisa Mae Alcott. New York: Morrow, 1975.

Weintraub, Rodelle. San Francisco Review of Books 1
(November 1975): 10-11. (Review of Behind a Mask.)

ALDRICH, THOMAS BAILEY

Montley, Patricia Ann. "Judith on Broadway: A Comparison of Twentieth Century Dramatic Adaptations
of the Biblical Book of Judith Produced on the New
York Stage (Volumes I and II)." Ph.D. Dissertation,
University of Minnesota, 1975.

ALFIERI, VITTORIO

> Herrera, Bertilia. "Racine, Alfieri, and Schiller: A Comparative Study of Heroines." Ph.D. Dissertation, University of California, Riverside, 1977.

ALGERIA, CIRO

> Jacquette, Jane S. "Literary Archetypes and Female Role Alternatives: The Woman and the Novel in Latin America." In Female and Male in Latin America: Essays, pp. 3-28. Edited by Ann Pescatello. Pittsburgh: University of Pittsburgh Press, 1973.

ALLART, HORTENSE

> Rabine, Leslie Ruth. "The Other Side of the Ideal: Women Writers of Mid-Nineteenth Century France (George Sand, Daniel Stern, Hortense Allart, and Flora Tristan)." Ph.D. Dissertation, Stanford University, 1973.

ALLEN, GRANT

> Calder, Jenni. Women and Marriage in Victorian Fiction. London: Thames & Hudson, 1976.

> Cunningham, A. R. "The 'New Woman Fiction' of the 1890's." Victorian Studies 17 (December 1973): 177-186.

> Fernando, Lloyd. "New Women" in the Late Victorian Novel. University Park: Pennsylvania State University Press, 1977.

ALTA

> Alta. "Like It Is." Small Press Review 3, no. 3 (1972): 1-6.

> "Alta." In The New Woman's Survival Sourcebook, pp. 116-117. Edited by Kirsten Grimstad and Susan Rennie. New York: Alfred A. Knopf, 1975.

> Juhasz, Suzanne. Naked and Fiery Forms: Modern American Poetry by Women, A New Tradition. New York: Harper & Row, 1976.

Piercy, Marge. Forward to I Am Not a Practicing Angel. Trumansburg, New York: Crossing Press, 1975.

Raeschild, Sheila. "Awakened: Sexuality in the New Women's Poetry (Judy Grahn, Alta, Diane Wakoski)." Paper presented at the MLA meeting, San Francisco, December 1975.

ALTHER, LISA

Adams, Alice. Harper 252 (May 1976): 94. (Review of Kinflicks.)

Clemons, Walter. Newsweek, 15 March 1976, p. 91. (Review of Kinflicks.)

Dickstein, Lore. "An Easy Lay, Spiritually Speaking." Ms. 4 (June 1976): 90-93. (Review of Kinflicks.)

Edwards, T. R. New York Review of Books, 1 April 1976, p. 34. (Review of Kinflicks.)

Gray, Paul. Time, 22 March 1976, p. 80. (Review of Kinflicks.)

Grumbach, Doris. Saturday Review, 20 March 1976, p. 22. (Review of Kinflicks.)

Larsen, Anne. "Reeling Through a Daughter's Decade." Village Voice, 8 March 1976, pp. 39-42. (Review of Kinflicks.)

Leonard, John. New York Times Book Review, 14 March 1976, p. 4. (Review of Kinflicks.)

Todd, Richard. Atlantic 237 (May 1976): 106. (Review of Kinflicks.)

AMADI, ELECHI

Brown, Lloyd W. "The African Woman as Writer." Canadian Journal of African Studies 9, no. 3 (1975): 493-502.

Nandakumar, Prema. "Another Image of African Womanhood (An Appreciation of Elechi Amadi's The

<u>Concubine</u>). " <u>African Quarterly</u> 13 (April-June 1973):
38-44.

AMADO, JORGE

Pescatello, Ann. "The <u>Brasileira</u>: Images and Realities
in Writings of <u>Machado de Assis</u> and Jorge Amado. "
In <u>Female and Male in Latin America</u>: Essays,
pp. 29-58. Edited by Ann Pescatello. Pittsburgh:
University of Pittsburgh Press, 1973.

Wolf, Donna M. "Women in Latin American Literature."
<u>Room of One's Own</u> 1 (Fall 1975): 73-83.

ANDERSON, MAXWELL

Loudin, Joanne Marie. "The Changing Role of the
Comic Heroine in American Drama from 1900 to
1940. " Ph.D. Dissertation, University of Washington, 1974.

Shafer, Y. B. "Liberated Women in American Plays of
the Past. " <u>Players Magazine</u> 49 (Spring 1974): 95-
100.

ANDERSON, ROBERT

Leone, Vivien. "Notes from an Accidentally Passionate
Playgoer. " <u>Drama and Theatre</u> 10 (1972): 134-136.

ANDERSON, SHERWOOD

Griffin, Gerald R. "Nature and 'Death in the Woods':
Threefold Emersonian Beauty and Anderson's Mrs.
Grimes. " Paper presented at the MLA meeting,
New York City, December 1976.

ANGELOU, MAYA

Angelou, Maya. "Maya Angelou. " North Hollywood:
The Center for Cassette Studies, n.d.

<u>Essence</u>, September 1974, p. 38. (Review of <u>Gather
Together in My Name</u>.)

Gilbert, S. M. <u>Poetry</u> 128 (August 1976): 290. (Review of <u>Oh Pray My Wings Are Gonna Fit Me Well</u>.)

Kent, George E. "Maya Angelou's I Know Why the Caged Bird Sings and Black Autobiographical Tradition." Kansas Quarterly 7, no. 3 (1975): 72-78.

Ryan, Beth Freeman. "Solzhenitsyn, Kesey and Angelou: Three for Freedom." Ph.D. Dissertation, The University of Nebraska-Lincoln, 1977.

ANGOFF, CHARLES

Baum, Charlotte, Paula Hyman and Sonya Michel. The Jewish Woman in America. New York: Dial Press, 1975.

Koltun, Elizabeth. The Jewish Woman: New Perspectives. New York: Schocken, 1976.

ANOUILH, JEAN

Spingler, Michael. "Anouilh's Little Antigone: Tragedy, Theatricalism, and the Romantic Self." Comparative Drama 8 (Fall 1974): 228-238.

Steiner, Lorraine Florence. "The Role of the Grande Dame in the Milieu of the French Salon, as Represented in Selected Works of Marcel Proust and Jean Anouilh." Ph.D. Dissertation, University of Minnesota, 1977.

Yim, Chol Kyu. "Mythological Figures in Ancient Greek and Modern Drama: Orestes and Antigone." Ph.D. Dissertation, Indiana University, 1975.

ANTHONY, FLORENCE see AI

ANTHONY, PIERS

Gower, Kathy. "Science Fiction and Women." In Mother Was Not a Person, pp. 98-101. Edited by Margret Andersen. Montreal: Content Publishing Limited and Black Rose Books, 1972.

APOLLODORUS

Fantham, Elaine. "Sex, Status, and Survival in Hellenistic Athens: A Study of Women in New Comedy." Phoenix 29 (Spring 1975): 44-74.

APULEIUS

Daghistany, Ann. "The Picara Nature." Women's
Studies 5, no. 1 (1977): 51-60.

AQUIN, HUBERT

Urbas, Jeannette. "La representation de la femme chez
Godbout, Aquin et Jasmin." Laurentian University
Review 9 (November 1976): [103]-113.

ARAGON, LOUIS

Becker, Lucille F. Louis Aragon. New York: Twayne,
1971.

ARDEN, JANE

Baker, Roger. In Contemporary Dramatists, pp. 42-43.
Edited by James Vinson. London and New York:
St. James Press and St. Martin's Press, 1973.

ARETINO, PIETRO

"How to Whore." Times Literary Supplement, 20 April
1973, p. 440.

ARGUEDAS, JOSE MARIE

Jaquette, Jane S. "Literary Archetypes and Female
Role Alternatives: The Woman and the Novel in
Latin America." In Female and Male in Latin Amer-
ica: Essays, pp. 3-28. Edited by Ann Pescatello.
Pittsburgh: University of Pittsburgh Press, 1973.

ARIOSTO

Hutchinson, Mary Anne. "The Devil's Gateway: The
Evil Enchantress in Ariosto, Tasso, Spenser, and
Milton." Ph.D. Dissertation, Syracuse University,
1975.

Tomalin, Margaret. "Bradamante and Marfisa: An
Analysis of the Guerrier of the Orlando furioso."
Modern Language Review 71 (July 1976): 540-552.

ARISTOPHANES

Pomeroy, Sarah B. Goddesses, Whores, Wives, and
Slaves: Women in Classical Antiquity. New York:
Schocken Books, 1975.

ARIYOSHI SAWAKO

Johnson, Eric W. "Modern Japanese Women Writers."
Literature East and West 8 (March 1974): [90]-102.

ARMAH, AYI KWEI

Staudt, Kathleen. "The Characterization of Women by
Soyinka and Armah." Afras Review (Sussex) 1, no.
1 (1975): 40-43.

Steele, Shelby. "Existentialism in the Novels of Ayi
Kwei Armah." Obsidian 3 (Spring 1977): 5-13.

ARNOLD, JUNE

Arnold, June, et al. "Lesbians and Literature." Sinister Wisdom 1 (Fall 1976): 20-23.

Miller, Dusty. Women 4, no. 4 (1976): 10-11. (Review of Sister Gin.)

ARNOLD, MATTHEW

Ball, Patricia M. The Heart's Events: The Victorian
Poetry of Relationships. London: University of
London, The Athlone Press, 1976.

Davis, Mary Myrd. "George Sand and the Poetry of
Matthew Arnold." Texas Studies in Literature and
Language 19 (Summer 1977): [204]-226.

Johnson, Wendell Stacy. Sex and Marriage in Victorian
Poetry. Ithaca: Cornell University Press, 1975.

Moers, Ellen. Literary Women. Garden City, N.Y.:
Doubleday, 1976.

Siegchrist, Mark. "The Role of Vivian in Arnold's
'Tristan and Iseult.'" Criticism 16 (1974): 136-152.

ARNOW, HARRIETTE

> Arnow, Harriette Simpson. Letter to Barbara H. Rigney. Frontiers: A Journal of Women Studies 1 (Spring 1976): 147.

> Baer, Barbara L. "Harriet Arnow's Chronicles of Destruction." Nation, 31 January 1976, pp. 117-120.

> Eckley, Wilton. Harriette Arnow. New York: Twayne, 1974.

> Goodman, Charlotte. "Images of American Rural Women in the Novel." University of Michigan Papers in Women's Studies 1 (June 1975): 57-70.

> Hobbs, Glenda. "Harriette Arnow's Kentucky Novels: Beyond Local Color." Kate Chopin Newsletter 2 (Fall 1976).

> New York Times Book Review, 24 January 1971, p. 2. (Review of The Dollmaker.)

> Rigney, Barbara. "Feminine Heroism in Harriette Arnow's The Dollmaker." Frontiers: A Journal of Women Studies 1 (Fall 1975): 81-85.

ASCH, SHALOM

> Baum, Charlotte, Paula Hyman and Sonya Michel. The Jewish Woman in America. New York: Dial Press, 1975.

ASSIS, MACHADO DE

> Pescatello, Ann. "The Brasileira: Images and Realities in Writings of Machado de Assis and Jorge Amado." In Female and Male in Latin America: Essays, pp. 29-58. Edited by Ann Pescatello. Pittsburgh: University of Pittsburgh Press, 1973.

ATHERTON, GERTRUDE

> Davidson, Colleen Tighe. "Beyond the Sentimental Heroine: The Feminist Character in American Novels, 1899-1937." Ph.D. Dissertation, University of Minnesota, 1975.

McClure, Charlotte S. "A Checklist of the Writings of and about Gertrude Atherton." American Literary Realism 9 (Spring 1976): 103-162.

_____. "Gertrude Atherton (1857-1948)." American Literary Realism 9 (Spring 1976): 95-101.

Maglin, Nan Bauer. "Rebel Women Writers, 1894-1925." Ph.D. Dissertation, Union Graduate School, 1975.

Richey, Elinor. "The Flappers Were Her Daughters: The Liberated, Literary World of Gertrude Atherton." American West 11 (July 1974): 4-10, 60-63.

Weir, Sybil. "Gertrude Atherton: The Limits of the Feminism in the 1890's." San Jose Studies 1 (February 1975): 24-31.

ATWOOD, MARGARET

Atwood, Margaret. "Paradoxes and Dilemmas: The Woman as Writer." In Women in the Canadian Mosaic, pp. 257-273. Edited by Gwen Matheson. Toronto: Peter Martin Associates, 1976.

Ayre, J. "Margaret Atwood and the End of Colonialism." Saturday Night 87 (November 1972): 23-26.

Bobak, E. L. Dalhousie Review 56 (Summer 1976): 404-406. (Review of Selected Poems.)

Browne, Rosellen. "The Poetry of Margaret Atwood." Nation, 28 June 1971, pp. 824-826.

Christ, Carol P. "Margaret Atwood: The Surfacing of Women's Spiritual Quest and Vision." Signs: Journal of Women in Culture and Society 2 (Winter 1976): 316-330.

Davidson, Cathy N. "Canadian Wry: Comic Vision in Atwood's Lady Oracle and Laurence's The Diviners." Regionalism and the Female Imagination 3 (Fall 1977/Winter 1977-78): 50-55.

_____. "Chopin and Atwood: Woman Drowning, Woman Surfacing." Kate Chopin Newsletter 1 (Winter 1975-76): 6-10.

Dilliott, Maureen. "Emerging from the Cold: Margaret Atwood's 'You Are Happy.' " Modern Poetry Studies 8 (Spring 1977): 73-90.

Foster, John Wilson. "The Poetry of Margaret Atwood." Canadian Literature no. 74 (Autumn 1977): 5-20.

Fulford, Robert. "The Images of Atwood." Malahat Review 41 (January 1977): 95-98.

Fulton, E. Margaret. "Out of Our Past: A New Future." Laurentian University Review 9 (November 1976): [87]-102.

Geddes, Gary. "Now You See It...." Books in Canada 5 (July 1976): 4-6. (Review of Selected Poems.)

Gibson, Mary Ellis. "A Conversation with Margaret Atwood." Chicago Review 27 (Spring 1976): 105-113.

Grumbach, Doris. Saturday Review, 18 September 1976, p. 28. (Review of Lady Oracle.)

Hofsess, John. "How to Be Your Own Best Survival." Malahat Review 41 (January 1977): 102-106.

Horne, Alan J. "A Preliminary Checklist of Writings by and about Margaret Atwood." Malahat Review 41 (January 1977): 195-222.

Irvine, Lorna Marie. "Hostility and Reconciliation: The Mother in English Canadian Fiction." Ph.D. Dissertation, The American University, 1977.

Kolodny, Annette. "Some Notes on Defining a 'Feminist Literary Criticism.' " Critical Inquiry 2 (Autumn 1975): 75-92.

Lauder, Scott. Canadian Forum 54 (November/December 1974): 17. (Review of You Are Happy.)

Laurel. "Toward a Woman Vision." Amazon Quarterly 2, no. 2, pp. 18-42.

Lefcowitz, Barbara. "The Search Motif in Some Contemporary Female Poets." University of Michigan Papers in Women's Studies 2, no. 3 (1977): 84-89.

Lyons, Bonnie. "Neither Victims nor Executioners in Margaret Atwood's Fiction." Paper presented at the MLA meeting, New York City, December 1976.

McLay, Catherine. "The Divided Self: Theme and Pattern in Margaret Atwood's Surfacing." Journal of Canadian Fiction 4, no. 1 (1975): 82-95.

Maclean's, 6 September 1976, p. 68. (Review of Lady Oracle.)

Macri, F. M. "Survival Kit: Margaret Atwood and the Canadian Scene." Modern Poetry Studies 5 (Autumn 1974): 187-195.

Mandel, Eli. "Atwood Gothic." Malahat Review 41 (January 1977): 165-174.

Marshall, Tom. "Atwood Under and Above Water." Malahat Review 41 (January 1977): 89-94.

Mathews, Robin. "Le roman engagé: The Social/Political Novel in English Canada." Laurentian University Review 9 (November 1976): [15]-31.

Miller, Karl. New York Review of Books, 28 October 1976, p. 30. (Review of Lady Oracle.)

Miner, Valerie. "Atwood in Metamorphosis: An Authentic Canadian Fairy Tale." In Her Own Woman: Profiles of Ten Canadian Women, pp. 173-194. Edited by Myrna Kostash, et al. Toronto: Macmillan of Canada, 1975.

Nichols, Marianna de Vinci. "Women on Women: The Looking Glass Novel." Denver Quarterly 11 (Autumn 1976): 1-13.

Northey, Margot Elizabeth. "Gothic and Grotesque Elements in Canadian Fiction." Ph.D. Dissertation, York University (Canada), 1974.

Onley, Gloria. "Power Politics in Bluebeard's Castle." Canadian Literature no. 60 (Spring 1974): 21-41.

Owen, I. M. "Queen of the Maze." Books in Canada 5 (September 1976): 3-5. (Review of Lady Oracle.)

Page, Sheila. "Supermarket Survival: A Critical Analysis of Margaret Atwood's The Edible Woman." Sphinx 1 (1974): 9-19.

Plaskow, Judith. "On Carol Christ on Margaret Atwood: Some Theological Reflections." Signs: Journal of Women in Culture and Society 2 (Winter 1976): 331-339. Margaret Atwood's reply, pp. 340-341.

Pollitt, Katha. New York Times Book Review, 26 September 1976, p. 7. (Review of Lady Oracle.)

Pritchard, W. H. Hudson Review 30 (Spring 1977): 147-160. (Review of Lady Oracle.)

Pritchard, William H. "Despairing at Styles." Poetry 127 (February 1976): 292-302. (Review Essay.)

Rigney, Barbara. Madness and Sexual Politics in the Feminist Novel: Studies of Charlotte Brontë, Virginia Woolf, Doris Lessing, and Margaret Atwood. Madison: University of Wisconsin Press, forthcoming.

Rogers, Linda. "Margaret the Magician." Canadian Literature no. 60 (Spring 1974): 83-85.

Rosengarten, Herbert. Canadian Literature no. 72 (Spring 1977): 84-87. (Review of Lady Oracle.)

Ross, Gary. "'The Circle Game.'" Canadian Literature no. 60 (Spring 1974): 51-63.

Rubenstein, Roberta. "Surfacing: Margaret Atwood's Journey to the Interior." Modern Fiction Studies 22 (Autumn 1976): 387-399.

Rule, Jane. "Life, Liberty and the Pursuit of Normalcy--The Novels of Margaret Atwood." Malahat Review 41 (January 1977): 42-49.

Sandler, Linda. "Interview with Margaret Atwood." Malahat Review 41 (January 1977): 7-27.

Saturday Night 91 (November 1976): 46. (Review of Lady Oracle.)

Savage, David. "Not Survival but Responsibility. " Dalhousie Review 55 (Summer 1975): 272-279.

Schreiber, Le Anne. Time, 11 October 1976, p. [97].
(Review of Lady Oracle.)

Skelton, Robin. "Timeless Constructions--A Note on
the Poetic Style of Margaret Atwood. " Malahat Review 41 (January 1977): 107-120.

Smith, Rowland. "Margaret Atwood: The Stoic Comedi-
an. " Malahat Review 41 (January 1977): 134-144.

Stevens, Peter. "Dark Mouth. " Canadian Literature
no. 50 (Autumn 1971): 91-92. (Review of Procedures
for Underground.)

Stimpson, Catharine R. "Don't Bother Me, I'm Dead. "
Ms. 5 (October 1976): 36, 40. (Review of Lady
Oracle.)

Struthers, J. R. "An Interview with Margaret Atwood. "
Essays on Canadian Writing no. 6 (Spring 1977): 18-27.

Sullivan, Rosemary. "Breaking the Circle. " Malahat
Review 41 (January 1977): 30-41.

_____. "Surfacing and Deliverance. " Canadian Lit-
erature no. 67 (Winter 1976): 6-20.

Swan, Susan. "Margaret Atwood: The Woman as Poet. "
In Communique: Women in Arts in Canada. Edited
by Terry Poulton. n. p. : Canadian Conference of
the Arts, May 1975.

Trueblood, Valerie. "Conscience and Spirit. " American Poetry Review 6, no. 2 (1977): 19-20. (Review of You Are Happy.)

Vender, Helen. New York Times Book Review, 6 April
1975, p. 4. (Review of You Are Happy.)

Walker, Cheryl. Nation, 13 September 1975, p. 215.
(Review of You Are Happy.)

Waters, Katherine E. "Margaret Atwood: Love on the
Dark Side of the Moon. " In Mother Was Not a

Person, pp. 102-119.   Edited by Margret Anderson. Montreal: Content Publishing Limited and Black Rose Books, 1972.

Weeks, Edward.   Atlantic Monthly (April 1973): 127. (Review of Surfacing.)

Woodcock, George, ed.   Essays from Canadian Litera- ture 1966-1974. London: Oxford, 1975.

_____.   "Margaret Atwood."   Literary Half-Yearly 13, no. 2 (July 1972): 233-242.

_____.   "Transformation Mask for Margaret Atwood." Malahat Review 41 (January 1977): 52-56.

Zonailo, Carolyn.   "Male Stereotypes in The Diviners and The Edible Woman."   Room of One's Own 3, no. 1 (1977): 70-72.

AUDOUX, MARGUERITE

Bleuzé, Ruth Allen.   "Romancières et Critiques: Etude du Prix Femina, 1904-1968." Ph.D. Dissertation, University of Colorado at Boulder, 1977.

AUROBINDO ASHRAM, SRI

Verma, K. D.   "Myth and Symbol in Aurobindo's Savi- tri: A Revaluation." Journal of South Asian Liter- ature 12 (Spring/Summer 1977): 67-72.

AUSTEN, JANE

Anderson, Walter E.   "Plot, Character, Speech, and Place in Pride and Prejudice." Nineteenth-Century Fiction 30 (December 1975): 367-382.

ApRoberts, Ruth.   "Sense and Sensibility, or Growing Up Dichotomous." Nineteenth-Century Fiction 30 (December 1975): 351-365.

Auerbach, Nina.   "Austen and Alcott on Matriarchy: New Women or New Wives?" Novel 10 (Fall 1976): 6-26.

Bauska, Kathy Anderson.   "The Feminine Dream of

Happiness: A Study of the Woman's Search for Intelligent Love and Recognition in Selected English Novels from Clarissa to Emma." Ph.D. Dissertation, University of Washington, 1977.

Bedick, David B. "The Changing Role of Anxiety in the Novel." Ph.D. Dissertation, New York University, 1975.

Beer, Patricia. "Jane Austen and Charlotte Brontë-- An Imaginary Conversation." Listener, 31 July 1975, pp. 144-147.

Berger, Carol. "The Rake and the Reader in Jane Austen's Novels." Studies in English Literature 15 (1975): 531-544.

Bompiani, Ginevra. "Il romanzo e il labrinto: Studio su Jane Austen." Nuovi Argomenti 43-44 (1975): 159-188.

Brenner, Gerry. "Mansfield Park: Reading for 'Improvement.' " Studies in the Novel 7 (Spring 1975): 24-32.

Brown, Julia Prewitt. "The Bonds of Irony: A Study of Jane Austen's Novels." Ph.D. Dissertation, Columbia University, 1975.

Burgam, Mary A. "Mr. Bennett and the Failures of Fatherhood in Jane Austen's Novels." Journal of English and German Philology 74 (1975): 536-552.

Burstall, Christopher, et al. " 'The Incident Is Not Closed'--A Conversation about Jane Austen." Listener, 25 December 1975 and 1 January 1976, p. 875.

Butler, Marilyn. Jane Austen and the Way of Ideas. Oxford: Clarendon, 1975.

Calder, Jenni. Women and Marriage in Victorian Fiction. London: Thames & Hudson, 1976.

Carter, Barbara Sue. "Jane Austen: The Moral Imperative." Ph.D. Dissertation, University of Maryland, 1976.

Chabot, C. Barry. "Jane Austen's Novels: The Vicissitudes of Desire." American Imago 32 (1975): 288-308.

Chandler, Alice. " 'A Pair of Fine Eyes': Jane Austen's Treatment of Sex." Studies in the Novel 7 (Spring 1975): 88-103.

Cohen, Sue Winters. "Threat and Resistance: Society vs. the Individual in the Novels of Jane Austen." Ph.D. Dissertation, The Ohio State University, 1975.

Collins, K. K. "Mrs. Smith and the Morality of Persuasion." Nineteenth-Century Fiction 30 (December 1975): 383-397.

Corwin, Laura J. "Character and Morality in the Novels of Jane Austen." Revue des Langues Vivantes 38, no. 4 (1972): 363-379.

Crowley, J. Donald. "Jane Austen Studies: A Portrait of the Lady and Her Critics." Studies in the Novel 7 (Spring 1975): 137-160. (Review Essay.)

Devlin, David Douglas. Jane Austen and Education. New York: Barnes & Noble, 1975.

Dry, Helen. "Syntax and Point of View in Jane Austen's Emma." Studies in Romanticism 16 (Winter 1977): 87-99.

Duffy, Joseph M. "The Politics of Love: Marriage and the Good Society in Pride and Prejudice." University of Windsor Review 11 (Spring-Summer 1976): 5-26.

Dylla, Sandra Marie. "Jane Austen and George Eliot: The Influence of Their Social Worlds on Their Women Characters." Ph.D. Dissertation, The University of Wisconsin-Milwaukee, 1975.

Ek, Grete. "Mistaken Conduct and Proper 'Feeling': A Study of Jane Austen's Pride and Prejudice." In Fair Forms: Essays in English Literature from Spenser to Jane Austen, pp. 178-202. Edited by Maren-Sofie Røstvig. Totowa, N.J.: Rowman & Littlefield, 1975.

Faulkner, Peter. Humanism in the English Novel. New York: Barnes & Noble, 1976.

Fergus, Jan Stockton. "Jane Austen's Early Novels: The Educating of Judgment and Sympathy." Ph.D. Dissertation, The City University of New York, 1975.

Flower, Annette. "Jane Austen Bicentennial: Janeites vs. Austenites." Ms. 4 (August 1975): 38-39. (Review of Sandition.)

Fowler, Marian E. "The Feminist Bias of Pride and Prejudice." Dalhousie Review 57 (Spring 1977): 47-64.

Francone, Carol Burr. "Women in Rebellion: A Study of the Conflict Between Self-Fulfillment and Self-Sacrifice in Emma, Jane Eyre, and The Mill on the Floss." Ph.D. Dissertation, Case Western Reserve University, 1975.

Friebe, Freimut. "Von Marianne Dashwood zu Anne Elliot: Empfindsame Motive bei Jane Austen." Anglia 91, no. 3 (1973): 314-341.

Gandesbery, Jean Johnson. "Versions of the Mother in the Novels of Jane Austen and George Eliot." Ph.D. Dissertation, University of California, Davis, 1976.

Garside, Peter and Elizabeth Macdonald. "Evangelicalism and Mansfield Park." Trivium 10 (May 1975): 34-50.

Gold, Joel J. "The Return to Bath: Catherine Morland to Anne Elliot." Genre 9 (Fall 1976): 215-229.

Hagan, John. "The Closure of Emma." Studies in English Literature 15, no. 4 (1975): 545-561.

Halperin, John and Janet Kunert. Plots and Characters in the Fiction of Jane Austen, the Brontës, and George Eliot. Hamden, Conn.: Shoe String Press, 1976.

Hardwick, John. A Guide to Jane Austen. New York: Scribners, 1974.

Harrison, Bernard. "Muriel Spark and Jane Austen." In The Modern English Novel: The Reader, The Writer, and The Work, pp. 225-251. Edited by Gabriel Josipovici. New York: Barnes & Noble, 1976.

Hart, Frances R. "The Spaces of Privacy: Jane Austen." Nineteenth-Century Fiction 30 (December 1975): 305-333.

Held, Leonard Edgar. "The Reader in Northanger Abbey." Ph.D. Dissertation, The University of New Mexico, 1976.

Hilliard, Raymond Francis. "Role-Playing and the Development of Jane Austen's Psychological Realism." Ph.D. Dissertation, The University of Rochester, 1976.

Jackel, David. "Leonora and Lady Susan: A Note on Maria Edgeworth and Jane Austen." English Studies in Canada 3 (Fall 1977): [278]-288.

"Jane Austen Special Number." Studies in the Novel 7, no. 1 (1975): special issue.

Kennedy, Alan. "Irony and Action in Mansfield Park." English Studies in Canada 3 (Summer 1977): [164]-175.

Kestner, Joseph. Jane Austen: Spatial Structure of Thematic Variations. Austria: University of Salzburg, 1974.

_____. "Sanditon or The Brothers: Nature into Art." Papers on Language and Literature 12 (Spring 1976): 161-166.

Kinkead-Weekes, Mark. "This Old Maid: Jane Austen Replies to Charlotte Brontë and D. H. Lawrence." Nineteenth-Century Fiction 30 (December 1975): 399-419.

Lachman, Michele Schurgin. "Jane Austen: Studies in Language and Values." Ph.D. Dissertation, Brandeis University, 1975.

LaJoy, Maureen. "No Laughing Matter: Women and Humor." Women 5, no. 1 (1976): 6-9.

Lauber, John. "Jane Austen's Fools." Studies in English Literature 14 (1975): 511-524.

Levin, Jane Aries. "Marriage in the Novels of Jane Austen." Ph. D. Dissertation. Yale University, 1975.

Levine, George. "Translating the Monstrous: Northanger Abbey." Nineteenth-Century Fiction 30 (December 1975): 335-350.

Lovenheim, Barbara. "Female as Subject and Object in Literature: From Austen to Jong." Deland, Florida: Everett/Edwards, n. d.

Magee, William H. "The Happy Marriage: The Influence of Charlotte Smith on Jane Austen." Studies in the Novel 7 (Spring 1975): 120-132.

Miles, Rosalind. The Fiction of Sex: Themes and Functions of Sex Difference in the Modern Novel. New York: Barnes & Noble, 1974.

Moers, Ellen. Literary Women. Garden City, N.Y.: Doubleday, 1976.

Monaghan, David M. "The Decline of the Gentry: A Study of Jane Austen's Attitude to Formality in Persuasion." Studies in the Novel 7 (Spring 1975): 73-87.

Morgan, Alice. "On Teaching Emma." Journal of General Education 24 (July 1972): 103-108.

Morgan, Susan. "Intelligence in Pride and Prejudice." Modern Philology 73 (August 1975): 54-68.

Morgan, Susan J. "Emma Woodhouse and the Charms of Imagination." Studies in the Novel 7 (Spring 1975): 33-48.

Nardin, Jane. "Charity in Emma." Studies in the Novel 7 (Spring 1975): 61-72.

O'Dowd, M. C. "Writing and Injustice." Contrast (Capetown, South Africa) 23 (1970): 48-61.

Patterson, Emily H. "Family and Pilgrimage Themes in Austen's Mansfield Park." CLA Journal 20 (September 1976): 14-18.

Price, Martin. "Manners, Morals, and Jane Austen." Nineteenth-Century Fiction 30 (December 1975): 261-280.

Raine, Craig. "Knotting." New Statesman, 25 July 1975, pp. 117-118. (Review of Sandition.)

Ram, Atma. "Marriage and Money in Jane Austen's Novels." Punjab University Research Bulletin 6 (1975): 9-18.

Rees, Joan. Jane Austen: Woman and Writer. New York: St. Martin's Press, 1976.

Sadoff, Diane F. "Forms of Female Contrition: The Heroine in Women's Nineteenth-Century English Novels." Paper presented at the MLA meeting, San Francisco, December 1976.

Scholes, Robert. "Dr. Johnson and Jane Austen." Philological Quarterly 54, no. 1 (1975): 380-390.

Shaw, Valerie. "Jane Austen's Subdued Heroines." Nineteenth-Century Fiction 30 (December 1975): 281-303.

Siefert, Susan Elizabeth. "The Dilemma of the Talented Woman: A Study in Nineteenth-Century Fiction." Ph.D. Dissertation, University of Marquette, 1974.

Skilton, David. The English Novel: Defoe to the Victorians. New York: Barnes & Noble, 1977.

Southam, B. C. Introduction to Sandition: An Unfinished Novel. Oxford: Clarendon, 1975.

Stowell, H. E. Quill Pens and Petticoats: A Portrait of Women of Letters. London: Wayland, 1970.

Taylor, Irene and Gina Luria. "Gender and Genre: Women in British Romantic Literature." In What Manner of Woman: Essays on English and American Life and Literature, pp. 98-124. Edited by Marlene

Springer. New York: New York University Press, 1977.

Taylor, Nancy McKeon. "Conscious Construction: The Concept of Plot in Five Novels by Women." Ph.D. Dissertation, Loyola University of Chicago, 1977.

Taylor, Roselle. "The Narrative Technique of Jane Austen: A Study in the Use of Point of View." Ph.D. Dissertation, The University of Texas at Austin, 1975.

Trowbridge, Hoyt. From Dryden to Jane Austen: Essays on English Critics and Writers, 1660-1818. Albuquerque: University of New Mexico Press, 1977.

Uffen, Ellen Serlen. "The Art of Mansfield Park." Women & Literature 5 (Fall 1977): 29-41.

Weinsheimer, Joel, ed. Jane Austen Today. Athens: University of Georgia Press, 1975.

Weissman, Judith. "Evil and Blunders: Human Nature in Mansfield Park and Emma." Women & Literature 4 (Spring 1976): 5-17.

Wherritt, T. Mildred. "For Better or for Worse: Marriage Proposals in Jane Austen's Novels." Midwest Quarterly 17 (April 1976): 229-244.

White, Edward M. "Freedom Is Restraint: The Pedagogical Problem of Jane Austen." San Jose Studies 2 (February 1976): 84-90.

Whitten, Benjamin. Jane Austen's Comedy of Telling: A Critical Analysis of "Persuasion." Ankara: Hacettepe University, 1974.

Wiesenfarth, Joseph. "History and Myth in Jane Austen's Persuasion." Literary Criterion 11, no. 3 (1975): 76-85.

Wilhelm, Albert E. "Three Word Clusters in Emma." Studies in the Novel 7 (Spring 1975): 49-60.

Williams, Ioan. The Realist Novel in England: A Study

in Development. Pittsburgh: University of Pittsburgh Press, 1974.

Youngren, Virginia Rotan. "Moral Life in Solitude: A
Study of Selected Novels of Jane Austen, Charlotte
Brontë, Elizabeth Gaskell and George Eliot. " Ph. D.
Dissertation, Rutgers University, The State Univer-
sity of New Jersey (New Brunswick), 1977.

Zimmerman, Eugenia Noik. "The Proud Princess Gets
Her Comeuppance: Structures of Patriarchal Order."
Canadian Review of Comparative Literature 3 (Fall
1976): [253]-268.

AUSTIN, Mary

Ballard, Rae Galbraith. "Mary Austin's Earth Horizon:
The Imperfect Circle. " Ph. D. Dissertation, Claremont Graduate School, 1977.

Berry, Wilkes. "Mary Austin: Sibylic Gourmet of the
Southwest. " Western Review 9, no. 2 (1972): 3-8.

Pannill, Linda Susanne. "The Artist-Heroine in American Fiction, 1890-1920. " Ph. D. Dissertation, The
University of North Carolina at Chapel Hill, 1975.

Waters, Lena W. "Mary Austin as Nature Essayist. "
Ph. D. Dissertation, Texas Tech University, 1974.

- B -

BAGNOLD, ENID

Hays, Janice. "Themes and Modes of Women's Drama
in the Twentieth Century. " Paper presented at the
MLA meeting. New York City, December 1976.
(Mimeographed.)

BAGRYANA, ELISAVETA

Knudsen, Erika. "The Counter-Points of Elisaveta Bagryana. " Canadian Slavonic Papers 16 (1974): 353-
370.

Moser, Charles A. A History of Bulgarian Literature.
The Hague: Mouton, 1972.

Mozejko, Edward. "The Private World of Elisaveta
Bagryana. " World Literature Today 51 (Spring
1977): 216-219.

BAILLIE, JOANNA

Haworth, H. E. "Romantic Female Writers and the
Critics. " Texas Studies in Literature and Language
17 (Winter 1976): 725-736.

BAINBRIDGE, BERYL

Clapp, Susannah. Times Literary Supplement, 3 October 1975, p. 1125. (Review of Sweet William.)

DeFeo, Ronald. National Review, 17 September 1976,
p. 1020. (Review of Sweet William.)

Kermode, Frank. New York Review of Books, 15 July
1975, p. 42. (Review of Sweet William.)

Neiditz, Elizabeth. San Francisco Review of Books 3
(May 1977): 15. (Review of A Quiet Life.)

Pollitt, Katha. New York Times Book Review, 17 May
1976, p. 4. (Review of Sweet William.)

Rosen, Norma. "A Quiet Life. " Ms. 6 (August 1977):
36-37. (Review of A Quiet Life.)

BAKER, DOROTHY

Rule, Jane. Lesbian Images. Garden City, N. Y. :
Doubleday, 1975.

BALDWIN, Emily Foote

Ward, Hazel Mae. "The Black Woman as Character:
Images in the American Novel, 1852-1953. " Ph. D.
Dissertation, The University of Texas at Austin,
1977.

Watts, Emily Stripes. The Poetry of American Women
from 1632 to 1945. Austin: University of Texas
Press, 1977.

BALDWIN, JAMES

Anderson, Mary Louise. "Black Matriarchy: Portrayal of Women in Three Plays." Negro American Literature Forum 10 (Fall 1976): 93-95.

Hoerchner, Susan Jane. " 'I Have to Keep the Two Things Separate': Polarity in Women in the Contemporary American Novel." Ph.D. Dissertation, Emory University, 1973.

Love, Theresa R. "The Black Woman in Afro-American Literature." Paper presented at the Midwest Modern Language Association meeting, Chicago, November 1975. (Mimeographed.)

Schulz, Elizabeth. " 'Free in Fact and at Last': The Image of the Black Woman in Black American Literature." In What Manner of Woman: Essays in English and American Life and Literature, pp. 316-344. Edited by Marlene Springer. New York: New York University Press, 1977.

Shinn, Shelma J. Wardrop. "A Study of Women Characters in Contemporary American Fiction 1940-1970." Ph.D. Dissertation, Purdue University, 1972.

BALZAC, HONORE de

Crane, Robert Arthur. "The Courtisane Character in the Nineteenth Century French Novel from Balzac to Zola." Ph.D. Dissertation, The University of North Carolina at Chapel Hill, 1976.

Holmberg, Arthur. "Balzac and Galdós: comment aiment les filles?" Comparative Literature 29 (Spring 1977): 109-123.

Moers, Ellen. Literary Women. Garden City, N.Y.: Doubleday, 1976.

Moss, Martha Caroline Niess. "Balzac: Sexual Polarity and the Origins of Character." Ph.D. Dissertation, The University of Michigan, 1975.

Ortali, Hélène. "Images of Women in Balzac's La Cousine Bette." Nineteenth-Century French Studies 4 (Spring 1976): 194-205.

Porter, Dennis. "Gustave Flaubert's Middle-Class Tragedy." Forum for Modern Language Studies 18 (January 1977): 59-69.

Steinberger, Eva Marie. "Balzac's Portrayal of Woman: A Study in the Role of Women in His Fictional Works Before 1842." Ph.D. Dissertation, City University of New York, 1977.

BAMBARA, TONI CADE

Abrahams, Roger D. "Negotiating Respect: Patterns of Presentation Among Black Women." Journal of American Folklore 88 (January-March 1975): 58-80.

Book World, 18 November 1973, p. 5. (Review of Gorilla, My Love.)

Dean, Nancy. "Feminist Short Fiction: New Forms and Styles." Paper presented at the MLA meeting, New York City, 1976. (Mimeographed.)

English Journal 63 (January 1974): 66. (Review of Gorilla, My Love.)

Mahone, Barbara D. "A Handsome Family Quilt." First World 1 (May/June 1977): 40-42. (Review of The Sea Birds Are Still Alive.)

Utamu, Imani. Black Books Bulletin 5 (Fall 1977): 36-37. (Review of The Sea Birds Are Still Alive.)

Washington, Mary Helen. "Blues Women of the Seventies." Ms. 6 (July 1977): 36, 38. (Review of The Sea Birds Are Still Alive.)

BARAKA, IMAMU AMIRI (LeRoi Jones)

Clayborne, Jon L. "Modern Black Drama and the Gay Image." College English 36 (November 1974): 381-384.

Miller, Jeanne-Marie A. "Images of Black Women in Plays by Black Playwrights." CLA Journal 20 (June 1977): 494-507.

_____. "The Plays of LeRoi Jones." CLA Journal 14 (March 1971): 331-339.

Mootry, Maria K. "Themes and Symbols in Two Plays by LeRoi Jones." Negro Digest 18 (April 1969): 42-47.

Reck, Tom S. "Archetypes in LeRoi Jones' Dutchman." Studies in Black Literature 1 (Spring 1970): 66-68.

Weisgram, Diane H. "Dutchman: Inter-Racial Ritual of Sexual Violence." American Imago 29 (Fall 1972): 215-232.

BARBAULD, ANNA LAETITIA

Mahl, Mary R. and Helen Koon, eds. The Female Spectator: English Women Writers Before 1800. Bloomington and Old Westbury, N.Y.: Indiana University Press and the Feminist Press, 1977.

BARKER, HARLEY GRANVILLE

Ritchie, Harry M. "Harley Granville Barker's The Madras House and the Sexual Revolution." Modern Drama 15 (September 1972): 150-158.

BARKER, JANE

Spacks, Patricia Meyer. Imagining a Self: Autobiography and Novel in Eighteenth-Century England. Cambridge: Harvard University Press, 1976.

BARNES, DJUNA

DeVore, Charles Lynn. "The Works of Djuna Barnes: A Literary Cosmos." Ph.D. Dissertation, The University of Tulsa, 1976.

Greiner, Donald J. "Djuna Barnes' Nightwood and the American Origins of Black Humor." Critique 17, no. 1 (1975): 41-54.

Hughes, Gillian. "Nightwood: Love Between the Oppressed." The Other Woman 2 (June 1974): n.p.

Johnsen, William A. "Modern Women Novelists: Nightwood and the Novel of Sensibility." Bucknell Review 21, no. 1 (1973): 29-42.

Kannenstine, Louis F. The Art of Djuna Barnes: Du-
ality and Damnation. New York: New York University Press, 1977.

_____. "The Halt Position of the Damned: A Study
of the Work of Djuna Barnes." Ph. D. Dissertation,
New York University, 1976.

Kolodny, Annette. "Some Notes on Defining a 'Feminist
Literary Criticism.'" Critical Inquiry 2 (Autumn
1975): 75-92.

Messerli, Douglas. Djuna Barnes: A Bibliography.
New York: David Lewis, 1976.

Nadeau, Robert L. "Nightwood and the Freudian Unconscious." International Fiction Review 2 (1975): 159-
163.

Rule, Jane. Lesbian Images. Garden City, N.Y.:
Doubleday, 1975.

Vella, Michael. "Djuna Barnes Gains Despite Critics'
Pall." Lost Generation Journal 4 (Winter 1976): 6-8.

BARNEY, NATALIE CLIFFORD

Klaich, Dolores. Woman + Woman: Attitudes Toward
Lesbianism. New York: Simon & Schuster, 1974.

BARRACK, BARBARA

Dean, Nancy. "Feminist Short Fiction: New Forms and
Styles." Paper presented at the MLA meeting, New
York City, 1976. (Mimeographed.)

BARRE, POULAINE de la

Seidel, Michael A. "Poulain de la Barre's The Woman
as Good as the Man." Journal of the History of
Ideas 35 (July-September 1974): 499-508.

BARRENO, MARIA ISABEL

Authors in the News, vol. 1. Detroit: Gale Research,
1976, p. 29.

BARRETT, ELIZABETH see BROWNING, ELIZABETH BAR-
RETT

BARROSO, MARIA ALICE

> Silverman, Malcolm. "Stylistic Evolution of Marie
> Alice Barroso's Works." Hispania 60 (September
> 1977): 478-485.

BARRY, PHILIP

> Loudin, Joanne Marie. "The Changing Role of the
> Comic Heroine in American Drama from 1900 to
> 1940." Ph. D. Dissertation, University of Washing-
> ton, 1974.

> Rinaldi, Frank Joseph. "Philip Barry: The Matter of
> Marriage." Ph. D. Dissertation, University of
> Massachusetts, 1975.

BARTH, JOHN

> Allen, Mary. The Necessary Blankness: Women in
> Major American Fiction of the Sixties. Urbana:
> University of Illinois Press, 1976.

> Fraustino, Daniel V. "The Country Wife Comes to The
> End of the Road: Wycherley Bewitches Barth."
> Arizona Quarterly 33 (Spring 1977): 76-85.

> Vanderbilt, Kermit. "From Passion to Impasse: The
> Structure of a Dark Romantic Theme in Hawthorne,
> Howells, and Barth." Studies in the Novel 8 (Win-
> ter 1976): 419-429.

BARTHELME, DONALD

> Dervin, Daniel A. "Breast Fantasy in Barthelme,
> Swift, and Philip Roth: Creativity and Psychoana-
> lytic Structure." American Imago 33 (Spring 1976):
> 102-122.

> Rother, James. "Parafiction: The Adjacent Universe
> of Barth, Barthelme, Pynchon, and Nabokov."
> Boundary 2 5 (Fall 1976): 21-43.

BASS, ELLEN

> Thurman, Judith. "Poetry: Notes from a Selfish
> Reader." Ms. 6 (November 1977): 30, 36-38. (Re-
> view of Of Separateness and Merging.)

BASSO, HAMILTON
    Seidel, Kathryn Lee. "The Southern Belle: Her Fall
        from the Pedestal in Fiction of the Southern Renais-
        sance. " Ph. D. Dissertation, University of Maryland,
        1976.

BAUDELAIRE, CHARLES

    Ahearn, Edward J. "Black Woman, White Poet: Exile
        and Exploitation in Baudelaire's Jeanne Duval Poems."
        French Review 51 (December 1977): 212-220.

    Fredrickson, Hélène. "Baudelaire: Héros et fils dualité
        et problèmes du travail dans les lettres à sa mère. "
        Ph. D. Dissertation, Northwestern University, 1975.

    Reff, Theodore. "The Influence of Flaubert's Queen of
        Sheba on Later Nineteenth-Century Literature. "
        Romanic Review 65 (November 1974): 249-265.

BAWDEN, NINA

    Miller, Jane. Times Literary Supplement, 8 October
        1976, p. 1268. (Review of Afternoon of a Good
        Woman.)

BEALS, MAY

    Maglin, Nan Bauer. "Rebel Women Writers, 1894-1925. "
        Ph. D. Dissertation, Union Graduate School, 1975.

BEATTIE, ANN

    Dean, Nancy. "Feminist Short Fiction: New Forms
        and Styles. " Paper presented at the MLA meeting,
        New York City, December 1976.

BEAUVOIR, SIMONE de

    Crossland, Margaret. Women of Iron and Velvet:
        French Women After George Sand. New York:
        Taplinger, 1976.

    Francis, Claude. "On Simone de Beauvoir. " Hecate 3
        (February 1977): 67-71.

    Harth, Erica. "The Creative Alienation of the Writer:

Sartre, Camus, and Simone de Beauvoir." <u>Mosaic</u>
8 (Spring 1975): 177-186.

Leighton, Jean. <u>Simone de Beauvoir on Woman</u>. Cranbury, N.J.: <u>Fairleigh Dickinson University</u> Press,
1975.

Marks, Elaine. " 'I Am My Own Heroine': Some
Thoughts About Women and Autobiography in France."
In <u>Female Studies IX: Teaching About Women in the
Foreign Languages</u>, pp. 1-10. Edited by Sidonie
Cassirer. Old Westbury, N.Y.: Feminist Press,
1975.

Rupprecht, Nancy E. "The Critics, Simone de Beauvoir
and <u>All Said and Done</u>. " <u>University of Michigan
Papers in Women's Studies</u> 1 (June 1975): 129-147.

Stineman, Esther F. 'Simone de Beauvoir: An Autobiographical Blueprint for Female Liberty. " <u>Uni-
versity of Michigan Papers in Women's Studies</u> 2,
no. 3 (1977): 99-122.

Terkel, Studs. 'Simone de Beauvoir." North Hollywood: The Center for Cassette Studies, n.d. (1960
interview.)

BECK, ROBERT

Graham, D. B. " 'Negative Glamour': The Pimp Hero
in the Fiction of Iceberg Slim. " <u>Obsidian</u> 1 (Spring
1975): 5-17.

BECKETT, SAMUEL

Fedor, Joan Roberta. "The Importance of the Female
in the Plays of Samuel Beckett, Harold Pinter, and
Edward Albee. " Ph.D. Dissertation, University of
Washington, 1976.

BECKLEY, ZOE

Maglin, Nan Bauer. 'Discovering Women's Activist Fiction." <u>University of Michigan Papers in Women's
Studies</u> 2, no. 2 (1976): 96-104.

_____. "Rebel Women Writers, 1894-1925. " Ph.D.
Dissertation, Union Graduate School, 1975.

BEERBOHM, MAX

Stein, Joseph. "The New Woman and the Decadent
Dandy." Dalhousie Review 55 (Spring 1975): 54-62.

BEHN, APHRA

Guffey, George. "Aphra Behn's Oroonoko: Occasion
and Accomplishment." In Two English Novelists:
Aphra Behn and Anthony Trollope, pp. 1-41. Introduction by M. E. Novak. Los Angeles: Wm. An-
drews Clark Memorial Library, 1975.

Hume, Robert D. "Marital Discord in English Comedy
from Dryden to Fielding." Modern Philology 74
(February 1977): 248-272.

_____. "The Myth of the Rake in 'Restoration' Com-
edy." Studies in the Literary Imagination 10 (Spring
1977): 25-55.

Jordan, Robert. "Mrs. Behn and Sir Anthony Love."
Restoration and 18th Century Theatre Research 12,
no. 1 (1973): 58-59.

Ludwig, Judith Karyn. "A Critical Edition of Aphra
Behn's Comedy The Feigned Courtesans (1679), with
Introduction and Notes." Ph.D. Dissertation, Yale
University, 1976.

Mahl, Mary R. and Helen Koon, eds. The Female
Spectator: English Women Writers Before 1800.
Bloomington and Old Westbury, N.Y.: Indiana Uni-
versity Press and The Feminist Press, 1977.

Novak, Maximillian E. "Margery Pinchwife's 'London
Disease': Restoration Comedy and the Libertine Of-
fensive in the 1670's." Studies in the Literary
Imagination 10 (Spring 1977): 1-24.

Root, Robert L., Jr. "Aphra Behn, Arranged Marriage,
and Restoration Comedy." Women & Literature 5
(Spring 1977): 3-14.

Woodcock, George. "Founding Mother of the English
Novel: Aphra Behn." Room of One's Own 2, no.
2/3 (1976): 31-44.

BEHRMAN, S. N.

> Klink, William Robert. "A Critical Analysis of Selected Plays of S. N. Behrman." Ph.D. Dissertation, Catholic University of America, 1972.

> Loudin, Joanne Marie. "The Changing Role of the Comic Heroine in American Drama from 1900 to 1940." Ph.D. Dissertation, University of Washington, 1974.

> Shafer, Yvonne B. "The Liberated Woman in American Plays of the Past." Players 49 (Spring 1974): 95-100.

BELL, THOMAS

> Davidson, Colleen Tighe. "Beyond the Sentimental Heroine: The Feminist Character in American Novels, 1899-1937." Ph.D. Dissertation, University of Minnesota, 1975.

BELLAMY, EDWARD

> Strauss, Sylvia. "Women in 'Utopia.' " South Atlantic Quarterly 75 (Winter 1976): 115-131.

BELLOCQ, LOUISE

> Bleuzé, Ruth Allen. "Romancières et Critiques: Etude du Prix Fémina, 1904-1968." Ph.D. Dissertation, University of Colorado at Boulder, 1977.

BELLOW, SAUL

> Jacobs, Rita D. " 'Truth on the Side of Life': Saul Bellow, Nobel Prize 1976." World Literature Today 51 (Spring 1977): 194-197.

> Lippitt, Noriko M. "A Perennial Survivor: Saul Bellow's Heroine in the Desert." Studies in Short Fiction 12 (Summer 1975): 281-283.

> Masinton, Martha and Charles G. Masinton. "Second-Class Citizenship: The Status of Women in Contemporary American Fiction." In What Manner of Woman: Essays in English and American Life and Literature, pp. 297-315. Edited by Marlene Springer. New York: New York University Press, 1977.

Rooke, Constance. "Saul Bellow's 'Leaving the Yellow House': The Trouble with Women." Studies in Short Fiction 14 (Spring 1977): 184-187.

Shinn, Thelma J. Wardrop. "A Study of Women Characters in Contemporary American Fiction 1940-1970." Ph.D. Dissertation, Purdue University, 1972.

Sullivan, Victoria. "The Battle of the Sexes in Three Bellow Novels." In Saul Bellow: A Collection of Critical Essays, pp. 101-114. Edited by Earl Rovit. Englewood Cliffs, N.J.: Prentice-Hall, 1975.

BENNETT, ARNOLD

Pearson, Judith Ann Siegel. "Marriage in the Novels of Arnold Bennett." Ph.D. Dissertation, Washington University, 1977.

BENNETT, GWENDOLYN

Rushing, Andrea Benton. "Images of Black Women in Afro-American Poetry." Black World 24 (September 1975): 18-30.

BENNETT, STEFANIE

Moorehead, Finola. "Goodbye Prince Hamlet: The New Australian Women's Poetry." Meanjin Quarterly 34 (Winter 1975): 169-179.

BERNSTEIN, HENRY

Montley, Patricia Ann. "Judith on Broadway: A Comparison of Twentieth Century Dramatic Adaptations of the Biblical Book of Judith Produced on the New York Stage (Volumes I and II)." Ph.D. Dissertation, University of Minnesota, 1975.

BERNSTEIN-ROSMER, ELSA

Novak, Sigrid Scholtz. "The Invisible Woman: The Case of the Female Playwright in German Literature." Journal of Social Issues 28, no. 2 (1972): 47-57.

BETTS, DORIS

Evans, Elizabeth. "Negro Characters in the Fiction of Doris Betts." Critique 17 (December 1975): 59-76.

BHANDARI, MANNU

Poulos, Steven Mark. "Feminine Sense and Sensibility: A Comparative Study of Six Modern Fiction Writers in Hindi and Urdu: Rashid Jahan, Ismat Chughtai, Qurratul-Ain Hyder, Mannu Bhandari, Usha Priyam-veda, Viday Chauhan." Ph.D. Dissertation, University of Chicago, 1975.

BHATTACHARYA, BHABANI

Bhattacharya, Bhabani. "Women in My Stories." Journal of South Asian Literature 12 (Spring-Summer 1977): 115-119.

Gemmill, Janet P. "An Interview with Bhabani Bhatta-charya." World Literature Written in English 14 (1975): 300-309.

BISHOP, ELIZABETH

Bertin, Célia. "A Novelist's Poet." World Literature Today 51 (Winter 1977): 16-17.

Brinnin, John Malcolm and Bill Read, eds. Twentieth Century Poetry: American and British (1900-1970), 2nd ed. New York: McGraw-Hill, 1970.

Bryan, Nancy L. "A Place for the Genuine: Elizabeth Bishop and the Factual Tradition in Modern American Poetry." Ph.D. Dissertation, Claremont College, 1974.

Estess, Sybil Pittman. "Discoveries of Travel: Elizabeth Bishop and the Poetry of Process." Ph.D. Dissertation, Syracuse University, 1976.

_____. "Shelters for 'What Is Within': Meditation and Epiphany in the Poetry of Elizabeth Bishop." Modern Poetry Studies 8 (Spring 1977): 50-60.

_____. "Toward the Interior: Epiphany in 'Cape

Breton.' " <u>World Literature Today</u> 51 (Winter 1977): 49-52.

Mazzaro, Jerome. "Elizabeth Bishop and the Poetics of Impediment." <u>Salmagundi</u> no. 27 (Summer-Fall 1974): [118]-144.

_____. "Elizabeth Bishop's Particulars." <u>World Literature Today</u> 51 (Winter 1977): 46-49.

Mortimer, Penelope. "Elizabeth Bishop's Prose." <u>World Literature Today</u> 51 (Winter 1977): 17-18.

Moss, Howard. "The Canada-Brazil Connection." <u>World Literature Today</u> 51 (Winter 1977): [29]-33.

Mullen, Kathleen Ruth. "Manipulation of Perspective in the Poetry of Elizabeth Bishop." Ph.D. Dissertation, The University of Texas at Austin, 1977.

Newman, Anne R. "Elizabeth Bishop's 'Songs for a Colored Singer.' " <u>World Literature Today</u> 51 (Winter 1977): 37-40.

Newman, Anne Royall. "Elizabeth Bishop: A Study of Form and Theme." Ph.D. Dissertation, University of South Carolina, 1974.

Paz, Octavio. "Elizabeth Bishop, or The Power of Reticence." <u>World Literature Today</u> 51 (Winter 1977): [15]-16.

Schwartz, Lloyd. "The Mechanical Horse and the Indian Princess: Two Poems from North & South." <u>World Literature Today</u> 51 (Winter 1977): [41]-44.

_____. "One Art: The Poetry of Elizabeth Bishop, 1971-76." <u>Ploughshares</u> 3, nos. 3 & 4 (1977): 30-52.

Slater, Candace. "Brazil in the Poetry of Elizabeth Bishop." <u>World Literature Today</u> 51 (Winter 1977): 33-36.

Smith, William Jay. "Geographical Questions: The Recent Poetry of Elizabeth Bishop." <u>Hollins Critic</u> 14 (February 1977): 1-11.

Spiegelman, Willard. "Landscape and Knowledge: The Poetry of Elizabeth Bishop." Modern Poetry Studies 6 (Winter 1975): 203-223.

Starbuck, George. "'The Work!': A Conversation with Elizabeth Bishop." Ploughshares 3, nos. 3 & 4 (1977): 11-29.

Taylor, Eleanor Ross. "Driving to the Interior: A Note on Elizabeth Bishop." World Literature Today 51 (Winter 1971): 44-46.

Vendler, Helen. "Domestication, Domesticity and the Other Worldly." World Literature Today 51 (Winter 1977): [23]-28.

Walker, Cheryl Lawson. "The Women's Tradition in American Poetry." Ph.D. Dissertation, Brandeis University, 1973.

World Literature Today 51 (Winter 1977): Elizabeth Bishop special issue.

BISHOP, JOHN PEALE

Seidel, Kathryn Lee. "The Southern Belle: Her Fall from the Pedestal in Fiction of the Southern Renaissance." Ph.D. Dissertation, University of Maryland, 1976.

BLACKWOOD, CAROLINE

Miller, Jane. Times Literary Supplement, 21 May 1976, p. 601. (Review of The Stepdaughter.)

Price, James. Encounter 47 (September 1976): 76. (Review of The Stepdaughter.)

BLAKE, WILLIAM

Fox, Susan. "The Female as Metaphor in William Blake's Poetry." Critical Inquiry 3 (Spring 1977): 507-519.

Radner, John B. "The Youthful Harlot's Curse: The Prostitute as Symbol of the City in 18th-Century English Literature." Eighteenth-Century Life 2 (March 1976): 59-64.

Wyatt, David M. "The Woman Jerusalem: Picture versus Poesis." Blake Studies 7, no. 2 (1975): 105-124.

BLANDIANA, ANA

Impey, Michael H. "Flights from Reality: Three Romanian Women Poets of the New Generation." Books Abroad 50 (Winter 1976): 16-33.

BLEEKER, ANN ELIZA

Watts, Emily Stipes. The Poetry of American Women from 1632 to 1945. Austin: University of Texas Press, 1977.

BLOWER, ELIZABETH

Portner, Ruth Lee. "A Study of Marriage in the English Novel." Ph.D. Dissertation, City University of New York, 1977.

BLOY, LEON

Birkett, Jennifer. "Barbey D'Aurevilly and Leon Bloy: Love and Morality in the Catholic Novel." Nottingham French Studies 14 (May 1975): 3-10.

_____. "The Theme of Love in the Work of Leon Bloy." Nottingham French Studies 14 (October 1975): 65-76.

BOCCACCIO, GIOVANNI

Cassell, Anthony K. "Il Corbaccio and the Secundus Tradition." Comparative Literature 25 (1973): 352-360.

Griffin, Robert. "Boccaccio's Fiammetta: Pictures at an Exhibition." Italian Quarterly 18 (Spring 1975): 75-94.

Moore, Cassandra Chrones. "The Romantic Triangle: A Study of Expanding Consciousness, (Volumes I and II)." Ph.D. Dissertation, The University of Michigan, 1975.

Still, Roger. <u>Love and Death in Renaissance Tragedy</u>.
Baton Rouge: Louisiana State University Press,
1976.

BODENHEIM, MAXWELL

Sacks, Arthur Bruce. "The Necessity of Rebellion: The
Novels of Maxwell Bodenheim." Ph.D. Dissertation,
The University of Wisconsin-Madison, 1975.

BOGAN, LOUISE

Bell, Pearl K. "A Woman of Letters." <u>New Leader</u>,
4 February 1974, pp. 23-24. (Review of <u>What the
Woman Lived.</u>)

Brinnin, John Malcolm and Bill Read, eds. <u>Twentieth
Century Poetry: American and British (1900-1970)</u>,
2nd ed. New York: McGraw-Hill, 1970.

Park, Clara Claiborne. "Poetry, Penetrable and Im-
penetrable." <u>Nation</u>, 3 September 1977, pp. 182-
186. (Review of <u>The Blue Estuaries: Poems 1923-
1968.</u>)

Perlmutter, Elizabeth P. "A Doll's Heart: The Girl in
the Poetry of Edna St. Vincent Millay and Louise
Bogan." <u>Twentieth Century Literature</u> 23 (May
1977): 157-179.

Ridgeway, Jaqueline Cecilia. "The Poetry of Louise
Bogan." Ph.D. Dissertation, University of California, Riverside, 1977.

Walker, Cheryl Lawson. "The Women's Tradition in
American Poetry." Ph.D. Dissertation, Brandeis
University, 1973.

BOGART, ELIZABETH

Watts, Emily Stipes. <u>The Poetry of American Women
from 1632 to 1945.</u> Austin: University of Texas
Press, 1977.

BOKER, GEORGE HENRY

Bennison, Martin J. and Barry B. Witham. "Sentimental

Love and the Nineteenth-Century American Drama. "
Players 49 (Summer 1974): 127-129.

BOLT, CAROL

Endres, Robin. "Not Fully Realized. " Canadian Forum
(May 1977): 38-39. (Review of Playwrights in Profile: Carol Bolt.)

Sarkar, Eileen. "Three Plays by Carol Bolt. " World
Literature Written in English 16 (November 1977):
366-367.

BOMBAL, MARIA LUISA

Welles, Marcia L. " 'El casamiento engañoso': Mar-
riage in the Novels of María Luisa Bombal, Silvina
Bullrich, and Elisa Serrana. " In Female Studies
IX: Teaching About Women in the Foreign Languages,
pp. 121-128. Edited by Sidonie Cassirer. Old
Westbury, N. Y. : Feminist Press, 1975.

BONNER, MARGERIE

Grace, Sherrill. "Margerie Bonner's Three Forgotten
Novels. " Journal of Modern Literature 6 (April
1977): 321-324.

BONTEMPS, ARNA

Love, Theresa R. "The Black Woman in Afro-American
Literature. " Paper presented at the Midwest Modern
Language Association meeting, Chicago, November
1975. (Mimeographed.)

BORKENSTEIN, HEINRICH

Sanders, Ruth Hetmanski. "The Virtuous Woman in the
Comedies of the Early German Enlightenment. "
Ph. D. Dissertation, State University of New York
at Stony Brook, 1975.

BOUCHER, SANDY

Arnold, June, et al. "Lesbians and Literature. " Sinister Wisdom 1 (Fall 1976): 20-23.

BOWEN, ELIZABETH

> Blodgett, Harriet. Patterns of Reality: Elizabeth Bowen's Novels. The Hague: Mouton, 1975.
>
> Kenney, Edwin J. Elizabeth Bowen. Lewisburg, Pa.: Bucknell University Press, 1974.
>
> Miles, Rosalind. The Fiction of Sex: Themes and Functions of Sex Difference in the Modern Novel. New York: Barnes & Noble, 1974.
>
> Nardella, Anna Gayle Ryan. "Feminism, Art, and Aesthetics: A Study of Elizabeth Bowen." Ph.D. Dissertation, State University of New York at Stony Brook, 1975.
>
> Noble, Linda Rae Willis. "A Critical Study of Elizabeth Bowen's Novels." Ph.D. Dissertation, University of Oregon, 1975.
>
> Rule, Jane. Lesbian Images. Garden City, N.Y.: Doubleday, 1975.

BOWER, BERTHA

> Davidson, Stanley R. "Chip of the Flying-U: The Author Was a Lady." Montana, The Magazine of Western History 23 (April 1973): 2-15.

BOYD, BLANCHE McCRARY

> Betsky, Celia. "Courting Time." Ms. 6 (November 1977): 39-43. (Review of Mourning the Death of Magic.)

BOYD, SHYLAH

> Garis, Leslie. "Books in Short." Ms. 4 (November 1975): 56. (Review of American Made.)

BOYLE, KAY

> Drew, Kathy. "Jails Don't Daunt Protesting Grandmother: Kay Boyle Dedicates Self to Human Dignity." Lost Generation Journal 4 (Winter 1976): 14.

Fay Stender with John Kelley. San Francisco Review of Books 1 (April 1975): 1, 10, 18. (Review of The Underground Woman.)

Fracchia, Charles. "Kay Boyle: A Profile." San Francisco Review of Books 1 (April 1976): 7-9.

Kay Boyle. San Francisco: San Francisco State University/The Poetry Center, n. d. (Video cassette.)

BRADDON, MARY

Behnken, Eloise. "Love, Desire, and Victorian Poets." Occasional Review Issue 6 (Summer 1977): [149]-157.

Bronfman, Judith. "The Griselda Legend in English Literature." Ph. D. Dissertation, New York University, 1977.

Garrison, Dee. "Immoral Fiction in the Late Victorian Library." American Quarterly 28 (Spring 1976): 71-89.

Keith, Sara. "The Athenaeum as Bibliographical Aid: Illustrated by Lady Audley's Secret and Other Novels." Victorian Periodicals Newsletter 8 (1975): 25-28.

Showalter, Elaine. "Desperate Remedies: Sensation Novels of the 1860s." Victorian Newsletter no. 49 (Spring 1976): [1]-5.

Wolff, Robert Lee. "Devoted Disciple: The Letters of Mary Elizabeth Braddon to Sir Edward Bulwer-Lytton, 1862-1873." Harvard Library Bulletin 12 (January 1974): 5-35; (April 1974): 129-161.

BRADSTREET, ANNE

Baldwin, Lewis M. "Moses and Mannerism: An Aesthetic for the Poetry of Colonial New England." Ph. D. Dissertation, Syracuse University, 1975.

Ball, Kenneth R. "Puritan Humility in Anne Bradstreet's Poetry." Cithara 13 (November 1973): [29]-41.

Dash, Irene. "The Literature of Birth and Abortion."
Regionalism and the Female Imagination 3 (Spring
1977): 8-13.

Eberwein, Jane Donahue. Early American Poetry.
Madison: University of Wisconsin Press, 1978.

Goldman, Maureen. "American Women and the Puritan
Heritage: Anne Hutchinson to Harriet Beecher Stowe."
Ph.D. Dissertation, Boston University Graduate
School, 1975.

Hornstein, Jacqueline. "Comic Vision in the Literature
of New England Women Before 1800." Regionalism
and the Female Imagination 3 (Fall 1977/Winter
1977-78): 11-19.

Moers, Ellen. Literary Women. Garden City, N.Y.:
Doubleday, 1976.

Stanford, Ann. Anne Bradstreet, the Worldly Puritan:
An Introduction to Her Poetry. New York: Franklin, 1974.

_____. "Images of Women in Early American Litera-
ture." In What Manner of Woman: Essays on English and American Life and Literature, pp. 185-210.
Edited by Marlene Springer. New York: New York
University Press, 1977.

Watts, Emily Stipes. The Poetry of American Women
from 1632 to 1945. Austin: University of Texas
Press, 1977.

Wess, Robert C. "Religious Tension in the Poetry of
Anne Bradstreet." Christianity and Literature 25
(Winter 1976): 30-36.

BRECHT, BERTOLT

Nussbaum, Laureen Klein. "The Image of Woman in the
Work of Bertolt Brecht." Ph.D. Dissertation, University of Washington, 1977.

BREMER, FREDIKA

Toth, Emily. "The Independent Woman and 'Free' Love."
Massachusetts Review 16 (Autumn 1975): 647-664.

BRETON, ANDRE

Balakian, Anna. André Breton: Magus of Surrealism. New York: Oxford University Press, 1971.

Sayegh, Alia Sayegh. "The Concept and Role of Woman in the Works of André Breton." Ph. D. Dissertation, University of Pennsylvania, 1974.

Smith, Susan Harris. "Breton's 'Femme et Oiseau': An Interpretation." Dada/Surrealism no. 6 (1976): 37-39.

BREWSTER, MARTHA

Watts, Emily Stipes. The Poetry of American Women from 1632 to 1945. Austin: University of Texas Press, 1977.

BRIET, MARGUERITE de

Baker, M. J. "France's First Sentimental Novel and Novels of Chivalry." Bibliothèque d'Humanisme et Renaissance 36, no. 1 (1974): 33-45.

BRØGGER, SUZANNE

Geng, Veronica. "Illuminating the Odd Assumption." Ms. 5 (February 1977): 40-41, 45. (Review of Deliver Us from Love: A Radical Feminist Speaks Out.)

Riley, Glenda. Best Sellers 36 (December 1976): 309. (Review of Deliver Us from Love.)

BRONTË, ANNE

Chitham, Edward. "Almost Like Twins." Brontë Society Transactions 16, no. 5 (1975): 365-373.

Halperin, John and Janet Kunert. Plots and Characters in the Fiction of Jane Austen, the Brontës, and George Eliot. Hamden, Conn.: Shoe String Press, 1976.

Karl, Frederick R. "The Brontës: The Self Defined, Redefined, and Refined." In The Victorian

Experience: The Novelists, pp. 121-150. Edited by Richard A. Levine. Athens: Ohio University Press, 1976.

Portner, Ruth Lee. "A Study of Marriage in the English Novel. " Ph.D. Dissertation, City University of New York, 1977.

Tiffany, Lewis K. "Charlotte and Anne's Literary Reputation. " Brontë Society Transactions 16, no. 4 (1974): 284-287.

Wilks, Brian. The Brontës. London: Hamlyn, 1975.

BRONTË, CHARLOTTE

Adams, Maurianne. "Jane Eyre: Woman's Estate. " In The Authority of Experience, pp. [137]-159. Edited by Arlyn Diamond and Lee R. Edwards. Amherst: University of Massachusetts Press, 1977.

Bedick, David B. "The Changing Role of Anxiety in the Novel. " Ph.D. Dissertation, New York University, 1975.

Beer, Patricia. "Jane Austen and Charlotte Brontë-- An Imaginary Conversation. " Listener, 31 July 1975, pp. 144-147.

Björk, Harriet. The Language of Truth: Charlotte Brontë, the Woman Question, and the Novel. Lund: Gleerup, 1974.

Blom, M. A. "Apprenticeship in 'The World Below': Charlotte Brontë's Juvenilia. " English Studies in Canada 1 (1975): 290-303.

Blom, Margaret Howard. Charlotte Brontë. New York: Twayne, 1977.

Calder, Jenni. Women and Marriage in Victorian Fiction. London: Thames & Hudson, 1976.

Cunningham, Valentine. Everywhere Spoken Against: Dissent in the Victorian Novel. Oxford: Clarendon Press, 1975.

Dessner, Lawrence J. The Homely Web of Truth: A
Study of Charlotte Brontë's Novels. The Hague:
Mouton, 1975.

Drabble, Margaret. "The Writer as Recluse: The
Theme of Solitude in the Works of the Brontës."
Brontë Society Transactions 16, no. 4 (1974): 259-
269.

Duthie, Enid L. The Foreign Vision of Charlotte Brontë.
London: Macmillan, 1975.

Eagleton, Terry. Myths of Power: A Marxist Study of
the Brontës. New York: Barnes & Noble, 1975.

Francone, Carol Burr. "Women in Rebellion: A Study
of the Conflict Between Self-Fulfillment and Self-
Sacrifice in Emma, Jane Eyre, and The Mill on the
Floss." Ph.D. Dissertation, Case Western Reserve
University, 1975.

Gates, Barbara. " 'Visionary Woe' and Its Revision:
Another Look at Jane Eyre's Pictures." Ariel 7
(October 1976): 36-49.

Goldfarb, Russell M. Sexual Repression and Victorian
Literature. Lewisburg: Bucknell University Press,
1970.

Grudin, Peter. "Jane and the Other Mrs. Rochester:
Excess and Restraint in Jane Eyre." Novel 10
(Winter 1977): [145]-157.

Gubar, Susan. "The Genesis of Hunger, According to
Shirley." Feminist Studies 3 (Spring-Summer 1976):
5-21.

Halperin, John and Janet Kunert. Plots and Characters
in the Fiction of Jane Austen, the Brontës, and
George Eliot. Hamden, Conn. : Shoe String Press,
1976.

Hart, Anne. "Studies, Time, the Author as Wife."
Brontë Society Transactions 16, no. 5 (1975): 376-
382.

Hoffeld, Laura Diamond. "The Servant Heroine in 18th

and 19th Century British Fiction: The Social Reality and Its Image in the Novel. " Ph. D. Dissertation, New York University, 1975.

Karl, Frederick R. "The Brontës: The Self Defined, Redefined, and Refined. " In The Victorian Experience: The Novelists, pp. 121-150. Edited by Richard A. Levine. Athens: Ohio University Press, 1976.

Lerner, Laurence. "The Tremulous Homely-Faced Creature: Charlotte Brontë and Her Critics. " Encounter (July 1975): 60-66. (Review essay.)

McDaniel, Judith. "Charlotte Brontë and the Feminist Novel. " University of Michigan Papers in Women's Studies 2, no. 3 (1977): 90-98.

_____. "Fettered Wings Half Loose: Female Development in the Victorian Novel. " Ph. D. Dissertation, Tufts University, 1975.

Martin, Robert K. "Jane Eyre and the World of Faery." Mosaic 10 (Summer 1977): [85]-95.

Miles, Rosalind. The Fiction of Sex: Themes and Functions of Sex Difference in the Modern Novel. New York: Barnes & Noble, 1974.

Moers, Ellen. Literary Women. Garden City, N.Y.: Doubleday, 1976.

Moglen, Helene. Charlotte Brontë: The Self Conceived. New York: Norton, 1976.

Natov, Roni L. "The Strong-Minded Heroine in Mid-Victorian Fiction. " Ph. D. Dissertation, New York University, 1975.

Ohmann, Carol. "Historical Reality and 'Divine Appointment' in Charlotte Brontë's Fiction. " Signs: Journal of Women in Culture and Society 2 (Summer 1977): 757-778.

Perry, Donna Marie. "From Innocence Through Experience: A Study of the Romantic Child in Five Nineteenth Century Novels. " Ph. D. Dissertation, Marquette University, 1976.

Peters, Margo. Unquiet Soul: A Biography of Charlotte Brontë. Garden City, N.Y.: Doubleday, 1975.

Pinion, F. B. A Brontë Companion: Literary Assess-
ment, Background and Reference. New York:
Barnes & Noble, 1975.

Platt, Carolyn V. "How Feminist Is Villette?" Women
& Literature 3 (Spring 1975): 16-27.

Rigney, Barbara. Madness and Sexual Politics in the
Feminist Novel: Studies of Charlotte Brontë, Virginia Woolf, Doris Lessing, and Margaret Atwood.
Madison: University of Wisconsin Press, forthcoming.

Schwartz, Roberta C. "Art as Ethic: A Study of Jane
Eyre." North Dakota Quarterly 44 (Winter 1976):
20-30.

Showalter, Elaine. A Literature of Their Own: British
Women Novelists from Brontë to Lessing. Princeton: Princeton University Press, 1977.

Siebenschuh, William R. "The Image of the Child and
the Plot of Jane Eyre." Studies in the Novel 8
(Fall 1976): 304-317.

Siefert, Susan Elizabeth. "The Dilemma of the Talented
Woman: A Study in Nineteenth-Century Fiction."
Ph.D. Dissertation, Marquette University, 1974.

Sigel, John Edwin. "Passionate Craftsmanship: The
Artistry of Charlotte Brontë's Jane Eyre and Vil-
lette." Ph.D. Dissertation, State University of New
York at Binghamton, 1976.

Simpson, Jacqueline. "The Function of Folklore in Jane
Eyre and Wuthering Heights." Folklore 85 (1975):
47-61.

Smith, LeRoy W. "Charlotte Brontë's Flight from
Eros." Women & Literature 4 (Spring 1976): 30-
44.

Springer, Marlene. "Angels and Other Women in Victorian Literature." In What Manner of Woman:

Essays on English and American Life and Literature, pp. 124-159. Edited by Marlene Springer. New York: New York University Press, 1977.

Stowell, H. E. Quill Pens and Petticoats: A Woman of Letters. London: Wayland, 1970.

Sullivan, Paula. "Rochester Reconsidered: Jane Eyre in the Light of the Samson Story." Brontë Society Transactions 16, no. 3 (1973): 192-198.

Taylor, Irene and Gina Luria. "Gender and Genre: Women in British Romantic Literature." In What Manner of Woman: Essays on English and American Life and Literature, pp. 98-124. Edited by Marlene Springer. New York: New York University Press, 1977.

Thorpe, Michael. " 'The Other Side': Wide Sargasso Sea and Jane Eyre. " Ariel: A Review of International English Literature 8 (July 1977): 99-110.

Tiffany, Lewis K. "Charlotte and Anne's Literary and Reputation." Brontë Society Transactions 16, no. 4 (1974): 284-287.

Toth, Emily. "The Independent Woman and 'Free' Love. " Massachusetts Review 16 (Autumn 1975): 647-664.

Wilks, Brian. The Brontës. London: Hamlyn, 1975.

Wilson, F. A. C. "The Primrose Wreath: The Heroes of the Brontë Novels. " Nineteenth-Century Fiction 29 (1975): 40-57.

Youngren, Virginia Rotan. "Moral Life in Solitude: A Study of Selected Novels of Jane Austen, Charlotte Brontë, Elizabeth Gaskell and George Eliot. " Ph. D. Dissertation, Rutgers University, The State University of New Jersey (New Brunswick), 1977.

Yuen, Maria. "Two Crises of Decision in Jane Eyre. " English Studies 57 (June 1976): 215-226.

BRONTË, EMILY

Beuersluis, John. "Love and Self-Knowledge: A Study of Wuthering Heights." English 24, no. 120 (1975): 77-82.

Blondel, Jacques. "Imagery in Wuthering Heights." Durham University Journal 37, no. 1 (1975): 1-7.

Bosco, Ronald. "Heathcliff: Societal Victim or Demon." Gypsy Scholar 2, no. 1 (1974): 5-12.

Chitham, Edward. "Almost Like Twins." Brontë Society Transactions 16, no. 5 (1975): 365-373.

Dingle, Herbert. The Mind of Emily Brontë. London: Martin Brian & O'Keeffe, 1974.

Halperin, John and Janet Kunert. Plots and Characters in the Fiction of Jane Austen, the Brontës, and George Eliot. Hamden, Conn.: Shoe String Press, 1976.

Hatch, Ronald B. "Heathcliff's 'Queer End' and Schopenhauer's Denial of the Will." Canadian Review of Comparative Literature 1 (1975): 49-64.

Karl, Frederick R. "The Brontës: The Self Defined, Redefined, and Refined." In The Victorian Experience: The Novelists, pp. 121-150. Edited by Richard A. Levine. Athens: Ohio University Press, 1976.

Leavis, Q. D. Introduction to Wuthering Heights, edited by William M. Sale, Jr. New York: Norton, 1972.

Miles, Rosalind. The Fiction of Sex: Themes and Functions of Sex Difference in the Modern Novel. New York: Barnes & Noble, 1974.

Moers, Ellen. Literary Women. Garden City, N.Y.: Doubleday, 1976.

O'Dowd, M. C. "Writing and Injustice." Contrast (Capetown, South Africa) 23 (1970): 48-61.

Petyt, K. M. " 'Thou' and 'You' in Wuthering Heights."

Brontë Society Transactions 16, no. 4 (1974): 291-293.

Reed, Walter. Meditations on the Hero. New Haven: Yale University Press, 1974.

Scrivner, Buford, Jr. "The Ethos of Wuthering Heights." Dalhousie Review 54 (Autumn 1974): 451-462.

Silver, Nancy. "To Be a Woman: Scarlett O'Hara Revisited: Looking Back at the Books That Taught Me to Be a Woman." Redbook 146 (December 1975): 52, 54, 56, 59.

Simpson, Jacqueline. "The Function of Folklore in Jane Eyre and Wuthering Heights." Folklore 85 (1975): 47-61.

Viswanathan, Jacqueline. "Point of View and Unreliability in Brontë's Wuthering Heights, Conrad's Under Western Eyes, and Mann's Doktor Faustus." Orbis Litterarum 29 (1974): 42-60.

Wilks, Brian. The Brontës. London: Hamlyn, 1975.

Wilson, F. A. C. "The Primrose Wreath: The Heroes of the Brontë Novels." Nineteenth-Century Fiction 29 (1975): 40-57.

BROOKE, FRANCES

Cunningham, A. R. "The 'New Woman Fiction' of the 1890's." Victorian Studies 17 (December 1973): 177-186.

New, William H. "The Old Maid: Frances Brooke's Apprentice Feminism." Journal of Canadian Fiction 2 (1973): 9-12.

BROOKS, GWENDOLYN

Authors in the News, vol. 1. Detroit: Gale Research, 1976, p. 63.

Callow, James T. and Robert Reilly. Guide to American Literature from Emily Dickinson to the Present. New York: Barnes & Noble, 1977.

Dash, Irene. "The Literature of Birth and Abortion." Regionalism and the Female Imagination 3 (Spring 1977): 8-13.

Hull, Gloria T. and Posey Gallagher. "Update on Part One: An Interview with Gwendolyn Brooks." CLA Journal 21 (September 1977): 19-40.

Juhasz, Suzanne. Naked and Fiery Forms: Modern American Poetry by Women, a New Tradition. New York: Harper & Row, 1976.

Lynch, Charles Henry. "Robert Hayden and Gwendolyn Brooks: A Critical Study." Ph.D. Dissertation, New York University, 1977.

McMahan, Elizabeth. "Gwendolyn Brooks: A Feminist Dilemma." Paper presented at the Midwest Modern Language Association meeting, Chicago, November 1975. (Mimeographed.)

Madhalreti, Safisha N. "Focus on Form in Gwendolyn Brooks." Black Books Bulletin 2, no. 1 (1975): 24-27.

Rushing, Andrea Benton. "Images of Black Women in Afro-American Poetry." Black World 24 (September 1975): 18-30.

Schraufnagel, Noel. From Apology to Protest: The Black American Novel. Deland, Florida: Everett/ Edwards, 1973.

Schulz, Elizabeth. " 'Free in Fact and at Last': The Image of the Black Woman in Black American Literature." In What Manner of Woman: Essays in English and American Life and Literature, pp. 316-344. Edited by Marlene Springer. New York: New York University Press, 1977.

Shinn, Thelma J. Wardrop. "A Study of Women Characters in Contemporary American Fiction 1940-1970." Ph.D. Dissertation, Purdue University, 1972.

Spillers, Hortense. "Gwendolyn the Terrible: Aspects of Style in the Poetry of Gwendolyn Brooks." Paper presented at the MLA convention, San Francisco, December 1975.

BROPHY, BRIGID

Burgess, Anthony. New York Times Book Review, 25 August 1974, p. 4. (Review of The Adventures of God in His Search for the Black Girl.)

Dock, Leslie. "An Interview with Brigid Brophy." Contemporary Literature 17 (Spring 1976): 151-170.

Walters, Margaret. New Republic, 28 December 1974, pp. 27-28. (Review of The Adventures of God in His Search for the Black Girl.)

Warnock, Mary. "A Hard Time for Satire." Listener, 6 December 1973, pp. 785-786. (Review of The Adventures of God in His Search for the Black Girl.)

BROUGHTON, RHODA

Garrison, Dee. "Immoral Fiction in the Late Victorian Library." American Quarterly 28 (Spring 1976): 71-89.

Showalter, Elaine. "Desperate Remedies: Sensation Novels of the 1860s." Victorian Newsletter no. 49 (Spring 1976): [1]-5.

_____. "The Double Standard: Criticism of Women Writers in England, 1845-1880." Ph.D. Dissertation, University of California, Davis, 1970.

_____. A Literature of Their Own: British Women Novelists from Brontë to Lessing. Princeton: Princeton University Press, 1977.

BROUMAS, OLGA

Gray, Paul. Time, 21 March 1977, p. 91. (Review of Beginning with O.)

Hall, Donald. Atlantic Monthly 240 (October 1977): 102-103. (Review of Beginning with O.)

Hudson Review 30 (Summer 1977): 459. (Review of Beginning with O.)

Sage, Lorna. Times Literary Supplement, 24 June 1977, p. 758.

Vendler, Helen. Yale Review 67 (Autumn 1977): 72-73.
(Review of Beginning with O.)

Village Voice, 29 August 1977, p. 41.

BROWN, ALICE

Langill, Ellen Detering. "Alice Brown: A Critical
Study. " Ph.D. Dissertation, The University of Wisconsin-Madison, 1975.

BROWN, CHARLES BROCKDEN

Clemon, John. "Ambiguous Evil: A Study of Villains
and Heroes in Charles Brockden Brown's Major
Novels. " Early American Literature 10 (Fall 1975):
190-219.

Hoekstra, Ellen Louise Jarvis. "The Characterization
of Women in the Novels of Charles Brockden Brown. "
Ph.D. Dissertation, Michigan State University,
1975.

Stanford, Ann. "Images of Women in Early American
Literature. " In What Manner of Woman: Essays on
English and American Life and Literature, pp. 185-
210. Edited by Marlene Springer. New York: New
York University Press, 1977.

BROWN, MARGERY FINN

Dean, Nancy. "Feminist Short Fiction: New Forms and
Styles. " Paper presented at the MLA meeting, New
York City, 1976. (Mimeographed.)

BROWN, RITA MAE

Core, Deborah. Sinister Wisdom 1 (Fall 1976): 87-88.
(Review of In Her Day.)

Larkin, Joan. "In Short: In Her Day. " Ms. 5 (April
1977): 44. (Review of In Her Day.)

Rule, Jane. Lesbian Images. Garden City, N.Y. :
Doubleday, 1975.

BROWN, ROSELLEN

Gargan, Carol. Best Sellers 37 (May 1977): 58. (Review of Cora Fry.)

Howes, Victor. Christian Science Monitor, 9 March 1977, p. 23. (Review of Cora Fry.)

BROWN, WILLIAM HILL

Davidson, Cathy N. "The Power of Sympathy Reconsidered: William Hill Brown as Literary Craftsman." Early American Literature 10 (Spring 1975): 14-29.

Stanford, Ann. "Images of Women in Early American Literature." In What Manner of Woman: Essays on English and American Life and Literature, pp. 185-210. Edited by Marlene Springer. New York: New York University Press, 1977.

BROWN, WILLIAM WELLS

Gayle, Addison, Jr. The Way of the New World: The Black Novel in America. Garden City, N.Y.: Anchor Press/Doubleday, 1975.

Ward, Hazel Mae. "The Black Woman as Character: Images in the American Novel, 1852-1953." Ph.D. Dissertation, The University of Texas at Austin, 1977.

BROWNING, ELIZABETH BARRETT

Behnken, Eloise. "Love, Desire, and Victorian Poets." Occasional Review Issue 6 (Summer 1977): [149]-157.

Donaldson, Sandra Marie. "Elizabeth Barrett Browning's Poetic and Feminist Philosophies in Aurora Leigh and Other Poems." Ph.D. Dissertation, The University of Connecticut, 1977.

_____. "Elizabeth Barrett's Two Sonnets to George Sand." Studies in Browning and His Circle 5 (Spring 1977): 19-22.

Heydon, Peter and Philip Keeley, eds. Elizabeth

Browning / 59

Browning: Letters to Mrs. David Ogilvy 1849-1861. London: Murray, 1974.

Johnson, Wendell Stacy. Sex and Marriage in Victorian Poetry. Ithaca and London: Cornell University Press, 1975, pp. 53-57.

Meredith, Michael. "The Wounded Heroine: Elizabeth Barrett's Sophocles." Studies in Browning and His Circle 3 (Fall 1975): 1-12.

Moers, Ellen. "Elizabeth Barrett Browning." Deland, Florida: Everett/Edwards, n.d. (Cassette no. 5523.)

_____. Literary Women. Garden City, N.Y.: Doubleday, 1976.

Showalter, Elaine. A Literature of Their Own: British Women Novelists from Brontë to Lessing. Princeton: Princeton University Press, 1977.

Springer, Marlene. "Angels and Other Women in Victorian Literature." In What Manner of Woman: Essays on English and American Life and Literature, pp. 124-159. Edited by Marlene Springer. New York: New York University Press, 1977.

Stowell, H. E. Quill Pens and Petticoats: A Portrait of Women of Letters. London: Wayland, 1970.

BROWNING, ROBERT

Adler, Joshua. "Structure and Meaning in Browning's 'My Last Duchess.'" Victorian Poetry 15 (Autumn 1977): 219-227.

Ball, Patricia M. The Heart's Events: The Victorian Poetry of Relationships. London: University of London, The Athlone Press, 1976.

Horne, Lewis B. "Action and Awareness in Pippa Passes." Studies in Browning and His Circle 3 (Fall 1975): 13-22.

Johnson, Wendell Stacy. Sex and Marriage in Victorian Poetry. Ithaca and London: Cornell University Press, 1975.

Locker, Kitty Colleen O'Donnell. "The Definition of Woman: A Major Motif in Browning's The Ring and the Book." Ph.D. Dissertation, University of Illinois at Urbana-Champaign, 1977.

Poston, Lawrence, III. " 'A novel grace and beauty strange': Browning's 'Women and Roses.' " Browning Studies Notes 5, no. 1 (1975): 15-17.

Siegchrist, Mark. "Pollyanna or Polyanthus: Clara de Millefleurs in Browning's Red Cotton Night-Cap Country." English Language Notes 11 (June 1974): 283-287.

BRUNTON, MARY

Taylor, Irene and Gina Luria. "Gender and Genre: Women in British Romantic Literature." In What Manner of Woman: Essays on English and American Life and Literature, pp. 98-124. Edited by Marlene Springer. New York: New York University Press, 1977.

BUCHANAN, THOMPSON

Loudin, Joanne Marie. "The Changing Role of the Comic Heroine in American Drama from 1900 to 1940." Ph.D. Dissertation, University of Washington, 1974.

BÜCHNER, GEORG

Drost, Carla Lowrey. "The Major Female Characters in Georg Büchner's Dramas." Ph.D. Dissertation, The Louisiana State University and Agricultural and Mechanical College, 1974.

BULGAKOV, MIKHAIL

Haber, Edythe C. "The Mythic Structure of Bulgakov's The Master and Margarita." Russian Review 34 (October 1975): 382-409.

BULLINS, ED

Kauffman. " 'The Taking of Miss Janie.' " New Republic, 7 June 1975; also in Persons of the Drama, pp. 251-252. New York: Harper, 1976.

MacKay, Barbara. Saturday Review, 12 July 1975, p. 52. (Review of The Taking of Miss Janie.)

Miller, Jeanne-Marie A. "Images of Black Women in Plays by Black Playwrights." CLA Journal 20 (June 1977): 494-507.

BULLRICH, SILVINA

Kaminsky, Amy. "The Real Circle of Iron: Mothers and Children; Children and Mothers, in Four Argentine Novels." Latin American Review 4 (Fall-Winter 1976): 77-86.

Tavenner, Anna C. "Aspectos de conflicto enajenamiento de la mujer en las novelas de Silvina Bullrich, Beatriz Guido y Clarice Lispector." Ph.D. Dissertation, Texas Tech University, 1977.

Welles, Marcia L. " 'El casamiento engañoso': Marriage in the Novels of María Luisa Bombal, Silvina Bullrich, and Elisa Serrana." In Female Studies IX: Teaching about Women in the Foreign Languages, pp. 121-128. Edited by Sidonie Cassirer. Old Westbury, N.Y.: Feminist Press, 1975.

BURGESS, ANTHONY

Fass, Barbara. La Belle Dame sans Merci & the Aesthetics of Romanticism. Detroit: Wayne State University Press, 1974.

BURGOS, CARMEN de

Starčerić, Elizabeth Deborah. "La mujer en la obra literaria de Carmen de Burgos." Ph.D. Dissertation, City University of New York, 1977.

BURKE, FIELDING see DARGAN, OLIVE TILFORD

BURNEY, FANNY (Fanny Burney d'Arblay)

Barker, Gerard A. "The Two Mrs. Selwyns: Evelina and The Man of the World." Papers on Language and Literature 13 (Winter 1977): 80-84.

Bodek, Evelyn Gordon. "Salonières and Bluestockings:

Educated Obsolescence and Germinating Feminism. " Feminist Studies 3 (Spring-Summer 1976): 183-199.

Calder, Jenni. Women and Marriage in Victorian Fiction. London: Thames & Hudson, 1976.

Copeland, Edward W. "Money in the Novels of Fanny Burney. " Studies in the Novel 8 (Spring 1976): 24-37.

Cutting, Rose Marie. "Defiant Women: The Growth of Feminism in Fanny Burney's Novels. " Studies in English Literature 17 (Summer 1977): [519]-530.

_____. "A Wreath for Fanny Burney's Last Novel: The Wanderer's Contribution to Women's Studies. " Illinois Quarterly 37, no. 3 (1975): 45-64.

Dobbs, Jeannine. "The Blue-Stockings: Getting It Together. " Frontiers 1 (Winter 1976): 81-93.

Fritz, Paul and Richard Morton, eds. Women in the Eighteenth Century and Other Essays. Toronto: Samuel Stevens Hakkert, 1976.

Glassman, Peter. "Acts of Enclosure. " Hudson Review 30 (Spring 1977): 138-146. (Review Essay.)

Glock, Waldo S. "Appearance and Reality: The Education of Evelina. " Essays in Literature 2 (Spring 1975): 32-41.

Haworth, H. E. "Romantic Female Writers and the Critics. " Texas Studies in Literature and Language 17 (Winter 1976): 725-736.

Moers, Ellen. Literary Women. Garden City, N.Y.: Doubleday, 1976.

Newton, Judith. "Evelina, or, the History of a Young Lady's Entrance into the Marriage Market. " Modern Language Studies 6 (Spring 1976): 48-56.

Patterson, Emily H. "Unearned Irony in Fanny Burney's Evelina. " Durham University Journal n.s. 36 (June 1975): 200-204.

Richetti, John J. "The Portrayal of Women in Restoration and Eighteenth-Century English Literature." In
What Manner of Woman: Essays on English and
American Life and Literature, pp. 65-97. Edited
by Marlene Springer. New York: New York University Press, 1977.

Skilton, David. The English Novel: Defoe to the Victorians. New York: Barnes & Noble, 1977.

Spacks, Patricia Meyer. Imagining a Self: Autobiography and Novel in Eighteenth-Century England. Cambridge: Harvard University Press, 1976.

Stowell, H. E. Quill Pens and Petticoats: A Portrait
of Women of Letters. London: Wayland, 1970.

Vopat, James B. "Evelina: Life as Art--Notes Toward
Becoming a Performer on the Stage of Life." Essays in Literature 2 (Spring 1975): 42-52.

BURR, ANNE

Hatch, Robert. Nation, 30 November 1974, p. 573.
(Review of Mert and Phil.)

Kalem, T. E. Time, 18 November 1974, p. 98. (Review of Mert and Phil.)

Kroll, Jack. "Papp's Platoons." Newsweek, 11 November 1974, pp. 121-122. (Review of Mert and Phil.)

Stasio, Marilyn. Ms. 4 (September 1975): 37-41. (Review of Mert and Phil.)

BURROWAY, JANET

Broyard, Anatole. New York Times Book Review, 10
April 1977, p. 14. (Review of Raw Silk.)

Jefferson, Margo. Newsweek, 14 April 1977, p. 88.
(Review of Raw Silk.)

Rinzler, Carol Eisen. "Books: Novel Reading." Ms.
6 (August 1977): 34-35. (Review of Raw Silk.)

BUZEA, CONSTANTA

> Impey, Michael H. "Flights from Reality: Three Romanian Women Poets of the New Generation." Books Abroad 50 (Winter 1976): 16-33.

BYRON, GEORGE GORDON, LORD

> Ball, Patricia M. The Heart's Events: The Victorian Poetry of Relationships. London: University of London, The Athlone Press, 1976.

> Kernberger, Katherine Anne. " 'A Lovely and a Fearful Thing': Byron's Sexual Politics in Don Juan." Ph.D. Dissertation, University of California, Los Angeles, 1977.

> Lisbeth, Terrence L. "The Motif of Imagination in Byron's Bluestocking Allusions." Massachusetts Studies in English 4 (Autumn 1974-Winter 1975): 34-42.

> Taylor, Irene and Gina Luria. "Gender and Genre: Women in British Romantic Literature." In What Manner of Woman: Essays on English and American Life and Literature, pp. 98-124. Edited by Marlene Springer. New York: New York University Press, 1977.

- C -

CABRERA INFANTE, GUILLERMO

> Siemens, William L. "Women as Cosmic Phenomena in Tres tristes tigres." Journal of Spanish Studies: Twentieth Century 3 (Winter 1975): 199-209.

CAHAN, ABRAHAM

> Baum, Charlotte, Paula Hyman and Sonya Michel. The Jewish Woman in America. New York: Dial Press, 1975.

> Chametzky, Jules. From the Ghetto: The Fiction of Abraham Cahan. Amherst: The University of Massachusetts Press, 1977.

Koltun, Elizabeth. The Jewish Woman: New Perspectives. New York: Schocken, 1976.

CAIN, GEORGE

Billingsley, R. G. "Forging New Directions: The Burden of the Hero in Modern Afro-American Literature." Obsidian 1 (Winter 1975): 5-21.

CAIRD, MONA

Cunningham, A. R. "The 'New Woman Fiction' of the 1890's." Victorian Studies 17 (December 1973): 177-186.

CALDERON DE LA BARCA, PEDRO

Dreyfuss, Cecilia Anne Stiborik. "Femina sapiens in Drama: Aeschylus to Grillparzer." Ph.D. Dissertation, The University of Michigan, 1975.

Honig, Edwin. Calderón and the Seizures of Honor. Cambridge: Harvard University Press, 1972.

Lavroff, Ellen C. "Who Is Rosaura? Another Look at La vida es sueño." Revue des Langues Vivantes 42, no. 5 (1976): 482-496.

Niera, David J. "Wife-Killing in Medieval Hispanic Letters: A Prelude to the Calderón-Honor-Vengeance Trilogy." Paper presented at the Tennessee Philological Association, March 1975. (Available from author, SUNY-Geneseo, Geneseo, N.Y. 14454.)

CALISHER, HORTENSE

Shinn, Thelma J. Wardrop. "A Study of Women Characters in Contemporary American Fiction 1940-1970." Ph.D. Dissertation, Purdue University, 1972.

CAMARA, EUGENIA

Haberly, David T. "Eugênia Câmara: The Life and Verse of an Actress." Luso-Brazilian Review 12 (Winter 1975): 162-174.

CAMPOS, JULIETA

>Young, Rinda Rebeca Stowell. "Six Representative Wo-
men Novelists of Mexico, 1960-1969. " Ph. D. Dissertation, University of Illinois at Urbana-Champaign,
1975.

CAMUS, ALBERT

>Shaw, Penelope Ann. "Camus: A Psychocritical Study
of the Image of the Mother. " Ph. D. Dissertation,
The University of Michigan, 1977.

CARROLL, LEWIS

>Auerbach, Nina. "Alice and Wonderland. " Victorian
Studies 17 (September 1973): 31-47.

>Little, Judith. "Liberated Alice: Dodgson's Female
Hero as Domestic Rebel. " Women's Studies 3, no.
2 (1976): 195-206.

>McGillis, Roderick. "Tenniel's Turned Rabbit: A Read-
ing of Alice with Tenniel's Help. " English Studies
in Canada 3 (Fall 1977): [326]-335.

CARTER, ELIZABETH

>Miner, Earl J. , ed. Stuart and Georgian Moments.
Berkeley: University of California Press, 1972.

CARY, ALICIA

>Wood, Ann D. "The 'Scribbling Women' and Fanny
Fern: Why Women Wrote. " American Quarterly
23 (Spring 1971): 3-24.

CARY, ELIZABETH (Viscountess Falkland)

>Mahl, Mary R. and Helen Koon, eds. The Female
Spectator: English Women Writers Before 1800.
Bloomington and Old Westbury, N. Y. : Indiana Uni-
versity Press and The Feminist Press, 1977.

>Pearse, Nancy Cotton. "Elizabeth Cary, Renaissance
Playwrights. " Texas Studies in Literature and
Language 18 (Winter 1977): [601]-608.

CARY, JOYCE

Dobbs, Jeannine. "The Blue-Stockings: Getting It Together." Frontiers 1 (Winter 1976): 81-93.

Kronenfeld, J. Z. "In Search of Mister Johnson: Creation, Politics, and Culture in Cary's Africa."
Ariel 7 (October 1976): 69-97.

Wells, Glenn Lawrence, Jr. "The Role of the Female
in Relation to the Artist in the Works of Joyce
Cary." Ph.D. Dissertation, The University of Mississippi, 1975.

CASTELLANOS, ROSARIO

Langford, Walter M. The Mexican Novel Comes of Age.
Notre Dame: University of Notre Dame Press, 1971.

Young, Rinda Rebeca Stowell. "Six Representative Women Novelists of Mexico, 1960-1969." Ph.D. Dissertation, University of Illinois at Urbana-Champaign,
1975.

CASTILLO SOLORZANO, ALONSO de

Pérez-Erdélyi, Mireya. "La imagen de las mujeres en
las novelas picaresco-cortesanas de María de Zayas
y Sotomayor y Alonso de Castillo Solórzano." Ph.D.
Dissertation, Rutgers University, The State University of New Jersey (New Brunswick), 1977.

Sánchez-Díez, Francisco Javier. "La novela picaresca
de protogonista femenino en España durante el siglo
XVII." Ph.D. Dissertation, University of North
Carolina, Chapel Hill, 1972.

CATHER, WILLA

Arnold, Marilyn. "Sapphira and the Slave Girl: Willa
Cather's Escape into Order." Paper presented at
the MLA convention, San Francisco, December 1975.

Bennett, Sandra Margaret. "Structure in the Novels of
Willa Cather." Ph.D. Dissertation, University of
Utah, 1976.

Bloom, Lillian D. "On Daring to Look Back with Wharton and Cather." Novel 10 (Winter 1977): [167]-178. (Review Essay.)

Brunauer, Dalma H. "The Problem of Point of View in A Lost Lady." Renascence 28 (Autumn 1975): 47-52.

Callow, James T. and Robert Reilly. Guide to American Literature from Emily Dickinson to the Present. New York: Barnes & Noble, 1977.

Davidson, Colleen Tighe. "Beyond the Sentimental Heroine: The Feminist Character in American Novels, 1899-1937." Ph.D. Dissertation, University of Minnesota, 1975.

Gerger, Philip. Willa Cather. New York: Twayne, 1975.

Goodman, Charlotte. "Images of American Rural Women in the Novel." University of Michigan Papers in Women's Studies 1 (June 1975): 57-70.

Hamner, Eugenie Lambert. "Affirmations in Willa Cather's A Lost Lady." Midwest Quarterly 17 (April 1976): 245-251.

Helmick, Evelyn. "The Broken World: Medievalism in A Lost Lady." Renascence 28 (Autumn 1975): 39-46.

_____. "The Mysteries of Antonia." Midwest Quarterly 17 (January 1976): 173-185.

Lathrop, Jo Anne. Willa Cather: A Checklist of Her Published Writing. Lincoln: University of Nebraska Press, 1975.

Maglin, Nan Bauer. "Rebel Women Writers, 1894-1925." Ph.D. Dissertation, Union Graduate School, 1975.

Meldrum, Barbara. "Images of Women in Western American Literature." Midwest Quarterly 17 (April 1976): 252-267.

Miller, Bruce E. "The Testing of Willa Cather's Humanism: A Lost Lady and Other Cather Novels." Kansas Quarterly 5 (Fall 1973): 43-50.

Miller, James E. "My Antonia and the American Dream." Prairie Schooner 48, no. 2 (1975): 112-123.

Moers, Ellen. Literary Women. Garden City, N.Y.: Doubleday, 1976.

O'Brien, Sharon. "The Limits of Passion: Willa Cather's Review of The Awakening." Women & Literature 3 (Fall 1975): 10-20.

Pannill, Linda Susanne. "The Artist-Heroine in American Fiction, 1890-1920." Ph.D. Dissertation, The University of North Carolina at Chapel Hill, 1975.

Parker, Jeri. Uneasy Survivors: Five Women Writers. Salt Lake City: Peregrine Smith, 1975.

Pers, Mona. "Repetition in Willa Cather's Early Writings: Clues to the Development of an Artist." American Studies in Scandinavia 8, no. 2 (1976): 55-66.

Rule, Jane. Lesbian Images. Garden City, N.Y.: Doubleday, 1975.

Shelton, Frank W. "The Image of the Rock and the Family in the Novels of Willa Cather." Markham Review 6 (Fall 1976): 9-14.

"Symposium: Women and Tragedy." Prairie Schooner 49 (Fall 1975): 227-236. (Participants: Lorraine M. Keilstrup, Betty Jochmans, JoAnna Lathrop.)

Watts, Emily Stipes. The Poetry of American Women from 1632 to 1945. Austin: University of Texas Press, 1977.

CATULLUS

Atkins, John. Sex in Literature: The Classical Experience of the Sexual Impulse, vol. 2. London: Calder & Boyers, 1973.

Luck, Georg. "The Woman's Role in Latin Love Poetry." In Perspectives of Roman Poetry, pp. 15-31. Edited by G. Karl Galinsky. Austin: University of Texas Press, 1974.

CAVENDISH, MARGARET (Duchess of Newcastle)

Mahl, Mary R. and Helene Koon, eds. The Female
Spectator: English Women Writers Before 1800.
Bloomington and Old Westbury, N. Y. : Indiana Uni-
versity Press and The Feminist Press, 1977.

CENTLIVRE, SUSANNA

Hume, Robert D. "Marital Discord in English Comedy
from Dryden to Fielding." Modern Philology 74
(February 1977): 248-272.

Lock, Frederick Peter. "The Dramatic Art of Susanna
Centlivre." Ph. D. Dissertation, McMaster University (Canada), 1975.

Mahl, Mary R. and Helen Koon, eds. The Female Spectator: English Women Writers Before 1800. Bloomington and Old Westbury, N. Y. : Indiana University
Press, and The Feminist Press, 1977.

CERVANTES SAAVEDRA, MIGUEL de

da Costa Fontes, Manual. "Love as an Equilizer in La
española inglesa." Romance Notes 16 (Spring 1975):
742-748.

CHALLE, ROBERT

Coulet, Henri. "Le Thème de 'La Madeleine repentie'
chez Robert Challe, Prévost et Diderot." Saggi e
Ricerche di Letterature Francese 14 (1975): 287-304.

Swiderski, Marie-Laure. "L'image de la femme dans
le roman au debut du XVIIIe siecle: Les 'Illustres
Francaises' de Robert Challe." Revue de l'Univer-
sité d'Ottawa 42 (Avril-Juin 1972): 259-271.

Webb, Shawncey Jay. "Aspects of Fidelity and Infidelity
in the Eighteenth Century French Novel from Chasles
to Laclos." Ph. D. Dissertation, Indiana University,
1977.

CHANG, EILEEN

Hales, Dell R. "Social Criticism in Modern Chinese

Essays and Novels. " Review of National Literatures 6 (Spring 1975): 39-59.

CHAO SHU-LI

Eber, Irene. "Images of Women in Recent Chinese Fiction: Do Women Hold Up Half the Sky?" Signs: Journal of Women in Culture and Society 2 (Autumn 1976): 24-34.

CHAPMAN, GEORGE

Mirenda, Angela Marie. "The Noble Lie: Selfhood and Tragedy in the Renaissance. " Ph. D. Dissertation, The Pennsylvania State University, 1977.

CHAPONE, HESTER

Bodek, Evelyn Gordon. "Salonières and Bluestockings: Educated Obsolescence and Germinating Feminism. " Feminist Studies 3 (Spring-Summer 1976): 183-199.

Dobbs, Jeannine. "The Blue-Stockings: Getting It Together. " Frontiers 1 (Winter 1976): 81-93.

CHAR, RENE

Aspel, Paulène. " 'La Rencontrée' of René Char: A Protean Female. " World Literature Today 51 (Summer 1977): 384-388.

Peyre, Henri. "René Char's Love Poetry. " World Literature Today 51 (Summer 1977): 366-369.

CHARLOTTE ELIZABETH see TONNA, CHARLOTTE ELIZABETH

CHASE, MARY

Zastrow, Sylvia Virginia Horning. "The Structure of Selected Plays by American Women Playwrights: 1920-1970. " Ph. D. Dissertation, Northwestern University, 1975.

CHASLES, EMILE see CHALLE, ROBERT

CHAUCER, GEOFFREY

Azelrod, Steven. "The Wife of Bath and the Clerk." Annuale Mediaevale 15 (1974): 109-124.

Beichner, Paul E. "Confrontation, Contempt of Court, and Chaucer's Cecilia." Chaucer Review 8 (Winter 1974): 198-204.

Beidler, Peter. "Conrad's 'Amy Foster' and Chaucer's Prioress." Nineteenth-Century Fiction 30 (1975): 111-115.

Boren, James. "Alysoun of Bath and the Vulgate 'Perfect Wife.'" Neuphilologische 76, no. 2 (1975): 247-256.

Bronfman, Judith. "The Griselda Legend in English Literature." Ph.D. Dissertation, New York University, 1977.

Brown, Emerson. "Biblical Women in the Merchant's Tale: Feminism, Antifeminism, and Beyond." Viator 5 (1974): 386-412.

Brown, Eric D. "Transformation and the Wife of Bath's Tale: A Jungian Discussion." Chaucer Review 10 (Spring 1976): 303-315.

Burlin, Robert B. Chaucerian Fiction. Princeton: Princeton University Press, 1977.

Cherniss, Michael D. "The Clerk's Tale and Envoy, the Wife of Bath's Purgatory, and the Merchant's Tale." Chaucer Review 6 (Spring 1972): 235-254.

Delasanta, Rodney. "Quoniam and the Wife of Bath." Papers on Language and Literature 8 (Spring 1972): 202-206.

Diamond, Arlyn. "Chaucer's Women and Women's Chaucer." In The Authority of Experience, [60]-83. Edited by Arlyn Diamond and Lee R. Edwards. Amherst: University of Massachusetts Press, 1977.

Fox, A. B. "The Traductio on Honde in the Wife of Bath's Prologue." Notre Dame English Journal 9, no. 1 (1975): 3-8.

Fries, Maureen. " 'Slydynge of Corage': Chaucer's Criseyde as Feminist and Victim." In The Authority of Experience, pp. [45]-59. Edited by Arlyn Diamond and Lee R. Edwards. Amherst: University of Massachusetts, 1977.

Gallagher, Joseph E. "Criseyde's Dream of the Eagle: Love and War in Troilus and Criseyde." Modern Language Quarterly 36 (June 1975): 115-132.

Gallick, Susan. "A Look at Chaucer and His Preachers." Speculum: A Journal of Medieval Studies 50 (July 1975): 456-476.

Grove, Robin. " 'The Merchant's Tale': Seeing, Knowing and Believing." Critical Review no. 18 (1976): [23]-38.

Hanning, Robert W. "From Eva and Ave to Eglentyne and Alisoun: Chaucer's Insight into the Roles Women Play." Signs: Journal of Women in Culture and Society 2 (Spring 1977): 580-599.

Haskell, Ann S. "The Portrayal of Women by Chaucer and His Age." In What Manner of Woman: Essays on English and American Life and Literature, pp. 1-14. Edited by Marlene Springer. New York: New York University Press, 1977.

Hawkins, Harriett. "The Victim's Side: Chaucer's Clerk's Tale and Webster's Duchess of Malfi." Signs: Journal of Women in Culture and Society 1 (Winter 1975): 339-361.

Kelly, Henry Ansgar. Love and Marriage in the Age of Chaucer. Ithaca and London: Cornell University Press, 1975.

Lockhart, Adrienne R. "Semantics, Moral and Aesthetic Degeneration in Troilus and Criseyde." Chaucer Review 8 (Fall 1973): 100-118.

Lunz, Elisabeth. "Chaucer's Prudence as the Ideal of the Virtuous Woman." Essays in Literature 4 (Spring 1977): 3-10.

Matthews, William. "The Wife of Bath and All Her Sect." Viator 5 (1974): 413-443.

Miller, Robert P. "Constancy Humanized: Trivet's Constance and the Man of Law's Custance." Costerus 3 (1975): 49-71.

Miskimin, Alice S. The Renaissance Chaucer. New Haven: Yale University Press, 1975.

Oberembt, Kenneth J. "Chaucer's Anti-Misogynist Wife of Bath." Chaucer Review 10 (Spring 1976): 287-302.

Palomo, Dolores. "The Fate of the Wife of Bath's 'Bad Husbands.'" Chaucer Review 9 (Spring 1975): 303-319.

Reisner, Thomas Andrew. "The Wife of Bath's Dower: A Legal Interpretation." Modern Philology 71 (February 1974): 301-302.

Rice, Nancy Hall. "Beauty and the Beast and the Little Boy: Clues About the Origins of Sexism and Racism from Folklore and Literature: Chaucer's 'The Prioress's Tale,' Sir Gawain and the Green Knight, the Alliterative Morte Arthure, Webster's The Duchess of Malfi, Shakespeare's Othello, Hawthorne's 'Rappaccini's Daughter,' Melville's 'Benito Cereno.'" Ph.D. Dissertation, University of Massachusetts, 1975.

Rudick, Michael. Western Humanities Review 30 (Winter 1976): 66-69. (Review of Love and Marriage in the Age of Chaucer by Henry Ansgar Kelly.)

Shapiro, Gloria K. "Dame Alice as Deceptive Narrator." Chaucer Review 6 (Fall 1971): 130-141.

Weissman, Hope Phyllis. "Antifeminism and Chaucer's Characterization of Women." In Geoffrey Chaucer, pp. 93-110. Edited by George D. Economou. New York: McGraw-Hill, 1975.

Witte, Stephen. "Muscipula Diaboli and Chaucer's Portrait of the Prioress." Papers on Language and Literature 13 (Summer 1977): 227-237.

CHAUHAN, VIJAY

Poulos, Steven Mark. "Feminine Sense and Sensibility: A Comparative Study of Six Modern Fiction Writers in Hindi and Urdu: Rashid Jahan, Ismat Chughtai, Qurratul-Ain Hyder, Mannu Bhandari, Usha Priyamvada, Vijay Chauhan." Ph.D. Dissertation, University of Chicago, 1975.

CHEDID, ANDREE

Accad, Evelyne. "Andrée Chédid's Poetry: A Reflection of Her Egyptian Cultural Heritage." Paper presented at the MMLA meeting, Chicago, October 1977. (Mimeographed.)

Izoard, Jacques. Andrée Chédid. Paris: Seghers, 1977.

CHEKHOV, ANTON

Armstrong, Judith. The Novel of Adultery. New York: Barnes & Noble, 1976.

Bayuk, Milla. "The Submissive Wife Stereotype in Anton Chekhov's Darling." CLA Journal 20 (June 1977): 533-538.

Hahn, Beverly. Chekhov: A Study of the Major Stories in Plays. London: Cambridge University Press, 1977.

Moss, Howard. "Three Sisters." Hudson Review 30 (Winter 1977-78): 525-543.

Paul, Barbara. "Chekhov's Five Sisters." Modern Drama 14 (February 1972): 436-440.

CHESNUTT, CHARLES

Cunningham, Joan. "The Uncollected Short Stories of Charles Waddell Chesnutt." Negro American Literature Forum 9 (Summer 1975): 57-58.

Gayle, Addison, Jr. The Way of the New World: The Black Novel in America. Garden City, N.Y.: Anchor Press/Doubleday, 1975.

Love, Theresa R. "The Black Woman in Afro-American Literature." Paper presented at the Midwest Modern Language Association meeting, Chicago, November 1975. (Mimeographed.)

Ogunyemi, Chikwenye Okonjo. "The Africanness of The Conjure Woman and Feather Woman of the Jungle." Ariel: A Review of International English Literature 8 (April 1977): [17]-30.

Schulz, Elizabeth. " 'Free in Fact and at Last': The Image of the Black Woman in Black American Literature." In What Manner of Woman: Essays in English and American Life and Literature, pp. 316-344. Edited by Marlene Springer. New York: New York University Press, 1977.

Ward, Hazel Mae. "The Black Woman as Character: Images in the American Novel, 1852-1953." Ph.D. Dissertation, The University of Texas at Austin, 1977.

CHILDRESS, ALICE

Anderson, Mary Louise. "Black Matriarchy: Portrayal of Women in Three Plays." Negro American Literature Forum 10 (Fall 1976): 93-95.

Arata, Esther S. and Nicholas J. Rotoli. Black American Playwrights, 1800 to the Present: A Bibliography. Metuchen, N.J.: Scarecrow Press, 1976.

Miller, Jeanne-Marie A. "Images of Black Women in Plays by Black Playwrights." CLA Journal 20 (June 1977): 494-507.

CHINO MASAKO

Ikuko Atsumi. "Modern Japanese Women Poets: After the Meiji Restoration." Iowa Review 7 (Spring/Summer 1976): 227-237.

CHIYOJO

Ikuko Atsumi. "Modern Japanese Women Poets: After the Meiji Restoration." Iowa Review 7 (Spring/Summer 1976): 227-237.

CHOPIN, KATE

Allen, Priscilla. "Old Critics and New: The Treatment of Chopin's The Awakening." In The Authority of Experience, pp. [224]-238. Edited by Arlyn Diamond and Lee R. Edwards. Amherst: University of Massachusetts Press, 1977.

Arner, Robert D. "Characterization and the Colloquial Style in Kate Chopin's 'Vagabonds.'" Markham Review 2 (May 1971).

_____. "Kate Chopin." Louisiana Studies 14, no. 1 (1975): 11-139.

_____. "Kate Chopin's Realism: 'At the 'Cadian Ball' and 'The Storm.'" Markham Review 2 (February 1970).

"Awakening in New Orleans: Kate Chopin." Distaff (New Orleans) 3 (March 15-April 15, 1975): 14.

Berggren, Paula S. "'A Lost Soul': Work Without Hope in The Awakening." Regionalism and the Female Imagination 3 (Spring 1977): 1-7.

Berke, Jacqueline. "Kate Chopin's Call to a Larger 'Awakening.'" Kate Chopin Newsletter 1 (Winter 1975-76): 1-5.

Bogarad, Carley Rees. "The Awakening: A Refusal to Compromise." University of Michigan Papers in Women's Studies 2, no. 3 (1977): 15-31.

Bonner, Thomas, Jr. "Kate Chopin: An Annotated Bibliography." Bulletin of Bibliography and Magazine Notes 32 (July-September 1975): 101-105.

_____. "Kate Chopin's European Consciousness." Paper presented at the MLA meeting, San Francisco, December 1976.

Borish, Elaine. "The Awakening Awakens England." Kate Chopin Newsletter 2 (Spring 1976): 1-5.

Chapin, Helen Geracimos. "Mythology and American Realism: Studies in Fiction by Henry Adams, Henry

James, and Kate Chopin. " Ph. D. Dissertation, The Ohio State University, 1975.

Culley, Margo. "Kate Chopin and Recent Obscenities. " Kate Chopin Newsletter 1 (Fall 1975): 28-29.

Dash, Irene. "The Literature of Birth and Abortion. " Regionalism and the Female Imagination 3 (Spring 1977): 8-13.

Davidson, Cathy N. "Chopin and Atwood: Woman Drowning, Woman Surfacing. " Kate Chopin Newsletter 1 (Winter 1975-76): 6-10.

Davidson, Colleen Tighe. "Beyond the Sentimental Heroine: The Feminist Character in American Novels, 1899-1937. " Ph. D. Dissertation, University of Minnesota, 1975.

Fryer, Judith. The Faces of Eve: Women in the Nineteenth Century American Novel. New York: Oxford University Press, 1976.

Gartner, Carol B. "Three Ednas. " Kate Chopin Newsletter 1 (Winter 1975-76): 11-20.

Gaudé, Pamela. "Kate Chopin's 'The Storm': A Study of Maupassant's Influence. " Kate Chopin Newsletter 1 (Fall 1975): 1-6.

Gornick, Vivian. "Too True, Too Soon. " Ms. 4 (November 1975): 52-54. (Review of The Storm and Other Stories.)

Jasenas, Elaine. "The French Influence in Kate Chopin's The Awakening. " Nineteenth-Century French Studies 4 (Spring 1976): 312-322.

Kolodny, Annette. "Some Notes on Defining a 'Feminist Literary Criticism. ' " Critical Inquiry 2 (Autumn 1975): 75-92.

Kuehl, Linda Kandel. "The Awakening. " Deland, Florida: Everett/Edwards, n. d. (Cassette no. 5307.)

Ladenson, J. R. "Paths to Suicide: Rebellion Against Victorian Womanhood in Kate Chopin's The Awakening. " Intellect 104 (July 1975): 52-55.

Moers, Ellen. Literary Women. Garden City, N.Y.:
Doubleday, 1976.

O'Brien, Sharon. "The Limits of Passion: Willa Cather's Review of The Awakening." Women & Literature 3 (Fall 1975): 10-20.

Ringe, Donald A. "Cane River World: Kate Chopin's
At Fault and Related Stories." Studies in American
Fiction 3 (Autumn 1975): 157-166.

Rowe, Anne. "A Note on Kate Chopin's 'Beyond the
Bayou.'" Paper presented at the MLA Convention,
San Francisco, December 1975. Published in Kate
Chopin Newsletter 1 (Fall 1975): 7-9.

Seyersted, Per. Introduction to The Storm and Other
Stories with The Awakening by Kate Chopin. Old
Westbury, N.Y.: Feminist Press, 1975.

Shroyer, David. "Eros and Civilization in Chopin's 'A
Vocation and a Voice.'" Paper presented at the
MLA meeting, San Francisco, December 1975.

Skaggs, Peggy. "The Man-Instinct of Possession: A
Persistent Theme in Kate Chopin's Stories."
Louisiana Studies 14, no. 3 (1975): 277-285.

_____. "Three Tragic Figures in Kate Chopin's The
Awakening." Louisiana Studies 13 (Winter 1974):
345-364.

Solomon, Barbara H. Introduction to The Awakening
and Selected Stories of Kate Chopin. New York:
New American Library, 1976.

Stafford, Jean. "Sensuous Women." New York Review
of Books, 23 September 1971, 33-35.

Tompkins, Jane P. "The Awakening: An Evaluation."
Feminist Studies 3 (Spring-Summer 1976): 22-29.

Toth, Emily. "The Cult of Domesticity and 'A Sentimental Soul.'" Kate Chopin Newsletter 1 (Fall
1975): 9-16.

_____. "The Independent Woman and 'Free' Love."
Massachusetts Review 16 (Autumn 1975): 647-664.

_____. "Kate Chopin Remembered. " Kate Chopin Newsletter 1 (Winter 1975-76): 21-27.

_____. "St. Louis and the Fiction of Kate Chopin. " Missouri Historical Society Bulletin 32 (1975): 33-50.

_____. "Women and Their Friends: Some Thoughts About Literature. " Cold Day in August 1 (November 1972): 1-3. Also in Women: A Journal of Liberation 3, no. 2 (1973): 44.

Van Sittert, Barbara Culver. "Social Institutions and Biological Determinism in the Fictional World of Kate Chopin. " Ph.D. Dissertation, Arizona State University, 1975.

Warnken, William. "Fire, Light, and Darkness in Kate Chopin's At Fault. " Kate Chopin Newsletter 1 (Fall 1975): 17-27.

_____. "Kate Chopin and Henrik Ibsen: A Study of The Awakening and A Doll's House. " Massachusetts Studies in English 4 (Autumn 1974/5-Winter 1975): 43-49.

Watson, Barbara Bellow. "On Power and the Literary Text. " Signs: Journal of Women in Culture and Society 1 (Autumn 1975): 111-118.

Zlotnick, Joan. "A Woman's Will: Kate Chopin on Selfhood, Wifehood, and Motherhood. " Markham Review 1 (October 1968): [1-5].

CHRETIEN DE TROYES

Noble, Peter. "The Character of Guinevere in the Arthurian Romances of Chrétien de Troyes. " Modern Language Review 67 (July 1972): 24-35.

CHUGHTAI, ISMAT

Poulos, Steven Mark. "Feminine Sense and Sensibility: A Comparative Study of Six Modern Fiction Writers in Hindi and Urdu: Rashid Jahan, Ismat Chughtai, Qurratul-Ain Hyder, Mannu Bhandari, Usha Priyamvada, Vijay Chauhan. " Ph.D. Dissertation, University of Chicago, 1975.

CIBBER, COLLEY

Boisaubin, Elizabeth Ann. "Identity and Difference in English and French Comedy: 1659-1722." Ph.D. Dissertation, Stanford University, 1975.

Greenberg, Joseph Lawrence. "English Marriage and Restoration Comedy, 1688-1710." Ph.D. Dissertation, Princeton University, 1976.

Hume, Robert D. "Marital Discord in English Comedy from Dryden to Fielding." Modern Philology 74 (February 1977): 248-272.

McDonald, Margaret Lamb. "The Independent Woman in the Restoration Comedy of Manners." Ph.D. Dissertation, University of Colorado, 1975.

Spacks, Patricia Meyer. Imagining a Self: Autobiography and Novel in Eighteenth-Century England. Cambridge: Harvard University Press, 1976.

CIXOUS, HELENE

Makward, Christiane. "Interview with Helen Cixous." Sub-Stance no. 13 (1976): 19-37.

_____. "Structures du silence/du délire: Duras/ Cixous." Paper presented at the MLA meeting, New York City, December 1976.

CLARE, JOHN

Todd, Janet M. "Mary in the Poetry of John Clare." Mary Wollstonecraft Newsletter 1 (July 1972): 12-18.

CLARIN

Dorwick, Thalia. "El amor y el matrimonio en la obra creacional de Clarín." Ph.D. Dissertation, Case Western Reserve University, 1973.

Ullman, Pierre L. "The Antifeminist Premises of Clarín's Su unico hijo." Estudos Ibero-Americanos (Pôrto Alegre, Brazil) 1 (1975): 57-91.

CLARK, WALTER VAN TILBURG

Meldrum, Barbara. "Images of Women in Western
American Literature." Midwest Quarterly 17 (April
1976): 252-267.

CLAUDE, CATHERINE

Crosland, Margaret. Women of Iron & Velvet: French
Women After George Sand. New York: Taplinger,
1976.

CLAUDEL, PAUL

Bugliani, Ann. Women and the Feminine Principle in
the Works of Paul Claudel. Madrid: Ediciones
José Porrúa Turanzas, S.A., n.d.

Cismaru, Alfred. "Alissa and Mara: Gide's and Claudel's Other 'partie nulle.'" Claudel Studies 4, no.
1 (1977): 68-75.

Rossi, Vinio. "Erato and Angèle: The Beatrice Figure
in the Early Works of Claudel and Gide." Claudel
Studies 4, no. 1 (1977): 38-47.

Witherell, Louise R. "Liberated Women in the Plays of
Paul Claudel." Paper presented at the Paul Claudel
Society, MLA meeting, San Francisco, December
1975.

CLELAND, JOHN

Miller, Nancy Kipnis. "Gender and Genre: An Analysis of Literary Femininity in the Eighteenth-Century
Novel." Ph.D. Dissertation, Columbia University,
1974.

Richetti, John J. "The Portrayal of Women in Restoration and Eighteenth-Century English Literature." In
What Manner of Woman: Essays on English and
American Life and Literature, pp. 65-97. Edited
by Marlene Springer. New York: New York University Press, 1977.

CLIFTON, LUCILLE

Brinnin, John Malcolm and Bill Read, eds. Twentieth Century Poetry: American and British (1900-1970), 2nd ed. New York: McGraw-Hill, 1970.

Scarupa, Harriet Jackson. "Lucille Clifton: Making the World 'Poem-Up.' " Ms. 5 (October 1976): 118, 120, 123.

Vendler, Helen. New York Times Book Review, 6 April 1975, p. 4. (Review of An Ordinary Woman.)

Williams, Sherley A. "The Blues Roots of Contemporary Afro-American Poetry." Massachusetts Review 18 (Autumn 1977): 542-554.

CLOUGH, ARTHUR HUGH

Ball, Patricia M. The Heart's Events: The Victorian Poetry of Relationships. London: University of London, The Athlone Press, 1976.

Behnken, Eloise. "Love, Desire, and Victorian Poets." Occasional Review Issue 6 (Summer 1977): [149]-157.

Johnson, Wendell Stacy. Sex and Marriage in Victorian Poetry. Ithaca and London: Cornell University Press, 1975.

COHEN, LEONARD

Venster, Dagmar de. "Leonard Cohen's Women." In Mother Was Not a Person, pp. 96-97. Edited by Margret Andersen. Montreal: Content Publishing Limited and Black Rose Books, 1972.

Wayman, Tom. "Cohen's Women." Canadian Literature no. 60 (Spring 1974): 89-93. (Review of The Energy of Slaves.)

COLERIDGE, SAMUEL

Flory, Wendy Stallard. "Fathers and Daughters: Coleridge and 'Christabel.' " Women & Literature 3 (Spring 1975): 5-15.

Kauvar, Gerald B. "The Psychological Structure of English Romantic Poetry. " Psychoanalytic Review 64 (Spring 1977): 21-40.

Kilday, Douglas Robert. "Christabel: The Way to the Poem. " Ph.D. Dissertation, The University of Wisconsin-Milwaukee, 1976.

COLETTE

Atkins, John. Sex in Literature: The Classical Experience of the Sexual Impulse, vol. 2. London: Calder & Boyars, 1973.

Benet, Mary Kathleen. Writers in Love: Katherine Mansfield, George Eliot, Colette, and the Men They Lived With. New York: Macmillan, 1977.

Crosland, Margaret. Women of Iron & Velvet: French Women After George Sand. New York: Taplinger, 1976.

Jong, Erica. Foreword to The Other Woman. New York: New American Library, 1975.

Klaich, Dolores. Woman + Woman: Attitudes Towards Lesbianism. New York: Simon & Schuster, 1974.

McCarty, V. Margaret Ward. "Colette: Theatrical Aspects of the Novel. " Ph.D. Dissertation, The University of Wisconsin-Madison, 1977.

Marks, Elaine. "Colette. " Deland, Florida: Everett/ Edwards, n.d. (Cassette no. 5503.)

_____. Foreword to Gigi and Selected Writings. New York: New American Library, 1973.

Mercier, Michel. Le roman féminin. Paris: P.U.F., 1976.

Mitchell, Yvonne. Colette: A Taste for Life. New York: Harcourt Brace Jovanovich, 1975.

Moers, Ellen. Literary Women. Garden City, N.Y.: Doubleday, 1976.

Resch, Yannick. Corps féminin, corps textual: essai sur le personnage féminin dans l'oeuvre de Colette. Paris: Librairie C. Klincksleck, 1973.

Rule, Jane. Lesbian Images. Garden City, N.Y.: Doubleday, 1975.

Schmitz, Betty Ann. "French Women Writers and Their Critics: An Analysis of the Treatment of Women Writers in Selected Histories of French Literature." Ph.D. Dissertation, The University of Wisconsin-Madison, 1977.

COLLET, CAMILLA

Berg, Karin Westmar. "Looking at Women in Literature." Scandinavian Review 63, no. 2 (1975): 48-55.

COLLINS, WILKIE

Brightman, William Lloyd. "A Study of The Woman in White." Ph.D. Dissertation, University of Washington, 1974.

Natov, Roni L. "The Strong-Minded Heroine in Mid-Victorian Fiction." Ph.D. Dissertation, New York University, 1975.

Reed, John R. Victorian Conventions. Athens: Ohio University Press, 1975.

Showalter, Elaine. A Literature of Their Own: British Women Novelists from Brontë to Lessing. Princeton: Princeton University Press, 1977.

Trudgill, Eric. Madonnas and Magdalens: The Origins and Development of Victorian Sexual Attitudes. New York: Holmes & Meier, 1976.

COMPTON-BURNETT, IVY

Duffy, Martha. "Household Tyrants." Time, 16 August 1971, p. 73.

Horn, Larry V. "Vision and Form in the Novels of I. Compton-Burnett." Ph.D. Dissertation, University of Arkansas, 1977.

Miles, Rosalind. The Fiction of Sex: Themes and
Functions of Sex Difference in the Modern Novel.
New York: Barnes & Noble, 1974.

Perry, Sandra Jeanne. "Disclosure and Ivy Compton-
Burnett: A Guide to Reading Her Dialogue Novels. "
Ph. D. Dissertation, University of Washington, 1977.

Rule, Jane. Lesbian Images. Garden City, N. Y. :
Doubleday, 1975.

Shaw, Elizabeth Baird. The Comic Novels of Ivy
Compton-Burnett and Nathalie Sarraute. Ph. D. Dissertation, University of Colorado, 1974.

Snitrow, Ann. "The Family in the Novels of Ivy Compton-Burnett. " Aphra 1 (Autumn 1970): 7-18.

Spriggs, Elizabeth. The Life of Ivy Compton-Burnett.
New York: Braziller, 1973.

Spurling, Hillary. Ivy When Young: The Family Life
of Compton-Burnett, 1884-1919. London: Gollancz,
1974.

CONGREVE, WILLIAM

Beless, Rosemary June. "Reflections of the Law in the
Comedies of Etherege, Wycherley, and Congreve. "
Ph. D. Dissertation, University of Utah, 1977.

Bratton, Clinton Woodrow. "The Use of Marriage in
the Comedies of Etherege, Wycherley, Dryden and
Congreve. " Ph. D. Dissertation, University of Colorado, 1975.

Greenberg, Joseph Lawrence. "English Marriage and
Restoration Comedy, 1688-1710. " Ph. D. Dissertation, Princeton University, 1976.

Hume, Robert D. "The Myth of the Rake in 'Restoration' Comedy. " Studies in the Literary Imagination
10 (Spring 1977): 25-55.

McCoy, Kathleen. "The Fallen Woman of Restoration
Comedy. " Paper presented at the MLA meeting,
New York City, December 1976; forthcoming in
Studies in Eighteenth-Century Culture.

McDonald, Margaret Lamb. "The Independent Woman in the Restoration Comedy of Manners." Ph.D. Dissertation, University of Colorado, 1975.

Richetti, John J. "The Portrayal of Women in Restoration and Eighteenth-Century English Literature." In What Manner of Woman: Essays on English and American Life and Literature, pp. 65-97. Edited by Marlene Springer. New York: New York University Press, 1977.

CONRAD, JOSEPH

Beidler, Peter. "Conrad's 'Amy Foster' and Chaucer's Prioress." Nineteenth-Century Fiction 30 (1975): 111-115.

Buczkowski, Yvonne. "Female Characters in Conrad's Novels and Short Stories: A Bibliographical Note." Modernist Studies 1 (1974-1975): 51-58.

Ford, Jane M. "The Father/Daughter/Suitor Triangle in Shakespeare, Dickens, James, Conrad, and Joyce." Ph.D. Dissertation, State University of New York at Buffalo, 1975.

Fries, Maureen. "Feminism-Antifeminism in Under Western Eyes." Conradiana 5, no. 2 (1973): 56-65.

Geary, Edward A. "Ashy Halo: Woman as Symbol in Heart of Darkness." Studies in Short Fiction 13 (Fall 1976): 499-506.

Inniss, Kenneth. "Conrad's Native Girl: Some Social Questions." Pacific Coast Philology 5 (April 1970): 39-45.

Meyers, Jeffrey. Married to Genius. New York: Barnes & Noble, 1977.

O'Connor, Peter D. "The Function of Nina in Alamayer's Folly." Conradiana 7, no. 3 (1973): 225-232.

Rose, Charles. "Romance and the Maiden Archetype." Conradiana 6 (1974): 183-188.

CONVERSE, FLORENCE

> Maglin, Nan Bauer. "Rebel Women Writers, 1894-
> 1925." Ph.D. Dissertation, Union Graduate School,
> 1975.

COOKE, MARGORIE BENTON

> Maglin, Nan Bauer. "Discovering Women's Activist
> Fiction." University of Michigan Papers in Women's
> Studies 2, no. 2 (1976): 96-104.

> _____. "Rebel Women Writers, 1894-1925." Ph.D.
> Dissertation, Union Graduate School, 1975.

COOKE, ROSE TERRY

> Davidson, Colleen Tighe. "Beyond the Sentimental Hero-
> ine: The Feminist Character in American Novels,
> 1899-1937." Ph.D. Dissertation, University of
> Minnesota, 1975.

> Toth, Susan Allen. "Character Studies in Rose Terry
> Cooke: New Faces for the Short Story." Kate
> Chopin Newsletter 2 (Spring 1976): 19-26.

> Voss, Arthur. The American Short Story: A Critical
> Survey. Norman: University of Oklahoma, 1973.

COOLBRITH, INA

> Morrow, Patrick D. "Power Behind the Throne: Ina
> Coolbrith and the Politics of Submission." Kate
> Chopin Newsletter 2 (Spring 1976): 13-18.

COOPER, JAMES FENIMORE

> Baym, Nina. "Portrayal of Women in American Liter-
> ature, 1790-1870." In What Manner of Woman:
> Essays on English and American Life and Litera-
> ture, pp. 211-234. Edited by Marlene Springer.
> New York: New York University Press, 1977.

> Haberly, David T. "Women and Indians: The Last of
> the Mohicans and the Captivity Tradition." Ameri-
> can Quarterly 28 (Fall 1976): 431-443.

Kolodny, Annette. The Lay of the Land: Metaphor as Experience and History in American Life and Letters. Chapel Hill: University of North Carolina Press, 1975.

Lander, Dawn. "Women and the Wilderness: Taboos in American Literature. " University of Michigan Papers in Women's Studies 2, no. 3 (1977): 62-83.

COOPER, JANE

Brown, Linda. "Books in Short. " Ms. 4 (November 1975): 59. (Review of Maps and Windows.)

Cooper, Jane. "Nothing Has Been Used in the Manufacture of This Poetry That Could Have Been Used in the Manufacture of Bread. " American Poetry Review (July/August 1974): 55-60.

Jane Cooper. San Francisco: San Francisco State University/The Poetry Center, n.d. (Video-cassette.)

Plumly, Stanley. Ohio Review 17 (Spring/Summer 1976): 105-107. (Review of Maps & Windows.)

Schulman, Grace. "Things of This World. " American Poetry Review 5 (May/June 1976): 41-42. (Review of Maps & Windows.)

CORNEILLE, PIERRE

Cloonan, William. "Women in Horace. " Romance Notes 16 (Spring 1975): 647-652.

Dreyfuss, Cecilia Anne Stiborik. "Femina sapiens in Drama: Aeschylus to Grillparzer. " Ph.D. Dissertation, The University of Michigan, 1975.

CORTAZAR, JULIO

Jaquette, Jane S. "Literary Archetypes and Female Role Alternatives: The Woman and the Novel in Latin America. " In Female and Male in Latin America: Essays, pp. 3-28. Edited by Ann Pescatello. Pittsburgh: University of Pittsburgh Press, 1973.

COTES, SARA JEANNETTE DUNCAN see DUNCAN, SARA
JEANNETTE

COZZENS, JAMES GOULD

Shinn, Thelma J. Wardrop. "A Study of Women Characters in Contemporary American Fiction 1940-
1970. " Ph.D. Dissertation, Purdue University,
1972.

CRABBE, GEORGE

Shearon, Forrest B. "The Muse of Hymen: George
Crabbe on Marriage. " Ph.D. Dissertation, University of Louisville, 1973.

CRADDOCK, CHARLES EGBERT see MURFREE, MARY
NOAILLES

CRAIGIN, ELISABETH

Rule, Jane. Lesbian Images. Garden City, N.Y.:
Doubleday, 1975.

CRAIK, DINAH MULOCK

Calder, Jenni. Women and Marriage in Victorian Fiction. London: Thames & Hudson, 1976.

Gartner, Carol B. "Three Ednas." Kate Chopin Newsletter 1 (Winter 1975-76): 11-20.

Mitchell, Sally. "Lost Women: Feminist Implications
of the Fallen in Works by Forgotten Women Writers
of the 1840's. " University of Michigan Papers in
Women's Studies 1 (June 1974): 110-124.

Showalter, Elaine Cottler. "The Double Standard:
Criticism of Women Writers in England, 1845-1880. "
Ph.D. Dissertation, University of California, Davis,
1970.

_____. A Literature of Their Own: British Women
Novelists from Brontë to Lessing. Princeton:
Princeton University Press, 1977.

CRANE, STEPHEN

Banta, Martha. "They Shall Have Faces, Minds, and (One Day) Flesh: Women in Late Nineteenth-Century and Early Twentieth-Century American Literature." In What Manner of Woman: Essays on English and American Life and Literature, pp. 235-270. Edited by Marlene Springer. New York: New York University Press, 1977.

Stimpson, Catharine. "Women as Scapegoats." In Female Studies V, pp. 7-16. Edited by Rae Lee Siporin. Pittsburgh: KNOW, Inc., 1972.

CRAPSSEY, ADELAIDE

Watts, Emily Stipes. The Poetry of American Women from 1632 to 1945. Austin: University of Texas Press, 1977.

CRAWFORD, ISABELLA VALANCY

Dunn, Margo. "Valancy Crawford: The Lifestyle of a Canadian Poet." Room of One's Own 2, no. 1 (1976): 11-19.

Hughes, Kenneth J. and Birk Sproxton. "Malcolm's Katie: Images and Songs." Canadian Literature no. 63 (Summer 1975): 55-64.

Livesay, Dorothy. "The Hunters Twain." Canadian Literature no. 55 (1973): 75-98.

_____. "Tennyson's Daughter or Wilderness Child? The Factual and the Literary Background of Isabella Valancy Crawford." Journal of Canadian Fiction 2, no. 3 (1973): 161-167.

Martin, Mary F. "The Short Life of Isabella Valancy Crawford." Dalhousie Review 52 (1972): 390-400.

Radu, Kenneth. "Patterns of Meaning: Isabella Crawford's Malcolm's Katie." Dalhousie Review 57 (Summer 1977): 322-331.

CREBILLON <u>fils</u>

Maidanek, John. "From Love and Virtue to Seduction and Degradation in the Works of Crébillon <u>fils</u>." Ph.D. Dissertation, The Florida State University, 1973.

Simmons, Sarah Tawil. "Attitudes de Hamilton, Marivaux, Crébillon <u>fils</u> et Laclos envers la femme d'apres leurs oeuvres romanesques." Ph.D. Dissertation, University of Colorado, 1970.

CRENNE, HELISENNE de

Mercier, Michel. <u>Le roman féminin</u>. Paris: P.U.F., 1976.

Wood, Diane Sylvia. "Literary Devices and Rhetorical Techniques in the Works of Hélisenne de Crenne." Ph.D. Dissertation, The University of Wisconsin-Madison, 1975.

CROSS, RUTH

Seidel, Kathryn Lee. "The Southern Belle: Her Fall from the Pedestal in Fiction of the Southern Renaissance." Ph.D. Dissertation, University of Maryland, 1976.

CROTHERS, RACHEL

Gottlieb, Lois C. "Obstacles to Feminism in the Early Plays of Rachel Crothers." <u>University of Michigan Papers in Women's Studies</u> 1 (June 1975): 71-84.

Kolb, Deborah S. "The Rise and Fall of the New Woman in American Drama." <u>Educational Theater Journal</u> 27 (1975): 149-160.

Loudin, Joanne Marie. "The Changing Role of the Comic Heroine in American Drama from 1900 to 1940." Ph.D. Dissertation, University of Washington, 1974.

Shafer, Y. B. "Liberated Women in American Plays of the Past." <u>Players Magazine</u> 49 (Spring 1974): 95-100.

Zastrow, Sylvia Virginia Horning. "The Structure of Selected Plays by American Women Playwrights: 1920-
1970. " Ph. D. Dissertation, Northwestern University, 1975.

CULLEN, COUNTEE

Brown, Martha Hursey. "Images of Black Women:
Family Roles in Harlem Renaissance Literature. "
D. A. Dissertation, Carnegie-Mellon University,
1976.

CULLINAN, ELIZABETH

Crain, J. L. New York Times Book Review, 17 April
1977, p. 13. (Review of Yellow Roses: Stories.)

CUMMINS, MARIA

Foster, Edward Halsey. The Civilized Wilderness:
Backgrounds to American Romantic Literature, 1817-
1860. New York: Free Press, 1975.

Hull, Raymona E. " 'Scribbling' Females and Serious
Males: Hawthorne's Comments from Abroad on
Some American Authors. " Nathaniel Hawthorne
Journal (1975): 35-58.

CUNNINGHAM, VERONICA

Sanchez, Rita. "Chicana Writer: Breaking Out of the
Silence. " La Cosecha: Literatura y la Mujer Chicana 3, no. 3 (1977): 31-37.

- D -

DADIE, BERNARD

Tidjani-Serpos, Nouréini. "L'image de la femme afri-
caine dans le théatre ivoirien: Le cas de Bernard
Dadié et de Charles NoKan. " Révue de Littérature
Comparée 48 (1974): 455-461.

DALY, AUGUSTIN

> Bennison, Martin J. and Barry B. Witham. "Sentimen-
> tal Love and the Nineteenth-Century American
> Drama." Players 49 (Summer 1974): 127-129.

DANIEL, SAMUEL

> Kau, Joseph. "Delia's Gentle Lover and the Eternizing
> Conceit in Elizabethan Sonnets." Anglia 92, nos.
> 3/4 (1974): 334-348.

DANTE

> Ferrante, Joan M. Woman as Image in Medieval Litera-
> ture from the Twelfth Century to Dante. New York
> and London: Columbia University Press, 1975.

> Shapiro, Marianne. Woman Earthly and Divine in the
> Comedy of Dante. Lexington: University Press of
> Kentucky, 1975.

DARGAN, OLIVE TILFORD (pseud.: Fielding Burke)

> Cook, Sylvia Jenkins. From Tobacco Road to Route 66:
> The Southern Poor White in Fiction. Chapel Hill:
> The University of North Carolina Press, 1976.

DARIO, RUBEN

> Schanzer, George O. "Rubén Darío and Ms. Crista."
> Journal of Spanish Studies: Twentieth Century 3
> (Fall 1975): 145-152.

DAUDET, ALPHONSE

> Crane, Robert Arthur. "The Courtisane Character in
> the Nineteenth Century French Novel from Balzac
> to Zola." Ph.D. Dissertation, The University of
> North Carolina at Chapel Hill, 1976.

DAVENPORT, ROBERT

> Leggatt, Alexander. Citizen Comedy in the Age of
> Shakespeare. Toronto: University of Toronto
> Press, 1973.

DAVIDSON, JOHN

    Fass, Barbara. <u>La Belle Dame sans Merci & the Aes-
thetics of Romanticism</u>. Detroit: Wayne State University Press, 1974.

DAVIDSON, LUCRETIA

    Wood, Ann D. "The 'Scribbling Women' and Fanny
Fern: Why Women Wrote." <u>American Quarterly</u>
23 (Spring 1971): 3-24.

DAVIS, OWEN

    Bonin, Jane. <u>Major Themes in Prize-Winning Ameri-
can Drama</u>. Metuchen, N.J.: Scarecrow Press,
1975.

DAY, MARTHA

    Wood, Ann D. "The 'Scribbling Women' and Fanny
Fern: Why Women Wrote." <u>American Quarterly</u>
23 (Spring 1971): 3-24.

DAZAI OSAMU

    Ueda, Makoto. <u>Modern Japanese Writers and the Nature
of Literature</u>. Stanford: Stanford University Press,
1976.

DEFOE, DANIEL

    Bell, Robert H. "Moll's Grace Abounding." <u>Genre</u> 8
(December 1975): 267-282.

    Bordner, Marsha. "Defoe's Androgynous Vision in <u>Moll
Flanders</u> and <u>Roxana</u>." <u>Gypsy Scholar</u> 2 (Spring
1975): 76-93.

    Byrd, Max. "The Madhouse, the Whorehouse, and the
Convent." <u>Partisan Review</u> 44, no. 2 (1977): 268-
278.

    Cohan, Steven. "Other Bodies: Roxana's Confession of
Guilt." <u>Studies in the Novel</u> 8 (Winter 1976): 406-
418.

Daghistany, Ann. "The Picara Nature." Women's
    Studies 5, no. 1 (1977): 51-60.

Faulkner, Peter. Humanism in the English Novel. New
    York: Barnes & Noble, 1976.

Fritz, Paul and Richard Morton, eds. Woman in the
    Eighteenth Century and Other Essays. Toronto:
    Samuel Stevens Hakkert, 1976.

Hoffeld, Laura Diamond. "The Servant Heroine in 18th
    and 19th Century British Fiction: The Social Reality
    and Its Image in the Novel." Ph.D. Dissertation,
    New York University, 1975.

Lerenbaum, Miriam. "Moll Flanders: 'A Woman on
    Her Own Account.'" In The Authority of Experience,
    pp. [101]-117. Edited by Arlyn Diamond and Lee
    R. Edwards. Amherst: University of Massachusetts
    Press, 1977.

Richetti, John J. "The Portrayal of Women in Restora-
    tion and Eighteenth-Century English Literature."
    In What Manner of Woman: Essays on English and
    American Life and Literature, pp. 65-97. Edited
    by Marlene Springer. New York: New York Uni-
    versity Press, 1977.

Sill, Geoffrey M. "Rogues, Strumpets, and Vagabonds:
    Defoe on Crime in the City." Eighteenth-Century
    Life 2 (June 1976): 74-78.

Snow, Malinda. "Diabolic Intervention in Defoe's Rox-
    ana." Essays in Literature 3 (Spring 1976): 52-60.

Spacks, Patricia Meyer. Imagining a Self: Autobiogra-
    phy and Novel in Eighteenth Century England.
    Cambridge: Harvard University Press, 1976.

DE FOREST, JOHN WILLIAM

Seidel, Kathryn Lee. "The Southern Belle: Her Fall
    from the Pedestal in Fiction of the Southern Renais-
    sance." Ph.D. Dissertation, University of Mary-
    land, 1976.

DEKKER, THOMAS

Bronfman, Judith. "The Griselda Legend in English Literature." Ph.D. Dissertation, New York University, 1977.

Leggatt, Alexander. Citizen Comedy in the Age of Shakespeare. Toronto: University of Toronto Press, 1973.

DELAND, MARGARET

Maglin, Nan Bauer. "Rebel Women Writers, 1894-1925." Ph.D. Dissertation, Union Graduate School, 1975.

Welter, Barbara. Dimity Convictions: The American Woman in the Nineteenth Century. Athens: Ohio University Press, 1976.

DELANY, SAMUEL

Russ, Joanna. "A Boy and His Dog: The Final Solution." Frontiers: A Journal of Women Studies 1 (Fall 1975): [153]-162.

DELARUE-MARDRUS, LUCIE

Crosland, Margaret. Women of Iron and Velvet: French Women after George Sand. New York: Taplinger, 1976.

DE MANDIARGUES, ANDRE PIEYRE

Charney, Diane Joy. "Woman as Mediatrix in the Prose Works of André Pieyre De Mandiargues." Ph.D. Dissertation, Duke University, 1976.

DEMBY, WILLIAM

Connelly, Joseph F. "William Demby's Fiction: The Pursuit of Muse." Negro American Literature Forum. 10 (Fall 1976): 100, 102-103.

DESBORDES-VALMORE, MARCELINE

Crosland, Margaret. Women of Iron and Velvet: French

Women after George Sand. New York: Taplinger, 1976.

DICKENS, CHARLES

Arakawa, Steven Ryoichi. "The Relationship of Father and Daughter in the Novels of Charles Dickens." Ph.D. Dissertation, Yale University, 1977.

Calder, Jenni. Women and Marriage in Victorian Fiction. London: Thames & Hudson, 1976.

Carey, John. The Violent Effigy: A Study of Dickens' Imagination. London: Faber & Feber, 1973.

Christ, Carol. "Victorian Masculinity and the Angel in the House." In A Widening Sphere: Changing Roles of Victorian Women, pp. 146-162. Edited by Martha Vicinus. Bloomington: Indiana University Press, 1977.

Cohan, Steven. " 'They Are All Secret': The Fantasy Content of Bleak House." Literature and Psychology 26, no. 2 (1976): 79-91.

Cunningham, Valentine. Everywhere Spoken Against: Dissent in the Victorian Novel. Oxford: Clarendon Press, 1975.

Ford, Jane M. "The Father/Daughter/Suitor Triangle in Shakespeare, Dickens, James, Conrad, and Joyce." Ph.D. Dissertation, State University of New York at Buffalo, 1975.

Frank, Lawrence. " 'Through a Glass Darkly': Esther Summerson and Bleak House." In Dickens Studies Annual IV, pp. 91-112. Edited by Robert B. Partlow, Jr. Carbondale and Edwardsville: Southern Illinois University Press, 1975.

Heatley, Edward. "The Redeemed Feminine of Little Dorit." In Dickens Studies Annual IV, pp. 153-164. Edited by Robert B. Partlow, Jr. Carbondale and Edwardsville: Southern Illinois University Press, 1975.

Hirsch, Gordon D. "The Mysterious in Bleak House."

In Dickens Studies Annual IV, pp. 132-152. Edited by Robert B. Partlow, Jr. Carbondale and Edwardsville: Southern Illinois University Press, 1975.

McDonald, Andrew. "The Preservation of Innocence in Dombey and Son: Florence's Identity and the Role of Walter Gay." Texas Studies in Literature and Language 18 (Spring 1976): [1]-19.

Manning, Sylvia. "Dickens, January, and May." The Dickensian 71 (May 1975): 67-75.

Miles, Rosalind. The Fiction of Sex: Themes and Functions of Sex Difference in the Modern Novel. New York: Barnes & Noble, 1974.

Moers, Ellen. Literary Women. Garden City, N.Y.: Doubleday, 1976.

Murphy, Mary Janice. "Dickens' 'Other Women': The Mature Women in His Novels." Ph.D. Dissertation, University of Louisville, 1975.

Natov, Roni L. "The Strong-Minded Heroine in Mid-Victorian Fiction." Ph.D. Dissertation, New York University, 1975.

Reed, John R. Victorian Conventions. Athens: Ohio University Press, 1975.

Rideal, C. F. Charles Dickens' Heroines. Brooklyn: Haskell House, 1974.

Showalter, Elaine. A Literature of Their Own: British Women Novelists from Brontë to Lessing. Princeton: Princeton University Press, 1977.

Slater, Michael. "Appreciating Mrs Nickleby." The Dickensian 71 (September 1975): 136-139.

Springer, Marlene. "Angels and Other Women in Victorian Literature." In What Manner of Woman: Essays on English and American Life and Literature, pp. 124-159. Edited by Marlene Springer. New York: New York University Press, 1977.

Welsh, Alexander. The City of Dickens. Oxford:
Clarendon Press, 1971.

Williams, Kristi Fayle. "The Idealized Heroine in Victorian Fiction. " Ph.D. Dissertation, Brown University, 1975.

Wing, George. "Mr F's Aunt: A Laughing Matter. "
English Studies in Canada 3 (Summer 1977): [206]-
215.

Yelin, Louise. "Women, Money, and Language: Dombey and Son and the 1840s. " Ph.D. Dissertation,
Columbia University, 1977.

DICKINSON, EMILY

Baym, Nina. "Portrayal of Women in American Literature, 1790-1870. " In What Manner of Woman: Essays on English and American Life and Literature,
pp. 211-234. Edited by Marlene Springer. New
York: New York University Press, 1977.

Buckingham, Willis J. "EDB Index 1968-1974. " Emily
Dickinson Bulletin 28 (1975): 79-103.

Callow, James T. and Robert Reilly. Guide to American Literature from Emily Dickinson to the Present.
New York: Barnes & Noble, 1977.

Drabble, Margaret. "A Vesuvian Family. " Listener,
6 May 1976, pp. 570-571. (Review of The Life of
Emily Dickinson by Richard B. Sewall and The Complete Poems of Emily Dickinson edited by Thomas
H. Johnson.

Faderman, Lillian. "Emily Dickinson's Letters to Sue
Gilbert. " Massachusetts Review 18 (Summer 1977):
197-225.

Ferlazzo, Paul J. Emily Dickinson. New York: Twayne,
1976.

Garrison, Joseph M. , Jr. "Emily Dickinson: From
Ballerina to Gymnast. " ELH 42 (Spring 1975): 107-
124.

Juhasz, Suzanne. Naked and Fiery Forms: Modern American Poetry by Women, A New Tradition. New York: Harper & Row, 1976.

_____. " 'A privilege so awful': Emily Dickinson as Woman Poet. " San Jose Studies 2 (May 1976): 94-107.

Moers, Ellen. Literary Women. Garden City, N.Y.: Doubleday, 1976.

Rich, Adrienne. "Vesuvius at Home: The Power of Emily Dickinson. " Parnassus: Poetry in Review 5 (Fall/Winter 1976): 49-74.

Sewall, Richard B. The Life of Emily Dickinson, 2 vols. New York: Farrar, Straus & Giroux, 1974.

Steinbrink, Jeffrey. "Emily Dickinson and Sylvia Plath: The Values of Mortality. " Women & Literature 4 (Spring 1976): 45-48.

Terris, Virginia. "Emily Dickinson as a Woman Poet. " Deland, Florida: Everett/Edwards, n.d. (Cassette no. 5519.)

Watts, Emily Stipes. The Poetry of American Women from 1632 to 1945. Austin: University of Texas Press, 1977.

Weisbuch, Robert. Emily Dickinson's Poetry. Chicago: University of Chicago Press, 1975.

DIDEROT, DENIS

Byrd, Max. "The Madhouse, the Whorehouse, and the Convent. " Partisan Review 44, no. 2 (1977): 268-278.

DIDION, JOAN

Authors in the News, no. 1. Detroit: Gale Research, 1976.

Braudy, Susan. "A Day in the Life of Joan Didion. " Ms. 5 (February 1977): 65-68, 108-109.

Didion, Joan. "Why I Write. " London Magazine 17 (June/July 1977): [84]-90.

Kolodny, Annette. "Some Notes on Defining a 'Feminist Literary Criticism. ' " Critical Inquiry 2 (Autumn 1975): 75-92.

Leider, Emily. "Joan Didion: Slouching Toward Sacramento. " San Francisco Review of Books 3 (May 1977): 13-14. (Review Essay.)

Masinton, Martha and Charles G. Masinton. "Second-Class Citizenship: The Status of Women in Contemporary American Fiction. " In What Manner of Woman: Essays in English and American Life and Literature, pp. 297-315. Edited by Marlene Springer. New York: New York University Press, 1977.

Samstag, Nicholas A. Saturday Review, 15 August 1970, p. 27. (Review of Play It As It Lays.)

DIOSDADO, ANA

Marqueríe, Alfredo. "Ana Diosdado. " Mundo Hispanico no. 315 (June 1974): 22-25.

DISRAELI, BENJAMIN

Calder, Jenni. Women and Marriage in Victorian Fiction. London: Thames & Hudson, 1976.

DIXON, THOMAS, Jr.

Seidel, Kathryn Lee. "The Southern Belle: Her Fall from the Pedestal in Fiction of the Southern Renaissance. " Ph. D. Dissertation, University of Maryland, 1976.

DODGSON, CHARLES F. see CARROLL, LEWIS

DONNE, JOHN

Snider, Clifton. "Jung's Psychology of the Conscious and the Unconscious. " Psychocultural Review 1 (Spring 1977): 216-242.

DOOLITTLE, HILDA see H. D.

DOS PASSOS, JOHN

Thornton, Patricia Elizabeth. "The Prison of Gender: Sexual Roles in Major American Novels of the 1920's." Ph. D. Dissertation, The University of New Brunswick, 1976.

DOSTOYEVSKY, FYODOR

Banerjee, Maria. "The Metamorphosis of an Icon: Woman in Russian Literature." In Female Studies IX: Teaching About Women in the Foreign Languages, pp. 228-235. Edited by Sidonie Cassirer. Old Westbury, N.Y.: Feminist Press, 1975.

Fort, Deborah. "Women in Dostoyevsky." Deland, Florida: Everett/Edward, n.d. (Cassette no. 5311.)

Kiremidjian, David. "Crime and Punishment: Matricide and the Woman Question." American Imago 33 (Winter 1976): 403-433.

Yaroslavtseva, Olga and Andrei Rumyantsev. "Women of Dostoyevsky's Time." Soviet Woman (December 1971): 34-35.

DRABBLE, MARGARET

Andzhaparidze, G. "Afterword to Russian Translation of The Garrick Year." Moscow: Progress, 1972.

Bonfond, Francois. "Margaret Drabble: How to Express Subjective Truth Through Fiction?" Revue des Langues Vivantes 40, no. 1 (1974): 41-55.

Casey, Constance. San Francisco Review of Books 1 (April 1976): 18-19. (Review of Realms of Gold.)

Clemons, Walter. Newsweek, 17 October 1977, p. 114. (Review of The Ice Age.)

Dean, Nancy. "Feminist Short Fiction: New Forms and Styles." Paper presented at the MLA meeting, New York City, 1976. (Mimeographed.)

Dickstein, Lore. New York Times Book Review, 16

November 1975, p. 5. (Review of The Realms of Gold.)

Gray, Paul. Time, 17 October 1977, p. 104. (Review of The Ice Age.)

Korn, Eric. Times Literary Supplement, 26 September 1975, p. 1077. (Review of The Realms of Gold.)

Libby, Marion Vlastos. "Fate and Feminism in the Novels of Margaret Drabble." Contemporary Literature 16 (Spring 1975): 175-192.

Little, Judy. "Satirizing the Norm: Comedy in Women's Fiction." Regionalism and the Female Imagination 3 (Fall 1977 and Winter 1977-78): 39-49.

Miles, Rosalind. The Fiction of Sex: Themes and Functions of Sex Difference in the Modern Novel. New York: Barnes & Noble, 1974.

Oates, Joyce Carol. Saturday Review, 15 November 1975, p. 20. (Review of The Realms of Gold.)

Poland, Nancy. "Margaret Drabble: 'There Must Be a Lot of People Like Me.'" Midwest Quarterly 16 (April 1975): 255-267.

Ricks, Christopher. New York Review of Books, 27 November 1975, p. 42. (Review of The Realms of Gold.)

Sale, Roger. "The Realms of Gold." Hudson Review 28 (Winter 1975-76): 616-628. (Review of The Realms of Gold.)

Showalter, Elaine. A Literature of Their Own: British Women Novelists from Brontë to Lessing. Princeton: Princeton University Press, 1977.

Standen, Michael. "New Fiction, Old Dissent." Stand (Newcastle on Tyne) 15, no. 1 (1974): 20-25.

Stephens, Evelyn Delores B. "The Novel of Personal Relationships: A Study of Three Contemporary British Women Novelists." Ph.D. Dissertation, Emory University, 1976.

Updike, John. New Yorker, 12 January 1976, p. 88.
(Review of The Realms of Gold.)

Wesker, Arnold. "Profile 10." New Review (London)
1 (February 1975): 25-30.

West, Rebecca. "And They All Lived Unhappily Ever
After." Times Literary Supplement, 26 July 1974,
p. 779.

DREISER, THEODORE

Banta, Martha. "They Shall Have Faces, Minds, and
(One Day) Flesh: Women in Late Nineteenth-Century
and Early Twentieth-Century American Literature."
In What Manner of Woman: Essays on English and
American Life and Literature, pp. 235-270. Edited
by Marlene Springer. New York: New York University Press, 1977.

Cohen, Lester H. "Locating One's Self: The Proble-
matics of Dreiser's Social World." Modern Fiction
Studies 23 (Autumn 1977): 355-368.

Davidson, Cathy N. and Arnold E. "Carrie's Sisters:
The Popular Prototypes for Dreiser's Heroine."
Modern Fiction Studies 23 (Autumn 1977): 395-407.

Forrey, Robert. "Theodore Dreiser: Oedipus Redivi-
vus." Modern Fiction Studies 23 (Autumn 1977):
341-354.

Griffith, Clark. "Sister Carrie: Dreiser's Wasteland."
American Studies 16 (Fall 1975): 41-47.

Lindborg, Mary Anne. "Dreiser's Sentimental Heroine,
Aileen Butler." American Literature 48 (January
1977): 590-593.

Pizer, Donald. The Novels of Theodore Dreiser: A
Critical Study. Minneapolis: University of Minnesota Press, 1976.

Price, Richard Alan. "The Culture of Despair: Characters and Society in the Novels of Edith Wharton and
Theodore Dreiser." Ph.D. Dissertation, The University of Rochester, 1976.

Weir, Sybil B. "The Image of Women in Dreiser's Fiction, 1900-1925." Pacific Coast Philology 7 (1972): 65-71.

Westbrook, Max. "Dreiser's Defense of Carrie Meeber." Modern Fiction Studies 23 (Autumn 1977): 381-393.

DREXLER, ROSALYN

Jefferson, Margo. Newsweek, 10 March 1975, pp. 74-76. (Review of The Cosmopolitan Girl.)

Sanborn, Sara. New York Times Book Review, 30 March 1975, p. 4. (Review of The Cosmopolitan Girl.)

Shapiro, Jane. "Making Woof-y." Ms. 4 (July 1975): 35-36. (Review of The Cosmopolitan Girl.)

DRYDEN, JOHN

Bratton, Clinton Woodrow. "The Use of Marriage in the Comedies of Etherege, Wycherley, Dryden and Congreve." Ph.D. Dissertation, University of Colorado, 1975.

Hume, Robert D. "Marital Discord in English Comedy from Dryden to Fielding." Modern Philology 74 (February 1977): 248-272.

_____. "The Myth of the Rake in 'Restoration' Comedy." Studies in the Literary Imagination 10 (Spring 1977): 25-55.

McCoy, Kathleen. "The Fallen Woman of Restoration Comedy." Paper presented at the MLA meeting, New York City, December 1976; forthcoming in Studies in Eighteenth-Century Culture.

McDonald, Margaret Lamb. "The Independent Woman in the Restoration Comedy of Manners." Ph.D. Dissertation, University of Colorado, 1975.

Novak, Maximillian E. "Margery Pinchwife's 'London Disease': Restoration Comedy and the Libertine Offensive in the 1670's." Studies in the Literary Imagination 10 (Spring 1977): 1-24.

Richetti, John J. "The Portrayal of Women in Restoration and Eighteenth-Century English Literature." In What Manner of Woman: Essays on English and American Life and Literature, pp. 65-97. Edited by Marlene Springer. New York: New York University Press, 1977.

Straulman, Ann. "Zempoalla, Lyndaraxa, and Nourmahal: Dryden's Heroic Female Villains." English Studies in Canada 1 (Spring 1975): 31-45.

DU BOIS, W. E. B.

Ward, Hazel Mae. "The Black Woman as Character: Images in the American Novel, 1852-1953." Ph.D. Dissertation, The University of Texas at Austin, 1977.

DUFFY, MAUREEN

Hays, Janice. "Themes and Modes of Women's Drama in the Twentieth Century." Paper presented at the MLA meeting, New York City, December 1976. (Mimeographed.)

Rule, Jane. Lesbian Images. Garden City, N.Y.: Doubleday, 1975.

DUMAS, ALEXANDER fils

Crane, Robert Arthur. "The Courtisane Character in the Nineteenth Century French Novel from Balzac to Zola." Ph.D. Dissertation, The University of North Carolina at Chapel Hill, 1976.

DUNBAR, PAUL LAURENCE

Ward, Hazel Mae. "The Black Woman as Character: Images in the American Novel, 1852-1953." Ph.D. Dissertation, The University of Texas at Austin, 1977.

DUNCAN, SARA JEANNETTE

Mathews, Robin. "Le roman engagé: The Social/Political Novel in English Canada." Laurentian University Review 9 (November 1976): [15]-31.

DUNNE, MARY CHARELITA (pseud.: George Egerton)

Fernando, Lloyd. "New Women" in the Late Victorian Novel. University Park: Pennsylvania State University Press, 1977.

Harris, Wendell V. "Egerton: Forgotten Realist." Victorian Newsletter (Spring 1968): 31-36.

Showalter, Elaine. A Literature of Their Own: British Women Novelists from Brontë to Lessing. Princeton: Princeton University Press, 1977.

DUNOIS, DOMINIQUE

Bleuzé, Ruth Allen. "Romancières et Critiques: Etude du Prix Fémina, 1904-1968." Ph.D. Dissertation, University of Colorado at Boulder, 1977.

DURAS, MARGUERITE

Crosland, Margaret. Women of Iron and Velvet: French Women After George Sand. New York: Taplinger, 1976.

Guers-Villate, Yvonne. "Marguerite Duras." Paper presented at the MLA Convention, San Francisco, December 1975.

Husserl-Kapit, Susan. "An Interview with Marguerite Duras." Signs: Journal of Women in Culture and Society 1 (Winter 1975): 423-434.

Makward, Christiane. "Structures du silence/du délire: Duras/Cixous." Paper presented at the MLA meeting, New York, December 1976.

Mercier, Michel. Le roman féminin. Paris: P.U.F., 1976.

Schwartz, Lucy M. "Social Rebellion in the Novels of Mme de Duras." North Dakota Quarterly 43 (Spring 1975): 45-49.

Watkins, Virginia Doris. "The Rebellious Heroine in the Novels of Marguerite Duras." Ph.D. Dissertation, Case Western Reserve University, 1975.

Zepp, Evelyn H. "Language as Ritual in Marguerite Duras's Moderato Cantabile." Symposium 30 (Fall 1976): 236-259.

- E -

EDGEWORTH, MARIA

Bronfman, Judith. "The Griselda Legend in English Literature." Ph.D. Dissertation, New York University, 1977.

Doubleday, Neal Frank. Variety of Attempt: British and American Fiction in the Early Nineteenth Century. Lincoln: University of Nebraska Press, 1976.

Eisenstadt, Elizabeth Rayment. "A Study of Maria Edgeworth's Fiction." Ph.D. Dissertation, Washington University, 1975.

Haworth, H. E. "Romantic Female Writers and the Critics." Texas Studies in Literature and Language 17 (Winter 1976): 725-736.

Hawthorne, Mark D. "Maria Edgeworth's Unpleasant Lesson: The Shaping of Character." Studies: An Irish Quarterly Review 64, no. 254 (1975): 167-177.

Jackel, David. "Leonora and Lady Susan: A Note on Maria Edgeworth and Jane Austen." English Studies in Canada 3 (Fall 1977): [278]-288.

Moers, Ellen. Literary Women. Garden City, N.Y.: Doubleday, 1976.

Paratte, Henri-Dominique. "Maria Edgeworth's Madame de Fleury, an Anglo-Irish View of the French Revolution." Cahiers Irlandais (Lille) 2-3 (1974): 69-82.

Portner, Ruth Lee. "A Study of Marriage in the English Novel." Ph.D. Dissertation, City University of New York, 1977.

Taylor, Irene and Gina Luria. "Gender and Genre:

Women in British Romantic Literature. " In What
Manner of Woman: Essays on English and American
Life and Literature, pp. 98-124. Edited by Marlene
Springer. New York: New York University Press,
1977.

EGERTON, GEORGE see DUNNE, MARY CHARELITA

EGGLESTON, GEORGE GARY

Seidel, Kathryn Lee. "The Southern Belle: Her Fall
from the Pedestal in Fiction of the Southern Renaissance. " Ph. D. Dissertation, University of Maryland, 1976.

EICHENDORFF, JOSEPH von

Fass, Barbara. La Belle Dame sans Merci & the Aesthetics of Romanticism. Detroit: Wayne State University Press, 1974.

Sheeran, Joan Garner. "Women and the Freedom-to-Be
in Selected Works of Schiller and the Romantics. "
Ph. D. Dissertation, University of Minnesota, 1976.

ELIOT, GEORGE

Androne, Mary Jane Petersen. "Legacies of Clerical
Life: A Study of Clerical, Artistic and Domestic
Figures in the Novels of George Eliot. " Ph. D.
Dissertation, University of Pennsylvania, 1977.

Argyle, Gisela. "The German Key to Life in Middlemarch. " Ariel 7 (October 1976): 51-68.

Auerbach, Nina. "The Power of Hunger: Demonism
and Maggie Tulliver. " Nineteenth-Century Fiction
30 (September 1975): [150]-171.

Austen, Zelda. "Why Feminist Critics Are Angry with
George Eliot. " College English 37 (February 1976):
549-561.

Beaty, Jerome. "On First Looking into George Eliot's
Middlemarch. " In The Victorian Experience: The
Novelists, pp. 151-176. Edited by Richard A. Le-
vine. Athens: Ohio University Press, 1976.

Bedick, David B. "The Changing Role of Anxiety in the Novel." Ph.D. Dissertation, New York University, 1975.

Benet, Mary Kathleen. Writers in Love: Katherine Mansfield, George Eliot, Colette, and the Men They Lived With. New York: Macmillan, 1977.

Blythe, David Everett. "Household Gods: Domesticity in the Novels of George Eliot." Ph.D. Dissertation, The University of North Carolina at Chapel Hill, 1977.

Bonaparte, Felicia. Will and Destiny: Morality and Tragedy in George Eliot's Novels. New York: New York University Press, 1975.

Bradley, Anthony G. "Family as Pastoral: The Garths in Middlemarch." Ariel 6 (October 1975): 41-51.

Calder, Jenni. Women and Marriage in Victorian Fiction. London: Thames & Hudson, 1976.

Cunningham, Valentine. Everywhere Spoken Against: Dissent in the Victorian Novel. Oxford: Clarendon Press, 1975.

Dylla, Sandra Marie. "Jane Austen and George Eliot: The Influence of Their Social Worlds on Their Women Characters." Ph.D. Dissertation, The University of Wisconsin-Milwaukee, 1974.

Edwards, Michael. "George Eliot and Negative Form." Critical Quarterly 17 (Summer 1975): [171]-179.

Eliasberg, Ann Pringle. "The Victorian Anti-Heroine: Her Role in Selected Novels of the 1860's and 1870's." Ph.D. Dissertation, The City University of New York, 1975.

Emery, Laura Comer. George Eliot's Creative Conflict: The Other Side of Silence. Berkeley, California: University of California Press, 1976.

Fairey, Wendy Westbrook. "The Relationship of Heroine, Confessor, and Community in the Novels of George Eliot." Ph.D. Dissertation, Columbia University, 1975.

Faulkner, Peter. Humanism in the English Novel. New York: Barnes & Noble, 1976.

Fernando, Lloyd. "New Women" in the Late Victorian Novel. University Park: Pennsylvania State University Press, 1977.

_____. "Special Pleading and Art in Middlemarch: The Relation Between the Sexes." Modern Language Review 67 (January 1972): 44-49.

Francone, Carol Burr. "Women in Rebellion: A Study of the Conflict Between Self-Fulfillment and Self-Sacrifice in Emma, Jane Eyre, and The Mill on the Floss." Ph.D. Dissertation, Case Western Reserve University, 1975.

Fulmer, Constance M. George Eliot: A Reference Guide. New York: G. K. Hall, 1977.

Gandesbery, Jean Johnson. "Versions of the Mother in the Novels of Jane Austen and George Eliot." Ph.D. Dissertation, University of California, Davis, 1976.

Haight, Gordon S. "The True Heroine of Middlemarch." George Eliot Fellowship Review 4 (1973): 8-10.

Halperin, John and Janet Kunert. Plots and Characters in the Fiction of Jane Austen, the Brontës, and George Eliot. Hamden, Conn.: Shoe String, 1976.

Hoffeld, Laura Diamond. "The Servant Heroine in 18th and 19th Century British Fiction: The Social Reality and Its Image in the Novel." Ph.D. Dissertation, New York University, 1975.

Jackson, Arlene M. "Dorothea Brooke of Middlemarch." Cithara 12 (May 1973): 91-102.

Jackson, R. L. P. "George Eliot, J. S. Mill and Women's Liberation." Quadrant: An Australian Bi-Monthly 94 (1975): 11-33.

Joyner, Nancy. "Eliot and Robinson: How to Write

About Women Without Being Trying." Presented at
the College English Association, Ashville, North
Carolina, October 1975.

LaJoy, Maureen. "No Laughing Matter: Women and
Humor." Women 5, no. 1 (1976): 6-9.

Levenson, Shirley Frank. "The Artist and the Woman
in George Eliot's Novels." Ph.D. Dissertation,
Brandeis University, 1975.

Longerbeam, Larry Simpson. "Seduction as Symbolic
Action: A Study of the Seduction Motif in Six Victorian Novels." Ph.D. Dissertation, George Peabody College for Teachers, 1975.

McDaniel, Judith Adair. "Fettered Wings Half Loose:
Female Development in the Victorian Novel." Ph.D.
Dissertation, Tufts University, 1975.

Miles, Rosalind. The Fiction of Sex: Themes and
Functions of Sex Difference in the Modern Novel.
New York: Barnes & Noble, 1974.

Moers, Ellen. Literary Women. Garden City, N.Y.:
Doubleday, 1976.

Natov, Roni L. "The Strong-Minded Heroine in Mid-
Victorian Fiction." Ph.D. Dissertation, New York
University, 1975.

Newton, K. M. "Historical Prototypes in Middlemarch."
English Studies 56 (October 1975): 403-408.

Perry, Donna Marie. "From Innocence Through Ex-
perience: A Study of the Romantic Child in Five
Nineteenth Century Novels." Ph.D. Dissertation,
Marquette University, 1976.

Portner, Ruth Lee. "A Study of Marriage in the English
Novel." Ph.D. Dissertation, City University of New
York, 1977.

Postlethwaite, Diana Lynn. "The Novelist as a Woman
of Science: George Eliot and Contemporary Psychology." Ph.D. Dissertation, Yale University,
1975.

Price, Theodore. "The Ugly Duckling: Recurrent Themes in George Eliot." Ph. D. Dissertation, Rutgers University, The State University of New Jersey, 1975.

Redinger, Ruby V. George Eliot: The Emergent Self. New York: Knopf, 1975.

Reed, John R. Victorian Conventions. Athens: Ohio University Press, 1975.

Rogal, Samuel J. "John Wesley's Women." Eighteenth-Century Life 1 (September 1974): 7-11.

Rooke, Constance. "Beauty in Distress: Daniel Deronda and The House of Mirth." Women & Literature 4 (Fall 1976): 28-39.

Rouslin, Virginia Watson. "Women's Sexuality in Brontë and Eliot." Room of One's Own 3, no. 1 (1977): 38-52.

Sadoff, Diane F. "Forms of Female Contrition: The Heroine in Women's Nineteenth-Century English Novels." Paper presented at the MLA meeting, New York City, December 1976. (Mimeographed.)

Showalter, Elaine. A Literature of Their Own: British Women Novelists from Brontë to Lessing. Princeton: Princeton University Press, 1977.

Siefert, Susan Elizabeth. "The Dilemma of the Talented Woman: A Study in Nineteenth-Century Fiction." Ph. D. Dissertation, Marquette University, 1974.

Speck, Paul. "Self and Self-Sacrifice in The Mill and the Floss." Innisfree 1 (1974): 21-28.

Springer, Marlene. "Angels and Other Women in Victorian Literature." In What Manner of Woman: Essays on English and American Life and Literature, pp. 124-159. Edited by Marlene Springer. New York: New York University Press, 1977.

Stowell, H. E. Quill Pens and Petticoats: A Portrait of Women of Letters. London: Wayland, 1970.

Taylor, Nancy McKeon. "Conscious Construction: The Concept of Plot in Five Novels by Women." Ph. D. Dissertation, Loyola University of Chicago, 1977.

Tomlinson, Thomas Brian. The English Middle-Class Novel. New York: Barnes & Noble, 1976.

Toth, Emily. "The Independent Woman and 'Free' Love." Massachusetts Review 16 (Autumn 1975): 647-664.

Trudgill, Eric. Madonnas and Magdalens: The Origins and Development of Victorian Sexual Attitudes. New York: Holmes & Meier, 1976.

Whitlock, Roger. "The Psychology of Consciousness in Daniel Deronda." Victorians Institute Journal (1957): 17-24.

Wiesenfarth, Joseph. "Legend in The Mill on the Floss." Texas Studies in Literature and Language 18 (Spring 1976): [20]-41.

Williams, Kristi Fayle. "The Idealized Heroine in Victorian Fiction." Ph. D. Dissertation, Brown University, 1975.

Woolf, Gabriel. "In the Vanguard of Women's Lib: George Eliot." George Eliot Fellowship Review 4 (1973): 11-13.

Yee, Carol Zonis. "Feminism and the Later Heroines of George Eliot." Ph. D. Dissertation, The University of New Mexico, 1977.

Youngren, Virginia Rotan. "Moral Life in Solitude: A Study of Selected Novels of Jane Austen, Charlotte Brontë, Elizabeth Gaskell and George Eliot." Ph. D. Dissertation, Rutgers University, The State University of New Jersey (New Brunswick), 1977.

Zimmerman, Bonnie S. "'Radiant as a Diamond': George Eliot, Jewelry and the Female Role." Criticism 19 (Summer 1977): 212-222.

ELIOT, T. S.

Gustafson, Richard. "'Time Is a Waiting Woman':

New Poetic Icons. '' Midwest Quarterly 16 (April 1975): 318-327.

Reed, John R. Victorian Conventions. Athens: Ohio University Press, 1975.

Smith, Carol. ''Women in Yeats and Eliot. '' Deland, Florida: Everett/Edwards, n. d. (Cassette no. 5321.)

ELLIOTT, SARAH BARNWELL

Maness, Dinford Gray. ''The Novels of Sarah Barnwell Elliott: A Critical Study. '' Ph. D. Dissertation, University of South Carolina, 1974.

ELLISON, RALPH

Shinn, Thelma J. Wardrop. ''A Study of Women Characters in Contemporary American Fiction 1940-1970. '' Ph. D. Dissertation, Purdue University, 1972.

Sylvander, Carolyn W. ''Ralph Ellison's Invisible Man and Female Stereotypes. '' Paper presented at the MLA meeting, New York City, December 1976.

EMECHETA, BUCHI

Clapp, Susannah. Times Literary Supplement, 11 June 1976, p. 689. (Review of The Bride Price.)

Collins, Harold. World Literature Today 51 (Summer 1977): 491. (Review of The Bride Price.)

Walker, Alice. ''A Writer Because of, Not in Spite of Her Children. '' Ms. 4 (January 1976): 40, 106. (Review of Second Class Citizen.)

ENCHI FUMIKO

Johnson, Eric W. ''Modern Japanese Women Writers. '' Literature East and West 8 (March 1974): [90]-102.

ENGEL, MARIAN

Appenzell, Anthony. ''The Great Bear. '' Canadian Literature 71 (Winter 1976): 105-107. (Review of Bear.)

Irvine, Lorna Marie. "Hostility and Reconciliation: The Mother in English Canadian Fiction. " Ph. D. Dissertation, The American University, 1977.

Mathews, Robin. "Le roman engagé: The Social/Political Novel in English Canada. " Laurentian University Review 9 (November 1976): [15]-31.

Morley, Patricia. "Marian Engel's Bear. " World Literature Written in English 16 (November 1977): 359-360.

Wiseman, Adele. "Pooh at Puberty. " Books in Canada 5 (April 1976): 6-8. (Review of Bear.)

ESCHENBACH, WOLFRAM von

Gibbs, Marion. Wîplîchez wîbes reht: A Study of the Women Characters in the Works of Wolfram von Eschenbach. Pittsburgh: Duquesne University Press, 1972.

ESTIENNE, NICOLE

Aronson, Nicole. "Nicole Estienne and Women's Liberation in the XVIth Century. " North Carolina Foreign Language Teacher 1 (Fall 1971): 22-29.

ETCHERELLI, CLAIRE

Bleuzé, Ruth Allen. "Romancières et Critiques: Etude du Prix Fémina, 1904-1968. " Ph. D. Dissertation, University of Colorado at Boulder, 1977.

Crosland, Margaret. Women of Iron and Velvet: French Women After George Sand. New York: Taplinger, 1976.

ETHEREGE, SIR GEORGE

Beless, Rosemary June. "Reflections of the Law in the Comedies of Etherege, Wycherley, and Congreve. " Ph. D. Dissertation, University of Utah, 1977.

Bratton, Clinton Woodrow. "The Use of Marriage in the Comedies of Etherege, Wycherley, Dryden and Congreve. " Ph. D. Dissertation, University of Colorado, 1975.

Corman, Brian. "Interpreting and Misinterpreting The Man of Mode." Papers on Language and Literature 13 (Winter 1977): 35-53.

Hume, Robert D. "The Myth of the Rake in 'Restoration' Comedy." Studies in the Literary Imagination 10 (Spring 1977): 25-55.

McDonald, Margaret Lamb. "The Independent Woman in the Restoration Comedy of Manners." Ph.D. Dissertation, University of Colorado, 1975.

Novak, Maximillian E. "Margery Pinchwife's 'London Disease': Restoration Comedy and the Libertine Offensive in the 1670's." Studies in the Literary Imagination 10 (Spring 1977): 1-24.

Suwannabha, Sumitra. "The Feminine Eye: Augustan Society as Seen by Selected Women Dramatists of the Restoration and Early Nineteenth Century." Ph.D. Dissertation, Indiana University, 1973.

EURIPIDES

Dreyfuss, Cecilia Anne Stiborik. "Femina sapiens in Drama: Aeschylus to Grillparzer." Ph.D. Dissertation, The University of Michigan, 1975.

Gelderman, Carol W. "The Male Nature of Tragedy." Prairie Schooner 49 (Fall 1975): 220-227.

Glenn, Justin. "The Phantasies of Phaedra: A Psychoanalytic Reading." Classical World 69 (April-May 1976): 435-442.

McDonald, William P. "The Blackness of Medea." CLA Journal 19 (September 1975): 20-37.

Méron, Evelyne. "De l'Hippolyte d'Euripide à la Phèdre de Racine: deux conceptions du tragique." XVII Siècle 100 (1973): 35-54.

Pomeroy, Sarah B. Goddesses, Whores, Wives, and Slaves: Women in Classical Antiquity. New York: Schocken Books, 1975.

Poole, Adrian. "Total Disaster: Euripides' The Trojan Women." Arion 3, no. 3 (1976): 257-287.

Smith, Louise Pearson. "Studies of Characterization
in Euripides: The Medeia, Elektra, and Orestes. " Ph. D. Dissertation, Princeton University,
1976.

EVANS, AUGUSTA JANE

Foster, Edward Halsey. The Civilized Wilderness:
Backgrounds to American Romantic Literature, 1817-
1960. New York: Free Press, 1975.

EVANS, MARI

Rushing, Andrea Benton. "Images of Black Women in
Afro-American Poetry. " Black World 24 (September 1975): 18-30.

EVTUSHENKO, E.

Babenko, Vickie A. "Women in Evtushenko's Poetry. "
Russian Review 36 (July 1977): 320-333.

- F -

FARQUHAR, GEORGE

Hume, Robert D. "Marital Discord in English Comedy
from Dryden to Fielding. " Modern Philology 74
(February 1977): 248-272.

_____. "The Myth of the Rake in 'Restoration'
Comedy. " Studies in the Literary Imagination 10
(Spring 1977): 25-55.

McDonald, Margaret Lamb. "The Independent Woman
in the Restoration Comedy of Manners. " Ph. D.
Dissertation, University of Colorado, 1975.

FAUCONNIER, GENEVIEVE

Bleuzé, Ruth Allen. "Romancières et Critiques: Etude
du Prix Fémina, 1904-1968. " Ph. D. Dissertation,
University of Colorado at Boulder, 1977.

FAULKNER, WILLIAM

Alldredge, Betty Jean Edwards. "Levels of Conscious- ness: Women in the Stream of Consciousness Novels of Joyce, Woolf, and Faulkner." Ph.D. Dissertation, University of Oregon, 1976.

Brooks, Cleanth. "The Image of Helen Baird in Early Faulkner." Sewanee Review 85 (April-June 1977): 218-234.

Castille, Philip Dubuisson. "Faulkner's Early Heroines." Ph.D. Dissertation, Tulane University, 1977.

Clark, Anderson Aubrey. "Courtly Love in the Writings of William Faulkner." Ph.D. Dissertation, Vander- bilt University, 1975.

Colson, Theodore. "Analogues of Faulkner's The Wild Palms and Hawthorne's 'The Birthmark.'" Dal- housie Review 56 (Autumn 1976): [510]-518.

Degenfelder, E. Pauline. "The Four Faces of Temple Drake: Faulkner's Sanctuary, Requiem for a Nun, and the Two Film Adaptations." American Quarter- ly 28 (Winter 1976): [544]-560.

Donovan, Josephine. "Feminism and Aesthetics." Critical Inquiry 3 (Spring 1977): 605-608.

Hill, Douglas B., Jr. "Faulkner's Caddy." Canadian Review of American Studies 7 (Spring 1976): 26-35.

Jaffe, Evelyn. "Endure and Prevail: Faulkner's Social Outcasts." Ph.D. Dissertation, University of Colo- rado at Boulder, 1977.

Kinney, Arthur F. "Faulkner and Flaubert." Journal of Modern Literature 6 (April 1977): 222-247.

Lander, Dawn. "Women and the Wilderness: Tabus in American Literature." University of Michigan Papers in Women's Studies 2, no. 3 (1977): 62-83.

McFarland, Holly. "The Mask Not Tragic ... Just Damned: The Women in Faulkner's Trilogy." Ball State University Forum 18 (Spring 1977): 27-50.

Milliner, Gladys. "The Third Eve: Caddy Compson." Midwest Quarterly 16 (April 1975): 268-275.

Muhlenfeld, Elisabeth S. "Shadows with Substance and Ghosts Exhumed: The Women in Absalom, Absalom!" Mississippi Quarterly 25 (Summer 1972): 289-304.

Page, Sally. "Faulkner's Women: A Defense Against His Critics." Deland, Florida: Everett/Edwards, n.d. (Cassette no. 5327.)

Peary, Charles A. " 'If I'd Just Had a Mother': Faulkner's Quentin Compson." Literature and Psychology 23 (1973): 114-121.

Sabiston, Elizabeth. "Women, Blacks, and Thomas Sutpen's Mythopoeic Drive in Absalom, Absalom!" Modernist Studies 1 (1974-75): 15-26.

Seidel, Kathryn Lee. "The Southern Belle: Her Fall from the Pedestal in Fiction of the Southern Renaissance." Ph.D. Dissertation, University of Maryland, 1976.

Thornton, Patricia Elizabeth. "The Prison of Gender: Sexual Roles in Major American Novels of the 1920's." Ph.D. Dissertation, The University of New Brunswick, 1976.

Traschen, Isadore. "The Tragic Form of The Sound and the Fury." Southern Review 12 (October 1976): 798-813.

Tuttleton, James W. " 'Combat in the Erogenous Zone': Women in the American Novel Between the Two World Wars." In What Manner of Woman: Essays in English and American Life and Literature, pp. 271-296. Edited by Marlene Springer. New York: New York University Press, 1977.

Waters, Maureen Anne. "The Role of Women in Faulkner's Yoknapatawpha." Ed.D. Dissertation, Columbia University, 1975.

Weinstein, Philip M. "Caddy Disparue: Exploring an Episode Common to Proust and Faulkner." Comparative Literature Studies 14 (March 1977): 38-52.

Williams, David. Faulkner's Women: The Myth and the Muse. Montreal: McGill-Queen's University Press, 1977.

FAUSET, JESSIE

Doyle, Sister Mary Ellen. "The Heroine of Black Novels." In Perspectives on Afro-American Women, pp. 112-125. Edited by Willa D. Johnson and Thomas L. Green. Washington, D.C.: ECCA Publications, 1975.

Ramsey, Priscilla Barbara Ann. "A Study of Black Identity in 'Passing' Novels of the Nineteenth and Early Twentieth Centuries." Ph.D. Dissertation, The American University, 1975.

Royster, Beatrice Horn. "The Ironic Vision of Four Black Women Novelists: A Study of the Novels of Jessie Fauset, Nella Larsen, Zora Neale Hurston, and Ann Petry." Ph.D. Dissertation, Emory University, 1975.

Ward, Hazel Mae. "The Black Woman as Character: Images in the American Novel, 1852-1953." Ph.D. Dissertation, The University of Texas at Austin, 1977.

FERBER, Edna

Davidson, Colleen Tighe. "Beyond the Sentimental Heroine: The Feminist Character in American Novels, 1899-1937." Ph.D. Dissertation, University of Minnesota, 1975.

Goodman, Charlotte. "Images of American Rural Women in the Novel." University of Michigan Papers in Women's Studies 1 (June 1975): 57-70.

FERN, FANNY

Douglas, Ann. The Feminization of American Culture. New York: Alfred A. Knopf, 1977.

Hull, Raymona E. " 'Scribbling' Females and Serious Males: Hawthorne's Comments from Abroad on Some American Authors." Nathaniel Hawthorne Journal (1975): 35-58.

FERNANDEZ, SEBASTIAN

Trisler, Barbara Jean. "A Comparative Study of the Character Portrayal of 'Celestina' and Other Golden Age Celestinesque Protagonists." Ph.D. Dissertation, The University of Oklahoma, 1977.

FERRIER, SUSAN

Doubleday, Neal Frank. Variety of Attempt: British and American Fiction in the Early Nineteenth Century. Lincoln: University of Nebraska Press, 1976.

Paxton, Nancy L. "Subversive Feminism: A Reassessment of Susan Ferrier's Marriage." Women & Literature 4 (Spring 1976): 18-29.

Portner, Ruth Lee. "A Study of Marriage in the English Novel." Ph.D. Dissertation, City University of New York, 1977.

Reed, John R. Victorian Conventions. Athens: Ohio University Press, 1975.

FEUILLET, OCTAVE

Armstrong, Judith. The Novel of Adultery. New York: Barnes & Noble, 1976.

FEYDEAU, ERNEST

Wood, Carol Colbert. "Ernest Feydeau: The Novelist as Social Historian." Ph.D. Dissertation, Fordham University, 1977.

FIAMENGO, MARYA

Bowering, Marilyn. "Stages of Poetry." Canadian Literature no. 74 (Autumn 1977): 102-104. (Review of In Praise of Old Women.)

FIELD, NATHAN

Leggatt, Alexander. Citizen Comedy in the Age of Shakespeare. Toronto: University of Toronto Press, 1973.

FIELDING, HENRY

Auty, Susan G.   The Comic Spirit of Eighteenth-Century
Novels. Port Washington, N.Y.: Kennikat Press,
1975.

Evans, James E.   "Fielding's Lady Booby and Fénelon's
Calypso. " Studies in the Novel 8 (Summer 1976):
210-213.

Hume, Robert D.   "Marital Discord in English Comedy
from Dryden to Fielding. " Modern Philology 74
(February 1977): 248-272.

Hunter, J. Paul. Occasional Form: Henry Fielding
and the Chains of Circumstance. Baltimore: Johns
Hopkins University Press, 1975.

Pykare, Nina Coombs.   "The Female Part of the
Species: A Study of Women in Fielding. " Ph.D.
Dissertation, Kent State University, 1976.

Radner, John B.   "The Youthful Harlot's Curse: The
Prostitute as Symbol of the City in 18th-Century English Literature. " Eighteenth-Century Life 2 (March
1976): 59-64.

Richetti, John J.   "The Portrayal of Women in Restoration and Eighteenth-Century English Literature. " In
What Manner of Woman: Essays on English and
American Life and Literature, pp. 65-97. Edited
by Marlene Springer. New York: New York University Press, 1977.

Spacks, Patricia Meyer. Imagining a Self: Autobiography and Novel in Eighteenth-Century England. Cambridge: Harvard University Press, 1976.

Swanson, Gayle Ruff.   "Henry Fielding and the Psychology of Womanhood. " Ph.D. Dissertation, University of South Carolina, 1976.

Williams, Murial Brittain. Marriage: Fielding's Mirror of Morality. University: University of Alabama
Press, 1973.

FIELDING, SARAH

Downs-Miers, Deborah Wheatley. "Labyrinths of the
Mind: A Study of Sarah Fielding. " Ph.D. Dissertation, University of Missouri-Columbia, 1975.

FILLEUL, NICOLAS

Goldman, Rachel Margaret. "The Lucretia Legend from
Livy to Rojas Zorrilla. " Ph.D. Dissertation, City
University of New York, 1976.

FISHER, VARDIS

Meldrum, Barbara. "Images of Women in Western
American Literature. " Midwest Quarterly 17 (April
1976): 252-267.

FITCH, CLYDE

Gottlieb, Lois C. "The Perils of Freedom: The New
Woman in Three American Plays of the 1900's. "
Canadian Review of American Studies 6 (Spring
1975): 84-98.

Loudin, Joanne Marie. "The Changing Role of the
Comic Heroine in American Drama from 1900 to
1940. " Ph.D. Dissertation, University of Washington, 1974.

FITZGERALD, F. SCOTT

Bedick, David B. "The Changing Role of Anxiety in the
Novel. " Ph.D. Dissertation, New York University,
1975.

Graham, Sheilah. The Real F. Scott Fitzgerald Thirty-
Five Years Later. New York: Grosset & Dunlap,
1976.

Greiff, Louis K. "Perfect Marriage in Tender Is the
Night: A Study in the Progress of a Symbol. " In
Fitzgerald/Hemingway Annual 1974, pp. 63-74.
Edited by Matthew J. Bruccoli and C. E. Frazer
Clark, Jr. Englewood, Colo. : Microcard Editions
Books, 1975.

Heath, Mary. "Marriages." In Woman: An Issue, pp. 281-288. Edited by Lee R. Edwards, Mary Heath, and Lisa Baskin. Boston and Toronto: Little, Brown, 1972.

Lewis, William F. "Masculine Inferiority Feelings of F. Scott Fitzgerald." Medical Aspects of Human Sexuality 7 (April 1973): 60.

Martin, Wendy. "Patterns of Mastery in Tender Is the Night." Paper presented at the MLA meeting, San Francisco, December 1975.

Meyers, Jeffrey. Married to Genius. New York: Barnes & Noble, 1977.

Stimpson, Catharine. "Women as Scapegoats." In Female Studies V, pp. 7-16. Edited by Rae Lee Siporin. Pittsburgh: KNOW, Inc., 1972.

Thornton, Patricia Elizabeth. "The Prison of Gender: Sexual Roles in Major American Novels of the 1920's." Ph.D. Dissertation, The University of New Brunswick, 1976.

Tuttleton, James W. "'Combat in the Erogenous Zone': Women in the American Novel Between the Two World Wars." In What Manner of Woman: Essays in English and American Life and Literature, pp. 271-296. Edited by Marlene Springer. New York: New York University Press, 1977.

Wasserstrom, William. "The Road of Guilt: Henry Adams, Scott and Zelda." Journal of Modern Literature 6 (April 1977): 289-310.

FITZGERALD, ZELDA

Anderson, W. R. "Rivalry and Partnership: The Short Fiction of Zelda Sayre Fitzgerald." Paper presented at the MLA meeting, San Francisco, December 1975.

Authors in the News, vol. 1. Detroit: Gale Research, 1976, pp. 146-153.

Davidson, Colleen Tighe. "Beyond the Sentimental

Heroine: The Feminist Character in American Novels, 1899-1937." Ph.D. Dissertation, University of Minnesota, 1975.

Evans, Jeff. "Zelda Fitzgerald in F. Scott Fitzgerald's Fiction." Paper presented at the MLA meeting, San Francisco, December 1975.

Heath, Mary. "Marriages." In Woman: An Issue, pp. 281-288. Edited by Lee R. Edwards, Mary Heath, and Lisa Baskin. Boston and Toronto: Little, Brown, 1972.

McCauley, Carole Spearin. "Zelda." Room of One's Own 1 (Fall 1975): 33-42.

Meyers, Jeffrey. Married to Genius. New York: Barnes & Noble, 1977.

Milford, Nancy. "Zelda." North Hollywood: The Center for Cassette Studies, n.d.

Seidel, Kathryn Lee. "The Southern Belle: Her Fall from the Pedestal in Fiction of the Southern Renaissance." Ph.D. Dissertation, University of Maryland, 1976.

FLAUBERT, GUSTAV

Armstrong, Judith. The Novel of Adultery. New York: Barnes & Noble, 1976.

Bart, Benjamin. "From Prostitute to Houri: The Image of the Prostitute from Balzac to Flaubert." Paper presented at the MLA meeting, New York City, December 1976.

Church, Margaret. "A Triad of Images: Nature in Madame Bovary." Mosaic 5 (Spring 1972): 203-213.

Crane, Robert Arthur. "The Courtisane Character in the Nineteenth Century French Novel from Balzac to Zola." Ph.D. Dissertation, The University of North Carolina at Chapel Hill, 1976.

Goodheart, Eugene. "Flaubert and the Powerlessness of Art." Centennial Review 19 (Summer 1975): 157-171.

Hamblin, Ellen N. "Adulterous Heroines in Nineteenth Century Literature: A Comparative Literature Study." Ph.D. Dissertation, The Florida State University, 1977.

Kumar, Prem. "Four Figures in Love: Anna Karenin, Emma Bovary, Constance Chatterly [sic], and Chitralekha." Journal of South Asian Literature 12 (Spring-Summer 1977): 73-80.

Manthey, Ethel Vern. "The Sentimentally Educated Hero: A Comparison of Some Aspects of the Hero of Gustave Flaubert with Two Leading Characters of Henry James." Ph.D. Dissertation, Case Western Reserve University, 1976.

Moravia, Alberto. "Emma Unglued." Saturday Review, 2 December 1972, pp. 53-55.

Pace, Jean. "Flaubert's Image of Woman." Southern Review 13 (January 1977): 114-130.

Porter, Dennis. "Gustave Flaubert's Middle-Class Tragedy." Forum for Modern Language Studies 18 (January 1977): 59-69.

Reff, Theodore. "The Influence of Flaubert's Queen of Sheba on Later Nineteenth-Century Literature." Romanic Review 65 (November 1974): 249-265.

Shriver, Margaret M. "Madame Bovary versus The Woman of Rome." Nineteenth-Century French Studies 1 (1973): 197-209.

Williams, D. A. "Water Imagery in Madame Bovary." Forum for Modern Language Studies 13 (January 1977): 70-84.

FLECKER, JAMES ELROY

Davis, M. B. "James Elroy Flecker's Don Juan." Durham University Journal 38 (June 1977): 271-277.

FLETCHER, JOHN

Forker, Charles R. "Wit Without Money: A Fletcherian Antecedent to Keep the Widow Waking." Comparative Drama 8 (Summer 1974): 172-183.

Hume, Robert D. "Marital Discord in English Comedy from Dryden to Fielding." Modern Philology 74 (February 1977): 248-272.

Leggatt, Alexander. Citizen Comedy in the Age of Shakespeare. Toronto: University of Toronto Press, 1973.

McDonald, Margaret Lamb. "The Independent Woman in the Restoration Comedy of Manners." Ph. D. Dissertation, University of Colorado, 1975.

FLORES, JOAN de

Sims, Edna Niecie. "El antifeminismo en la literatura española hasta 1560." Ph. D. Dissertation, Catholic University, 1970.

FLORIAN, RODRIGUEZ

Trisler, Barbara Jean. "A Comparative Study of the Character Portrayal of 'Celestina' and Other Golden Age Celestinesque Protagonists." Ph. D. Dissertation, The University of Oklahoma, 1977.

FONTANE, THEODORE

Rose, Ingrid Barbara. "Social Stereotypes and Female Actualities: A Dimension of the Social Criticism in Selected Works by Fontane, Hauptmann, Wedekind, and Schnitzler." Ph. D. Dissertation, Princeton University, 1976.

FOOTE, MARY HALLOCK

Meldrum, Barbara. "Images of Women in Western American Literature." Midwest Quarterly 17 (April 1976): 252-267.

FORD, FORD MADOX

DeKoven, Marianne. "Valentine Wannop and Thematic Structure in Ford Madox Ford's Parade's End." English Literature in Transition 20, no. 2 (1977): 56-68.

FORD, JOHN

Hogan, A. P. " 'Tis Pity She's a Whore: The Overall Design. " Studies in English Literature 1500-1900 17 (Spring 1977): [303]-316.

Kaye, Melanie. "The Sword Philippan: Woman as Hero in Stuart Tragedy. " Ph. D. Dissertation, University of California, Berkeley, 1976.

Mirenda, Angela Marie. "The Noble Lie: Selfhood and Tragedy in the Renaissance. " Ph. D. Dissertation, The Pennsylvania State University, 1977.

Roper, Derek, ed. Introduction to 'Tis Pity She's a Whore. New York: Barnes & Noble, 1975.

Shaw, Sharon K. "Medea on Pegasus: Some Speculations on the Parallel Rise of Women and Melodrama on the Jacobean Stage. " Ball State University Forum 14, no. 4 (1973): 13-21.

Still, Roger. Love and Death in Renaissance Tragedy. Baton Rouge: Louisiana State University Press, 1976.

Stone, Carl Warren. "John Ford's Women: The Moral Center of His Drama. " Ph. D. Dissertation, Kent State University, 1975.

Ure, Peter. Elizabethan and Jacobean Drama. Edited by J. C. Maxwell. New York: Barnes & Noble, 1974.

FORRESTER, MRS. (Mrs. Colonel Bridges)

Garrison, Dee. "Immoral Fiction in the Late Victorian Library. " American Quarterly 28 (Spring 1976): 71-89.

FORSTER, E. M.

Gish, Robert. "Mr. Forster and Mrs. Woolf: Aspects of the Novelist as Critic. " Virginia Woolf Quarterly 2 (Summer & Fall 1976): 255-269.

Kennard, Jean E. "Victims of Convention. " Pacific Coast Philology 8 (1973): 23-27.

McDowell, Frederick P. "Forster's Posthumously Published Tales and Some Reflections on His Fiction." Virginia Woolf Quarterly 2 (Summer & Fall 1976): 270-280.

Showalter, Elaine. "A Passage to India as 'Marriage Fiction': Forster's Sexual Politics." Women & Literature 5 (Fall 1977): 3-16.

Wallace, Ronald. "The Inclusion of Merriment: Comedy in A Passage to India." Essays in Literature 4 (Spring 1977): 37-48.

FORSTER, MARGARET

Miles, Rosalind. The Fiction of Sex: Themes and Functions of Sex Difference in the Modern Novel. New York: Barnes & Noble, 1974.

FOTHERGILL, JESSIE

Garrison, Dee. "Immoral Fiction in the Late Victorian Library." American Quarterly 28 (Spring 1976): 71-89.

FOWLES, JOHN

Sullivan, Karen Lever. "The Muse of Fiction: Fatal Women in the Novels of W. M. Thackeray, Thomas Hardy, and John Fowles." Ph.D. Dissertation, The Johns Hopkins University, 1973.

FRAME, JANET

Delbaere-Grant, Jeanne. "Daphne's Metamorphoses in Janet Frame's Early Novels." Ariel 6 (April 1975): 23-37.

Hankin, Cherry. "Language as Theme in Owls Do Cry." Landfall 28 (June 1974): 91-110.

Henden, Josephine. New York Times Book Review, 27 August 1972, p. 5. (Review of Daughter Buffalo.)

Leiter, Robert. "Reconsideration." New Republic, 31 May 1975, pp. 21-22.

McCracken, Jill. "Janet Frame: It's Time for France." New Zealand Listener, 27 October 1973, pp. 20-21.

FRANCE, ANATOLE

> Reff, Theodore. "The Influence of Flaubert's Queen of Sheba on Later Nineteenth-Century Literature." Romanic Review 65 (November 1974): 249-265.

FRANKEN, ROSE

> Shafer, Y. B. "Liberated Women in American Plays of the Past." Players Magazine 49 (Spring 1974): 95-100.

FRANKLIN, J. E.

> Miller, Jeanne-Marie A. "Images of Black Women in Plays by Black Playwrights." CLA Journal 20 (June 1977): 494-507.

FRASER, SYLVIA

> Irvine, Lorna Marie. "Hostility and Reconciliation: The Mother in English Canadian Fiction." Ph.D. Dissertation, The American University, 1977.

> Mansbridge, Francis. "A Better Hard Centre." Canadian Literature no. 71 (Winter 1976): 104-105. (Review of The Candy Factory.)

FRECHETTE, ANNIE HOWELLS see HOWELLS, ANNIE

FREDERIC, HAROLD

> Blackall, Jean Frantz. "Frederic's Gloria Mundi as a Novel of Education." Markham Review 3 (May 1972): 41-46.

> Witt, Stanley Pryor. "Harold Frederic as a Purveyor of American Myth: An Approach to His Novels." Ph.D. Dissertation, The University of Arizona, 1976.

FREEMAN, GILLIAN

> Loprete, N. J. Best Sellers 35 (October 1975): 194. (Review of The Marriage Machine.)

> Miller, Jane. Times Literary Supplement, 4 July 1975, p. 714. (Review of The Marriage Machine.)

FREEMAN, MARY E. WILKINS

Brand, Alice Giarden. "Mary Wilkins Freeman: Misanthropy as Propaganda. " New England Quarterly 50 (March 1977): 83-100.

Callow, James T. and Robert Reilly. Guide to American Literature from Emily Dickinson to the Present. New York: Barnes & Noble, 1977.

Clark, Michelle. "Afterword. " In The Revolt of Mother and Other Stories by Mary E. Wilkins Freeman. Old Westbury, N.Y. : Feminist Press, 1974.

Crowley, John W. "Freeman's Yankee Tragedy: 'Amanda and Love. ' " Markham Review 5 (Spring 1976): 58-60.

Davidson, Colleen Tighe. "Beyond the Sentimental Heroine: The Feminist Character in American Novels, 1899-1937. " Ph. D. Dissertation, University of Minnesota, 1975.

Dullea, Gerard John. "Two New England Voices: Sarah Orne Jewett and Mary Wilkins Freeman. " Ph. D. Dissertation, Syracuse University, 1975.

Ehrlich, Carol. "Evolutionism and the Female in Selected American Novels, 1885-1900. " Ph. D. Dissertation, University of Iowa, 1974.

Gasser, Larry Winston. "Social Reform in the Late Nineteenth-Century American Strike Novel. " Ph. D. Dissertation, University of Denver, 1975.

Lee, Susan. "Another Find From the Feminist Press. " Ms. 4 (December 1975): 50. (Review of The Revolt of Mother and Other Stories.)

Maglin, Nan Bauer. "Rebel Women Writers, 1894-1925." Ph. D. Dissertation, Union Graduate School, 1975.

Voss, Arthur. The American Short Story: A Critical Survey. Norman: University of Oklahoma, 1973.

FRENCH, MARILYN

New York Times Book Review, 16 October 1977, p. 7;

13 November 1977, p. 95. (Review of The Women's Room.)

Robertson, Nan. Milwaukee Journal, 20 November 1977, p. 6. (Review of The Women's Room.)

Sokolov, Raymond. Newsweek, 24 October 1977, p. 121, 124. (Review of The Women's Room.)

FRENEAU, PHILIP

Kolodny, Annette. The Lay of the Land: Metaphor as Experience and History in American Life and Letters. Chapel Hill: University of North Carolina Press, 1975.

FRIEDEL, JOHANN

Horwath, Peter. "Richardsonian Characters and Motifs in Johann Friedel's Novel Eleonore." Forum for Modern Language Studies 13 (April 1977): [97]-107.

FRISCH, MAX

Knight, Eunice Edna. "The Role of Women in the Don Juan and Faust Literature." Ph.D. Dissertation, Florida State University, 1973.

Musgrave, Marian E. "Kürmann, His Wives, and 'Helen, the Mulatta' in Max Frisch's Biographie: Ein Spiel." CLA Journal 18 (March 1975): 341-347.

FROMBERG, SUSAN see SCHAEFFER, SUSAN FROMBERG

FROST, ROBERT

Bacon, Helen. "For Girls: From 'Birches' to 'Wild Grapes.' " Yale Review 67 (Autumn 1977): [13]-29.

House, Elizabeth Balkman. "Robert Frost on Women and Marriage." Ph.D. Dissertation, University of South Carolina, 1975.

Marcus, Mordecai. "The Whole Pattern of Robert Frost's 'Two Witches': Contrasting Psycho-Sexual Modes." Literature and Psychology 26, no. 2 (1976): 69-78.

Wallace, Patricia. "The 'Estranged Point of View'...."

In Frost: Centennial Essays II, pp. 177-95. Ed.
by Jac Tharpe. Jackson: University Press of Mississippi, 1976.

FUCHS, DAVID

Baum, Charlotte, Paula Hyman and Sonya Michel. The Jewish Woman in America. New York: Dial Press, 1975.

Koltun, Elizabeth. The Jewish Woman: New Perspectives. New York: Schocken, 1976.

FUENTES, CARLOS

Bland, Carole E. "Carlos Fuentes' Cambio de piel:
The Quest for Rebirth." Journal of Spanish Studies:
Twentieth Century 4 (Fall 1976): 77-88.

Chrzanowski, Joseph. "The Double in 'Las dos Elenas'
by Carlos Fuentes." Romance Notes 18 (Fall 1977):
6-10.

Gyurko, Lanin A. "The Pseudo-Liberated Woman in
Fuentes' Zona Sagrada." Journal of Spanish Studies:
Twentieth Century 3 (Spring 1975): 17-43.

Jaquette, Jane S. "Literary Archetypes and Female
Role Alternatives: The Woman and the Novel in
Latin America." In Female and Male in Latin Amer-
ica: Essays, pp. 3-28. Edited by Ann Pescatello.
Pittsburgh: University of Pittsburgh Press, 1973.

Meyer, Victoria Junco. "The Images of Women in Contemporary Mexican Literature." In Beyond Intellectual Sexism: A New Woman, A New Reality, pp.
210-228. Edited by Joan Roberts. New York:
David McKay, 1976.

- G -

GADKARI, RAM GANESH

Junghare, Indira Y. "Women in Gadkari's Premasan-
yas." Literature East and West 17 (June, September & December 1973): 228-237.

GAINES, ERNEST

>Bryant, Jerry H. "Ernest Gaines: Change, Growth, and History." Southern Review 10 (October 1974): 851-864.

>Schulz, Elizabeth. " 'Free in Fact and at Last': The Image of the Black Woman in Black American Literature." In What Manner of Woman: Essays in English and American Life and Literature, pp. 316-344. Edited by Marlene Springer. New York: New York University Press, 1977.

GALDOS, BENITO PEREZ

>Del Busto, Margarita. "La mujer liberada en la obra de Galdós." Ph.D. Dissertation, University of Miami, 1974.

>Holmberg, Arthur. "Balzac and Galdós: comment aiment les filles?" Comparative Literature 29 (Spring 1977): 109-123.

>Ledesma, Enrique. "Isabel II: Semblanza historica y creacion literaria." Ph.D. Dissertation, New York University, 1976.

>Ormes, Margot De La Mater. "La mujer del pueblo en algunas novelas de Benito Pérez Galdós." Ph.D. Dissertation, University of Virginia, 1975.

>Orsag, Shirley Ann. "Galdós' Presentation of Women in Light of Naturalism." Ph.D. Dissertation, University of Pittsburgh, 1971.

>Petit, Marie-Claire. "Les personnages féminins dans les romans de Benito Pérez Galdós. Etude sociale, psychologique et littéraire des personnages féminins dans ses 76 romans et Episodios nacionales." Doctorat d'Etat, Université de Paris-Sorbonne, 1971.

>Sinnigen, John H. "Resistance and Rebellion in Tristana." MLN 91 (March 1976): 277-291.

GALE, ZONA

>Bonin, Jane. Major Themes in Prize-Winning American Drama. Metuchen, N.J.: Scarecrow Press, 1975.

Maglin, Nan Bauer. "Discovering Women's Activist Fiction." University of Michigan Papers in Women's Studies 2, no. 2 (1976): 96-104.

_____. "Rebel Women Writers, 1894-1925." Ph.D. Dissertation, Union Graduate School, 1975.

Zastrow, Sylvia Virginia Horning. "The Structure of Selected Plays by American Women Playwrights: 1920-1970." Ph.D. Dissertation, Northwestern University, 1975.

GALLANT, MAVIS

Ayre, John. "The Sophisticated World of Mavis Gallant." Saturday Night (September 1973): 33-36.

GALLEGOS, ROMULO

Wolf, Donna M. "Women in Latin American Literature." Room of One's Own 1 (Fall 1975): 73-83.

GALVEZ, MANUEL

Smith, Elyzabeth Marie-Pierre Richer. "Nana, Santa, et Nacha Regules: trois courtisanes modernes." Ph.D. Dissertation, University of Georgia, 1974.

GALZY, JEANNE

Grosland, Margaret. Women of Iron and Velvet: French Women After George Sand. New York: Taplinger, 1976.

GAMBARO, GRISELDA

Holzapfel, Tamara. Latin American Theatre Review 4 (Fall 1970): 7. (Review of The Folly.)

GAMBOA, FEDERICO

Smith, Elyzabeth Marie-Pierre Richer. "Nana, Santa, et Nacha Regules: trois courtisanes modernes." Ph.D. Dissertation, University of Georgia, 1974.

138 / More Women in Literature

GARCIA LORCA, FEDERICO

McBride, Charles. "The Metropolis and García Lorca's
Tragic View of Woman." Romance Notes 16 (Winter
1975): 479-482.

Morris, C. B. "Lorca's Yerma: Wife Without an Anchor." Neophilologus 56 (July 1972): 285-297.

Platt, Joseph. "The Maternal Theme in García Lorca's
Folk Tragedies." Ph.D. Dissertation, University
of Southern California, 1973.

GARCIA MARQUEZ, GABRIEL

Gantt, Barbara N. "The Women of Macondo: Feminine
Archetypes in García Márquez Cien años de Soledad."
Ph.D. Dissertation, The Florida State University,
1977.

Jaquette, Jane S. "Literary Archetypes and Female
Role Alternatives: The Woman and the Novel in
Latin America." In Female and Male in Latin
America: Essays, pp. 3-28. Edited by Ann Pes-
catello. Pittsburgh: University of Pittsburgh Press,
1973.

Wolf, Donna M. "Women in Latin American Literature."
Room of One's Own 1 (Fall 1975): 73-83.

GARCIA PAVON, FRANCISCO

O'Connor, Patricia W. "Eros and Thanatos in Francisco García Pavon's El último sábado." Journal of
Spanish Studies: Twentieth Century 3 (1975): 175-
185.

GARLAND, HAMLIN

Bray, Robert. "Hamlin Garland's Rose of Dutcher's
Coolly." Great Lakes Review 3 (Summer 1976): 1-
14.

GARRIQUE, JEAN

Brinnin, John and Bill Read, eds. Twentieth Century
Poetry: American and British (1900-1970), 2nd ed.
New York: McGraw-Hill, 1970.

GARRO, ELENA

Young, Rinda Rebeca Stowell. "Six Representative Women Novelists of Mexico, 1960-1969. " Ph.D. Dissertation, University of Illinois at Urbana-Champaign, 1975.

GASHE, MARINA (Mrs. Elimo Njau)

Brown, Lloyd W. "The African Woman as Writer. " Canadian Journal of African Studies 9, no. 3 (1975): 493-502.

GASKELL, ELIZABETH C.

Anjum, A. R. "Social Problems as Themes for Fiction. " Explorations 2, no. 1 (1975): 13-21.

Auerbach, Nina. "Elizabeth Gaskell's 'Sly Javelins': Governing Women in Cranford and Haworth. " Modern Language Quarterly 38 (September 1977): 276-291.

Barr, Marleen. "A Dual Analysis of Mary Barton: Mrs. Gaskell's Portrayals of Stereotypical Feminine Personality Traits and Idealized Conceptions of Women's Working Conditions in Victorian England. " Paper presented at the Michigan Women's Studies Association Conference, 1976. (Available from the author, 127 W. Northrup Place, Buffalo, N.Y. 14214.)

Calder, Jenni. Women and Marriage in Victorian Fiction. London: Thames & Hudson, 1976.

Crick, Brian. "Mrs. Gaskell's Ruth: A Reconsideration. " Mosaic 9 (Winter 1976): 85-104.

Cunningham, Valentine. Everywhere Spoken Against: Dissent in the Victorian Novel. Oxford: Clarendon Press, 1975.

Eagleton, Terry. "Sylvia's Lovers and Legality. " Essays in Criticism 26 (January 1976): 17-27.

Eliasberg, Ann Pringle. "The Victorian Anti-Heroine: Her Role in Selected Novels of the 1860's and

1870's. " Ph. D. Dissertation, The City University of New York, 1975.

Lansbury, Coral. Elizabeth Gaskell: The Novel of Social Crisis. New York: Barnes & Noble, 1975.

Lucas, John. "Mrs. Gaskell and the Nature of Social Change. " Literature and History no. 1 (March 1975): 3-27.

McDaniel, Judith Adair. "Fettered Wings Half Loose: Female Development in the Victorian Novel. " Ph. D. Dissertation, Tufts University, 1975.

Moers, Ellen. Literary Women. Garden City, N. Y. : Doubleday, 1976.

Rance, Nicholas. The Historical Novel and Popular Politics in Nineteenth-Century England. New York: Barnes & Noble, 1975.

Sawdey, Barbara Christiane Meihoefer. "Between Two Worlds: A Study of the Heroine in the Novels of Elizabeth Gaskell. " Ph. D. Dissertation, University of Illinois at Urbana-Champaign, 1975.

Shelston, A. J. "Ruth: Mrs. Gaskell's Neglected Novel. " Bulletin of the John Rylands Library 58 (1975): 173-192.

Showalter, Elaine. A Literature of Their Own: British Women Novelists from Brontë to Lessing. Princeton: Princeton University Press, 1977.

Skilton, David. The English Novel: Defoe to the Victorians. New York: Barnes & Noble, 1977.

Stowell, H. E. Quill Pens and Petticoats: A Portrait of Women of Letters. London: Wayland, 1970.

Sucksmith, Harvey Peter. "Mrs. Gaskell's Mary Barton and William Mudford's The Iron Shroud. " Nineteenth-Century Fiction 29 (1975): 460-463.

Tomlinson, Thomas Brian. The English Middle-Class Novel. New York: Barnes & Noble, 1976.

Trudgill, Eric. Madonnas and Magdalens: The Origins and Development of Victorian Sexual Attitudes. New York: Holmes & Meier, 1976.

Wheeler, Michael D. "The Writer as Reader in Mary Barton." Durham University Journal 36 (1975): 92-102.

Youngren, Virginia Rotan. "Moral Life in Solitude: A Study of Selected Novels of Jane Austen, Charlotte Brontë, Elizabeth Gaskell and George Eliot." Ph.D. Dissertation, Rutgers University, The State University of New Jersey (New Brunswick), 1977.

GASS, GÜNTER

Shinn, Thelma J. Wardrop. "A Study of Women Characters in Contemporary American Fiction 1940-1970." Ph.D. Dissertation, Purdue University, 1972.

GASS, WILLIAM

Blau, Marion. " 'How I Would Brood Upon You': The Lonesome Wife of William Gass." Great Lakes Review 2 (Summer 1975): 40-50.

GAUTIER, JUDITH

Crosland, Margaret. Women of Iron and Velvet: French Women After George Sand. New York: Taplinger, 1976.

GAUTIER, THEOPHILE

Brians, Paul. "Sexuality and the Opposite Sex: Variations on a Theme by Théophile Gautier and Anaïs Nin." Essays in Literature 4 (Spring 1977): 122-137.

Crane, Robert Arthur. "The Courtisane Character in the Nineteenth Century French Novel from Balzac to Zola." Ph.D. Dissertation, The University of North Carolina at Chapel Hill, 1976.

Reff, Theodore. "The Influence of Flaubert's Queen of Sheba on Later Nineteenth-Century Literature." Romanic Review 65 (November 1974): 249-265.

GELLERT, CHRISTIAN FÜRCHTEGOTT

Sanders, Ruth Hetmanski. "The Virtuous Woman in the Comedies of the Early German Enlightenment." Ph.D. Dissertation, State University of New York at Stony Brook, 1975.

GENET, JEAN

Bermel, Albert. "Society as a Brothel: Genet's Satire in The Balcony." Modern Drama 19 (September 1976): 265-280.

GENNARI, GENEVIEVE

Robinson, Jean H. "Genevieve Gennari." Paper presented at the MLA meeting, San Francisco, December 1975.

_____. "A Thematic Analysis of the Novels of Genevieve Gennari." Ph.D. Dissertation, University of Kansas, 1977.

GHELDERODE, MICHEL de

Althofer, Beth Adelsberg. "Aspects of the Archetypal Feminine in the Plays of Michel de Ghelderode." Ph.D. Dissertation, University of California, Berkeley, 1976.

GIDE, ANDRE

Cismaru, Alfred. "Alissa and Mara: Gide's and Claudel's Other 'partie nulle.'" Claudel Studies 4, no. 1 (1977): 68-75.

Gontier, Fernande. "Les images de la femme dans le roman français de l'entre-deux-guerres." Ph.D. Dissertation, University of Virginia, 1973.

Rossi, Vinio. "Erato and Angele: The Beatrice Figure in the Early Works of Claudel and Gide." Claudel Studies 4, no. 1 (1977): 38-47.

Sonnenfeld, Albert. "On Readers and Reading in La porte étroite and L'Immoraliste." Romanic Review 67 (May 1976): 172-186.

GIDLOW, ELSA

"Elsa Gidlow. " In The New Woman's Survival Sourcebook, p. 115. Edited by Kirsten Grimstad and
Susan Rennie. New York: Alfred A. Knopf, 1975.

GILBOORD, MARGARET GIBSON

Wolfe, Morris. "Sad, Mad, and Good. " Books in Canada 5 (July 1976): 7. (Review of The Butterfly
Ward.)

GILMAN, CHARLOTTE PERKINS

Hedges, Elaine R. "Afterword. " The Yellow Wallpaper
by Charlotte Perkins Gilman. Old Westbury, N. Y.:
Feminist Press, 1973.

MacPike, Loralee. "Environment as Psychopathological
Symbolism in 'The Yellow Wallpaper. ' " Paper presented at the MLA meeting, San Francisco, December 1975.

Maglin, Nan Bauer. "Rebel Women Writers, 1894-
1925. " Ph. D. Dissertation, Union Graduate School,
1975.

Wells, Judith. "Daddy's Little Girl and the Enemy: A
Study of Charlotte Perkins Gilman's 'The Yellow
Wallpaper. ' " Paper presented at the MLA meeting,
New York City, December 1976.

GINZBURG, NATALIA

Soave-Bowe, Clotilde. International P. E. N. 24, no. 1
(1973): 14-15. (Review of Dear Michael.)

_____. "Natalia Ginzburg's Plays as a Portrait of
the Italian Bourgeoisie. " International P. E. N. 24,
no. 2 (1973): 49-53.

GIOSEFFI, DANIELA

Schechter, Harold. "The Return of Demeter: The Poetry of Daniela Gioseffi. " Psychocultural Review 1
(Fall 1977): 452-458.

GIOVANNI, NIKKI

Domash, Lynne and Suzanne Juhasz. "A Talk with Nikki Giovanni." Frontiers: A Journal of Women Studies 1 (Fall 1975): 147-150.

Juhasz, Suzanne. Naked and Fiery Forms: Modern American Poetry by Women, A New Tradition. New York: Harper & Row, 1976.

_____. " 'A Sweet Inspiration ... of My People': The Art of Nikki Giovanni." Frontiers: A Journal of Women Studies 1 (Fall 1975): 130-146.

McGeehin, Robert. Best Sellers 35 (January 1976): 318. (Review of The Women and the Men.)

Salaam, Kalamu Ya. Black World 23 (July 1974): 64-70. (Review of My House.)

GIRAUDOUX, JEAN

Fass, Barbara. La Belle Dame sans Merci & the Aesthetics of Romanticism. Detroit: Wayne State University Press, 1974.

Gontier, Fernande. "Les images de la femme dans le roman français de l'entre-deux-guerres." Ph.D. Dissertation, University of Virginia, 1973.

Lemaitre, Georges. Jean Giraudoux: The Writer and His Work. New York: Frederick Ungar, 1971.

Montley, Patricia Ann. "Judith on Broadway: A Comparison of Twentieth Century Dramatic Adaptations of the Biblical Book of Judith Produced on the New York Stage (Volumes I and II)." Ph.D. Dissertation, University of Minnesota, 1975.

Schuler, Marilyn. "Giraudoux as Feminist." Paper presented at the MLA meeting, San Francisco, December 1975.

GISSING, GEORGE

Calder, Jenni. Women and Marriage in Victorian Fiction. London: Thames & Hudson, 1976.

Fernando, Lloyd. "New Women" in the Late Victorian Novel. University Park: Pennsylvania State University Press, 1977.

Fox, Marcia Rose. "The Woman Question in Selected Victorian Fiction, 1883-1900." Ph.D. Dissertation, The City University of New York, 1975.

Goode, John. George Gissing. New York: Barnes & Noble, 1977.

Halperin, John. "The Gissing Revival, 1961-1974." Studies in the Novel 8 (Spring 1976): 103-120.

_____. "How to Read Gissing." English Literature in Transition 20, no. 4 (1977): 188-198.

Korg, Jacob. "George Gissing: Humanist in Exile." In The Victorian Experience: The Novelists, pp. 239-273. Edited by Richard A. Levine. Athens: Ohio University Press, 1976.

Scanlon, Leone. "The New Woman in the Literature of 1883-1909." University of Michigan Papers in Women's Studies 2, no. 1 (1976): 133-159.

Showalter, Elaine. A Literature of Their Own: British Women Novelists from Brontë to Lessing. Princeton: Princeton University Press, 1977.

GLASGOW, ELLEN

Auchincloss, Louis. "Ellen Glasgow." In American Writers, vol. 2, pp. 173-195. Edited by Leonard Unger. New York: Charles Scribner's Sons, 1974.

Cook, Sylvia Jenkins. From Tobacco Road to Route 66: The Southern Poor White in Fiction. Chapel Hill: The University of North Carolina Press, 1976.

Davidson, Colleen Tighe. "Beyond the Sentimental Heroine: The Feminist Character in American Novels, 1899-1937." Ph.D. Dissertation, University of Minnesota, 1975.

Golts, Rita R. "The Face of Everywoman in the Writings of Ellen Glasgow." Ph.D. Dissertation, Temple University, 1977.

Goodman, Charlotte. "Images of American Rural Women in the Novel." University of Michigan Papers
in Women's Studies 1 (June 1975): 57-70.

Murr, Judy Smith. "History in Barren Ground and Vein
of Iron: Theory, Structure and Symbol." Southern
Literary Journal 8 (Fall 1975): 39-54.

Pannill, Linda Susanne. "The Artist-Heroine in American Fiction, 1890-1920." Ph.D. Dissertation, The
University of North Carolina at Chapel Hill, 1975.

Raper, J. R. "Glasgow's Psychology of Deceptions and
The Sheltered Life." Southern Literary Journal 8
(Fall 1975): 27-38.

Raper, Julius Rowan. "Invisible Things: The Short
Stories of Ellen Glasgow." Southern Literary Journal 9 (Spring 1977): [66]-90.

Seidel, Kathryn Lee. "The Southern Belle: Her Fall
from the Pedestal in Fiction of the Southern Renaissance." Ph.D. Dissertation, University of Maryland, 1976.

GLASPELL, SUSAN

Bach, Gerhard P. "Susan Glaspell: Supplementary
Notes." American Literary Realism 5 (1972): 71-
73.

Dean, Nancy. "Feminist Short Fiction: New Forms
and Styles." Paper presented at the MLA meeting,
New York City, 1976. (Mimeographed.)

Jones, Betty H. and Alberta Arthurs. "The American
Eve: A New Look at American Heroines and Their
Critics." International Journal of Women's Studies
1 (January/February 1978): 1-12.

Noe, Marcia Ann. "A Critical Biography of Susan Glaspell." Ph.D. Dissertation, The University of Iowa,
1976.

Sochen, June. The New Woman: Feminism in Green-
wich Village, 1910-1920. New York: Quadrangle,
1972.

Zastrow, Sylvia Virginia Horning. "The Structure of Selected Plays by American Women Playwrights: 1920-1970. " Ph. D. Dissertation, Northwestern University, 1975.

GLASS, MONTAGUE

Baum, Charlotte, Paula Hyman and Sonya Michel. The Jewish Woman in America. New York: Dial Press, 1975.

GLENN, ISA

Seidel, Kathryn Lee. "The Southern Belle: Her Fall from the Pedestal in Fiction of the Southern Renaissance. " Ph. D. Dissertation, University of Maryland, 1976.

GLÜCK, LOUISE

Bedient, Calvin. Sewanee Review 8 (Spring 1976): 351. (Review of The House on Marshland.)

Landis, Joan Hutton. "The Poems of Louise Glück. " Salmagundi no. 36 (Winter 1977): [140]-148.

Louise Glück. San Francisco: San Francisco State University/The Poetry Center, n. d. (Videocassette.)

McClatchy, J. D. Yale Review 65 (Autumn 1975): 95. (Review of The House on Marshland.)

Pritchard, William H. "Despairing at Styles. " Poetry 127 (February 1976): 292-302.

Schulman, Grace. "Life-Death-Life: A Poetic Dialectic. " Ms. (October 1975): 82-83. (Review of The House on Marshland.)

GODBOUT, JACQUES

Urbas, Jeannette. "La representation de la femme chez Godbout, Aquin et Jasmin. " Laurentian University Review 9 (November 1976): [103]-113.

GODWIN, GAIL

> Avant, J. A. New Republic, 25 January 1975, p. 26.
> (Review of The Odd Woman.)

> Dickstein, Lore. New York Times Book Review, 20
> October 1974, p. 4. (Review of The Odd Woman.)

> Edwards, T. R. New York Review of Books, 20 Febru-
> ary 1975, p. 34. (Review of The Odd Woman.)

> Gardiner, Judith Kegan. "Gail Godwin and Feminist
> Fiction. " North American Review 260 (Summer
> 1975): 83-86. (Review of The Odd Woman.)

GODWIN, WILLIAM

> Bauska, Kathy Anderson. "The Feminine Dream of
> Happiness: A Study of the Woman's Search for In-
> telligent Love and Recognition in Selected English
> Novels from Clarissa to Emma. " Ph. D. Disserta-
> tion, University of Washington, 1977.

> Bedick, David B. "The Changing Role of Anxiety in the
> Novel. " Ph. D. Dissertation, New York University,
> 1975.

> Gold, Alex, Jr. "It's Only Love: The Politics of Pas-
> sion in Godwin's Caleb Williams. " Texas Studies
> in Literature and Language 19 (Summer 1977): [135]-
> 160.

GOETHE, JOHANN WOLFGANG

> Ames, Carol. "Love Triangles in Fiction: The Under-
> lying Fantasies. " Ph. D. Dissertation, State Uni-
> versity of New York at Buffalo, 1973.

> Borchardt, Frank L. "Goethe, Schiller, Sphinx, Cen-
> taur, and Sex. " Monatshefte 64 (February 1972):
> 247-255.

> Dreyfuss, Cecilia Anne Stiborik. "Femina sapiens in
> Drama: Aeschylus to Grillparzer. " Ph. D. Disser-
> tation, The University of Michigan, 1975.

> Knight, Eunice Edna. "The Role of Women in the Don

Juan and Faust Literature. " Ph. D. Dissertation, Florida State University, 1973.

Zipser, Richard A. "Bulwer-Lytton and Goethe's Mignon. " Modern Language Notes 89 (April 1974): 465-468.

GOGOL, NIKOLAY

Lindstrom, Thaïs S. Nikolay Gogol. New York: Twayne, 1974.

GOLDSMITH, OLIVER

Radner, John B. "The Youthful Harlot's Curse: The Prostitute as Symbol of the City in 18th-Century English Literature. " Eighteenth-Century Life 2 (March 1976): 59-64.

GOMES, ALFREDO DIAS

Bailey, Dale S. Latin American Theatre Review 6 (Fall 1972): 35-36. (Review of The Redeemer of Pledges.)

GOMEZ, GASPAR

Trisler, Barbara Jean. "A Comparative Study of the Character Portrayal of 'Celestina' and Other Golden Age Celestinesque Protagonists. " Ph. D. Dissertation, The University of Oklahoma, 1977.

GOMEZ DE AVELLANEDA, GERTRUDIS

Moore, Suzanne Shelton. "Themes and Characterization in the Dramatic Words of Gertrudis Gómez de Avellaneda. " Ph. D. Dissertation, Tulane University, 1976.

GONCOURT, EDMOND and JULES

Crane, Robert Arthur. "The Courtisane Character in the Nineteenth Century French Novel from Balzac to Zola. " Ph. D. Dissertation, The University of North Carolina at Chapel Hill, 1976.

Michot-Dietrick, Hela. "Blindness to 'Goodness': The Critics' Chauvinism? An Analysis of Four Novels

by Zola and the Goncourts." Modern Fiction Studies
21 (Summer 1975): 215-222.

GONZALES, SYLVIA

Alva, Jorge Klor de. "Critique of National Character
vs. Universality in Chicana Poetry." La Cosecha:
Literatura y la Mujer Chicana 3, no. 3 (1977): 20-
24.

Gaitan, Marcella Trujillo. "The Dilemma of the Modern
Chicana Artist and Critic." La Cosecha: Literatura
y la Mujer Chicana 3, no. 3 (1977): 38-48.

GOODHUE, WILLIS MAXWELL

Shafer, Y. B. "Liberated Women in American Plays of
the Past." Players Magazine 49 (Spring 1974): 95-
100.

GORBANEVSKAYA, NATALYA

Rich, Adrienne. "Caryatid: A Column." American
Poetry Review 2 (September/October 1973): 42-43.

GORDIMER, NADINE

Geng, Veronica. "Disputed Territory." Ms. 4 (July
1975): 39-41. (Review of The Conservationist.)

Glover, Elaine. Stand 16, no. 3 (1975). (Review
of The Conservationist.)

Lomberg, Alan. "Withering into the Truth: The Romantic Realism of Nadine Gordimer." Africa in
English 3 (March 1976): 1-12.

GORDON, CAROLINE

Brown, Jane Gibson. "The Early Novels of Caroline
Gordon: Myth and History as a Fictional Technique." Southern Review 13 (Spring 1977): 289-298.

McDowell, Frederick P. W. "Caroline Gordon." In
American Writers, vol. 2, pp. 196-222. Edited by
Leonard Unger. New York: Charles Scribner's
Sons, 1974.

Shinn, Thelma J. Wardrop. "A Study of Women Characters in Contemporary American Fiction 1940-
1970." Ph.D. Dissertation, Purdue University,
1972.

Stanford, Donald. "Caroline Gordon." In Contemporary
Novelists. Edited by James Vinson. New York:
St. Martin's Press, 1972.

Seidel, Kathryn Lee. "The Southern Belle: Her Fall
from the Pedestal in Fiction of the Southern Renaissance." Ph.D. Dissertation, University of Maryland, 1976.

GORE, CATHERINE

Anderson, Bonnie. "The Writings of Catherine Gore."
Journal of Popular Culture 10 (Fall 1976): 404-423.

GOTTSCHED, LUISE VICTORIE ADELGUNDE

Sanders, Ruth Hetmanski. "The Virtuous Woman in the
Comedies of the Early German Enlightenment."
Ph.D. Dissertation, State University of New York
at Stony Brook, 1975.

GOULD, LOIS

Glass, John, Jr. "Fish Story." Chronicles of Culture
1 (September 1977): 10-11. (Review of A Sea-
Change.)

Gottlieb, Annie. Village Voice, 30 August 1976, pp. 33-
34. (Review of A Sea-Change.)

Lieber, Joel. Saturday Review, 13 June 1970, p. 43.
(Review of Such Good Friends.)

Nichols, Marianna de Vinci. "Women on Women: The
Looking Glass Novel." Denver Quarterly 11
(Autumn 1976): 1-13.

GOYTISOLO, JUAN

Schwartz, Kessel. "Women in the Novels of Juan Goytisolo." Symposium 31 (Winter 1977): 357-367.

GRACQ, JULIEN

Gaudon, Sheila. "Julien Gracq's Un balcon en foret:
The Ambiguities of Initiation." Romanic Review 67
(March 1976): 132-146.

GRAHN, JUDY

"Judy Grahn." In The New Woman's Survival Sourcebook, p. 117. Edited by Kirsten Grimstad and Susan
Rennie. New York: Alfred A. Knopf, 1975.

Judy Grahn/Diane Wakoski. San Francisco: San Francisco State University/The Poetry Center, n.d.
(Videocassette.)

Raeschild, Sheila. "Awakened: Sexuality in the New
Women's Poetry (Judy Grahn, Alta, Diane Wakoski)."
Paper presented at the MLA meeting, San Francisco,
December 1975.

GRAND, MRS. SARAH

Cunningham, A. R. "The 'New Woman Fiction' of the
1890's." Victorian Studies 17 (December 1973): 177-
186.

Showalter, Elaine. A Literature of Their Own: British
Women Novelists from Brontë to Lessing. Princeton: Princeton University Press, 1977.

GRAU, SHIRLEY ANN

Hall, Joan Joffe. "Lives Alone." New Republic, 24
November 1973, pp. 30-31.

Shinn, Thelma J. Wardrop. "A Study of Women Characters in Contemporary American Fiction 1940-
1970." Ph.D. Dissertation, Purdue University,
1972.

GRAVES, ROBERT

Grant, Patrick. "The Dark Side of the Moon: Robert
Graves as Mythographer." Malahat Review no. 35
(July 1975): 143-165.

Newlin, Margaret. " 'Unhelpful Hymen!': Marianne
Moore and Hilda Doolittle. " Essays in Criticism
27 (July 1977): 216-230.

Vickery, John B. Robert Graves and the White Goddess.
Lincoln: University of Nebraska Press, 1972.

GRAY, FRANCINE DU PLESSIX

Rivers, Caryl. "Starved for Transcendence. " Ms. 5
(November 1976): 42, 44. (Review of Lovers and
Tyrants.)

Trafton, Dain A. "The Liberation of a Free Woman. "
Chronicles of Culture 1 (September 1977): 6-7. (Review of Lovers and Tyrants.)

GREEN, ANNA KATHERINE

Welter, Barbara. Dimity Convictions: The American
Woman in the Nineteenth Century. Athens: Ohio
University Press, 1976.

GREEN, ROBERT

Dean, J. S. , Jr. "Robert Green's Romantic Heroines:
Caught Up in Knowledge and Power?" Ball State
University Forum 14, no. 4 (1973): 3-12.

Larson, Charles H. "Robert Greene's Ciceronis Amor:
Fictional Biography in the Romance Genre. " Studies
in the Novel 6 (Fall 1974): 256-267.

GREENBERG, JOANNE

Olson, Carol Booth. "Madness in the Contemporary
American Novel. " Ph. D. Dissertation, University
of California, Los Angeles, 1977.

GREENE, GAEL

Fox, Mary Ellen. "An Epitome of Junk. " Chronicles
of Culture 1 (September 1977): 12-13. (Review of
Blue Skies, No Candy.)

Weller, Sheila. "A Glutton for Sex, or: A Bad Case
of Heartburn. " Ms. 5 (October 1976): 42, 44, 47.
(Review of Blue Skies, No Candy.)

GREENE, WARD

> Seidel, Kathryn Lee. "The Southern Belle: Her Fall
> from the Pedestal in Fiction of the Southern Renais-
> sance." Ph.D. Dissertation, University of Mary-
> land, 1976.

GREENWOOD, GRACE

> Hull, Raymona E. " 'Scribbling' Females and Serious
> Males: Hawthorne's Comments from Abroad on
> Some American Authors." Nathaniel Hawthorne
> Journal (1975): 35-58.

GREGORY, LADY

> Stevenson, Mary Lou Kohfeldt. "Lady Gregory: A
> Character Study." Ph.D. Dissertation, The Univer-
> sity of North Carolina at Chapel Hill, 1977.

GRIFFIN, SUSAN

> Arnold, June, et al. "Lesbians and Literature." Sinis-
> ter Wisdom 1 (Fall 1976): 20-33.

> Choice 14 (May 1977): 371. (Review of Like the Iris of
> an Eye.)

> Jordan, June. "Susan Griffin: Poet of Plain Magic--
> The Black Poet Speaks of Poetry." American Poe-
> try Review 5, no. 6 (1976): 19-20.

> Rich, Adrienne. Introduction to Voices by Susan Griffin.
> Old Westbury, N.Y.: Feminist Press, 1975.

> "Susan Griffin." In The New Woman's Survival Source-
> book, p. 116. Edited by Kirsten Grimstad and
> Susan Rennie. New York: Alfred A. Knopf, 1975.

GRIFFITH, MRS

> Portner, Ruth Lee. "A Study of Marriage in the Eng-
> lish Novel." Ph.D. Dissertation, City University
> of New York, 1977.

GRIGGS, SUTTON

> Schulz, Elizabeth. " 'Free in Fact and at Last': The

Image of the Black Woman in Black American Literature. " In What Manner of Woman: Essays in English and American Life and Literature, pp. 316-344. Edited by Marlene Springer. New York: New York University Press, 1977.

Ward, Hazel Mae. "The Black Woman as Character: Images in the American Novel, 1852-1953. " Ph. D. Dissertation, The University of Texas at Austin, 1977.

GRILLPARZER, FRANZ

Dreyfuss, Cecilia Anne Stiborik. "Femina sapiens in Drama: Aeschylus to Grillparzer. " Ph. D. Dissertation, The University of Michigan, 1975.

Stenberg, Peter. "Strindberg and Grillparzer: Contrasting Approaches to the War of the Sexes. " Canadian Review of Comparative Literature 1 (1974): 65-75.

GRIMM, JAKOB LUDWIG KARL and WILHELM KARL

Zimmerman, Eugenia Noik. "The Proud Princess Gets Her Comeuppance: Structures of Patriarchal Order." Canadian Review of Comparative Literature 3 (Fall 1976): [253]-268.

GRIMMELSHAUSEN, JOHANN VON

Daghistany, Ann. "The Picara Nature. " Women's Studies 5, no. 1 (1977): 51-60.

GROVE, FREDERICK PHILIP

Arnold, Armin. English Studies in Canada 3 (Summer 1977): [241]-243. (Review of The Master Mason's House.)

Fulton, E. Margaret. "Out of Our Past: A New Future. " Laurentian University Review 9 (November 1976): [87]-102.

McMullen, Lorraine. "Women in Grove's Novels. " In The Grove Symposium, pp. 67-76. Edited by John Nause. Ottawa: University of Ottawa Press, 1974.

GUIDACCI, MARGHERITA

> Beckage, Donna. "Sea Imagery in Margherita Guidacci's Poetry." Modern Poetry Studies 5 (Spring 1974): 145-156.

GUIDO, BEATRIZ

> Tavenner, Anna C. "Aspectos de conflicto y enajenamiento de la mujer en las novelas de Silvina Bullrich, Beatriz Guido y Clarice Lispector." Ph.D. Dissertation, Texas Tech University, 1977.

GUINEY, LOUISE

> Walker, Cheryl Lawson. "The Women's Tradition in American Poetry." Ph.D. Dissertation, Brandeis University, 1973.

> Watts, Emily Stipes. The Poetry of American Women from 1632 to 1945. Austin: University of Texas Press, 1977.

GUTHRIE, A. B.

> Lander, Dawn. "Women and the Wilderness: Tabus in American Literature." University of Michigan Papers in Women's Studies 2, no. 3 (1977): 62-83.

> Meldrum, Barbara. "Images of Women in Western American Literature." Midwest Quarterly 17 (April 1976): 252-267.

GUTZKOW, KARL FERDINAND

> Flavell, M. Kay. "Women and Individualism: A Reexamination of Schlegel's Lucinde and Gutzkow's Wally die Zweiflerin." Modern Language Review 70 (July 1975): 550-566.

- H -

H. D. (Hilda Doolittle)

Harmer, J. B. Victory in Limbo: Imagism, 1908-1917. New York: St. Martin's Press, 1975.

Holland, Norman H. Poems in Persons: An Introduction to the Psychoanalysis of Literature. New York: Norton, 1975.

Klaich, Dolores. Woman + Woman: Attitudes Toward Lesbianism. New York: Simon & Schuster, 1974.

Newlin, Margaret. " 'Unhelpful Hymen!': Marianne Moore and Hilda Doolittle." Essays in Criticism 27 (July 1977): 216-230.

Peck, John. "Passio Perpetuae." Parnassus: Poetry in Review 3 (Spring/Summer 1975): 42-74.

Quinn, Vincent. "H. D. 's 'Hermetic Definition': The Poet as Archetypal Mother." Contemporary Literature 18 (Winter 1977): 51-61.

Watts, Emily Stipes. The Poetry of American Women from 1632 to 1945. Austin: University of Texas Press, 1977.

HACKS, PETER

Tilton, Helga. "Virgins and Other Victims: Aspects of German Middle-Class Theatre." In Female Studies IX: Teaching About Women in Foreign Languages, pp. 180-186. Edited by Sidonie Cassirer. Old Westbury, N. Y.: Feminist Press, 1975.

HAGGERTY, JOAN

Rule, Jane. Lesbian Images. Garden City, N. Y.: Doubleday, 1975.

HALE, SARAH JOSEPHA

Riley, Glenda Gates. "The Subtle Subversion: Changes in the Traditionalist Image of the American Woman." Historian 32 (February 1970): 210-227.

Seidel, Kathryn L.   "The Southern Belle as an Antebellum Ideal. "   Southern Quarterly 15 (July 1977): 387-401.

_____.   "The Southern Belle: Her Fall from the Pedestal in Fiction of the Southern Renaissance. " Ph. D. Dissertation, University of Maryland, 1976.

Wood, Ann D.   "The 'Scribbling Women' and Fanny Fern: Why Women Wrote. " American Quarterly 23 (Spring 1971): 3-24.

HALL, RADCLYFFE

Atkins, John.   Sex in Literature: The Classical Experience of the Sexual Impulse.   London: Calder & Boyars, 1973.

Klaich, Dolores.   Woman + Woman: Attitudes Toward Lesbianism.   New York: Simon & Schuster, 1974.

Miles, Rosalind.   The Fiction of Sex: Themes and Functions of Sex Difference in the Modern Novel.   New York: Barnes & Noble, 1974.

Rule, Jane.   Lesbian Images.   Garden City, N. Y. : Doubleday, 1975.

Showalter, Elaine.   A Literature of Their Own: British Women Novelists from Brontë to Lessing.   Princeton: Princeton University Press, 1977.

HALPER, ALBERT

Baum, Charlotte, Paula Hyman and Sonya Michel.   The Jewish Woman in America.   New York: Dial Press, 1975.

HANSBERRY, LORRAINE

Anderson, Mary Louise.   "Black Matriarchy: Portrayal of Women in Three Plays. " Negro American Literature Forum 10 (Fall 1976): 93-95.

Arata, Esther S. and Nicholas J. Rotoli.   Black American Playwrights 1800 to the Present: A Bibliography.   Metuchen, N. J. : Scarecrow Press, 1976.

Cheney, Anne. "Lorraine Hansberry: Young, Gifted, and Black." Paper presented at the MLA meeting, New York City, December 1976.

Curb, Rosemary Keefe. "The Idea of the American Dream in Afro-American Plays of the Nineteen Sixties." Ph. D. Dissertation, University of Arkansas, 1977.

Harrison, Paul Carter. The Drama of Nommo. New York: Grove Press, 1972.

Hays, Peter L. "Raisin in the Sun and Juno and the Paycock." Phylon 33 (Summer 1972): 175-176.

Lorraine Hansberry: The Black Experience in the Creation of Drama. Princeton, N.J.: Films for the Humanities, n.d. (16 mm color.)

Love, Theresa R. "The Black Woman in Afro-American Literature." Paper presented at the Midwest Modern Language Association meeting, Chicago, November 1975. (Mimeographed.)

Miller, Jeanne-Marie A. "Images of Black Women in Plays by Black Playwrights." CLA Journal 20 (June 1977): 494-507.

Ness, David E. "The Sign in Sidney Brustein's Window: A Black Playwright Looks at White America." Freedomways 11 (Fourth Quarter 1971): 359-366.

Zastrow, Sylvia Virginia Horning. "The Structure of Selected Plays by American Women Playwrights: 1920-1970." Ph. D. Dissertation, Northwestern University, 1975.

HAO JAN

Eber, Irene. "Images of Women in Recent Chinese Fiction: Do Women Hold Up Half the Sky?" Signs: Journal of Women in Culture and Society 2 (Autumn 1976): 24-34.

HARDY, THOMAS

Armstrong, Judith. The Novel of Adultery. New York: Barnes & Noble, 1976.

Calder, Jenni. Women and Marriage in Victorian Fiction. London: Thames & Hudson, 1976.

Couch, Ruth Lazelle. "Women and Thomas Hardy: A Study of Sex-Linked Qualities in the Characters." Ph.D. Dissertation, Oklahoma State University, 1975.

Ebbatson, J. R. "Thomas Hardy and Lady Chatterley." Ariel: A Review of International English Literature 8 (April 1977): [85]-95.

Fass, Barbara. La Belle Dame sans Merci & the Aesthetics of Romanticism. Detroit: Wayne State University Press, 1974.

Fernando, Lloyd. "New Women" in the Late Victorian Novel. University Park: Pennsylvania State University Press, 1977.

Fox, Marcia Rose. "The Woman Question in Selected Victorian Fiction, 1883-1900." Ph.D. Dissertation, The City University of New York, 1975.

Gordon, Jan B. "Origins, History, and the Reconstitution of the Family: Tess's Journey." ELH 43 (Fall 1976): 66-88.

Grace, Charles Clyde, Jr. "Hardy's Tess of the D'Urbervilles: A Reconsideration." Ph.D. Dissertation, Cornell University, 1975.

Hardwick, Elizabeth. "Sue and Arabella." In The Genius of Thomas Hardy, pp. 67-73. Edited by Margaret Drabble. New York: Alfred A. Knopf, 1976.

Hoffeld, Laura Diamond. "The Servant Heroine in 18th and 19th Century British Fiction: The Social Reality and Its Image in the Novel." Ph.D. Dissertation, New York University, 1975.

Jacobus, Mary. "Sue the Obscure." Essays in Criticism 25 (July 1975): 304-328.

_____. "Tess's Purity." Essays in Criticism 26 (October 1976): 318-338.

Kramer, Dale. Thomas Hardy: The Forms of Tragedy.
Detroit: Wayne State University Press, 1975.

Longerbeam, Larry Simpson. "Seduction as Symbolic
Action: A Study of the Seduction Motif in Six Victorian Novels. " Ph.D. Dissertation, George Peabody College for Teachers, 1975.

May, Charles E. "Hardy's Diabolical Dames: A Generic Consideration. " Genre 7 (December 1974): 307-
321.

Mickelson, Anne Z. Thomas Hardy's Women and Men:
The Defeat of Nature. Metuchen, N.J.: Scarecrow
Press, 1976.

Miles, Rosalind. The Fiction of Sex: Themes and
Functions of Sex Difference in the Modern Novel.
New York: Barnes & Noble, 1974.

Paris, Bernard J. "Experiences of Thomas Hardy. "
In The Victorian Experience: The Novelists, pp.
203-237. Edited by Richard A. Levine. Athens:
Ohio University Press, 1976.

Philbin, Alice Irene. "The Literary Femme Fatale--A
Social Fiction: The Willful Female in the Deterministic Vision of Thomas Hardy and in the Psychological Vision of Henry James. " Ph.D. Dissertation,
Southern Illinois University at Carbondale, 1977.

Pinion, F. B. Thomas Hardy: Art and Thought. London: Macmillan, 1977.

Reed, John R. Victorian Conventions. Athens: Ohio
University Press, 1975.

Richert, Ethel Susanne. "Perception of Women's Roles
in Thomas Hardy's Novels. " Ph.D. Dissertation,
Brown University, 1976.

Rogers, Katharine. "Women in Thomas Hardy. " Centennial Review 19 (Fall 1975): 249-258.

Scanlon, Leone. "The New Woman in the Literature of
1883-1909. " University of Michigan Papers in Women's Studies 2, no. 2 (1976): 133-159.

Spector, Judith Ann. "Sexual Dialectic in Four Novels: The Mythos of the Masculine Aesthetic. " Ph. D. Dissertation, Indiana University, 1977.

Springer, Marlene. "Angels and Other Women in Victorian Literature. " In What Manner of Woman: Essays on English and American Life and Literature, pp. 124-159. Edited by Marlene Springer. New York: New York University Press, 1977.

Sullivan, Karen Lever. "The Muse of Fiction: Fatal Women in the Novels of W. M. Thackeray, Thomas Hardy, and John Fowles. " Ph. D. Dissertation, The Johns Hopkins University, 1973.

HARRIS, BERTHA KELLY

Glover, Erma Williams. "Salt of the Earth: Plain People in the Novels of Bernice Kelly Harris. " Ph. D. Dissertation, The University of North Carolina at Chapel Hill, 1977.

Larkin, Joan. "In Short: Lover. " Ms. 5 (April 1977): 42. (Review of Lover.)

Willis, Julia. Sinister Wisdom 1 (Fall 1976): 86-87. (Review of Lover.)

HARRIS, CORRA

Maglin, Nan Bauer. "Rebel Women Writers, 1894-1925. " Ph. D. Dissertation, Union Graduate School, 1975.

HARRIS, JANE

Frym, Gloria. "Tough and Tender: Lady Punk Poets. " San Francisco Review of Books, 3 (October 1977): 20-30.

HARRISON, CONSTANCE CARY

Maxwell, Sherrolyn. "Constance Cary Harrison: American Woman of Letters, 1843-1920. " Ph. D. Dissertation, The University of North Carolina at Chapel Hill, 1977.

HARTE, BRET

Meldrum, Barbara. "Images of Women in Western American Literature." Midwest Quarterly 17 (April 1976): 252-267.

HARRIS, JOSEPH

Hume, Robert D. "Marital Discord in English Comedy from Dryden to Fielding." Modern Philology 74 (February 1977): 248-272.

HAUGHTON, WILLIAM

Leggatt, Alexander. Citizen Comedy in the Age of Shakespeare. Toronto: University of Toronto Press, 1973.

HAUPTMANN, GERHART

Rose, Ingrid Barbara. "Social Stereotypes and Female Actualities: A Dimension of the Social Criticism in Selected Works by Fontane, Hauptmann, Wedekind, and Schnitzler." Ph.D. Dissertation, Princeton University, 1976.

HAUSER, MARIANNE

Cooke, Michael G. "Recent Novels: Women Bearing Violence." Yale Review 66 (Autumn 1976): 146-155. (Review of The Talking Room.)

HAWKES, JOHN

Hawkes, John and Robert Scholes. "A Conversation on The Blood Oranges." Novel 5 (Spring 1972): 197-207.

HAWTHORNE, NATHANIEL

Andola, John A. "Pearl: Symbolic Link Between Two Worlds." Ball State University Forum 13 (Winter 1972): 60-67.

Armstrong, Judith. The Novel of Adultery. New York: Barnes & Noble, 1976.

164 / More Women in Literature

Baym, Nina. "Portrayal of Women in American Literature, 1790-1870." In What Manner of Woman: Essays on English and American Life and Literature, pp. 211-234. Edited by Marlene Springer. New York: New York University Press, 1977.

Baym, Nina. The Shape of Hawthorne's Career. Ithaca: Cornell University Press, 1976.

Brenzo, Richard. "Beatrice Rappaccini: A Victim of Male Love and Horror." American Literature 48 (May 1976): 152-164.

Callison, Helen V. "Hester Prynne: A Study in Misanthropy and Mysticism." Wisconsin English Journal 15 (April 1973): 23-29.

Colacurcio, Michael J. "Footsteps of Ann Hutchinson: The Context of the Scarlet Letter." ELH 39 (September 1972): 459-494.

Cromphout, Gustaaf von. "Blithedale and the Androgyne Myth: Another Look at Zenobia." ESQ 18, no. 3 (1972): 141-145.

Dryden, Edgar A. Nathaniel Hawthorne: The Poetics of Enchantment. Ithaca: Cornell University Press, 1977.

Eakin, Paul John. The New England Girl: Cultural Ideals in Hawthorne, Stowe, Howells, and James. Athens: University of Georgia Press, 1976.

Fryer, Judith. The Faces of Eve: Women in the Nineteenth-Century American Novel. New York: Oxford University Press, 1976.

Hamblin, Ellen N. "Adulterous Heroines in Nineteenth Century Literature: A Comparative Literature Study." Ph.D. Dissertation, The Florida State University, 1977.

Hull, Raymona E. "'Scribbling' Females and Serious Males: Hawthorne's Comments from Abroad on Some American Authors." Nathaniel Hawthorne Journal (1975): 35-58.

Hull, Richard Jon. "Equality in Hawthorne." Ph.D. Dissertation, University of Washington, 1975.

Lander, Dawn. "Women and the Wilderness: Tabus in American Literature." University of Michigan Papers in Women's Studies 2, no. 3 (1977): 62-83.

Morgan, Ellen E. "The Erotization of Male Dominance/ Female Submission." University of Michigan Papers in Women's Studies 2 (September 1975): 112-145.

Person, Leland, Jr. "Aesthetic Headaches and European Women in The Marble Faun and The American." Studies in American Fiction 4 (Spring 1976): 65-79.

Rice, Nancy Hall. "Beauty and the Beast and the Little Boy: Clues about the Origins of Sexism and Racism from Folklore and Literature: Chaucer's 'The Prioress's Tale,' Sir Gawain and the Green Knight, the Alliterative Morte Arthure, Webster's The Duchess of Malfi, Shakespeare's Othello, Hawthorne's 'Rappaccini's Daughter,' Melville's 'Benito Cereno.'" Ph.D. Dissertation, University of Massachusetts, 1975.

Stimpson, Catharine. "Women as Scapegoats." In Female Studies V, pp. 7-16. Edited by Rae Lee Siporin. Pittsburgh: KNOW, Inc., 1972.

Vanderbilt, Kermit. "From Passion to Impasse: The Structure of a Dark Romantic Theme in Hawthorne, Howells, and Barth." Studies in the Novel 8 (Winter 1976): 419-429.

Walter, James. "A Farewell to Blithedale; Coverdale's Aborted Pastoral." South Atlantic Quarterly 76 (Winter 1977): [73]-92.

HAYASHI FUMIKO

Johnson, Eric W. "Modern Japanese Women Writers." Literature East and West 8 (March 1974): [90]-102.

Reich, Pauline C. and Atsuko Fukuda, trans. "Japan's Literary Feminists: The Seito Group." Signs: Journal of Women in Culture and Society 2 (Autumn 1976): 280-287.

HAYDEN, ANNA THOMPSON

> Watts, Emily Stipes. The Poetry of American Women
> from 1632 to 1945. Austin: University of Texas
> Press, 1977.

HAYDEN, ESTHER

> Watts, Emily Stipes. The Poetry of American Women
> from 1632 to 1945. Austin: University of Texas
> Press, 1977.

HAYWOOD, ELIZA

> Woodcock, George. "Founding Mothers of the English
> Novel: Mary Manley and Eliza Haywood." Room
> of One's Own 2, no. 4 (1977): 49-65.

HEAD, BESSIE

> Larson, Charles R. The Novel in the Third World.
> Washington, D.C.: Inscape, 1976.

HEBBEL, FRIEDICH

> Ross, Carol Jean. "Schiller and Hebbel: Characters
> and Ideas and the Portrayal of Women." Ph.D.
> Dissertation, University of Toronto, 1974.

> Tilton, Helga. "Virgins and Other Victims: Aspects
> of German Middle-Class Theatre." In Female
> Studies IX: Teaching About Women in Foreign
> Languages, pp. 180-186. Edited by Sidonie Cassi-
> rer. Old Westbury, N.Y.: Feminist Press, 1975.

HEBERT, ANNE

> Amprimoz, Alexandre. "Four Writers and Today's
> Quebec." Tamarack Review no. 70 (1977): 72-80.

> Downes, G. V. "Hébert in English." Canadian Litera-
> ture 71 (Winter 1976): 87-89. (Review of Poems by
> Anne Hébert.)

> Mezei, Kathy. "Anne Hébert: A Pattern Repeated."
> Canadian Literature no. 72 (Spring 1977): 29-40.

Hecht / 167

_____. "Commands and Desires." Canadian Litera-
ture 70 (Autumn 1976): 79-81. (Review of Les En-
fants du sabbat.)

Russell, D. W. "Anne Hébert: Les Invites au procès."
Canadian Literature no. 74 (Autumn 1977): 30-39.

Stratford, Philip. "Kamouraska and The Diviners."
Review of National Literatures 7 (1976): 110-126.

HECHT, BEN

Baum, Charlotte, Paula Hyman and Sonya Michel. The
Jewish Woman in America. New York: Dial Press,
1975.

HEINE, HEINRICH

Fass, Barbara. La Belle Dame sans Merci & the Aesthetics of Romanticism. Detroit: Wayne State University Press, 1974.

Kellogg, Patricia Rossworm. "The Myth of Salome in
Symbolist Literature and Art." Ph.D. Dissertation,
New York University, 1975.

HELLMAN, LILLIAN

Authors in the News, vol. 1. Detroit: Gale Research,
1976, pp. 217-219.

Authors in the News, vol. 2. Detroit: Gale Research,
1976, pp. 142-143.

Carlson, Eugene Tunney. "Lillian Hellman's Plays as
a Reflection of the Southern Mind." Ph.D. Dissertation, University of Southern California, 1975.

Gornick, Vivian. "Neither Forgotten Nor Forgiven."
Ms. 5 (August 1976): 46-47. (Review of Scoundrel
Time.)

Hellman, Lillian. "Lillian Hellman." North Hollywood:
The Center for Cassette Studies, n.d.

Moody, Richard. Lillian Hellman: Playwright. Indian-
apolis: Pegasus, 1972.

Patraka, Vivian Mary. "Lillian Hellman, Dramatist of the Second Sex. " Ph. D. Dissertation, The University of Michigan, 1977.

Zastrow, Sylvia Virginia Horning. "The Structure of Selected Plays by American Women Playwrights: 1920-1970. " Ph. D. Dissertation, Northwestern University, 1975.

HEMINGWAY, ERNEST

Crozier, Robert D. "For Thine Is the Power and the Glory: Love in For Whom the Bells Toll. " Papers in Linguistics and Literature 10 (Winter 1974): 76-97.

Davidson, Arnold E. "The Ambivalent End of Francis Macomber's Short Happy Life. " Hemingway Notes 2 (Spring 1972): 14-16.

Fetterley, Judith. "A Farewell to Arms: Ernest Hemingway's 'Resentful Cryptogram. ' " In The Authority of Experience, pp. 257-273. Edited by Arlyn Diamond and Lee R. Edwards. Amherst: University of Massachusetts Press, 1977.

Herndon, Jerry A. "No 'Maggie's Drawers' for Margot Macomber. " In Fitzgerald/Hemingway Annual 1975, pp. 289-291. Edited by Matthew J. Bruccoli and C. E. Frazer Clark, Jr. Englewood, Colorado: Microcard Editions, 1975.

Lander, Dawn. "Women and the Wilderness: Tabus in American Literature. " University of Michigan Papers in Women's Studies 2, no. 3 (1977): 62-83.

Lefcourt, Charles R. "The Macomber Case. " Revue des langues vivantes 43, no. 4 (1977): 341-347.

Meyer, William E. , Jr. "Hemingway's Novels: The Shift in Orthodoxy and Symbolism. " Arizona Quarterly 33 (Summer 1977): 141-155.

Meyers, Jeffrey. Married to Genius. New York: Barnes & Noble, 1977.

Miles, Rosalind. The Fiction of Sex: Themes and

Functions of Sex Difference in the Modern Novel.
New York: Barnes & Noble, 1974.

Shaw, Sharon. "Hemingway's Mis-treatment of Women
Characters." Moving Out 4, no. 1 (1974): 42-43.

Thornton, Patricia Elizabeth. "The Prison of Gender:
Sexual Roles in Major American Novels of the 1920's."
Ph.D. Dissertation, The University of New Bruns-
wick, 1976.

Tuttleton, James W. " 'Combat in the Erogenous Zone':
Women in the American Novel Between the Two
World Wars." In What Manner of Woman: Essays
in English and American Life and Literature, pp.
271-296. Edited by Marlene Springer. New York:
New York University Press, 1977.

Wagner, Linda Welshimer. "The Marinating of For
Whom the Bell Tolls." In Hemingway: 5 Decades
of Criticism, pp. 201-212. Edited by Linda Welshimer Wagner. East Lansing: Michigan State University Press, 1974. (Reprinted from Journal of
Modern Literature 2 (November 1972): 533-546.)

Watson, James Gray. " 'A Sound Basis of Union':
Structural and Thematic Balance in 'The Short Happy
Life of Francis Macomber.' " In Fitzgerald/Heming-
way Annual 1974, pp. 215-228. Edited by Matthew
J. Bruccoli and C. E. Frazer, Jr. Englewood,
Colorado: Microcard Editions, 1975.

Whitlow, Roger. "The Destruction/Prevention of the
Family Relationship in Hemingway's Fiction." Literary Review 20 (Fall 1976): 5-16.

Wyrick, Jean. "Fantasy as Symbol: Another Look at
Hemingway's Catherine." Massachusetts Studies in
English 4 (Fall 1973): 42-47.

HENRYSON, ROBERT

Adamson, Jane. "Henryson's Testament of Cresseid:
'Fyre' and 'Cauld.' " Critical Review no. 18 (1976):
[39]-60.

HENTZ, CAROLINE LEE

Garrison, Dee. "Immoral Fiction in the Late Victorian Library. " American Quarterly 28 (Spring 1976): 71-89.

Ruoff, John C. "Frivolity to Consumption: Or, Southern Womanhood in Antebellum Literature. " Civil War History 18 (September 1972): 213-229.

Seidel, Kathryn L. "The Southern Belle as an Antebellum Ideal. " Southern Quarterly 15 (July 1977): 387-401.

_____. "The Southern Belle: Her Fall from the Pedestal in Fiction of the Southern Renaissance. " Ph. D. Dissertation, University of Maryland, 1976.

Wood, Ann D. "The 'Scribbling Women' and Fanny Fern: Why Women Wrote. " American Quarterly 23 (Spring 1971): 3-24.

HERBERT, FRANK

Gower, Kathy. "Science Fiction and Women. " In Mother Was Not a Person, pp. 98-101. Edited by Margret Andersen. Montreal: Content Publishing Limited and Black Rose Books, 1972.

HERBERT, MARY SIDNEY (Countess of Pembroke)

Hogrefe, Pearl. Women of Action in Tudor England: Nine Biographical Sketches. Ames: Iowa State University Press, 1977.

Mahl, Mary R. and Helen Koon, eds. The Female Spectator: English Women Writers Before 1800. Bloomington and Old Westbury, N. Y. : Indiana University Press and The Feminist Press, 1977.

HERBST, JOSEPHINE

Bevilacqua, Winifred Farrant. "The Novels of Josephine Herbst. " Ph. D. Dissertation, The University of Iowa, 1977.

HERNANDEZ, BARBARA

Sanchez, Rita. "Chicana Writer: Breaking Out of the Silence. " La Cosecha: Literatura y la Mujer Chicana 3, no. 3 (1977): 31-37.

HERNE, JAMES

Bennison, Martin J. and Barry B. Witham. "Sentimental Love and the Nineteenth-Century American Drama. " Players 49 (Summer 1974): 127-129.

Kolb, Deborah S. "The Rise and Fall of the New Woman in American Drama. " Educational Theater Journal 27 (1975): 149-160.

HERVIEU, LOUISE

Bleuzé, Ruth Allen. "Romancières et Critiques: Etude du Prix Fémina, 1904-1968. " Ph. D. Dissertation, University of Colorado at Boulder, 1977.

HESIOD

Marquardt, Patricia Ann. "Ambivalence in Hesiod and Its Relationship to Feminine Deities. " Ph. D. Dissertation, The University of Wisconsin-Madison, 1976.

Pomeroy, Sarah B. Goddesses, Whores, Wives, and Slaves: Women in Classical Antiquity. New York: Schocken Books, 1975.

HESSE, HERMANN

Remys, Edmund. "Hermann Hesse's Das Glasperlenspiel: A Concealed Defence of the Mother World. " Ph. D. Dissertation, University of Cincinnati, 1975.

HEWETT, DOROTHY

Porter, Pip. "Dorothy Hewett: An Interview. " Hecate 3 (February 1977): 6-15.

HEWITT, MARY E.

Watts, Emily Stipes. The Poetry of American Women

from 1632 to 1945. Austin: University of Texas
Press, 1977.

HEYWOOD, ELIZA

Mahl, Mary R. and Helen Koon, eds. The Female
Spectator: English Women Writers Before 1800.
Bloomington and Old Westbury, N.Y.: Indiana Uni-
versity Press and The Feminist Press, 1977.

HEYWOOD, THOMAS

Goldman, Rachel Margaret. "The Lucretia Legend from
Livy to Rojas Zorrilla." Ph.D. Dissertation, City
University of New York, 1976.

Helton, Tinsley. Review of Images of Women in the
Works of Thomas Heywood by Marilyn L. Johnson.
Seventeenth Century News 23 (Fall 1975): 67-68.

Johnson, Marilyn L. Images of Women in the Works of
Thomas Heywood. Salzburg Studies in English Lit-
erature: Jacobean Drama Studies 42. Salzburg:
Institut für Englische Sprache und Literatur, 1974.

Leggatt, Alexander. Citizen Comedy in the Age of
Shakespeare. Toronto: University of Toronto
Press, 1973.

Still, Roger. Love and Death in Renaissance Tragedy.
Baton Rouge: Louisiana State University Press,
1976.

Ure, Peter. Elizabethan and Jacobean Drama. Edited
by J. C. Maxwell. New York: Barnes & Noble,
1974.

Waith, Eugene M. "Heywood's Women Worthies." In
Concepts of the Hero in the Middle Ages and the
Renaissance, pp. 222-238. Edited by Norman T.
Burns and Christopher J. Reagon. Albany: State
University of New York Press, 1975.

HIGUCHI ICHIYO

Reich, Pauline C. and Atsuko Fukada, trans. "Japan's
Literary Feminists: The Seito Group." Signs:

Journal of Women in Culture and Society 2 (Autumn 1976): 280-287.

HIMES, CHESTER

Lee, A. Robert. "Real and Imagined Violence in the Novels of Chester Himes. " Negro American Literature Forum 10 (Spring 1976): 13-22.

HIRSH, CHARLOTTE TELLER

Maglin, Nan Bauer. "Discovering Women's Activist Fiction. " University of Michigan Papers in Women's Studies 2, no. 2 (1976): 96-104.

_____. "Rebel Women Writers, 1894-1925. " Ph.D. Dissertation, Union Graduate School, 1975.

HOBSON, LAURA

Betsky, Celia. "Courting Time. " Ms. 6 (November 1977): 39-43. (Review of Endangered Species.)

Fadiman, Edwin. Saturday Review, 16 January 1971, p. 34. (Review of The Tenth Month.)

HOGE, PHYLLIS

Stewart, Frank. "Islands: An Interview with Phyllis Hoge. " Modern Poetry Studies 8 (Spring 1977): 29-46.

HOLLAND, BARBARA A.

Cabral, Olga. "A Wry Romantic (The Poems of Barbara A. Holland). " Feminist Art Journal 4 (Fall 1975): 31-33.

HOLLEY, MARIETTA

Curry, Jane Anne. "Women as Subjects and Writers of Nineteenth Century American Humor. " Ph.D. Dissertation, The University of Michigan, 1975.

HOLMES, MARY JANE

Garrison, Dee. "Immoral Fiction in the Late Victorian

Library. " American Quarterly 28 (Spring 1976): 71-89.

HOMER

Gross, Nicholas P. "Nausicaa: A Feminine Threat. " Classical World 69 (February 1976): 311-317.

HORACE

Minadeo, R. W. "Sexual Symbolism in Horace's Love Odes. " Latomus 34 (April-June 1975): 392-424.

HORTA, MARIA TERESA

Authors in the News, vol. 1. Detroit: Gale Research, 1976, p. 29.

HORVATH, ÖDÖN VON

Neikirk, Joan Cantwell. "The Role of the Woman in the Works of Ödön von Horváth. " Ph. D. Dissertation, The University of Wisconsin, 1971.

HOWAR, BARBARA

Brandy, Susan. "She Only Laughs When It Hurts. " Ms. 4 (June 1976): 95-96. (Review of Making Ends Meet.)

Jong, Erica. New York Times Book Review, 25 April 1976, p. 2. (Review of Making Ends Meet.)

O'Reilly, Jane. Viva 3 (June 1976): 38-39. (Review of Making Ends Meet.)

Washington Magazine 11 (June 1976): 252-253. (Review of Making Ends Meet.)

HOWES, BARBARA

Brinnin, John Malcolm and Bill Read, eds. Twentieth Century Poetry: American and British (1900-1970), 2nd ed. New York: McGraw-Hill, 1970.

HOWARD, ELIZABETH JANE

Grumbach, Doris. " 'A Cage Went in Search of a

Bird.' " Ms. 4 (April 1976): 39-40. (Review of Mr. Wrong.)

Miles, Rosalind. The Fiction of Sex: Themes and Functions of Sex Difference in the Modern Novel. New York: Barnes & Noble, 1974.

Rule, Jane. Lesbian Images. Garden City, N.Y.: Doubleday, 1975.

HOWARD, SIDNEY

Bonin, Jane F. Major Themes in Prize-Winning American Drama. Metuchen, N.J.: Scarecrow Press, 1975.

Loudin, Joanne Marie. "The Changing Role of the Heroine in American Drama from 1900 to 1940." Ph.D. Dissertation, University of Washington, 1974.

HOWELLS, ANNIE

Doyle, James. "Howells' Canadian Sister." Canadian Literature no. 74 (Autumn 1977): 58-62.

HOWELLS, WILLIAM DEAN

Bremer, Sidney H. "Invalids and Actresses: Howell's Duplex Imagery for American Women." American Literature 47 (January 1976): 599-614.

Bromberger, Eric Aldridge. "An Odour of Old Maid Boston as Literary Symbol." Ph.D. Dissertation, University of California, Los Angeles, 1976.

Crowley, John W. "An Interoceanic Episode: The Lady of Aroostook." American Literature 49 (May 1977): 180-191.

Dockery, Michael Anthony. "Orphan Figures in the Works of William Dean Howells: The Kitty Ellison-Bartley Hubbard Dilemma." Ph.D. Dissertation, Southern Illinois University of Carbondale, 1977.

Eakin, Paul John. The New England Girl: Cultural Ideals in Hawthorne, Stowe, Howells, and James. Athens: University of Georgia Press, 1976.

Fryer, Judith. The Faces of Eve: Women in the Nineteenth Century American Novel. New York: Oxford University Press, 1976.

Habegger, Alfred. "The Autistic Tyrant: Howell's Self-Sacrificial Woman and Jamesian Renunciation. " Novel 10 (Fall 1976): 27-39.

_____. "W. D. Howells and the 'American Girl.' " Texas Quarterly 19 (Winter 1976): 149-156.

Hunt, Gary Alan. "Feminism and the Modern Family: Howells as Domestic Realist. " Ph. D. Dissertation, Brandeis University, 1976.

Long, Robert Emmet. "Transformations: The Blithedale Romance to Howells and James. " American Literature 47 (January 1976): 552-571.

Stein, Allen F. "Marriage in Howell's Novels. " American Literature 48 (January 1977): 501-524.

Vanderbilt, Kermit. "From Passion to Impasse: The Structure of a Dark Romantic Theme in Hawthorne, Howells, and Barth. " Studies in the Novel 8 (Winter 1976): 419-429.

HOWITT, MARY

Mitchell, Sally. "Lost Women: Feminist Implications of the Fallen in Works by Forgotten Women Writers of the 1840's. " University of Michigan Papers in Women's Studies 1 (June 1974): 110-124.

HUGHES, LANGSTON

Doyle, Sister Mary Ellen. "The Heroine of Black Novels. " In Perspectives on Afro-American Women, pp. 112-125. Edited by Willa D. Johnson and Thomas L. Green. Washington, D. C. : ECCA Publications, 1975.

Love, Theresa R. "The Black Woman in Afro-American Literature. " Paper presented at the Midwest Modern Language Association Meeting, Chicago, November 1975. (Mimeographed.)

Miller, R. Baxter. " 'Done Made Us Leave Our Home':
Langston Hughes's Not Without Laughter--Unifying
Images and Three Dimensions. " Phylon 37 (December 1976): 362-369.

_____. " 'No Crystal Stair': Unity, Archetype and
Symbol in Langston Hughes's Poems on Women. "
Negro American Literature Forum 9 (Winter 1975):
109-114.

Schraufnagel, Noel. From Apology to Protest: The
Black American Novel. Deland, Florida: Everett/
Edwards, 1973.

Senghor, Léopold Sédar. "The African in the Black
American. " Third Press Review 1 (September/October 1975): 6-9, 63.

HUGO, RICHARD

Rich, Adrienne. "Caryatid: A Column. " American Poetry Review 2 (May/June 1973): 10-11.

HUGO, VICTOR

Wildgen, Kathryn E. "Romance and Myth in Notre-Dame
de Paris. " French Review 49 (February 1976): 319-327.

HUNT, VIOLET

Gibson, Susan Monteith. "Love and the Vote: Fiction
of the Suffrage Movement in Edwardian England. "
Ph.D. Dissertation, University of Massachusetts,
1975.

Secor, Marie. "Violet Hunt, Novelist: A Reintroduction. " English Literature in Transition 1880-1920
19, no. 1 (1976): 25-34.

HUNTER, KRISTIN

Authors in the News, vol. 1. Detroit: Gale Research,
1976, p. 236.

Schatt, Stanley. "The Ghetto in Recent American Literature. " Journal of Ethnic Studies 1 (Spring 1973):
44-54.

Schultz, Elizabeth. " 'Free in Fact and at Last': The
Image of the Black Woman in Black American Liter-
ature. " In What Manner of Woman: Essays in Eng-
lish and American Life and Literature, pp. 316-344.
Edited by Marlene Springer. New York: New York
University Press, 1977.

Williams, Gladys Margaret. "Blind and Seeing Eyes in
the Novel God Bless the Child. " Obsidian 1 (Summer 1975): 18-26.

HURSTON, ZORA NEALE

Abrahams, Roger D. "Negotiating Respect: Patterns
of Presentation Among Black Women. " Journal of
American Folklore 88 (January-March 1975): 58-80.

Bone, Robert. Down Home: A History of Afro-American Short Fiction from Its Beginnings to the End of
the Harlem Renaissance. New York: G. P. Put-
nam's Sons, 1975.

Brown, Martha Hursey. "Images of Black Women:
Family Roles in Harlem Renaissance Literature. "
D. A. Dissertation, Carnegie-Mellon University,
1976.

Burke, Virginia M. "Zora Neale Hurston and Fannie
Hurst as They Saw Each Other. " CLA Journal 20
(June 1977): 435-447.

Davidson, Colleen Tighe. "Beyond the Sentimental Heroine: The Feminist Character in American Novels,
1899-1937. " Ph. D. Dissertation, University of
Minnesota, 1975.

Davis, Arthur P. From the Dark Tower. Washington:
Howard University Press, 1974.

Doyle, Sister Mary Ellen. "The Heroine of Black
Novels. " In Perspectives on Afro-American Women, pp. 112-125. Edited by Willa D. Johnson
and Thomas L. Green. Washington, D. C. : ECCA
Publications, 1975.

Harris, Trudier. "Zora Neale Hurston, Folklorist. "
Paper presented at the MLA meeting, San Francisco,
December 1975.

Hemenway, Robert. "Discoveries in the Hurston Biography." Paper presented at the MLA meeting, San Francisco, December 1975.

_____. Zora Neale Hurston: A Literary Biography. Urbana: University of Illinois Press, 1977.

Howard, Lillie. "A New Look at Zora Neale Hurston's Seraph on the Sewannee." Paper presented at the MLA meeting, New York City, December 1976.

_____. "Zora Neale Hurston: A Non-Revolutionary Black Artist." Ph.D. Dissertation, The University of New Mexico, 1975.

Love, Theresa R. "The Black Woman in Afro-American Literature." Paper presented at the Midwest Modern Language Association meeting, Chicago, November 1975. (Mimeographed.)

Rambeau, James. "The Fiction of Zora Neale Hurston." Markham Review 5 (Summer 1976): 61-64.

Schraufnagel, Noel. From Apology to Protest: The Black American Novel. Deland, Florida: Everett/ Edwards, 1973.

Schulz, Elizabeth. "'Free in Fact and at Last': The Image of the Black Woman in Black American Literature." In What Manner of Woman: Essays in English and American Life and Literature, pp. 316-344. Edited by Marlene Springer. New York: New York University Press, 1977.

Schwalbenberg, Peter. "Time as Point of View in Zora Neale Hurston's Their Eyes Were Watching God." Negro American Literature Forum 10 (Fall 1976): 104-105, 107.

Shange, Ntozake. "Black Women Writing/Where Truth Becomes Hope/Cuz It's Real." Margins no. 17 (February 1975): 50-54, 59-60.

Smith, Barbara. "The Fiction of Zora Neale Hurston." Paper presented at the MLA meeting, San Francisco, December 1975.

HUYSMANS, J. K.

Nuccitelli, Angela. "A rebours's Symbol of the 'femme fleur': A Key to des Esseintes's Obsession." Symposium 28 (Winter 1974): 336-345.

Reff, Theodore. "The Influence of Flaubert's Queen of Sheba on Later Nineteenth-Century Literature." Romanic Review 65 (November 1974): 249-265.

HYDER, QURRATUL-AIN

Poulos, Steven Mark. "Feminine Sense and Sensibility: A Comparative Study of Six Modern Fiction Writers in Hindi and Urdu: Rashid Jahan, Ismat Chughtai, Qurratul-Ain Hyder, Mannu Bhandari, Usha Priyamveda, Vijay Chauhan." Ph.D. Dissertation, University of Chicago, 1975.

HYMER, JOHN B.

Shafer, Y. B. "Liberated Women in American Plays of the Past." Players Magazine 49 (Spring 1974): 95-100.

- I -

IBSEN, HENRIK

Balice, Vincent J. Ibsen's Feminine Mystique. New York: Vantage, 1975.

Brown, Lorraine A. "Swan and Mermaid: Love's Comedy and The Lady from the Sea." Scandinavian Studies 47 (Summer 1975): 352-363.

Jones, David Richard. "The Virtues of Hedda Gabler." Educational Theatre Journal 29 (December 1977): 447-462.

Kester, Dolores A. "Shaw and the Victorian 'Problem' Genre: The Woman Side." Ph.D. Dissertation, University of Wisconsin, 1971.

Magoun, Francis P. "Ibsen: Women's Votes and Women's Lib." Neuphilologische Mitteilungen 74 (1973):
727-729.

Rosengarten, David. "The Lady from the Sea: Ibsen's
Submerged Allegory." Educational Theatre Journal
29 (December 1977): 463-476.

Saari, Sandra E. "Hedda Gabler: The Past Recaptured."
Modern Drama 20 (September 1977): 299-316.

Schwarcz, Vera. "Ibsen's Nora: The Promise and the
Trap." Bulletin of Concerned Asian Scholars 7
(January-March 1975): 3-5.

Warnken, William P. "Kate Chopin and Henrik Ibsen:
A Study of The Awakening and A Doll's House."
Massachusetts Studies in English 4 (Autumn 1974-
Winter 1975): 43-49.

IDRIS, YUSUF

Cobham, Catherine. "Sex and Society in Yūsuf Idrīs:
'Qā'al-Madīna.' " Journal of Arabic Literature 6
(1975): 78-100.

Mikhail, Mona N. "The Search for the Authentic Self
Within Idris's City." Mundus Artium 10, no. 1
(1977): 89-99.

INCHBALD, ELIZABETH

Kelly, Gary. The English Jacobin Novel 1780-1805.
Oxford: Clarendon Press, 1976.

Rogers, Katharine M. "Inhibitions on Eighteenth-Century
Women Novelists: Elizabeth Inchbald and Charlotte
Smith." Eighteenth-Century Studies 11 (Fall 1977):
63-78.

ISHIGAKI RIN

Ikuko Atsumi. "Five Modern Women Poets on Love."
Literature East and West 8 (March 1974): [58]-75.

_____. "Modern Japanese Women Poets: After the
Meiji Restoration." Iowa Review 7 (Spring/Summer
1976): 227-237.

ISHWARA SHINTARO

Wagatsuma Hiroshi. "Ishwara Shintaro's Early Novels
and Japanese Male Psychology. " Journal of Nervous
and Mental Disease 157 (November 1973): 358-369.

IYACUN, IFA

Shange, Ntozake. "Black Women Writing/Where Truth
Becomes Hope/Cuz It's Real. " Margins no. 17
(February 1975): 50-54, 59-60.

IZUMI SHIKIBU NIKKI

Walker, Janet A. "Poetic Ideal and Fictional Reality in
the Izumi Shikibu nikki. " Harvard Journal of Asiatic Studies 37 (June 1977): 135-182.

- J -

JACKSON, HELEN HUNT

Walker, Cheryl Lawson. "The Women's Tradition in
American Poetry. " Ph.D. Dissertation, Brandeis
University, 1973.

Watts, Emily Stipes. The Poetry of American Women
from 1632 to 1945. Austin: University of Texas
Press, 1977.

JACKSON, LAURA RIDING see RIDING, LAURA

JACKSON, SHIRLEY

Hoffman, Steven K. "Individuation and Character Development in the Fiction of Shirley Jackson. " Hartford Studies in Literature 8, no. 3 (1976): 190-208.

Shinn, Thelma J. Wardrop. "A Study of Women Characters in Contemporary American Fiction 1940-
1970. " Ph.D. Dissertation, Purdue University,
1972.

Thomas, Deborah. "The Motif of the Alienated Woman

in the Novels of Shirley Jackson. " Paper presented
at the MLA meeting, New York City, December
1976.

JACOBSEN, JOSEPHINE

Hahn, Claire. Commonweal, 29 November 1974, p. 217.
(Review of The Shade-Seller.)

Martin, James. "Questions of Style. " Poetry 126
(May 1975): 103-115. (Review of The Shade-Seller.)

Meinke, Peter. New Republic, 4-11 January 1975, p.
26. (Review of The Shade-Seller.)

JAHAN, RASHID

Poulos, Steven Mark. "Feminine Sense and Sensibility:
A Comparative Study of Six Modern Fiction Writers
in Hindi and Urdu: Rashid Jahan, Ismat Chughtai,
Qurratul-Ain Hyder, Mannu Bhandari, Usha Priyamvada, Vijay Chauhan. " Ph. D. Dissertation, University of Chicago, 1975.

JAHNN, HANS HENRY

McDonald, William P. "The Blackness of Medea. "
CLA Journal 19 (September 1975): 20-37.

JAKOBSDOTTIR, SVAVA

Magnússon, Sigurdur A. "The Icelandic Short Story:
Svava Jakobsdóttir. " Scandinavian Studies 49 (Spring
1977): 208-212.

JAMES, HENRY

Armstrong, Judith. The Novel of Adultery. New York:
Barnes & Noble, 1976.

Banta, Martha. "They Shall Have Faces, Minds, and
(One Day) Flesh: Women in Late Nineteenth-Century
and Early Twentieth-Century American Literature. "
In What Manner of Woman: Essays on English and
American Life and Literature, pp. 235-270. Edited
by Marlene Springer. New York: New York University Press, 1977.

Baym, Nina. "Revision and Thematic Change in The Portrait of a Lady." Modern Fiction Studies 22 (Summer 1976): 183-200.

Beauchamp, Andrea Louise Roberts. "The Heroine of Our Common Scene: Portrayals of American Women in Four Novels by Edith Wharton and Henry James." Ph.D. Dissertation, The University of Michigan, 1976.

Bedick, David B. "The Changing Role of Anxiety in the Novel." Ph.D. Dissertation, New York University, 1975.

Benert, Annette Larson. "Passion and Perception: A Jungian Reading of Henry James." Ph.D. Dissertation, Lehigh University, 1975.

Bobbitt, Joan. "Aggressive Innocence in The Portrait of a Lady." Massachusetts Studies in English 4 (Spring 1973): 31-37.

Bromberger, Eric Aldridge. "An Odour of Old Maid Boston as Literary Symbol." Ph.D. Dissertation, University of California, Los Angeles, 1976.

Chapin, Helen Geracimos. "Mythology and American Realism: Studies in Fiction by Henry Adams, Henry James, and Kate Chopin." Ph.D. Dissertation, The Ohio State University, 1975.

Collins, Martha. "Narrator, the Satellites, and Isabel Archer: Point of View in The Portrait of a Lady." Studies in the Novel 8 (Summer 1976): 142-157.

Crosby, Patricia Lauer. "Growth to Fulfillment: A Psychological Analysis of Six Heroines of Henry James." Ph.D. Dissertation, Miami University, 1975.

Crowley, John W. "The Wiles of a 'Witless' Woman: Tina in The Aspern Papers." ESQ: A Journal of the American Renaissance 22 (Third Quarter 1976): 159-168.

Eakin, Paul John. The New England Girl: Cultural Ideals in Hawthorne, Stowe, Howells, and James. Athens: University of Georgia Press, 1976.

Fass, Barbara. La Belle Dame sans Merci & the Aesthetics of Romanticism. Detroit: Wayne State University Press, 1974.

Faulkner, Peter. Humanism in the English Novel. New York: Barnes & Noble, 1976.

Fernando, Lloyd. "New Women" in the Late Victorian Novel. University Park: Pennsylvania State University Press, 1977.

Ford, Jane M. "The Father/Daughter/Suitor Triangle in Shakespeare, Dickens, James, Conrad, and Joyce." Ph.D. Dissertation, State University of New York at Buffalo, 1975.

Fowler, Virginia Carol. "The Renunciatory Heroine in Henry James." Ph.D. Dissertation, University of Pittsburgh, 1976.

Fryer, Judith. The Faces of Eve: Women in the Nineteenth Century American Novel. New York: Oxford University Press, 1976.

Gargano, James W. "Washington Square: A Study in the Growth of an Inner Self." Studies in Short Fiction 13 (Summer 1976): 355-362.

Getz, Thomas Theodore. "Henry James: The Novel as an Act of Self-Consciousness and Conscience." Ph.D. Dissertation, The University of Iowa, 1976.

Gustafson, Judith A. "The Wings of the Dove or, A Gathering of Pigeons." Gypsy Scholar 3 (Fall 1975): 13-19.

Hall, Sallie J. "Henry James and the Bluestockings: Satire and Morality in The Bostonians." In Aeolian Harps, pp. 207-225. Edited by Donna G. Fricke and Douglas C. Fricke. Bowling Green: Bowling Green University Press, 1976.

Hoffeld, Laura Diamond. "The Servant Heroine in 18th and 19th Century British Fiction: The Social Reality and Its Image in the Novel." Ph.D. Dissertation, New York University, 1975.

Horwitz, B. D. "The Sense of Desolation in Henry James." Psychocultural Review 1 (Fall 1977): 466-492.

Jones, Granville H. Henry James's Psychology of Experience. Paris: Mouton, 1975.

Kaston, Carren Osna. "Houses of Fiction in 'What Maisie Knew.'" Criticism 18 (Winter 1976): 27-42.

Korenman, Joan S. "Henry James and the Murderous Mind." Essays in Literature 4 (Fall 1977): 198-211.

Krier, William J. "The 'Latent Extravagance' of The Portrait of a Lady." Mosaic 9 (Spring 1976): 57-65.

Krupnick, Mark L. "The Golden Bowl: Henry James's Novel About Nothing." English Studies 57 (December 1976): 533-540.

Lay, Mary M. "Parallels: Henry James's The Portrait of a Lady and Nella Larsen's Quicksand." CLA Journal 20 (June 1977): 475-486.

Long, Robert Emmet. "Transformations: The Blithedale Romance to Howells and James." American Literature 47 (January 1976): 552-571.

MacNaughton, W. R. "Turning the Screw of Ordinary Virtue: The Governess and the First-Person Narrators." Canadian Review of American Studies 5, no. 1 (1975): 18-25.

Manthey, Ethel Vern. "The Sentimentally Educated Hero: A Comparison of Some Aspects of the Hero of Gustave Flaubert with Two Leading Characters of Henry James." Ph.D. Dissertation, Case Western Reserve University, 1976.

Menikoff, Barry. "A House Divided: A New Reading of The Bostonians." CLA Journal 20 (June 1977): 459-474.

Morgan, Ellen. "Isabel Archer: Resistance to the Patriarchal Order." University of Michigan Papers in Women's Studies 1 (June 1975): 95-106.

Nance, William L. "What Maisie Knew: The Myth of the Artist." Studies in the Novel 8 (Spring 1976): 88-102.

Nethery, Wallace. "Tragedy of Errors: A Note on The Bostonians." Coranto: Journal of Friends of the Libraries 8, no. 2 (1973): 34-41.

Niemtzow, Annette. "Marriage and the New Woman in The Portrait of a Lady." American Literature 47 (November 1975): 377-395.

Parrill, Anna S. "Portraits of Ladies." In Tennessee Studies in Literature, pp. 92-99. Knoxville: The University of Tennessee Press, 1975.

Perry, Donna Marie. "From Innocence Through Experience: A Study of the Romantic Child in Five Nineteenth Century Novels." Ph.D. Dissertation, Marquette University, 1976.

Person, Leland, Jr. "Aesthetic Headaches and European Women in The Marble Faun and The American." Studies in American Fiction 4 (Spring 1976): 65-79.

Philbin, Alice Irene. "The Literary Femme Fatale--A Social Fiction: The Willful Female in the Deterministic Vision of Thomas Hardy and in the Psychological Vision of Henry James." Ph.D. Dissertation, Southern Illinois University of Carbondale, 1977.

Reid, Maynard. "The Image of Venice in Milly Theale's American Dream of Europe." Studies in the Humanities 3 (October 1972): 45-50.

Schriber, Mary S. "Isabel Archer and Victorian Manners." Studies in the Novel 8 (Winter 1976): 441-457.

Snider, Clifton. "Jung's Psychology of the Conscious and the Unconscious." Psychocultural Review 1 (Spring 1977): 216-242.

Stein, William Bysshe. "The Wings of the Dove: James's Eucharist of Punch." Centennial Review 21 (Summer 1977): 236-260.

Tintner, Adeline R. "Henry James's Salomé and the Arts of the Fin de Siècle." Markham Review 5 (Fall 1975): 5-10.

_____. "Isabel's Carriage-Image and Emma's Day Dream." Modern Fiction Studies 22 (Summer 1976): 227-231.

_____. "James and Balzac: The Bostonians and 'La fille aux yeux d'or.'" Comparative Literature 29 (Summer 1977): 241-254.

_____. "Sleeping Beauty and Victorian Fantasies: Henry James's Use of Doré and Burne-Jones." Paper presented at the MLA meeting, New York City, December 1976.

Wallace, Ronald. Henry James and the Comic Form. Ann Arbor: University of Michigan Press, 1975.

Zuckert, Catherine H. "American Women and Democratic Morals: The Bostonians." Feminist Studies 3 (Spring-Summer 1976): 30-50.

JARDIEL PONCELA, ENRIQUE

DiMaio, Carlo. "Antifeminism in Selected Works of Enrique Jardiel Poncela." Ph.D. Dissertation, The Louisiana State University and Agricultural and Mechanical College, 1974.

JASMIN, CLAUDE

Urbas, Jeannette. "La representation de la femme chez Godbout, Aquin et Jasmin." Laurentian University Review 9 (November 1976): [103]-113.

JENNINGS, KATE

Moorhead, Finola. "Goodbye Prince Hamlet: The New Australian Women's Poetry." Meanjin Quarterly 34 (Winter 1975): 169-179.

JEWETT, SARAH ORNE

Callow, James T. and Robert Reilly. Guide to American Literature from Emily Dickinson to the Present. New York: Barnes & Noble, 1977.

Davidson, Colleen Tighe. "Beyond the Sentimental Heroine: The Feminist Character in American Novels,
1899-1937." Ph.D. Dissertation, University of Minnesota, 1975.

Dullea, Gerard John. "Two New England Voices: Sarah
Orne Jewett and Mary Wilkins Freeman." Ph.D.
Dissertation, Syracuse University, 1975.

Eppard, Philip B. " 'Dan's Wife': A Newly Discovered
Sarah Orne Jewett Story." Colby Library Quarterly
12 (June 1976): 101-102.

Moers, Ellen. Literary Women. Garden City, N.Y.:
Doubleday, 1976.

Schaefer, Anita Jeanne. "Three Significant Motifs in
the New England Stories and Sketches of Sarah Orne
Jewett." Ph.D. Dissertation, The Florida State
University, 1975.

Thorp, Margaret Farrand. "Sarah Orne Jewett." In
American Writers, vol. 2, pp. 391-414. Edited by
Leonard Ungar. New York: Charles Scribner's
Sons, 1974.

Voss, Arthur. The American Short Story: A Critical
Survey. Norman: University of Oklahoma, 1973.

JHABVALA, R. PRAWER

Bell, P. K. New York Times Book Review, 4 April
1976, p. 7. (Review of Heat and Dust.)

Chesnick, Eugene. Nation, 28 August 1976, p. 149.
(Review of Heat and Dust.)

Cooke, Michael G. "Recent Novels: Women Bearing
Violence." Yale Review 66 (Autumn 1976): 146-155.
(Review of Heat and Dust.)

Gemmill, Janet Powers. "Ruth Prawer Jhabvala's How
I Became a Holy Mother." World Literature Written in English 16 (November 1977): 380-381.

Glamour 74 (August 1976): 26+. (Review of Heat and
Dust.)

Harrison, Barbara Grizzuti. "We're Off to See the Guru. " Ms. 2 (December 1973): 28-31.

_____. "Why Olivia (Now Dead) Left Her Calm, Controlled, English Husband. " Ms. 5 (July 1976): 42-44. (Review of Heat and Dust.)

Kermode, Frank. New York Review of Books, 15 July 1976, pp. 42-44. (Review of Heat and Dust.)

Mewshaw, Michael. Texas Monthly 4 (July 1976): 46-49. (Review of Heat and Dust.)

Price, James. Encounter 46 (February 1976): 65. (Review of Heat and Dust.)

Updike, John. New Yorker, 5 July 1976, p. 81. (Review of Heat and Dust.)

Winegarten, Renee. "Ruth Prawer Jhabvala: A Jewish Passage to India. " Midstream, March 1974, pp. 72-79.

JOAQUIN, NICK

Constantino, Josefina D. "Illusion and Reality in Nick Joaquin. " In Philippine Fiction, pp. 13-24. Edited by Joseph A. Galdon. Quezon City: Ateneo de Manila at the University Press, 1972.

Garcia-Groyon, Regina. "Joaquin's Connie Escobar: Fall and Rise. " In Philippine Fiction, pp. 25-44. Edited by Joseph A. Galdon. Quezon City: Ateneo de Manila at the University Press, 1972.

JOHNSON, CHARLES

Gottlieb, Annie. New York Times Book Review, 12 January 1975, p. 6. (Review of Faith and the Good Thing.)

Skow, John. "Smoky Legend. " Time, 6 January 1975, p. 92. (Review of Faith and the Good Thing.)

JOHNSON, DIANE

Casey, Constance. "Interview with Diane Johnson. "

San Francisco Review of Books 1 (January 1976): 15-20.

JOHNSON, GEORGIA D.

   Rushing, Andrea Benton. "Images of Black Women in Afro-American Poetry." Black World 24 (September 1975): 18-30.

JOHNSON, SAMUEL

   Molin, Sven Eric. "Dr. Johnson on Marriage, Chastity, and Fidelity." Eighteenth-Century Life 1 (September 1974): 15-18.

   Radner, John B. "The Youthful Harlot's Curse: The Prostitute as Symbol of the City in 18th-Century English Literature." Eighteenth-Century Life 2 (March 1976): 59-64.

JOHNSTONE, SIR HARRY

   Higgins, Susan. "The Suffragettes in Fiction." Hecate 2 (July 1976): 31-47.

JONES, GAYL

   Avant, J. A. New Republic, 28 June 1975, p. 27. (Review of Corregidora.)

   Coast 17 (November 1976): 27. (Review of Corregidora.)

   Cooke, Michael G. "Recent Novels: Women Bearing Violence." Yale Review 66 (Autumn 1976): 146-155. (Review of Eva's Man.)

   Dixon, Melvin. Obsidian 3 (Spring 1977): 72-74. (Review of Corregidora.)

   Encore, 7 June 1976, p. 44. (Review of Eva's Man.)

   Gayle, Addison. Black Books Bulletin 4 (Winter 1976): 48-52. (Review of Eva's Man.)

   Golden, Bernette. Black World 25 (February 1976): 82. (Review of Corregidora.)

Hairston, Loyle. Freedomways 16 (Second Quarter 1976): 133-135. (Review of Eva's Man.)

Jordan, June. New York Times Book Review, 16 May 1976, pp. 36-37. (Review of Eva's Man.)

Sokolov, Raymond. New York Times Book Review, 25 May 1975, p. 21. (Review of Corregidora.)

Updike, John. New Yorker, 9 August 1976, p. 74. (Review of Eva's Man.)

JONES, SUZANNE HOLLY

Higgins, Sue. "Breaking the Rules: New Fiction by Australian Women." Meanjin Quarterly 34 (December 1975): 415-420.

JONG, ERICA

Authors in the News, vol. 1. Detroit: Gale Research, 1976, pp. 102-103, 256.

Denne, Constance Ayers, and Katharine M. Rogers, Moderators. "Women Novelists: A Distinct Group?" Women's Studies 3 (1975): 5-28.

Frym, Gloria. "With Ovaries on Our Sleeves." San Francisco Review of Books 3 (Summer 1977): 18-19. (Review of How to Save Your Own Life.)

Gross, Martin. Interview. Book Digest 3 (January 1976): 18-31.

Kazin, Alfred. "The Writer as Sexual Show-Off; or, Making Press Agents Unnecessary." New York, 9 June 1975, pp. 36-40.

Klinkowitz, Jerome. North American Review 260 (Summer 1975): 88-90. (Review of Fear of Flying.)

Koltun, Elizabeth. The Jewish Woman: New Perspectives. New York: Schocken, 1976.

Lovenheim, Barbara. "Female as Subject and Object in Literature: From Austen to Jong." Deland, Florida: Everett/Edwards, n.d. (Cassette no. 5315.)

Manfred, Freya. <u>Moons and Lion Tailes</u> 2, no. 1
(1976): 93-97. (Review of <u>Loveroot.</u>)

Meyer, Ellen Hope. "The Aesthetic of 'Dear Diary.' "
<u>Nation</u>, 12 January 1974, pp. 55-56. (Review of
<u>Fear of Flying.</u>)

Modleski, Tania. "Why Do We Still Fear Flying." <u>Uni</u>-
<u>versity of Michigan Papers in Women's Studies</u> 1
(June 1975): 107-112.

Moers, Ellen. <u>Literary Women.</u> Garden City, N.Y.:
Doubleday, 1976.

Nichols, Marianna de Vinci. "Women on Women: The
Looking Glass Novel." <u>Denver Quarterly</u> 11 (Autumn
1976): 1-13.

Perloff, Margorie. "The Joy of Jong." <u>Washington
Post</u>, 6 July 1975, pp. 1-2. (Review of <u>Here Comes</u>
and <u>Loveroot.</u>)

Straight, N. A. "Girl Crazy." <u>New York Review of
Books</u>, 2 October 1975, pp. 39-41.

Toth, Emily. "Dorothy Parker, Erica Jong, and New
Feminist Humor." <u>Regionalism and the Female
Imagination</u> 3 (Fall 1977 and Winter 1977-78): 70-85.

Vendler, Helen. <u>New York Times Book Review</u>, 7 September 1975, p. 6. (Review of <u>Loveroot.</u>)

Walker, Cheryl. "Welcome Eumenides: Contemporary
Feminist Poets." <u>Feminist Art Journal</u> 2 (Winter
1973-74): 6-7.

Widner, Eleanor Rackow. "Poppa Freud, Dr. Yussel,
and the Great American Novelist." <u>Arts in Society</u>
12, no. 1 (1975): 122-126.

Wixen, Joan. "A Frank Interview with Erica Jong."
<u>Family Circle</u> 89 (September 1976): 132-136.

JONSON, BEN

Drew-Bear, Annette. "Cosmetics and Attitudes Towards
Women in the Seventeenth Century." <u>Journal of
Popular Culture</u> 9 (Summer 1975): 31-37.

204 / More Women in Literature

Dreyfuss, Cecilia Anne Stiborik. "Femina sapiens in Drama: Aeschylus to Grillparzer." Ph.D. Dissertation, The University of Michigan, 1975.

Kay, W. David. "Bartholomew Fair: Ben Jonson in Praise of Folly." English Literary Renaissance 6 (Spring 1976): 299-316.

Leggatt, Alexander. Citizen Comedy in the Age of Shakespeare. Toronto: University of Toronto Press, 1973.

JORDON, JUNE

Rushing, Andrea Benton. "Images of Black Women in Afro-American Poetry." Black World 24 (September 1975): 18-30.

JOYCE, JAMES

Alldredge, Betty Jean Edwards. "Levels of Consciousness: Women in the Stream of Consciousness Novels of Joyce, Woolf, and Faulkner." Ph.D. Dissertation, University of Oregon, 1976.

Benstock, Shari. "The Daughter Relationships of Joyce's Issy." Paper presented at the MLA meeting, New York City, December 1976.

Eggers, Tilly. "Darling Milly Bloom." James Joyce Quarterly 12 (Summer 1975): 386-395.

Ferrara, Peter. "Why Molly Menstruates: The Language of Desire." Sub-Stance no. 4 (Fall 1972): 51-62.

Ford, Jane M. "The Father/Daughter/Suitor Triangle in Shakespeare, Dickens, James, Conrad, and Joyce." Ph.D. Dissertation, State University of New York at Buffalo, 1975.

_____. "Why Is Milly in Mullingar?" James Joyce Quarterly 14 (Summer 1977): 436-449.

Freeman, Alma Susan. "The Androgynous Ideal: A Study of Selected Novels by D. H. Lawrence, James Joyce, and Virginia Woolf." Ed.D.

Dissertation, Rutgers University, The State University of New Jersey, 1974.

Honton, Margaret. "Molly's Mistresstroke. " James Joyce Quarterly 14 (Fall 1976): 25-29.

Meyers, Jeffrey. Married to Genius. New York: Barnes & Noble, 1977.

Nebeker, H. E. "James Joyce's 'Clay': The Well-Wrought Urn. " Renascence 28 (Spring 1976): 123-138.

Paterakis, Deborah Tannen. "Keylessness, Sex and the Promised Land: Associated Themes in Ulysses. " Eire-Ireland 8 (Spring 1973): 97-108.

Roberts, Dorothy Hutcherson. "James Joyce's Ulysses: A Study of the Motifs of Androgyny. " Ph. D. Dissertation, University of South Florida, 1977.

Shilts, John A. "To Him She Would Unveil Her Shy Soul's Nakedness: A Study of Sexual Imagery in Joyce and Proust. " Ph. D. Dissertation, The Pennsylvania State University, 1975.

Solomen, Albert J. "The Bird Girls of Ireland. " Colby College Quarterly 10 (March 1974): 259-269.

Spector, Judith Ann. "Sexual Dialectic in Four Novels: The Mythos of the Masculine Aesthetic. " Ph. D. Dissertation, Indiana University, 1977.

Steinberg, Erwin. "To Whom Did Molly Say Yes?" James Joyce Quarterly 11 (1974): 171-172.

Unkeless, Elaine Rapp. "Leopold Bloom as a Womanly Man. " Modernist Studies 2 (1976): 35-44.

Voelker, Joseph Craig. "James Joyce's Penelope: A Study of the Influence of Scholastic Psychology and the Metaphysics of Giordano Bruno on the Character of Molly Bloom. " Ph. D. Dissertation, Yale University, 1975.

_____. " 'Nature it is': The Influence of Giordano Bruno on James Joyce's Molly Bloom. " James Joyce Quarterly 14 (Fall 1976): 39-48.

JU CHIH-CHÜAN

Eber, Irene. "Images of Women in Recent Chinese
Fiction: Do Women Hold Up Half the Sky?" Signs:
Journal of Women in Culture and Society 2 (Autumn
1976): 24-34.

JUANA INEZ DE LA CRUZ, SOR

Schwartz, Kessel. " 'Primero Sueño'--A Reinterpreta-
tion." Kentucky Romance Quarterly 22, no. 4
(1975): 473-490.

Wolf, Donna M. "Women in Latin American Literature."
Room of One's Own 1 (Fall 1975): 73-83.

JUVENAL

Atkins, John. Sex in Literature, vol. 2: The Classical
Experience of the Sexual Impulse. London: Calder
& Boyers, 1973.

- K -

KĀLIDĀSA, ABHIGNANA-SAKUNTALA

Robinson, Richard H. "Humanism Versus Asceticism
in Aśvaghosa and Kālidāsa." Journal of South Asian
Literature 12 (Spring-Summer 1977): 1-10.

KARAMZIN, NIKOLAI

Banerjee, Maria. "The Metamorphosis of an Icon:
Woman in Russian Literature." In Female Studies
IX: Teaching About Women in the Foreign Lan-
guages. Edited by Sidonie Cassirer. Old Westbury,
N.Y.: Feminist Press, 1975.

KARAPANOUR, MARGARITA

Charyn, Jerome. New York Times Book Review, 25
July 1976, p. [13]. (Review of Kassandra and the
Wolf.)

Cooke, Michael G. "Recent Novels: Women Bearing Violence." Yale Review 66 (Autumn 1976): 146-155. (Review of Kassandra and the Wolf.)

KASA, LADY

Ikuko Atsumi. "Modern Japanese Women Poets: After the Meiji Restoration." Iowa Review 7 (Spring/ Summer 1976): 227-237.

KAUFMAN, SUE

Nichols, Marianna de Vinci. "Women on Women: The Looking Glass Novel." Denver Quarterly 11 (Autumn 1976): 1-13.

KAWABATA YASUNARI

Ueda, Makoto. Modern Japanese Writers and the Nature of Literature. Stanford: Stanford University Press, 1976.

KAZANTZAKIS, NIKOS

Poulakidas, Andreas K. "Kazantzakis' Recurrent Victim: Woman." Southern Humanities Review 6 (Spring 1972): 177-189.

KEATS, JOHN

Fass, Barbara. La Belle Dame sans Merci and the Aesthetics of Romanticism. Detroit: Wayne State University Press, 1974.

Noonan, Paula E. "The Nature of Dream Experience in Keats's Narrative Poetry." Gypsy Scholar 3 (Spring 1976): 84-95.

Smith, Louise Z. "The Material Sublime: Keats and Isabella." Studies in Romanticism 13 (Fall 1974): 299-311.

Snider, Clifton. "Jung's Psychology of the Conscious and the Unconscious." Psychocultural Review 1 (Spring 1977): 216-242.

Stephenson, William Curtis. "The Fall From Innocence

in Keats' 'Lamia.' " Papers on Language and Literature 10 (Winter 1974): 35-50.

Taylor, Irene and Gina Luria. "Gender and Genre: Women in British Romantic Literature." In What Manner of Woman: Essays on English and American Life and Literature, pp. 98-124. Edited by Marlene Springer. New York: New York University Press, 1977.

Twitchell, James. "La Belle Dame as Vampire." CEA Critic 37 (May 1975): 31-33.

Ward, Arthur Douglas. "Death and Eroticism in the Poetry of Keats and Tennyson." Ph. D. Dissertation, University of California, Berkeley, 1975.

KELLEY, EDITH SUMMERS

Cheuse, Alan. Nation, 26 April 1975, p. 536. (Review of The Devil's Hand.)

Cook, Sylvia Jenkins. From Tobacco Road to Route 66: The Southern Poor White in Fiction. Chapel Hill: The University of North Carolina Press, 1976.

Goodman, Charlotte. "Images of American Rural Women in the Novel." University of Michigan Papers in Women's Studies 1 (June 1975): 57-70.

_____. "Widening Perspectives, Narrowing Possibilities: The Trapped Woman in Edith Summers Kelley's Weeds." Regionalism and the Female Imagination 3 (Spring 1977): 14-20.

Miller, Jane. Times Literary Supplement, 7 February 1975, p. 129. (Review of The Devil's Hand.)

KELLY, GEORGE

Bonin, Jane F. Major Themes in Prize-Winning American Drama. Metuchen, N.J.: Scarecrow Press, 1975.

Kolb, Deborah S. "The Rise and Fall of the New Woman in American Drama." Educational Theater Journal 27 (1975): 149-160.

Loudin, Joanne Marie. "The Changing Role of the Comic Heroine in American Drama from 1900 to 1940. " Ph. D. Dissertation, University of Washington, 1974.

KELLY, MYRA

Baum, Charlotte, Paula Hyman and Sonya Michel. The Jewish Woman in America. New York: Dial Press, 1975.

KENNEDY, ADRIENNE

Arata, Esther S. and Nicholas J. Rotoli. Black American Playwrights, 1800 to the Present: A Bibliography. Metuchen, N. J. : Scarecrow Press, 1976.

Benston, Kimberly W. "Cities in Bezique: Adrienne Kennedy's Expressionistic Vision. " CLA Journal 20 (December 1976): 235-244.

Brown, Lorraine A. " 'For the Characters Are Myself': Adrienne Kennedy's Funnyhouse of a Negro. " Negro American Literature Forum 9 (1975): 86-88.

Curb, Rosemary Keefe. "The Idea of the American Dream in Afro-American Plays of the Nineteen Sixties. " Ph. D. Dissertation, University of Arkansas, 1977.

Miller, Jeanne-Marie A. "Images of Black Women in Plays by Black Playwrights. " CLA Journal 20 (June 1977): 494-507.

Ogunbiyi, Yemi. "New Black Playwrights in America (1960-1975): Essays in Theatrical Criticism. " Ph.D. Dissertation, New York University, 1976.

Tener, Robert L. "Theatre of Identity: Adrienne Kennedy's Portrait of the Black Woman. " Studies in Black Literature 6 (Summer 1975): 1-5.

Valgamae, Mardi. "Expressionism and the New American Drama. " Twentieth Century Literature 17 (October 1971): 227-234.

KESEY, KEN

Allen, Mary. The Necessary Blankness: Women in

Major American Fiction of the Sixties. Urbana: University of Illinois Press, 1976.

Crump, G. B. "D. H. Lawrence and the Immediate Present: Kurt Vonnegut, Jr., Ken Kesey, and Wright Morris." D. H. Lawrence Review 10 (Summer 1977): 103-141.

Forrey, Robert. "Ken Kesey's Psychopathic Savior: A Rejoinder." Modern Fiction Studies 21 (Summer 1975): 222-230.

Holly, Marcia. "Consciousness and Authenticity: Toward a Feminist Aesthetic." In Feminist Literary Criticism, pp. 38-47. Edited by Josephine Donovan. Lexington: University of Kentucky Press, 1975.

McMahon, Elizabeth E. "The Big Nurse as Ratchet: Sexism in Kesey's Cuckoo's Nest." CEA Critic 37 (May 1975): 25-27.

Martin, Terence. "One Flew Over the Cuckoo's Nest and the High Cost of Living." Modern Fiction Studies 19 (Spring 1973): 43-55.

Shinn, Thelma J. Wardrop. "A Study of Women Characters in Contemporary American Fiction 1940-1970." Ph.D. Dissertation, Purdue University, 1972.

Widmer, Kingsley. "The Post-Modernist Art of Protest: Kesey and Mailer as American Expressions of Rebellion." Centennial Review 19 (Summer 1975): 121-135.

KILLENS, JOHN OLIVER

Gayle, Addison, Jr. The Way of the New World: The Black Novel in America. Garden City, N.Y.: Anchor Press/Doubleday, 1975.

Schulz, Elizabeth. " 'Free in Fact and at Last': The Image of the Black Woman in Black American Literature." In What Manner of Woman: Essays in English and American Life and Literature, pp. 316-344. Edited by Marlene Springer. New York: New York University Press, 1977.

KING, GRACE

Bush, Robert, ed. "Grace King (1852-1932). " American Literary Realism 8 (Winter 1975): [43]-51.

_____. "Grace King: The Emergence of a Southern Intellectual Woman. " Southern Review 13 (Spring 1977): 272-288.

_____. Introduction to Grace King of New Orleans: A Selection of Her Writings. Baton Rouge: Louisiana State University Press, 1973.

Slayton, Gail Cathy. "Grace Elizabeth King: Her Life and Works. " Ph. D. Dissertation, University of Pennsylvania, 1974.

KINGSLEY, CHARLES

Hartley, Allan John. The Novels of Charles Kingsley: A Christian Social Interpretation. Folkestone: Hour-Glass Press, 1977.

Reed, John R. Victorian Conventions. Athens: Ohio University Press, 1975.

KISS, ANNA

Promogátis, Béla. "Kiss Anna vermítoszai. " Alföld 28 (April 1977): 58-61.

KIZER, CAROLYN

Stimpson, Catharine. "Carolyn Kizer: A Rare Sort of Poetry. " Ms. 1 (October 1972): 23-25.

Wallace, Ronald. "Alone with Poems. " Colorado Quarterly 23 (1975): 341-353.

Whiteside, George. "Sine Pro Femina. " Modern Poetry Studies 4 (Spring 1973): 116-118. (Review of Midnight Was My Cry: New and Selected Poems.)

KLEIST, HEINRICH von

Dreyfuss, Cecilia Anne Stiborik. "Femina sapiens in Drama: Aeschylus to Grillparzer. " Ph. D. Dissertation, The University of Michigan, 1975.

202 / More Women in Literature

Fries, Thomas. "Impossible Object: The Feminine, the Narrative." MLN 91 (December 1976): 1296-1326.

Sheeran, Joan Garner. "Women and the Freedom-to-Be in Selected Works of Schiller and the Romantics." Ph.D. Dissertation, University of Minnesota, 1976.

Silz, Walter. "Kleist's Natalie." MLN 91 (April 1976): 531-537.

Weiss, H. F. "Precarious Idylls: The Relationship Between Father and Daughter in Heinrich von Kleist's Die marquise von O." MLN 91 (April 1976): 538-542.

KLEPFISZ, IRENE

Sherman, Susan. Sinister Wisdom 1 (Fall 1976): 81-85. (Review of periods of stress.)

KNIGHT, SARAH KEMBLE

Stanford, Ann. "Images of Women in Early American Literature." In What Manner of Woman: Essays on English and American Life and Literature, pp. 185-210. Edited by Marlene Springer. New York: New York University Press, 1977.

Watts, Emily Stipes. The Poetry of American Women from 1632 to 1945. Austin: University of Texas Press, 1977.

KŌDA AYA

Johnson, Eric W. "Modern Japanese Women Writers." Literature East and West 8 (March 1974): [90]-102.

KOLLONTAI, ALEXANDRA

Toth, Emily. "The Independent Woman and 'Free' Love." Massachusetts Review 16 (Autumn 1975): 647-664.

KOLMAR, GERTRUD

Smith, Henry. Introduction to Dark Soliloquy: The

Selected Poems of Gertrud Kolmar. New York: Seabury Press, 1975.

KOOLISH, LYNDA

Savery, Pancho. "Conversations with the Self. " Epoch 23 (Fall 1973): 120-123.

KOZAI SHIKIN

Yamaguchi, Reiko. "Kozai Shikin no koto. " Bungaku 43 (1975): 1134-1140.

KROETSCH, ROBERT

Fulton, E. Margaret. "Out of Our Past: A New Future." Laurentian University Review 9 (November 1976): [87]-102.

KROLL, JUDITH

Klappert, Peter. "Knowing It. " Parnassus 3 (Fall/ Winter 1974): 93-96. (Review of In the Temperate Zone.)

Parisi, Joseph. "Personae, Personalities. " Poetry 126 (July 1975): 239-241. (Review of In the Temperate Zone.)

KUAN HUA

Eber, Irene. "Images of Women in Recent Chinese Fiction: Do Women Hold Up Half the Sky?" Signs: Journal of Women in Culture and Society 2 (Autumn 1976): 24-34.

KUJŌ TAKEKO

Ikuko Atsumi. "Modern Japanese Women Poets: After the Meiji Restoration. " Iowa Review 7 (Spring/ Summer 1976): 227-237.

KUMIN, MAXINE

Authors in the News, vol. 2. Detroit: Gale Research, 1976, pp. 171-172.

Howard, Jane. New York Times Book Review, 23 June 1974, p. 10. (Review of The Designated Heir.)

Maxine Kumin/Carol Berge. San Francisco: San Francisco State University/The Poetry Center, n. d. (Videocassette.)

Meek, Martha George. "An Interview with Maxine Kumin." Massachusetts Review 16 (Spring 1975): 317-327.

Ryan, F. L. Best Sellers, 15 November 1971, p. 382. (Review of The Abduction.)

Showalter, Elaine and Carol Smith. "A Nurturing Relationship: A Conversation with Anne Sexton and Maxine Kumin, April 15, 1974." Women's Studies 4, no. 1 (1976): 115-135.

Walker, Cheryl Lawson. "The Women's Tradition in American Poetry." Ph.D. Dissertation, Brandeis University, 1973.

KUMMER, CLARE

Loudin, Joanne Marie. "The Changing Role of the Comic Heroine in American Drama from 1900 to 1940." Ph.D. Dissertation, University of Washington, 1974.

Zastrow, Sylvia Virginia Horning. "The Structure of Selected Plays by American Women Playwrights: 1920-1970." Ph.D. Dissertation, Northwestern University, 1975.

KUO LIANG-HUI

Tung, Constantine. "Romance in the Fiction of Kuo Liang-hui, a Woman Novelist in Taiwan." Paper presented at the MLA meeting, San Francisco, December 1975.

KURAHASHI YUMIKO

Mori, Jōji. "Drag the Doctors into the Area of Metaphysics: An Introduction to Kurahashi Yumiko." Literature East and West 8 (March 1974): [76]-89.

KYD, THOMAS

Still, Roger. Love and Death in Renaissance Tragedy.
Baton Rouge: Louisiana State University Press,
1976.

- L -

LABE, LOUISE

Tucker, Cynthia G. "Rilke's Eternal Woman and the
Translation of Louise Labé." Modern Language
Notes 89 (October 1974): 829-839.

Woods, Charlotte Lee. "The Three Faces of Louise
Labé." Ph. D. Dissertation, Syracuse University,
1976.

LACLOS, CHODERLOS de

Fries, Thomas. "Impossible Object: The Feminine,
the Narrative." Modern Language Notes 91 (December 1976): 1296-1326.

LeGates, Marlene. "The Cult of Womanhood in Eighteenth-Century Thought." Eighteenth-Century Studies
10 (Fall 1976): 21-39.

Miller, Nancy K. "Female Sexuality and Narrative
Structure in La Nouvelle Héloïse and Les liaisons
dangereuses." Signs: Journal of Women in Culture
and Society 1 (Spring 1976): 609-638.

Sartori, Eva Martin. "Nature and Forms of Anxiety in
the Works of Pierre Choderlos de Laclos." Ph. D.
Dissertation, Boston University Graduate School,
1975.

Webb, Shawncey Jay. "Aspects of Fidelity and Infidelity
in the Eighteenth Century French Novel from Chasles
to Laclos." Ph. D. Dissertation, Indiana University,
1977.

LACROSIL, MICHELE

>Smith, Robert P. , Jr. "Michèle Lacrosil: Novelist
with a Color Complex. " French Review 47 (March
1974): 783-790.

LAFAYETTE, MME de

>Crosland, Margaret. Women of Iron and Velvet: French
Women After George Sand. New York: Taplinger,
1976.

>Greene, M. S. "Victorian Romanticizing of Sex:
Changes in English Translations of Madame de Lafayette's La Princesse de Clèves. " Bibliographical
Society of American Papers 70 (October 1976): 501-
511.

>Grieder, Josephine. "La Morlière's Motifs de retraite:
An Eighteenth-Century Metamorphosis of La Princesse
de Clèves. " French Review 51 (October 1977): 10-
14.

>Kusch, Manfred. "Narrative Technique and Cognitive
Modes in La princesse de Clèves. " Symposium 30
(Winter 1976): 308-324.

>Maurin, Mario. "Un modèle h'Indiana?" French Re-
view 50 (1976-77): 317-320.

>Moore, Cassandra Chrones. "The Romantic Triangle:
A Study of Expanding Consciousness, (Volumes I and
II). " Ph. D. Dissertation, The University of Michi-
gan, 1975.

>Rodino, Sandra. "Mme de Lafayette and the Italian Tra-
dition of the Courtier. " Ph. D. Dissertation, City
University of New York, 1977.

>Scanlan, Timothy M. "Comic Elements in La Princesse
de Clèves. " Romance Notes 17 (Spring 1977): 281-
285.

>Schmitz, Betty Ann. "French Women Writers and Their
Critics: An Analysis of the Treatment of Women
Writers in Selected Histories of French Literature. "
Ph. D. Dissertation, The University of Wisconsin-
Madison, 1977.

Singerman, Alan J. "History as Metaphor in Mme de Lafayette's La Princesse de Clèves." Modern Language Quarterly 36 (September 1975): 261-271.

LAFORET, CARMEN

Hadjopoulos, Theresa Mary. "Four Women Novelists of Postwar Spain: Matute, Lafôret, Quiroga, and Medio." Ph. D. Dissertation, Columbia University, 1974.

Illanes Adaro, Graciela. La Novelística de Carmen Lafôret. Madrid: Gredos, 1971.

Jones, Margaret W. "Dialectical Movements as Feminist Techniques." Paper presented at the MLA meeting, New York City, December 1976.

Newberry, Wilma. "The Solstitial Holidays in Carmen Lafôret's Nada: Christmas and Midsummer." Romance Notes 17 (Fall 1976): 76-81.

Schyfter, Sara E. "The Male Mystique and Its Victims in Nada." Paper presented at the MLA meeting, New York City, December 1976.

LAHOR, JEAN

Reff, Theodore. "The Influence of Flaubert's Queen of Sheba on Later Nineteenth-Century Literature." Romanic Review 65 (November 1974): 249-265.

LAMMING, GEORGE

Cash, Earl A. CLA Journal 15 (March 1972): 381-382. (Review of Natives of My Person.)

Larson, Charles R. The Novel in the Third World. Washington, D. C. : Inscape, 1976.

LANG, BUNNY

Lurie, Alison. "The Life and Death of Bunny Lang." New Review 2 (June 1975): 9-33.

LARBAUD, VALERY

Grace, Jane Opper. "Geography as Metaphor: Larbaud's

Fiction Revisited. " Romanic Review 67 (November 1976): 300-307.

LARKIN, JOAN

Lapidus, Jacqueline. Sinister Wisdom 1 (Fall 1976): 73-76. (Review of Housework.)

Rich, Adrienne. " 'There Is a Fly in This House.' " Ms. 5 (February 1977): 46-47, 105-106. (Review of Housework.)

LARSEN, NELLA

Brown, Martha Hursey. "Images of Black Women: Family Roles in Harlem Renaissance Literature. " D.A. Dissertation, Carnegie-Mellon University, 1976.

Davidson, Colleen Tighe. "Beyond the Sentimental Heroine: The Feminist Character in American Novels, 1899-1937. " Ph.D. Dissertation, University of Minnesota, 1975.

Doyle, Sister Mary Ellen. "The Heroine of Black Novels. " In Perspectives on Afro-American Women, pp. 112-125. Edited by Willa D. Johnson and Thomas L. Green. Washington, D.C.: ECCA Publications, 1975.

Klotman, Phyllis Rauch. Another Man Gone: The Black Runner in Contemporary Afro-American Literature. Port Washington, N.Y.: Kennikat Press, 1977.

Lay, Mary M. "Parallels: Henry James's The Portrait of a Lady and Nella Larsen's Quicksand. " CLA Journal 20 (June 1977): 475-486.

Perry, Margaret. Silence to the Drums: A Survey of the Literature of the Harlem Renaissance. Contributions in Afro-American and African Studies, no. 18. Westport, Conn.: Greenwood Press, 1976.

Ramsey, Priscilla Barbara Ann. "A Study of Black Identity in 'Passing' Novels of the Nineteenth and Early Twentieth Centuries. " Ph.D. Dissertation, The American University, 1975.

_____. "A Study of Black Identity in 'Passing' Novels
of the Nineteenth and Early Twentieth Centuries. "
Studies in Black Literature 7 (Winter 1976): 1-7.

Royster, Beatrice Horn. "The Ironic Vision of Four
Black Women Novelists: A Study of the Novels of
Jessie Fauset, Nella Larsen, Zora Neale Hurston,
and Ann Petry. " Ph.D. Dissertation, Emory University, 1975.

Schulz, Elizabeth. " 'Free in Fact and at Last': The
Image of the Black Woman in Black American Lit-
erature. " In What Manner of Woman: Essays in
English and American Life and Literature, pp. 316-
344. Edited by Marlene Springer. New York: New
York University Press, 1977.

Singh, Amritjit. The Novels of the Harlem Renaissance:
Twelve Black Writers, 1923-1933. University Park:
Pennsylvania State University Press, 1976.

Stetson, Earlene. "The Mulatto Motif in Black Fiction. "
Ph.D. Dissertation, State University of New York
at Buffalo, 1976.

LATHEN, EMMA

Bakerman, Jane S. "Women and Wall Street: Portraits
of Women in Novels by Emma Lathen. " Armchair
Detective 8 (1975): 36-41.

LAURENCE, MARGARET

Atherton, Stan. "Margaret Laurence's Progress. " International Fiction Review 2 (January 1975): 61-64.

Atwood, Margaret. "Face to Face with Margaret Laurence. " Maclean's 87 (May 1974): 38-39.

Bruce, Phyllis. Canadian Forum 54 (May/June 1974):
15. (Review of The Diviners.)

Davidson, Cathy N. "Canadian Wry: Comic Vision in
Atwood's Lady Oracle and Laurence's The Diviners. "
Regionalism and the Female Imagination 3 (Fall
1977/Winter 1977-78): 50-55.

_____. "Geography as Psychology in the Writings of Margaret Laurence." Paper presented at the MLA meeting, New York City, December 1976.

Frank, Sheldon. New Republic, 27 July-3 August 1974, p. 28. (Review of The Diviners.)

Fulton, E. Margaret. "Out of Our Past: A New Future." Laurentian University Review 9 (November 1976): [87]-102.

Gom, Leona M. "Laurence and the Use of Memory." Canadian Literature no. 71 (Winter 1976): 48-58.

_____. "Margaret Laurence and the First Person." Dalhousie Review 55 (Summer 1975): 236-251.

Grace, Sherrill E. "Crossing Jordan: Time and Memory in the Fiction of Margaret Laurence." World Literature Written in English 16 (November 1977): 328-339.

Hehner, Barbara. "River of Now and Then: Margaret Laurence's Narratives." Canadian Literature no. 74 (Autumn 1977): 40-57.

Irvine, Lorna Marie. "Hostility and Reconciliation: The Mother in English Canadian Fiction." Ph. D. Dissertation, The American University, 1977.

New, W. H. Articulating West: Essays on Purpose and Form in Modern Canadian Literature. Toronto: New Press, 1972.

Piercy, Marge. New York Times Book Review, 23 June 1974, p. 6. (Review of The Diviners.)

Quill & Quire (Toronto) 42, no. 15 (1976): 30. (Review of Heart of a Stranger.)

Saturday Night 91 (November 1976): 49-50. (Review of Heart of a Stranger.)

Savage, David. "Not Survival but Responsibility." Dalhousie Review 55 (Summer 1975): 272-279.

Thomas, Clara. The Manawaka World of Margaret Laurence. Toronto: McClelland & Stewart, 1975.

_____. "The Wild Garden and the Manawaka World."
Modern Fiction Studies 22 (Autumn 1976): 401-411.

LAWRENCE, D. H.

Adamowski, T. H. "Being Perfect: Lawrence, Sartre,
and Women in Love." Critical Inquiry 2 (Winter
1975): 345-368.

Alinei, Tamara. "Imagery and Meaning in D. H. Lawrence's The Rainbow." Yearbook of English Studies
2 (1972): 205-211.

Bassoff, Bruce. "Metaphysical Desire in Women in
Love." Revue des Langues Vivantes 42, no. 3
(1976): 227-236.

Braendlin, Bonnie Hoover. "The 'New Woman' in the
Bildungsromane of Somerset Maugham, H. G. Wells,
and D. H. Lawrence." Paper presented at the MLA
meeting, New York City, December 1976.

Ebbatson, J. R. "Thomas Hardy and Lady Chatterley."
Ariel: A Review of International English Literature
8 (April 1977): 85-95.

Fernando, Lloyd. "New Women" in the Late Victorian
Novel. University Park: Pennsylvania State University Press, 1977.

Finney, Brian and Michael L. Ross. "The Two Versions of 'Sun': An Exchange." D. H. Lawrence
Review 8 (Fall 1975): 371-374.

Freeman, Alma Susan. "The Androgynous Ideal: A
Study of Selected Novels by D. H. Lawrence, James
Joyce, and Virginia Woolf." Ed. D. Dissertation,
Rutgers University, The State University of New
Jersey, 1974.

Green, Eleanor H. "Schopenhauer and D. H. Lawrence
on Sex and Love." D. H. Lawrence Review 8, 9
(Fall 1975): 329-345.

Haegert, John W. "Brothers and Lovers: D. H. Lawrence and the Theme of Friendship." Southern Review (Adelaide) 8 (March 1975): 39-50.

Harris, Janice H.   "Sexual Antagonism in D. H. Lawrence's Early Leadership Fiction." Modern Language Studies 7 (Spring 1977): 43-52.

Heldt, Lucia Henning.   "Lawrence on Love: The Courtship and Marriage of Tom Brangwen and Lydia Lensky." D. H. Lawrence Review 8 (Fall 1975): 358-370.

Heywood, Christopher.   "Olive Schreiner's The Story of an African Farm: Prototype of Lawrence's Early Novels." English Language Notes 14 (September 1976): 44-50.

Higgins, Susan.   "The Suffragettes in Fiction." Hecate 2 (July 1976): 31-47.

Hinz, Evelyn J.   "The Rainbow: Ursula's 'Liberation.' " Contemporary Literature 17 (Winter 1976): 24-43.

Howe, Marguerite Beede.   The Art of the Self in D. H. Lawrence. Athens, Ohio: Ohio University Press, 1976.

Hyde, Virginia.   "Will Brangwen and Paradisal Vision in The Rainbow and Women in Love." D. H. Lawrence Review 8 (Fall 1975): 346-357.

Kay, Wallace G.   "Women in Love and The Man Who Died: Resolving Apollo and Dionysus." Southern Quarterly 10 (July 1972): 325-339.

Kumar, Prem.   "Four Figures in Love: Anna Karenin, Emma Bovary, Constance Chatterly [sic], and Chitralekha." Journal of South Asian Literature 12 (Spring-Summer 1977): 73-80.

MacDonald, Robert.   "The Union of Fire and Water: An Examination of the Imagery of The Man Who Died." D. H. Lawrence Review 10 (Spring 1977): 34-51.

Mandel, Jerome.   "Medieval Romance and Lady Chatterley's Lover." D. H. Lawrence Review 10 (Spring 1977): 20-33.

Meyers, Jeffrey.   Married to Genius. New York: Barnes & Noble, 1977.

Miles, Rosalind. The Fiction of Sex: Themes and Functions of Sex Difference in the Modern Novel. New York: Barnes & Noble, 1974.

Morrison, Kristin. "Lawrence, Beardsley, Wilde: The White Peacock and Sexual Ambiguity." Western Humanities Review 30 (Autumn 1976): 241-248.

Panken, Shirley. "Some Psychodynamics in Sons and Lovers: A New Look at the Oedipal Theme." Psychoanalytic Review 61 (Winter 1974-75): 571-590.

Peters, Joan K. "The Gentleman Doth Protest Too Much: An Analysis of Female Alliances in D. H. Lawrence's Tales." Paper presented at the MLA meeting, San Francisco, December 1975.

Portner, Ruth Lee. "A Study of Marriage in the English Novel." Ph.D. Dissertation, City University of New York, 1977.

Ross, Charles L. "D. H. Lawrence's Use of Greek Tragedy: Euripides and Ritual." D. H. Lawrence Review 10 (Spring 1977): 1-19.

Ross, Michael L. "Lawrence's Second 'Sun.'" D. H. Lawrence Review 8 (Spring 1975): 1-18.

Rossman, Charles. "'You are the call and I am the answer': D. H. Lawrence and Women." D. H. Lawrence Review 8/9 (Fall 1975): 255-328.

Ruderman, Judith G. "The Fox and the 'Devouring Mother.'" D. H. Lawrence Review 10 (Fall 1977): 251-269.

_____. "The Making of The Fox: A Study of the 'Devouring Mother' Figure as It Relates to D. H. Lawrence's Ideal of Leadership." Ph.D. Dissertation, Duke University, 1976.

Snider, Clifton. "Jung's Psychology of the Conscious and the Unconscious." Psychocultural Review 1 (Spring 1977): 216-242.

Solecki, Sam. Dalhousie Review 57 (Spring 1977): 191-193. (Review of Thought, Words and Creativity: Art and Thought in Lawrence by F. R. Leavis.)

Spector, Judith Ann. "Sexual Dialectic in Four Novels: The Mythos of the Masculine Aesthetic." Ph.D. Dissertation, Indiana University, 1977.

Spilka, Mark. "Lessing and Lawrence: The Battle of the Sexes." Contemporary Literature 16 (Spring 1975): 218-240.

Unrue, Darlene H. "Lawrence's Vision of Evil: The Power-Spirit in The Rainbow and Women in Love." Dalhousie Review 55 (Winter 1975-76): 643-654.

Watson, Barbara Bellow. "On Power and the Literary Text." Signs: Journal of Women in Culture and Society 1 (Autumn 1975): 111-118.

LAYE, CAMARA

Brown, Lloyd W. "Mannequins and Mermaids--The Contemporary Writer and Sexual Images in the Consumer Culture." Women's Studies 5, no. 1 (1977): 1-12.

LAZARUS, ESTHER

Watts, Emily Stipes. The Poetry of American Women from 1632 to 1945. Austin: University of Texas Press, 1977.

LEDUC, VIOLETTE

Aury, Dominique. "Violette Leduc." La Nouvelle Revue Francaise no. 255 (March 1974): 114-116.

Brooks, Peter. New York Times Book Review, 3 October 1971, p. 4. (Review of Mad in Pursuit.)

Contemporary Authors--Permanent Series, vol. 1.

Crosland, Margaret. Women of Iron and Velvet: French Women After George Sand. New York: Taplinger, 1976.

Marks, Elaine. "'I Am My Own Heroine': Some Thoughts About Women and Autobiography in France." In Female Studies IX: Teaching About Women in the Foreign Languages, pp. 1-10. Edited by Sodonie Cassirer. Old Westbury, N.Y.: Feminist Press, 1975.

Rule, Jane. Lesbian Images. Garden City, N.Y.:
Doubleday, 1975.

LEE, SOPHIA

Roberts, Bette B. "The Gothic Romance: Its Appeal
to Women Writers and Readers in Late Eighteenth-
Century England." Ph.D. Dissertation, University
of Massachusetts, 1975.

LEE, VERNON

Briggs, Julia. Night Visitors: The Rise and Fall of
the English Ghost Story. London: Faber, 1977.

LeGUIN, URSULA K.

Authors in the News, vol. 1. Detroit: Gale Research,
1976, p. 302.

Hipolito, Jane. "Flatland and Beyond: Characterization
in Science Fiction." CEA Chap Book 1 (November
1974): 18-21.

Jameson, Fredric. "World Reduction in LeGuin: The
Emergence of Utopian Narrative." Science-Fiction
Studies 2 (November 1975): 221-230.

LeGuin, Ursula. "Ursula LeGuin: Woman of Science
Fiction." North Hollywood: The Center for Cassette Studies, n.d.

Levin, Jeff. "Ursula K. LeGuin: A Select Bibliography."
Science-Fiction Studies 2 (November 1975): 204-208.

Russ, Joanna. "Reflections on Science Fiction." Quest
2 (Summer 1975): 40-49.

"Ursula LeGuin." In The New Woman's Survival Sourcebook, p. 132. Edited by Kirsten Grimstad and Susan
Rennie. New York: Alfred A. Knopf, 1975.

LEHMAN, ROSAMOND

Coopman, Tony. "Symbolism in Rosamond Lehmann's
The Echoing Grove." Revue des Langues Vivantes
50, no. 2 (1974): 116-121.

Dorosz, Wiktoria. Subjective Vision and Human Relationships in the Novels of Rosamond Lehmann. Stockholm: Almqvist & Wiksell, 1975.

Franklin, Olga. "Why Novelist Rosamond Is Writing Again." Daily Telegraph (London), 5 January 1977, p. 11.

Kaplan, Sydney Janet. The Feminine Consciousness and the British Novel. Urbana: University of Illinois Press, 1975.

LENNOX, CHARLOTTE

Eastham, Leah Raye. "Charlotte Ramsay Lennox: A Critical Study of Her Novels." Ph.D. Dissertation, University of Arkansas, 1977.

Skilton, David. The English Novel: Defoe to the Victorians. New York: Barnes & Noble, 1977.

Spacks, Patricia Meyer. Imagining a Self: Autobiography and Novel in Eighteenth-Century England. Cambridge: Harvard University Press, 1976.

LESAGE, RENE

Daghistany, Ann. "The Picara Nature." Women's Studies 5, no. 1 (1977): 51-60.

LESSING, DORIS

Barnouw, Dagmar. "Disorderly Company: From the Golden Notebook to the Four-Gated City." In Contemporary Women Novelists: A Collection of Critical Essays, pp. 30-54. Edited by Patricia Meyer Spacks. Englewood Cliffs, N.J.: Prentice-Hall, 1977.

Bedick, David B. "The Changing Role of Anxiety in the Novel." Ph.D. Dissertation, New York University, 1975.

Brown, Lloyd W. "Mannequins and Mermaids--The Contemporary Writer and Sexual Images in the Consumer Culture." Women's Studies 5, no. 1 (1977): 1-12.

_____. "The Shape of Things: Several Images and the Sense of Form in Doris Lessing's Fiction." World Literature Written in English 14, no. 1 (1975): 176-186.

Christ, Carol P. "Explorations with Doris Lessing in Quest of the Four-Gated City." In Women and Religion: Proceedings, rev. ed., pp. 31-61. Edited by Judith Plaskow and Joan A. Romero. Missoula: Scholar's Press, 1974.

_____. "Spiritual Quest and Women's Experience." Anima: An Experimental Journal of Celebration 1 (Spring 1974): 4-14.

Clements, Frances M. "Lessing's 'One Off the Short List' and the Definition of the Self." Frontiers: A Journal of Women Studies 1 (Fall 1975): 106-109.

Cohen, Mary. " 'Out of the chaos, a new kind of strength': Doris Lessing's The Golden Notebook." In The Authority of Experience, pp. [178]-193. Edited by Arlyn Diamond and Lee R. Edwards. Amherst: University of Massachusetts Press, 1977.

Dinnage, Rosemary. "In the Disintegrating City." New York Review of Books, 17 July 1975, pp. 38-39.

Draine, Mary Elizabeth. "Stages of Consciousness in Doris Lessing's Fiction." Ph.D. Dissertation, Temple University, 1977.

Driver, C. J. "Profile 8." New Review (London) 1 (November 1974): 17-23.

Grant, Velma Fudge. "The Quest for Wholeness in Novels by Doris Lessing." Ed.D. Dissertation, Rutgers University, The State University of New Jersey, 1974.

Kaplan, Sydney Janet. The Feminine Consciousness and the British Novel. Urbana: University of Illinois Press, 1975.

Karl, Frederick R. "Doris Lessing in the Sixties: The New Anatomy of Melancholy." In Contemporary Women Novelists: A Collection of Critical Essays,

pp. 55-74. Edited by Patricia Meyer Spacks.
Englewood Cliffs, N.J.: Prentice-Hall, 1977.

Lang, Frances. "Doris Lessing: Madness as Ideology."
Off Our Backs, December 1972, pp. 10-11.

Laurel. "Toward a Woman Vision." Amazon Quarterly
2, no. 2, pp. 18-42.

Lefcowitz, Barbara F. "Dream and Action in Lessing's
Summer Before the Dark." Critique 17, no. 2
(1975): 107-120.

Libby, Marion. "Sex and the New Woman in The Golden
Notebook." Iowa Review 5 (1974): 106-120.

Lightfoot, Margorie J. "Breakthrough in The Golden
Notebook." Studies in the Novel 7 (Summer 1975):
277-284.

McLaughlin, Marilou Briggs. "The Love Dialectic."
Ph.D. Dissertation, State University of New York
at Binghamton, 1976.

Miles, Rosalind. The Fiction of Sex: Themes and
Functions of Sex Difference in the Modern Novel.
New York: Barnes & Noble, 1974.

Rapping, Elayne Antler. "Unfree Women: Feminism in
Doris Lessing's Novels." Women's Studies 3 (1975):
29-44.

Rigney, Barbara. Madness and Sexual Politics in the
Feminist Novel: Studies of Charlotte Brontë, Virginia Woolf, Doris Lessing, and Margaret Atwood.
Madison: University of Wisconsin Press, forthcoming.

Rose, Ellen Cronan. "The Eriksonian Bildungsroman:
An Approach Through Doris Lessing." Hartford
Studies in Literature 7 (1975): 1-17.

_____. "The Tree Outside the Window: Doris Less-
ing's 'Children of Violence.'" Hanover, N.H.:
University Press of New England, 1976.

Rubenstein, Roberta. "Doris Lessing's The Golden

Notebook: The Meaning of Its Shape." American Imago 32 (Spring 1975): 40-58.

_____. "Outer Space, Inner Space: Doris Lessing's Metaphor of Science Fiction." World Literature Written in English 14, no. 1 (1975): 187-197.

Ryf, Robert S. "Beyond Ideology: Doris Lessing's Mature Vision." Modern Fiction Studies 21 (Summer 1975): 193-201.

Schaeffer, Susan. "When Walls Tumble Down." Chicago Review 27 (Winter 1975): 132-137. (Review of Memoirs of a Survivor.)

Seligman, Claudia Dee. "The Autobiographical Novels of Doris Lessing." Ph.D. Dissertation, Tufts University, 1975.

Showalter, Elaine. A Literature of Their Own: British Women Novelists from Brontë to Lessing. Princeton: Princeton University Press, 1977.

Singleton, Mary Ann. The City and the Veld: The Fiction of Doris Lessing. Lewisburg: Bucknell University Press, 1977.

Spacks, Patricia Meyer, ed. Contemporary Women Novelists: A Collection of Critical Essays. Englewood Cliffs, N.J.: Prentice-Hall, 1977.

Spilka, Mark. "Lessing and Lawrence: The Battle of the Sexes." Contemporary Literature 16 (Spring 1975): 218-240.

Taylor, Nancy McKeon. "Conscious Construction: The Concept of Plot in Five Novels by Women." Ph.D. Dissertation, Loyola University of Chicago, 1977.

Tiger, Virginia. "Doris Lessing." Deland, Florida: Everett/Edwards, n.d. (Cassette no. 5521.)

Tuathaigh, Seamus O. "Query on Doris Lessing." Dublin Magazine 9, no. 1 (1971): 67.

Watson, Barbara Bellow. "On Power and the Literary Text." Signs: Journal of Women in Culture and Society 1 (Autumn 1975): 111-118.

West, Rebecca. "And They All Lived Unhappily Ever
   After. " Times Literary Supplement, 26 July 1974,
   p. 779.

LESSING, G. E.

   Marshall, Madeleine Forell. "Millwood and Marwood:
      Fallen Women and the Moral Interest of Sentimental
      Tragedy. " Mary Wollstonecraft Journal 22 (May
      1974): 2-12.

   Tilton, Helga. "Virgins and Other Victims: Aspects of
      German Middle-Class Theatre. " In Female Studies
      IX: Teaching About Women in Foreign Languages,
      pp. 180-186. Edited by Sidonie Cassirer. Old
      Westbury, N. Y. : Feminist Press, 1975.

LeSUEUR, MERIDEL

   Hampl, Patricia. "Meridel LeSueur: Voice of the
      Prairie. " Ms. (August 1975): 62-66, 96.

LEVERTOV, DENISE

   Beis, Patricia Sharon. "Cold Fire: Some Contemporary
      American Women Poets. " Ph. D. Dissertation, Saint
      Louis University, 1972.

   Brinnin, John Malcolm and Bill Read, eds. Twentieth
      Century Poetry: American and British (1900-1970),
      2nd ed. New York: McGraw-Hill, 1970.

   Denise Levertov. San Francisco: San Francisco State
      University/The Poetry Center, n. d. (Videocassette.)

   Deren, Jane Martha. "Denise Levertov's Postmodern
      Poetic: A Study in Theory and Criticism. " Ph. D.
      Dissertation, Temple University, 1977.

   DuPlessis, Rachel Blau. "The Critique of Consciousness
      and Myth in Levertov, Rich, and Rukeyser. " Femi-
      nist Studies 3 (Fall 1975): [199]-221.

   Gitzen, Julian. "From Reverence to Attention: The
      Poetry of Denise Levertov. " Midwest Quarterly 16
      (April 1975): 328-341.

Halbritter, Rudolf. "Zur Inhalt-Form-Problematik in Denise Levertovs engagierten Gedichten [Problems of the Form-Content Relationship in Denise Levertov's Poetry of Political Commitment.]" Amerikastudien/American Studies 22, no. 1 (1977): 167-189.

Hampl, Patricia. "A Witness of Our Time." Moons and Lion Tailes 2, no. 1 (1976): 47-53. (Review of The Freeing of the Dust.)

Ignatow, David. New York Times Book Review, 30 November 1975, p. 54. (Review of The Freeing of the Dust.)

Juhasz, Suzanne. Naked and Fiery Forms: Modern American Poetry by Women, A New Tradition. New York: Harper & Row, 1976.

Levertov, Denise. "The Poet in the World." American Poetry Review 1 (November/December 1972): 16-18.

Mersmann, James F. "Out of the Vortex: A Study of Poets and Poetry Against the Vietnam War." Ph.D. Dissertation, University of Kansas, 1972.

Nelson, Rudolph Lorens. "The Search for Transcendence in Contemporary American Poetry." Ph.D. Dissertation, Brown University, 1971.

Phillips, Martha Jean Payne. "The Dissenting Voice: A Rhetorical Analysis of Denise Levertov's Engagé Poetry." Ph.D. Dissertation, The University of Texas at Austin, 1975.

Wagner, Linda. "Levertov and Rich: The Later Poems." Paper presented at the MLA meeting, San Francisco, December 1975.

Walker, Cheryl. "A Poetic License to Kill--And Live." Ms. 4 (April 1976): 42-43. (Review of The Freeing of the Dust.)

Wallace, Ronald. "Alone with Poems." Colorado Quarterly 23 (1975): 341-353.

Younkins, Ronald. "Denise Levertov and the Hasidic Tradition." Descant 19, no. 1 (1975): 40-48.

Zverev, A. "Introduction to Russian Translation of Selections from Denise Levertov." Inostrannaya Literature (Moscow) Part 10 (1972): 57-63.

LEVIN, MEYER

Baum, Charlotte, Paula Hyman and Sonya Michel. The Jewish Woman in America. New York: Dial Press, 1975.

Koltun, Elizabeth. The Jewish Woman: New Perspectives. New York: Schocken, 1976.

LEWIS, MATTHEW GREGORY

Byrd, Max. "The Madhouse, the Whorehouse, and the Convent." Partisan Review 44, no. 2 (1977): 268-278.

Longerbeam, Larry Simpson. "Seduction as Symbolic Action: A Study of the Seduction Motif in Six Victorian Novels." Ph.D. Dissertation, George Peabody College for Teachers, 1975.

Mise, Raymond Winfield. "The Gothic Heroine and the Nature of the Gothic Novel." Ph.D. Dissertation, University of Washington, 1970.

LEWIS, SINCLAIR

Tuttleton, James W. " 'Combat in the Erogenous Zone': Women in the American Novel Between the Two World Wars." In What Manner of Woman: Essays in English and American Life and Literature, pp. 271-296. Edited by Marlene Springer. New York: New York University Press, 1977.

LI CHUN

Eber, Irene. "Images of Women in Recent Chinese Fiction: Do Women Hold Up Half the Sky?" Signs: Journal of Women in Culture and Society 2 (Autumn 1976): 24-34.

LI FANG-LING

Eber, Irene. "Images of Women in Recent Chinese

Fiction: Do Women Hold Up Half the Sky?" Signs:
Journal of Women in Culture and Society 2 (Autumn
1976): 24-34.

LI YU

Eber, Irene. "Images of Women in Recent Chinese Fiction: Do Women Hold Up Half the Sky?" Signs:
Journal of Women in Culture and Society 2 (Autumn
1976): 24-34.

LILLO, GEORGE

Marshall, Madeleine Forell. "Millwood and Marwood:
Fallen Women and the Moral Interest of Sentimental
Tragedy." Mary Wollstonecraft Journal 22 (May
1974): 2-12.

Tilton, Helga. "Virgins and Other Victims: Aspects of
German Middle-Class Theatre." In Female Studies
IX: Teaching About Women in Foreign Languages,
pp. 180-186. Edited by Sidonie Cassirer. Old
Westbury, N.Y.: Feminist Press, 1975.

LIN YUTANG

Hagman, Lorri. "Two Famous Courtesans: Vasantesena
and Miss Tu." Journal of South Asian Literature
12 (Spring-Summer 1977): 31-36.

LINTON, ELIZA LYNN

Calder, Jenni. Women and Marriage in Victorian Fiction. London: Thames & Hudson, 1976.

Showalter, Elaine. A Literature of Their Own: British
Women Novelists from Brontë to Lessing. Princeton: Princeton University Press, 1977.

Speegle, Katherine Sloan. "God's Newer Will: Four
Examples of Victorian Angst Resolved by Humani-
tarianism." Ph.D. Dissertation, North Texas State
University, 1975.

LISPECTOR, CLARICE

Cypress, Sandra. "Clarice Lispector and Women

Writers in Brazil." Paper presented at the MLA
meeting, San Francisco, December 1975.

Fitz, Earl Eugene. "Clarice Lispector: The Nature
and Form of the Lyrical Novel." Ph.D. Dissertation, City University of New York, 1977.

Tavenner, Anna C. "Aspectos de Conflicto y enajenamiento de la mujer en las novelas de Silvina Bullrich, Beatriz Guido y Clarice Lispector." Ph.D.
Dissertation, Texas Tech University, 1977.

LIVESAY, DOROTHY

Authors in the News, vol. 2. Detroit: Gale Research,
1976, p. 177.

Foulks, Debbie. "Livesay's Two Seasons of Love."
Canadian Literature no. 74 (Autumn 1977): 63-73.

Harrison, R. T. "Taking the Prairies Seriously: Dorothy Livesey's A Winnipeg Childhood...." World
Literature Written in English 13 (November 1974):
266-274.

LIVY

Piper, Linda J. "Livy's Portrayal of Early Roman
Women." Classical Bulletin 48 (December 1971):
26-28.

LO PIN-CHI

Eber, Irene. "Images of Women in Recent Chinese Fiction: Do Women Hold Up Half the Sky?" Signs:
Journal of Women in Culture and Society 2 (Autumn
1976): 24-34.

LODGE, THOMAS

Larson, Charles. "Lodge's Rosalind: Decorum in Arden." Studies in Short Fiction 14 (Spring 1977):
117-127.

LONDON, JACK

Forrey, Robert. "Male and Female in London's The

Sea Wolf. " Literature and Psychology 24, no. 4
(1974): 135-143.

_____. "Three Modes of Sexuality in London's The
Big Little Lady of the Big House. " Literature and
Psychology 26, no. 2 (1976): 52-60.

Lachtman, Howard. "Man and Superwoman in Jack
London's 'The Kanaka Surf. ' " Western American
Literature 7 (Summer 1972): 101-110.

Stasz, Clarice. "Androgyny in the Novels of Jack London. " Western American Literature 11 (Summer
1976): 121-134.

LOOS, ANITA

Blom, T. E. "Anita Loos and Sexual Economics:
'Gentlemen Prefer Blondes. ' " Canadian Review of
American Studies 7 (Spring 1976): 36-47.

LaJoy, Maureen. "No Laughing Matter: Women and
Humor. " Women 5, no. 1 (1976): 6-9.

LOPE DE VEGA CARPIO, FELIX

Dreyfuss, Cecilia Anne Stiborik. "Femina sapiens in
Drama: Aeschylus to Grillparzer. " Ph. D. Dissertation, The University of Michigan, 1975.

Friesner, Esther Mona. "The Mirror of Queens: The
Queen in the Theatre of Lope de Vega. " Ph. D.
Dissertation, Yale University, 1977.

Hesse, Everett W. "The Perversion of Love in Lope
de Vega's El castigo sin venganza. " Hispania 60
(September 1977): 430-435.

Trisler, Barbara Jean. "A Comparative Study of the
Character Portrayal of 'Celestina' and Other Golden
Age Celestinesque Protagonists. " Ph. D. Disserta-
tion, The University of Oklahoma, 1977.

LOPEZ DE UBEDA, FRANCISCO

Sánchez-Díez, Francisco Javier. "La novela picaresca
de protagonista feminino en España durante el siglo

XVII. " Ph.D. Dissertation, University of North Carolina, Chapel Hill, 1972.

LORCA, FEDERICO GARCIA see GARCIA LORCA, FEDERICO

LORDE, AUDRE

Cernwell, Anita. " 'So Who's Giving Guarantees?' An Interview with Audre Lorde. " Sinister Wisdom no. 4 (Fall 1977): 15-21.

Larkin, Joan. "Nothing Safe: The Poetry of Audre Lorde. " Margins no. 23 (August 1975): 23-25.

Mberi, Antar S. K.   Freedomways 16 (Third Quarter 1976): 194-196. (Review of Oal.)

Piercy, Marge. "From Where I Work. " American Poetry Review 5, no. 2 (1976): 11-12.

Vendler, Helen. New York Times Book Review, 7 September 1975, p. 6. (Review of The New York Head Shop and Museum.)

LORRIS, GUILLAUME

Ferrante, Joan M.   Woman As Image in Medieval Literature from the Twelfth Century to Dante. New York: Columbia University Press, 1975.

LOUŸS, PIERRE

Rudluff, Sandra Lillian Mutina. "The Woman as a Figure in the Works of Pierre Louÿs. " Ph.D. Dissertation, Tulane University, 1975.

LOWELL, AMY

Callow, James T. and Robert Reilly. Guide to American Literature from Emily Dickinson to the Present. New York: Barnes & Noble, 1977.

Flint, F. Cudworth. "Amy Lowell. " In American Writers, vol. 2, pp. 511-533. Edited by Leonard Unger. New York: Charles Scribner's Sons, 1974.

Gould, Jean. Amy: The World of Amy Lowell and the Imagist Movement. New York: Dodd, Mead, 1975.

Healey, Claire. "Amy Lowell Visits London. " New England Quarterly 46 (September 1973): 439-453.

Hirsch, John C. "John Gould Fletcher and Amy Lowell: New Evidence of Their Relationship. " Harvard Library Bulletin 2 (January 1974): 72-75.

Ruihley, Glenn Richard. The Thorn of a Rose: Amy Lowell Reconsidered. Hamden, Conn.: Archon Books, 1975.

Watts, Emily Stipes. The Poetry of American Women from 1632 to 1945. Austin: University of Texas Press, 1977.

LOWTHER, PAT

Ryan, Sean. "Florence McNeil and Pat Lowther. " Canadian Literature no. 74 (Autumn 1977): 21-29.

LUMPKIN, GRACE

Cook, Sylvia Jenkins. From Tobacco Road to Route 66: The Southern Poor White in Fiction. Chapel Hill: The University of North Carolina Press, 1976.

LURIE, ALISON

Aldridge, John. "How Good Is Alison Lurie?" Commentary 9, no. 1 (1975): 79-81.

Nichols, Marianna de Vinci. "Women on Women: The Looking Glass Novel. " Denver Quarterly 11 (Autumn 1976): 1-13.

Times Literary Supplement, 21 June 1974, p. 657. (Review of The War Between the Tates.)

LYLY, JOHN

Gannon, C. C. "Lyly's Endimion: From Myth to Allegory. " English Literary Renaissance 6 (Spring 1976): 220-243.

Lenz, Carolyn Ruth Swift. "The Allegory of Wisdom in
Lyly's Endimion." Comparative Drama 10 (Fall
1976): 235-257.

LYN

Redmond, Eugene. "Five Black Poets: History, Consciousness, Love, and Harshness." Parnassus:
Poetry in Review 3 (Spring/Summer 1975): 153-172.

LYNCH, MARTA

Billman, Lynne Lois. "The Political Novels of Lucila
Palacios and Marta Lynch." Ph.D. Dissertation,
The Catholic University of America, 1976.

Kaminsky, Amy Sue Katz. "Marta Lynch: The Expand-
ing Political Consciousness of an Argentine Woman
Writer." Ph.D. Dissertation, The Pennsylvania
State University, 1975.

_____. "The Real Circle of Iron: Mothers and
Children, Children and Mothers, in Four Argentine
Novels." Latin American Literary Review 4 (Fall-
Winter 1976): 77-86.

- M -

MA FENG

Eber, Irene. "Images of Women in Recent Chinese Fiction: Do Women Hold Up Half the Sky?" Signs:
Journal of Women in Culture and Society 2 (Autumn
1976): 24-34.

McCARTHY, MARY

Cornwell, Ethel F. "Virginia Woolf, Nathalie Sarraute,
and Mary McCarthy: Three Approaches to Character in Modern Fiction." International Fiction Review 4 (January 1977): 3-10.

Mailer, Norman. "The Case Against McCarthy: A Review of The Group." In Contemporary Women

Novelists: A Collection of Critical Essays, pp. 75-
84. Edited by Patricia Meyer Spacks. Englewood
Cliffs, N.J.: Prentice-Hall, 1977.

Miles, Rosalind. The Fiction of Sex: Themes and
Functions of Sex Difference in the Modern Novel.
New York: Barnes & Noble, 1974.

Myers, Mitzi. "You Can't Catch Me: Mary McCarthy's
Evasive Comedy." Regionalism and the Female
Imagination 3 (Fall 1977 and Winter 1977-1978): 58-
69.

Shinn, Thelma J. Wardrop. "A Study of Women Characters in Contemporary American Fiction 1940-1970."
Ph.D. Dissertation, Purdue University, 1972.

Spacks, Patricia Meyer. "Mary McCarthy: Society's
Demands." In Contemporary Women Novelists: A
Collection of Critical Essays, pp. 85-91. Edited by
Patricia Meyer Spacks. Englewood Cliffs, N.J.:
Prentice-Hall, 1977.

Stock, Irvin. "Mary McCarthy." In American Writers,
pp. 558-584. Edited by Leonard Unger. New York:
Charles Scribner's Sons, 1974.

McCLUNG, NELLIE L.

Fulton, E. Margaret. "Out of Our Past: A New Future." Laurentian University Review 9 (November
1976): [87]-102.

Mathews, Robin. "Le roman engagé: The Social/Politi-
cal Novel in English Canada." Laurentian University
Review 9 (November 1976): [15]-31.

McCULLERS, CARSON

Broughton, Panthea Reid. "Rejection of the Feminine
in Carson McCullers' The Ballad of the Sad Cafe."
Twentieth Century Literature 20 (January 1974): 34-
43.

Carr, Virginia S. "Carson McCullers: The Lonely
Hunter." Paper presented at the MLA meeting,
New York City, December 1976.

_____. The Lonely Hunter: A Biography of Carson
  McCullers.   Garden City, N.Y.: Doubleday, 1975.

Cook, Richard M.   Carson McCullers.   New York:
  Ungar, 1975.

Grauer, Lawrence.   "Carson McCullers." In American
  Writers, vol. 2, pp. 585-608.   Edited by Leonard
  Unger: New York: Scribners, 1974.

Perrine, Laurence.   "Restoring 'A Domestic Dilemma.'"
  Studies in Short Fiction 11, no. 1 (1975): 101-104.

Shapiro, Adrian Michael.   "Carson McCullers: A De-
  scriptive Bibliography." Ph.D. Dissertation, Indiana University, 1977.

Shinn, Thelma J. Wardrop.   "A Study of Women Characters in Contemporary American Fiction 1940-1970."
  Ph.D. Dissertation, Purdue University, 1972.

Smith, Christopher Michael.   "Self and Society: The
  Dialectic of Themes and Forms in the Novels of
  Carson McCullers." Ph.D. Dissertation, University
  of North Carolina at Greensboro, 1976.

Wallace, Harry Joseph.   " 'Lifelessness Is the Only Ab-
  normality': A Study of Love, Sex, Marriage, and
  Family in the Novels of Carson McCullers." Ph.D.
  Dissertation, University of Maryland, 1976.

Whitt, Mary Alice.   "A Study of the Adolescent in Carson McCullers' Fiction." Ph.D. Dissertation, The
  University of Alabama, 1974.

MACDONALD, ROSS

Wolfe, Peter.   Dreamers Who Live Their Dreams: The
  World of Ross Macdonald's Novels.   Bowling Green:
  Bowling Green University Popular Press, 1976.

MacEWEN, GWENDOLYN

Warwick, Ellen D.   "To Seek a Single Symmetry."
  Canadian Literature no. 71 (Winter 1976): 21-34.

McKAY, CLAUDE

Brown, Martha Hursey. "Images of Black Women:
Family Roles in Harlem Renaissance Literature. "
D.A. Dissertation, Carnegie-Mellon University,
1976.

Gayle, Addison, Jr. The Way of the New World: The
Black Novel in America. Garden City, N.Y. :
Anchor Press/Doubleday, 1975.

Ward, Hazel Mae. "The Black Woman as Character:
Images in the American Novel, 1852-1953. " Ph. D.
Dissertation, The University of Texas at Austin,
1977.

MACKENZIE, HENRY

Platzner, Robert L. "Mackenzie's Martyr: The Man
of Feeling as Saintly Fool. " Novel 10 (Fall 1976):
59-64.

MACKEY, MARY

Frym, Gloria. "Tough and Tender: Lady Punk Poets. "
San Francisco Review of Books 3 (October 1977):
29-30.

MacLENNON, HUGH

Fulton, E. Margaret. "Out of Our Past: A New Future. " Laurentian University Review 9 (November
1976): [87]-102.

Mathews, Robin. "Le roman engagé: The Social/Politi-
cal Novel in English Canada. " Laurentian University Review 9 (November 1976): [15]-31.

McNEIL, FLORENCE

Ryan, Sean. "Florence McNeil and Pat Lowther. "
Canadian Literature no. 74 (Autumn 1977): 21-29.

MAHFUZ, NAJIB

Allen, Roger. "Introduction to 'The Chase: A Play by
Najib Mahfuz. ' " Mundus Artium 10, no. 1 (1977):
134-137.

Jayyusi, Salma Khadra. "Two Types of Hero in Contemporary Arabic Literature." Mundus Artium 10, no. 1 (1977): 35-49.

MAIDEN, JENNIFER

Moorhead, Finola. "Goodbye Prince Hamlet: The New Australian Women's Poetry." Meanjin Quarterly 34 (Winter 1975): 169-179.

MAILER, NORMAN

Barnes, Annette. "Norman Mailer: A Prisoner of Sex." Massachusetts Review 13 (Winter-Spring 1972): 269-274.

Djikstra, Bea. "Une rêve américain: Norman Mailer et l'ésthetique de la domination." Les Temps Modernes no. 309 (Avril 1972): 1680-1694.

Masinton, Martha and Charles G. Masinton. "Second-class Citizenship: The Status of Women in Contemporary American Fiction." In What Manner of Woman: Essays in English and American Life and Literature, pp. 297-315. Edited by Marlene Springer. New York: New York University Press, 1977.

Raines, Helon Howell. "Norman Mailer's Sergius O'Shaugnessy, Villain and Victim." Frontiers 2 (Spring 1977): [71]-75.

Widmer, Kingsley. "The Post-Modernist Art of Protest: Kesey and Mailer as American Expressions of Rebellion." Centennial Review 19 (Summer 1975): 121-135.

MALAMUD, BERNARD

Shinn, Thelma J. Wardrop. "A Study of Women Characters in Contemporary American Fiction 1940-1970." Ph.D. Dissertation, Purdue University, 1972.

MALGONKAR, MANOHAR

Dayananda, James Y. "The Image of Women in Manohar Malgonkar's Novels." Journal of South Asian Literature 12 (Spring-Summer 1977): 109-113.

MALKIEL, THERESA SERBER

Maglin, Nan Bauer. "Rebel Women Writers, 1894-1925." Ph.D. Dissertation, Union Graduate School, 1975.

MALLARME, STEPHANE

Hunting, Claudine. "Quelques aspects de la femme dans l'oeuvre poétique de Mallarmé." Claudel Studies 3, no. 1 (1976): 48-63.

Kellogg, Patricia Rossworm. "The Myth of Salome in Symbolist Literature and Art." Ph.D. Dissertation, New York University, 1975.

Reff, Theodore. "The Influence of Flaubert's Queen of Sheba on Later Nineteenth-Century Literature." Romanic Review 65 (November 1974): 249-265.

MALLET-JORIS, FRANÇOISE

Crosland, Margaret. Women of Iron and Velvet: French Women After George Sand. New York: Taplinger, 1976.

MALORY, SIR THOMAS

Kimball, Arthur Samuel. "Merlin's Miscreation and the Repetition Compulsion in Malory's Morte d'Arthur." Literature and Psychology 25, no. 1 (1975): 27-33.

MALRAUX, ANDRE

Robbins, Kittye Delle. "Legends of Good Women: Medieval Images in the Novels of André Malraux." Mélanges Malraux Miscellany 5, no. 2 (1973): 3-8.

MANLEY, MARY de la RIVIERE

Lock, Frederick Peter. "The Dramatic Art of Susanna Centilivre." Ph.D. Dissertation, McMaster University (Canada), 1975.

Mahl, Mary R. and Helene Koon, eds. The Female Spectator: English Women Writers Before 1800. Bloomington and Old Westbury, N.Y.: Indiana University Press and The Feminist Press, 1977.

Woodcock, George. "Foundling Mothers of the English Novel: Mary Manley and Eliza Haywood." Room of One's Own 2, no. 4 (1977): 49-65.

MANN, HEINRICH

Theurer, Walter. "Heinrich Mann and the Femme Fatale." Ph.D. Dissertation, Columbia University, 1976.

MANN, THOMAS

Fass, Barbara. La Belle Dame sans Merci and the Aesthetics of Romanticism. Detroit: Wayne State University Press, 1974.

Knight, Eunice Edna. "The Role of Women in the Don Juan and Faust Literature." Ph.D. Dissertation, Florida State University, 1973.

MANSFIELD, KATHERINE

Benet, Mary Kathleen. Writers in Love: Katherine Mansfield, George Eliot, Colette, and the Men They Lived With. New York: Macmillan, 1977.

Lederman, Marie Jean. "Through the Looking-Glass: Queens, Dreams, Fears in the Fiction of Katherine Mansfield." Women's Studies 5, no. 1 (1977): 35-50.

Meyers, Jeffrey. Married to Genius. New York: Barnes & Noble, 1977.

Michael-Michot, P. "Katherine Mansfield's 'The Fly': An Attempt to Capture the Boss." Studies in Short Fiction 11 (1974): 85-92.

Miles, Rosalind. The Fiction of Sex: Themes and Functions of Sex Difference in the Modern Novel. New York: Barnes & Noble, 1974.

O'Sullivan, Vincent. Katherine Mansfield's New Zealand. London: Muller, 1975.

_____. "The Magnetic Chain: Notes and Approaches to Katherine Mansfield." Landfall 29 (1975): 95-131.

Showalter, Elaine. A Literature of Their Own: British Women Novelists from Brontë to Lessing. Princeton: Princeton University Press, 1977.

Verzea, Ileana. "Katherine Manfield, An Innovator of the Short Story." Revista de Istorie si Theorie Literara 23 (1974): 79-85.

MAO TUN (Shen Yen-ping)

Eber, Irene. "Images of Women in Recent Chinese Fiction: Do Women Hold Up Half the Sky?" Signs: Journal of Women in Culture and Society 2 (Autumn 1976): 24-34.

MARGUERITE DE NAVARRE

Davis, Betty Jean. "The Devisants and Their Personal Relationships in Marguerite de Navarre's Heptaméron." Ph.D. Dissertation, Columbia University, 1974.

Moore, Cassandra Chrones. "The Romantic Triangle: A Study of Expanding Consciousness, (Volumes I and II)." Ph.D. Dissertation, The University of Michigan, 1975.

Romer, Bessie Jane Wells. "The Heptaméron of Marguerite de Navarre: Scriptural Context and Structure." Ph.D. Dissertation, The University of North Carolina at Chapel Hill, 1977.

Schmitz, Betty Ann. "French Women Writers and Their Critics: An Analysis of the Treatment of Women Writers in Selected Histories of French Literature." Ph.D. Dissertation, The University of Wisconsin-Madison, 1977.

MARIE DE FRANCE

Cowling, Samuel T. "The Image of the Tournament in Marie de France's Le Chaitivel." Romance Notes 16 (Spring 1975): 686-691.

Crosland, Margaret. Women of Iron and Velvet: French Women After George Sand. New York: Taplinger, 1976.

Green, Robert B. "Marie de France's 'Laustic': Love's Victory Through Symbolic Expression." Romance Notes 16 (Spring 1975): 695-699.

Hieatt, Constance B. "Eliduc Revisited: John Fowles and Marie de France." English Studies in Canada 3 (Fall 1977): [351]-358.

Ireland, Patrick John. "The Narrative Unity of the Lanval of Marie de France." Studies in Philology 74 (April 1977): 130-145.

MARIVAUX, PIERRE CARLET DE CHAMBLAIN DE

Whatley, Janet. "L'Age équivoque: Marivaux and the Middle-Aged Woman." University of Toronto Quarterly 46 (Fall 1976): 68-82.

MARKANDAYA, KAMALA

Adkins, Joan F. "Kamala Markandaya: Indo-Anglian Conflict as Unity." Journal of South Asian Literature 10 (Fall 1974): 89-101.

Kirkpatrick, Joanna. "Women in Indian-English Literature: The Question of Individuation." Journal of South Asian Literature 12 (Spring-Summer 1977): 121-129.

Larson, Charles R. The Novel in the Third World. Washington, D.C.: Inscape, 1976.

Murad, Orlene. International Fiction Review 4 (January 1977): 73-76. (Review of Nectar in a Sieve.)

Rao, K. S. Narayana. "Love, Sex, Marriage and Morality in Kamala Markandaya's Novels." Osmajia Journal of English Studies 10 (1973): 69-77.

_____. "Religious Elements in Kamala Markandaya's Novels." Ariel: A Review of International English Literature 8 (January 1977): [35]-50.

MARLATT, DAPHNE

Lillard, Charles. Malahat Review no. 38 (April 1976): 148-150. (Review of Steveston.)

MARLOW, CHRISTOPHER

Knight, Eunice Edna. "The Role of Women in the Don Juan and Faust Literature." Ph.D. Dissertation, Florida State University, 1973.

Mirenda, Angela Marie. "The Noble Lie: Selfhood and Tragedy in the Renaissance." Ph.D. Dissertation, The Pennsylvania State University, 1977.

Still, Roger. Love and Death in Renaissance Tragedy. Baton Rouge: Louisiana State University Press, 1976.

MARQUEZ, GARCIA

Levine, Suzanne Jill. "One Hundred Years of Solitude and Pedro Páramo: A Parallel." Books Abroad 47 (Summer 1973): 490-495.

MARRYAT, FLORENCE (Mrs. Florence [Marryat] Church Lean)

Garrison, Dee. "Immoral Fiction in the Late Victorian Library." American Quarterly 28 (Spring 1976): 71-89.

MARSHALL, PAULE

Benston, Kimberly. "Architectural Imagery and Unity in Paule Marshall's Brown Girl, Brownstones." Negro American Literature Forum 9 (Fall 1975): 67-76.

Brown, Lloyd W. "Mannequins and Mermaids--The Contemporary Writer and Sexual Images in the Consumer Culture." Women's Studies 5, no. 1 (1977): 1-12.

Keizs, Marcia. "Themes and Style in the Works of Paule Marshall." Negro American Literature Forum 9 (Fall 1975): 67, 71-76.

Love, Theresa R. "The Black Woman in Afro-American Literature." Paper presented at the Midwest Modern Language Association meeting, Chicago, November 1975. (Mimeographed.)

Reilly, John M. In Contemporary Novelists. Edited by
James Vinson. New York: St. Martin's Press,
1976.

Rosenblatt, Roger. Black Fiction. Cambridge: Harvard University Press, 1974.

Schraufnagel, Noel. From Apology to Protest: The
Black American Novel. Deland, Florida: Everett/
Edwards, 1973.

Schultz, Elizabeth. " 'Free in Fact and at Last': The
Image of the Black Woman in Black American Litera-
ture. " In What Manner of Woman: Essays in Eng-
lish and American Life and Literature, pp. 316-344.
Edited by Marlene Springer. New York: New York
University Press, 1977.

MARSTON, JOHN

Leggatt, Alexander. Citizen Comedy in the Age of
Shakespeare. Toronto: University of Toronto Press,
1973.

Shaw, Sharon K. "Medea on Pegasus: Some Speculations on the Parallel Rise of Women and Melodrama
on the Jacobean Stage. " Ball State University
Forum 14, no. 4 (1973): 13-21.

Still, Roger. Love and Death in Renaissance Tragedy.
Baton Rouge: Louisiana State University Press,
1976.

MARTIN, HELEN R.

Maglin, Nan Bauer. "Rebel Women Writers, 1894-
1925. " Ph.D. Dissertation, Union Graduate School,
1975.

MARTINEAU, HARRIET

Lever, Sir Tresham. "Harriet Martineau and Her
Novel Oliver Weld. " Brontë Society Transactions
16, no. 4 (1974): 270-273.

Moers, Ellen. Literary Women. Garden City, N.Y.:
Doubleday, 1976.

Martínez / 239

Pichanick, Valerie Kossew. "An Abominable Submission: Harriet Martineau's Views on the Role and Place of Woman. " Women's Studies 5, no. 1 (1977): 13-32.

Showalter, Elaine. A Literature of Their Own: British Women Novelists from Brontë to Lessing. Princeton: Princeton University Press, 1977.

Skilton, David. The English Novel: Defoe to the Victorians. New York: Barnes & Noble, 1977.

Tarantelli, Carole Beebe. "The Working Class in the 'Social Problem' Novel: 1830-1855. " Ph. D. Dissertation, Brandeis University, 1975.

Williams, Ione. The Realist Novel in England: A Study of Development. Pittsburgh: University of Pittsburgh Press, 1974.

MARTINEZ, ALFONSO

Sims, Edna N. "El antifeminismo en la literatura española hasta 1560. " Ph. D. Dissertation, Catholic University, 1970.

_____. "The Antifeminist Element in the Works of Alfonso Martínez and Juan Luis Vives. " CLA Journal 18 (September 1974): 52-68.

MARTINEZ RUIZ, JOSE

Ibarra, Fernando. "Clarín y Azorín: El matrimonio y el papel de la mujer española. " Hispania 55 (March 1972): 45-54.

MARTINEZ SIERRA, GREGORIO

O'Connor, Patricia W. "A Spanish Precursor to Women's Lib: The Heroine in Gregorio Martínez Sierra's Theater. " Hispania 55 (December 1972): 865-872.

MATHERS, HELEN M. (Mrs. Helen B. Reeves)

Garrison, Dee. "Immoral Fiction in the Late Victorian Library. " American Quarterly 28 (Spring 1976): 71-89.

MATUTE, ANA MARIE

Diaz, Janet. Ana María Matute. New York: Twayne,
1971.

Hadjopoulos, Theresa Mary. "Four Women Novelists of
Postwar Spain: Matute, Lafôret, Quiroga, and Medio. " Ph. D. Dissertation, Columbia University,
1974.

Jones, Margaret E. W. The Literary World of Ana
María Matute. Lexington: University Press of Kentucky, 1970.

MAUGHAM, SOMERSET

Braendlin, Bonnie Hoover. "The 'New Woman' in the
Bildungsromane of Somerset Maugham, H. G. Wells,
and D. H. Lawrence. " Paper presented at the MLA
meeting, New York City, December 1976.

MAUPASSANT, GUY de

Armstrong, Judith. The Novel of Adultery. New York:
Barnes & Noble, 1976.

MAURIAC, FRANCOIS

Nevo, Natan. "Anna Karénine et Thérèse Desqueyroux:
Parallèles. " Comparative Literature Studies 14
(September 1977): 214-222.

MEAKERS, MARIJANE

Rule, Jane. Lesbian Images. Garden City, N.Y. :
Doubleday, 1975.

MEDIO, DOLORES

Hadjopoulos, Theresa Mary. "Four Women Novelists of
Postwar Spain: Matute, Lafôret, Quiroga, and
Medio. " Ph. D. Dissertation, Columbia University,
1974.

Jones, Margaret E. Dolores Medio. Twayne, 1974.

MELVILLE, HERMAN

Barber, Patricia. "What If Bartleby Were a Woman?"
In The Authority of Experience, pp. [212]-223. Edited by Arlyn Diamond and Lee R. Edwards. Amherst: University of Massachusetts Press, 1977.

Baym, Nina. "Portrayal of Women in American Literature, 1790-1870." In What Manner of Woman: Essays on English and American Life and Literature,
pp. 211-234. Edited by Marlene Springer. New
York: New York University Press, 1977.

Douglas, Ann. The Feminization of American Culture.
New York: Alfred A. Knopf, 1977.

Fryer, Judith. The Faces of Eve: Women in the Nineteenth Century American Novel. New York: Oxford
University Press, 1976.

Kellner, Robert Scott. "Toads and Scorpions: Women
and Sex in the Writings of Herman Melville." Ph.D.
Dissertation, University of Massachusetts, 1977.

MENANDER

Fantham, Elaine. "Sex, Status, and Survival in Hellenistic Athens: A Study of Women in New Comedy."
Phoenix 29 (Spring 1975): 44-74.

MENDOZA, RITA

Sanchez, Rita. "Chicana Writer: Breaking Out of the
Silence." La Cosecha: Literatura y la Mujer Chicana 3, no. 3 (1977): 31-37.

MENKEN, ADAH ISAACS

Watts, Emily Stipes. The Poetry of American Women
from 1632 to 1945. Austin: University of Texas
Press, 1977.

MEREDITH, GEORGE

Armstrong, Judith. The Novel of Adultery. New York:
Barnes & Noble, 1976.

Ball, Patricia M. The Heart's Events: The Victorian
    Poetry of Relationships. London: University of
    London, The Athlone Press, 1976.

Calder, Jenni. Women and Marriage in Victorian Fic-
    tion. London: Thames & Hudson, 1976.

Comstock, Margaret von Szeliski. "George Meredith,
    Virginia Woolf, and Their Feminist Comedy. "
    Ph. D. Dissertation, Stanford University, 1975.

Fernando, Lloyd. "New Women" in the Late Victorian
    Novel. University Park: Pennsylvania State Univer-
    sity Press, 1977.

Fox, Marcia Rose. "The Woman Question in Selected
    Victorian Fiction, 1883-1900. " Ph. D. Dissertation,
    The City University of New York, 1975.

Johnson, Wendell Stacy. Sex and Marriage in Victorian
    Poetry. Ithaca: Cornell University Press, 1975.

Longerbeam, Larry Simpson. "Seduction as Symbolic
    Action: A Study of the Seduction Motif in Six Vic-
    torian Novels. " Ph. D. Dissertation, George Pea-
    body College for Teachers, 1975.

McCullen, M. L. "Handsome Heroes and Healthy Hero-
    ines: Patterns of the Ideal in George Meredith's
    Later Novels. " Cithara 14 (December 1974): 95-106.

McElligott, Mary Bradley. "English Novels of the
    Eighteen-Seventies. " Ph. D. Dissertation, New York
    University, 1975.

Marcus, Jane. " 'Clio in Calliope': History and Myth
    in Meredith's Diana of the Crossways. " Bulletin of
    the New York Public Library 79 (Winter 1976): 167-
    192.

Parrill, Anna S. "Portraits of Ladies. " In Tennessee
    Studies in Literature, pp. 92-99. Knoxville: The
    University of Tennessee Press, 1975.

Rance, Nicholas. The Historical Novel and Popular Pol-
    itics in Nineteenth-Century England. New York:
    Barnes & Noble, 1975.

Reed, John. Victorian Conventions. Athens: Ohio University Press, 1975.

Stevenson, Lionel. "Meredith and the Art of Implication." In The Victorian Experience: The Novelists, pp. 177-201. Edited by Richard A. Levine. Athens: Ohio University Press, 1976.

Williams, David. George Meredith: His Life and Lost Love. London: Hamish Hamilton, 1977.

Wilson, Phillip E. "Affective Coherence, a Principle of Abated Action, and Meredith's Modern Love." Modern Philology 72 (November 1974): 151-171.

Wilt, Judith. "Meredith's Diana: Freedom, Fiction, and the Female." Texas Studies in Literature and Language 18 (Spring 1976): 42-62.

MERIMEE, PROSPER

Fass, Barbara. La Belle Dame sans Merci and the Aesthetics of Romanticism. Detroit: Wayne State University Press, 1974.

MERIWETHER, LOUISE

Harper, Clifford Doyl. "A Study of the Disunity Theme in the Afro-American Experience: An Examination of Five Representative Novels." Ph.D. Dissertation, Saint Louis University, 1974.

Schraufnagel, Noel. From Apology to Protest: The Black American Novel. Deland, Florida: Everett/Edwards, 1973.

Schulz, Elizabeth. " 'Free in Fact and at Last': The Image of the Black Woman in Black American Literature." In What Manner of Woman: Essays in English and American Life and Literature, pp. 316-344. Edited by Marlene Springer. New York: New York University Press, 1977.

MERRIAM, EVE

Epstein, Renee. "Theatre: The Club: A Musical Double Take in Drag." Ms. 5 (March 1977): 34, 36. (Review of The Club.)

Schwartz, L. S. New Republic, 9 October 1976, p. 41. (Review of A Husband's Notes about Her.)

METEYARD, ELIZA

Mitchell, Sally. "Lost Women: Feminist Implications of the Fallen in Works by Forgotten Women Writers of the 1840's." University of Michigan Papers in Women's Studies 1 (June 1974): 110-124.

MEUN, JEAN de

Ferrante, Joan M. Woman as Image in Medieval Literature from the Twelfth Century to Dante. New York: Columbia University Press, 1975.

MIDDLETON, THOMAS

Batchelor, J. B. "The Pattern of Women Beware Women." Yearbook of English Studies 2 (1972): 78-88.

Champion, Larry S. "Tragic Vision in Middleton's Women Beware Women." English Studies 57 (October 1976): 410-424.

Childres, Clare Fooshee. "Feminine Character and Sexual Roles in the Plays of Thomas Middleton (1580-1627)." Ph.D. Dissertation, Northwestern University, 1975.

Duffy, Joseph M. "Madhouse Optics: The Changeling." Comparative Drama 8 (Summer 1974): 184-198.

Hallett, Charles. "The Psychological Drama of Women Beware Women." Studies in English Literature, 1500-1900 12 (Spring 1972): 375-390.

Kistner, A. L. and M. K. "Will, Fate, and the Social Order in Women Beware Women." Essays in Literature 3 (Spring 1976): 17-31.

Kaye, Melanie. "The Sword Philippan: Woman as Hero in Stuart Tragedy." Ph.D. Dissertation, University of California, Berkeley, 1976.

Leggatt, Alexander. Citizen Comedy in the Age of Shakespeare. Toronto: University of Toronto Press, 1973.

McDonald, Margaret Lamb. "The Independent Woman in the Restoration Comedy of Manners." Ph.D. Dissertation, University of Colorado, 1975.

Mulryne, J. R. Introduction to Women Beware Women. New York: Barnes & Noble, 1975.

Still, Roger. Love and Death in Renaissance Tragedy. Baton Rouge: Louisiana State University Press, 1976.

Ure, Peter. Elizabethan and Jacobean Drama. Edited by J. C. Maxwell. New York: Barnes & Noble, 1974.

Wigler, Stephen. "Penitent Brothel Reconsidered: The Place of the Grotesque in Middleton's A Mad World, My Masters." Literature and Psychology 25, no. 1 (1975): 17-25.

MIELKE, MARGARET

Chandonnet, Ann. "Margaret Mielke: Alaska's First Poet Laureate." Alaska Journal 6 (Winter 1976): 12-16.

MIEN YING

Eber, Irene. "Images of Women in Recent Chinese Fiction: Do Women Hold Up Half the Sky?" Signs: Journal of Women in Culture and Society 2 (Autumn 1976): 24-34.

MIQUEIS, RODRIGUES

Kerr, John Austin, Jr. "Some Considerations on Rodrigues Miquéis's 'Leah.'" World Literature Today 51 (Spring 1977): 220-223.

MIHURA, MIGUEL

Davison, Darlyn D. "The Role of the Woman in Miguel Mihura's Plays." Ph.D. Dissertation, The Florida State University, 1974.

MILLAY, EDNA ST. VINCENT

Ash, Adrienne. "Edna St. Vincent Millay: A Re-

Evaluation." Paper presented at the MLA meeting, New York City, December 1976.

Callow, James T. and Robert Reilly. Guide to American Literature from Emily Dickinson to the Present. New York: Barnes & Noble, 1977.

Fetterley, Judith. "Feminist Criticism and New Criticism." Paper presented at the MLA meeting, New York City, December 1976. (Mimeographed.)

Gray, James. "Edna St. Vincent Millay." In American Writers, vol. 3, pp. 122-144. Edited by Leonard Unger. New York: Charles Scribner's Sons, 1974.

Millay at Steepletop. Princeton, N.J.: Films for the Humanities, n.d. (54-minute, 16mm b&w film.)

Perlmutter, Elizabeth P. "A Doll's Heart: The Girl in the Poetry of Edna St. Vincent Millay and Louise Bogan." Twentieth Century Literature 23 (May 1977): 157-179.

"On Writing and Writers." Los Angeles, Calif.: Pacifica Tape Library, 1975.

Watts, Emily Stipes. The Poetry of American Women from 1632 to 1945. Austin: University of Texas Press, 1977.

MILLER, ALICE DUER

Maglin, Nan Bauer. "Rebel Women Writers, 1894-1925." Ph.D. Dissertation, Union Graduate School, 1975.

MILLER, ARTHUR

Bonin, Jane. Major Themes in Prize-Winning American Drama. Metuchen, N.J.: Scarecrow Press, 1975.

MILLICAN, ARTHENIA BATES

Ward, Jerry W. "Legitimate Resources of the Soul: An Interview with Arthenia Bates Millican." Obsidian 3 (Spring 1977): 14-34.

MILNER, RON

Miller, Jeanne-Marie A. "Images of Black Women in Plays by Black Playwrights." CLA Journal 20 (June 1977): 494-507.

MILTON, JOHN

Asals, Heather R. "In Defense of Dalila: Samson Agonistes and the Reformation Theology of the Word." Journal of English and Germanic Philology 74 (April 1975): 183-194.

Brodwin, Leonora Leet. "Milton and the Renaissance Circe." In Milton Studies VI, pp. 21-84. Edited by James D. Simmonds. Pittsburgh: University of Pittsburgh Press, 1975.

Demaray, John G. "Love's Epic Novel in Paradise Lost: A Theatrical Vision of Marriage." Modern Language Quarterly 38 (March 1977): 3-20.

Demetrakopoulos, S. A. "Eve as a Circean and Courtly Fatal Woman." Milton Quarterly 9 (December 1975): 99-107.

Gallagher, Philip J. " 'Real or Allegoric': The Ontology of Sin and Death in Paradise Lost." English Literary Renaissance 6 (Spring 1976): 317-335.

Hartman, Joan. "Milton's Women, I and II." Deland, Florida: Everett/Edwards, n. d. (Cassette nos. 5313, 5314.)

Hutchinson, Mary Anne. "The Devil's Gateway: The Evil Enchantress in Ariosto, Tasso, Spenser, and Milton." Ph. D. Dissertation, Syracuse University, 1975.

Latt, David J. "Raising Virtuous Ladies: The Literary Image and Historical Reality in Seventeenth-century England." In What Manner of Woman: Essays on English and American Life and Literature, pp. 39-64. Edited by Marlene Springer. New York: New York University Press, 1977.

Lewalski, Barbara K. "Milton on Women--Yet Once

More. " In Milton Studies VI, pp. 3-20. Edited by
James D. Simmonds. Pittsburgh: University of
Pittsburgh Press, 1975.

Lindenbaum, Peter. "Lovemaking in Milton's Paradise. "
In Milton Studies VI, pp. 277-306. Edited by James
D. Simmonds. Pittsburgh: University of Pittsburgh
Press, 1975.

Mollenkott, Virginia Ramey. "Some Implications of Milton's Androgynous Muse. " [An abstract of a paper
read at the New England Renaissance Conference.]
Seventeenth-Century News 33 (Fall 1975): 72-73.

Savage, J. B. "Comus and Its Traditions. " English
Literary Renaissance 5 (Winter 1975): 58-80.

MISHIMA YUKIO

Flood, Cynthia. "Images of Women in Modern Japanese
Fiction. " Room of One's Own 1 (Spring 1975): 18-
25.

Ueda, Makoto. Modern Japanese Writers and the Nature
of Literature. Stanford: Stanford University Press,
1976.

MITCHELL, LANGDON

Loudin, Joanne Marie. "The Changing Role of the
Comic Heroine in American Drama from 1900 to
1940. " Ph. D. Dissertation, University of Washington, 1974.

MITCHELL, MARGARET

Seidel, Kathryn Lee. "The Southern Belle: Her Fall
from the Pedestal in Fiction of the Southern Renaissance. " Ph. D. Dissertation, University of Maryland, 1976.

Silver, Nancy. "To Be a Woman: Scarlett O'Hara Revisited: Looking Back at the Books that Taught Me
How to Be a Woman. " Redbook 146 (December
1975): 52, 54, 56, 59.

Wells, Charles E. "The Hysterical Personality and the

Feminine Character: A Study of Scarlett O'Hara."
Comprehensive Psychiatry 17 (March-April 1976):
353-360.

MITFORD, MARY RUSSELL

Doubleday, Neal Frank. Variety of Attempt: British
and American Fiction in the Early Nineteenth Century. Lincoln: University of Nebraska Press, 1976.

MITSUHASHI TAKAJO

Ikuko Atsumi. "Modern Japanese Women Poets: After
the Meiji Restoration." Iowa Review 7 (Spring/Sum-
mer 1976): 227-237.

MIYAMOTO YURIKO

Johnson, Eric W. "Modern Japanese Women Writers."
Literature East and West 8 (March 1974): [90]-102.

Nee, Britt. "Translator's Note." Bulletin of Concerned
Asian Scholars 7 (October-December 1975): 44-46.

Reich, Pauline C. and Atsuko Fukuda, trans. "Japan's
Literary Feminists: The Seito Group." Signs:
Journal of Women in Culture and Society 2 (Autumn
1976): 280-287.

MOFFETT, JUDITH

Bromwich, David. "Verse Chronicle." Hudson Review
30 (Summer 1977): 290-292. (Review essay.)

MOISE, PENINA

Watts, Emily Stipes. The Poetry of American Women
from 1632 to 1945. Austin: University of Texas
Press, 1977.

MOIX, ANA MARIA

Jones, Margaret E. W. "Ana María Moix: Literary
Structures and the Enigmatic Nature of Reality."
Journal of Spanish Studies: Twentieth Century 4
(Fall 1976): 105-116.

MOLETTE, BARBARA and CARLTON

Arata, Esther S. and Nicholas J. Rotoli. Black American Playwrights, 1800 to the Present: A Bibliography. Metuchen, N.J.: Scarecrow Press, 1976.

Oliver, Edith. "Off Broadway: The N. E. C. Back in Stride." New Yorker, 30 January 1971, p. 54, 56-57.

Riley, Clayton. "My Quarrels Notwithstanding, I Liked Them." New York Times, 7 February 1971, II, p. 3.

MOLIERE

Albanese, Ralph, Jr. "Pedagogie et didactisme dans L'école des femmes." Romance Notes 16 (August 1974): 114-123.

Boisaubin, Elisabeth Ann. "Identity and Difference in English and French Comedy: 1659-1722." Ph.D. Dissertation, Stanford University, 1975.

Dreyfuss, Cecilia Anne Stiborik. "Femina sapiens in Drama: Aeschylus to Grillparzer." Ph.D. Dissertation, The University of Michigan, 1975.

Knight, Eunice Edna. "The Role of Women in the Don Juan and Faust Literature." Ph.D. Dissertation, Florida State University, 1973.

Knutson, Harold C. Molière: An Archetypal Approach. Toronto: University of Toronto Press, 1976.

Suther, Judith D. "The Tricentennial of Molière's Femmes savantes." French Review 45 (Special Issue, No. 4, Spring 1972): 31-38.

Uber, David Merrill. "Family Structure in Molière's Theater." Ph.D. Dissertation, Rice University, 1977.

Zimmerman, Eugenia Noik. "The Proud Princess Gets Her Comeuppance: Structures of Patriarchal Order." Canadian Review of Comparative Literature 3 (Fall 1976): [253]-268.

MONNET, ANNE-MARIE

Bleuzé, Ruth Allen. "Romancières et Critiques: du Prix Fémina, 1904-1968." Ph.D. Dissertation, University of Colorado at Boulder, 1977.

MONTAGU, LADY MARY WORTLEY

Fritz, Paul and Richard Morton, eds. Woman in the Eighteenth Century and Other Essays. Toronto: Samuel Stevens Hakkert, 1976.

LaJoy, Maureen. "No Laughing Matter: Women and Humor." Women 5, no. 1 (1976): 6-9.

Spacks, Patricia Meyer. Imagining a Self: Autobiography and Novel in Eighteenth-Century England. Cambridge: Harvard University Press, 1976.

MONTAGUE, ELIZABETH

Dobbs, Jeannine. "The Blue-Stockings: Getting It Together." Frontiers 1 (Winter 1976): 81-93.

MONTALES, EUGENIO

Cambon, Glauco. "The New Montale." Books Abroad 45 (Autumn 1971): 639-645.

MONTGOMERY, L. M.

Willis, Lesley. "The Bogus Ugly Duckling: Anne Shirley Unmasked." Dalhousie Review 56 (Summer 1976): [247]-251.

MOODIE, SUSANNA

Mathews, Robin. "Le roman engagé: The Social/Political Novel in English Canada." Laurentian University Review 9 (November 1976): [15]-31.

MOODY, ANNE

Abrahams, Roger D. "Negotiating Respect: Patterns of Presentation Among Black Women." Journal of American Folklore 88 (January-March 1975): 58-80.

Butterfield, Stephen. Black Autobiography in America. Amherst: University of Massachusetts Press, 1974.

Kent, George E. "The Radical Strain in Black Autobiography." Paper presented at the Midwest Modern Language meeting, Chicago, November 1975.

Spacks, Patricia Meyer. "Reflecting Women." Yale Review 63 (October 1973): 26-42.

MOODY, WILLIAM VAUGHN

Gottlieb, Lois C. "The Perils of Freedom: The New Woman in Three American Plays of the 1900's." Canadian Review of American Studies 6 (Spring 1975): 84-98.

MOORE, BRIAN

Grosskurth, Phyllis. "A Woman Is a Woman Is a Woman." Canadian Literature no. 72 (Spring 1977): 77-80. (Review of The Doctor's Wife.)

McSweeney, Kerry. "Brian Moore: Past and Present." Critical Quarterly 18 (Summer 1976): 53-66.

Marshall, Douglas. "Toujours le Moore." Books in Canada 5 (October 1976): 8-9. (Review of The Doctor's Wife.)

Staines, David. "Observance Without Belief." Canadian Literature no. 73 (Summer 1977): 8-24.

MOORE, GEORGE

Burkhart, Charles. "George Moore and His Critics." Literature in Transition 20, no. 4 (1977): 199-203.

Fernando, Lloyd. "New Women" in the Late Victorian Novel. University Park: Pennsylvania State University Press, 1977.

Hoffeld, Laura Diamond. "The Servant Heroine in 18th and 19th Century British Fiction: The Social Reality and Its Image in the Novel." Ph.D. Dissertation, New York University, 1975.

Longerbeam, Larry Simpson. "Seduction as Symbolic
Action: A Study of the Seduction Motif in Six Vic-
torian Novels." Ph.D. Dissertation, George Peabody
College for Teachers, 1975.

Newell, Kenneth B. " 'The Wedding Gown' Group in
George Moore's The Untilled Field." Eire-Ireland
8 (Winter 1973): 70-83.

Reed, John R. Victorian Conventions. Athens: Ohio
University Press, 1975.

Solomen, Albert J. "The Bird Girls of Ireland." Colby
College Quarterly 10 (March 1974): 259-269.

MOORE, MARIANNE

Brinnin, John Malcolm and Bill Read, eds. Twentieth
Century Poetry: American and British (1900-1970),
2nd ed. New York: McGraw-Hill, 1970.

Callow, James T. and Robert Reilly. Guide to American Literature from Emily Dickinson to the Present.
New York: Barnes & Noble, 1977.

Hadas, Pamela White. Marianne Moore: Poet of Affec-
tion. Syracuse: Syracuse University Press, 1977.

Juhasz, Suzanne. Naked and Fiery Forms: Modern
American Poetry by Women, A New Tradition. New
York: Harper & Row, 1976.

Newlin, Margaret. " 'Unhelpful Hymen!': Marianne
Moore and Hilda Doolittle." Essays in Criticism
27 (July 1977): 216-230.

Watts, Emily Stipes. The Poetry of American Women
from 1632 to 1945. Austin: University of Texas
Press, 1977.

MOORSOM, SASHA

Johnson, Marigold. Times Literary Supplement, 11 June
1976, p. 689. (Review of Lavender Burning.)

MORAVIA, ALBERTO

Cottrell, Jane E. Alberto Moravia. New York: Frederick Ungar, 1974.

Ross, Joan and Donald Freed. The Existentialism of Alberto Moravia. Carbondale and Edwardsville: Southern Illinois University Press, 1972.

Shriver, Margaret M. "Madame Bovary versus The Woman of Rome." Nineteenth-Century French Studies 1 (September 1973): 197-210.

MORE, HANNAH

Bodek, Evelyn Gordon. "Salonières and Bluestockings: Educated Obsolescence and Germinating Feminism." Feminist Studies 3 (Spring-Summer 1976): 183-199.

Dobbs, Jeannine. "The Blue-Stockings: Getting It Together." Frontiers 1 (Winter 1976): 81-93.

Mahl, Mary R. and Helen Koon, eds. The Female Spectator: English Women Writers Before 1800. Bloomington and Old Westbury, N.Y.: Indiana University Press and The Feminist Press, 1977.

MORENO, DORINDA

Sanchez, Rita. "Chicana Writer: Breaking Out of the Silence." La Cosecha: Literatura y la Mujer Chicana 3, no. 3 (1977): 31-37.

MORGAN, CLAIRE

Rule, Jane. Lesbian Images. Garden City, N.Y.: Doubleday, 1975.

MORGAN, ROBIN

Cooper, Helen. "Lust for Deliverance." Ms. 5 (March 1977): 47-48. (Review of Lady of the Beasts.)

Grimstad, Kirsten and Susan Rennie, interviewers. "Adrienne Rich and Robin Morgan Talk About Poetry and Women's Culture." In The New Woman's Survival Sourcebook, pp. 106-111. Edited by Kirsten

Grimstad and Susan Rennie. New York: Alfred A. Knopf, 1975.

Gustafson, Richard. " 'Time Is a Waiting Woman': New Poetic Icons. " Midwest Quarterly 16 (April 1975): 318-327.

Parini, Jay. "The Small Valleys of Our Living. " Poetry 130 (August 1977): 293-303. (Review of Lady of the Beasts.)

MORI MARI

Johnson, Eric W. "Modern Japanese Women Writers. " Literature East and West 8 (March 1974): [90]-102.

MORRIS, WILLIAM

Balch, Dennis R. "Guenevere's Fidelity to Arthur in 'The Defence of Guenevere' and 'King Arthur's Tomb.' " Victorian Poetry 13 (Fall-Winter 1975): 61-70.

Black, Judith Booher. "A Critical Look at William Morris' Guenevere. " D.A. Dissertation, University of Miami, 1975.

Fass, Barbara. La Belle Dame sans Merci and the Aesthetics of Romanticism. Detroit: Wayne State University Press, 1974.

Strauss, Sylvia. "Women in 'Utopia.' " South Atlantic Quarterly 75 (Winter 1976): 115-131.

MORRIS, WRIGHT

Crump, G. B. "D. H. Lawrence and the Immediate Present: Kurt Vonnegut, Jr. , Ken Kesey, and Wright Morris. " D. H. Lawrence Review 10 (Summer 1977): 103-141.

MORRISON, TONI

Bell, Roseann P. Obsidian 2 (Winter 1976): 93-95. (Review of Sula.)

Bischoff, Joan. "The Novels of Toni Morrison: Studies

in Thwarted Sensitivity." Studies in Black Literature 6 (Fall 1975): 21-23.

Chafe, William H. "Sex and Race: The Analogy of Social Control." Massachusetts Review 18 (Spring 1977): 147-176.

Contemporary Authors, 29/32.

"Conversation with Alice Childress and Toni Morrison." Black Creation 6 (Annual 1974-1975): 90-92.

David, Faith. Harvard Advocate 107, no. 4 (1974): 61-62. (Review of Sula.)

Frederick, Earl. Nation, 19 November 1977, p. 536. (Review of Song of Solomon.)

Harris, Jessica. "Toni Morrison." Essence 7 (December 1976): 54+.

Jefferson, Margo. Newsweek, 12 September 1977, pp. 93, 96. (Review of Song of Solomon.)

Lardner, Susan. New Yorker, 7 November 1977, p. 217. (Review of Song of Solomon.)

Martin, Odette C. "The Novels of Toni Morrison: Sula." First World 1 (Winter 1977): 34-44.

Price, Reynolds. New York Times Book Review, 11 September 1977, p. 1. (Review of Song of Solomon.)

Royster, Philip M. "The Novels of Toni Morrison: The Bluest Eye." First World 1 (Winter 1977): 34-44.

Schulz, Elizabeth. " 'Free in Fact and at Last': The Image of the Black Woman in Black American Literature." In What Manner of Woman: Essays in English and American Life and Literature, pp. 316-344. Edited by Marlene Springer. New York: New York University Press, 1977.

Simama, Jabari. "Acute Depiction of Bourgeois Reality." First World 1 (Winter 1977): 45-48. (Review of Song of Solomon.)

Smith, Cynthia J. "Black Fiction by Black Females."
Cross Currents 26 (Fall 1976): 340-343. (Review
of Sula.)

Stepto, Robert. " 'Intimate Things in Place': A Conversation with Toni Morrison." Massachusetts Review 18 (Autumn 1977): 473-489.

Wigan, Angela. "Native Daughter." Time, 12 September 1977, p. 76. (Review of Song of Solomon.)

MORTIMER, PENELOPE

Little, Judy. "Satirizing the Norm: Comedy in Women's Fiction." Regionalism and the Female Imagination 3 (Fall 1977 and Winter 1977-1978): 38-49.

Nichols, Mariana de Vinci. "Women on Women: The
Looking Glass Novel." Denver Quarterly 11 (Autumn
1976): 1-13.

Stephens, Evelyn Delores B. "The Novel of Personal
Relationships: A Study of Three Contemporary
British Women Novelists." Ph.D. Dissertation,
Emory University, 1976.

Times Literary Supplement, 24 September 1971, p. 1137.
(Review of The Home.)

West, Rebecca. "And They All Lived Unhappily Ever
After." Times Literary Supplement, 26 July 1974,
p. 779. (Review of Long Distance.)

MOWATT, MRS

Curry, Jane Anne. "Women as Subjects and Writers of
Nineteenth Century American Humor." Ph.D. Dissertation, The University of Michigan, 1975.

Hull, Raymona E. " 'Scribbling' Females and Serious
Males: Hawthorne's Comments from Abroad on
Some American Authors." Nathaniel Hawthorne
Journal (1975): 35-58.

MUKHERJEE, BHARATI

Klass, Rosanne. "Indian Wife Lives Soap-Opera Life."
Ms. (October 1975): 83-88. (Review of Wife.)

Ricks, Christopher. New York Review of Books, 9
March 1972, p. 23. (Review of The Tiger's Daughter.)

Sandler, Linda. "Violence as a Device for Problem-Solving." Saturday Night, October 1975, pp. 75-76.
(Review of The Tiger's Daughter and Wife.)

MULOCK, DINAH see CRAIK, DINAH MULOCK

MUNDT, THEODOR

Sammons, Jeffrey. "Theodor Mundt and Women's Heroism in Early Nineteenth-Century Germany." Yale
University Gazette 47 (1972): 109-111.

MUNRO, ALICE

Allentuck, Marcia. "Resolution and Independence in the
Work of Alice Munro." World Literature Written
in English 16 (November 1977): 340-343.

Authors in the News, vol. 2. Detroit: Gale Research,
1976, p. 210.

Dobbs, Kildare. "New Directions for Alice Munro."
Saturday Night (July 1974): 28.

Irvine, Lorna Marie. "Hostility and Reconciliation:
The Mother in English Canadian Fiction." Ph.D.
Dissertation, The American University, 1977.

Macdonald, Rae McCarthy. "A Madman Loose in the
World: The Vision of Alice Munro." Modern Fiction Studies 22 (Autumn 1976): 365-374.

Monaghan, David. "Confinement and Escape in Alice
Munro's 'The Flats Road.'" Studies in Short Fiction 14 (Spring 1977): 165-168.

MURASAKI SHIKIBU

Ikuko Atsumi. "Modern Japanese Women Poets: After
the Meiji Restoration." Iowa Review 7 (Spring/
Summer 1976): 227-237.

Mercier, Michel. Le roman féminin. Paris: P.U.F.,
1976.

Seidensticker, Edward G. Introduction to The Tale of Genji by Murasaki Shikibu. New York: Alfred A. Knopf, 1976.

_____. "Murasaki Shikibu and Her Diary and Her Other Writings." Literature East and West 8 (March 1974): [1]-7.

Ury, Marian. "The Complete Genji." Harvard Journal of Asiatic Studies 37 (June 1977): 135-182.

Yu, Diana, trans. "The Tale of Genji and 'The Song of Enduring Woe.'" Renditions, no. 5 (Autumn 1975): 38-49.

MURDOCH, IRIS

Goshgarian, Gary. "Feminist Values in the Novels of Iris Murdoch." Revue des Langues Vivantes 40 (1974): 522, 526-527.

Henderson, Gloria Ann Mason. "Dionysus and Apollo: Iris Murdoch and Love." Ph.D. Dissertation, Georgia State University School of Arts and Sciences, 1974.

Kmetz, Gail. "People Don't Do Such Things: Business-as-Usual in the Novels of Iris Murdoch." Ms. 5 (July 1976): 70-72, 85-87.

Kuehl, Linda. "Iris Murdoch: The Novelist as Magician/The Magician as Artist." In Contemporary Women Novelists: A Collection of Critical Essays, pp. 92-107. Edited by Patricia Meyer Spacks. Englewood Cliffs, N.J.: Prentice-Hall, 1977.

Little, Judy. "Satirizing the Norm: Comedy in Women's Fiction." Regionalism and the Female Imagination 3 (Fall 1977 and Winter 1977-78): 39-49.

Miles, Rosalind. The Fiction of Sex: Themes and Functions of Sex Difference in the Modern Novel. New York: Barnes & Noble, 1974.

Obumselu, Ben. "Iris Murdoch and Sartre." ELH 42 (Summer 1975): 296-317.

Packer, P. A. "The Theme of Love in the Novels of Iris Murdoch." Durham University Journal 38 (June 1977): 217-224.

Randall, Julia. "Against Consolation: Some Novels of Iris Murdoch." Hollins Critic 13 (February 1976): 1-15.

Sullivan, Zohreh Tawakuli. "Enchantment and the Demonic in Iris Murdoch: The Flight from the Enchanter." Midwest Quarterly 16 (April 1975): 276-297.

_____. "Iris Murdoch's Self-Conscious Gothicism: The Time of the Angels." Arizona Quarterly 33 (Spring 1977): [47]-60.

Tominaga, Thomas T. and Wilma Schneidermeyer. Iris Murdoch and Muriel Spark: A Bibliography. Metuchen, N.J.: Scarecrow Press, 1976.

West, Rebecca. "And They All Lived Unhappily Ever After." Times Literary Supplement, 26 July 1974, p. 779.

MURFREE, MARY NOAILLES

Carleton, Reese Monroe. "Conflict in Direction: Realistic, Romantic, and Romanticistic Elements in the Fiction of Mary N. Murfree." Ph.D. Dissertation, The University of Wisconsin-Madison, 1976.

_____. "Mary Noailles Murfree (1850-1922): An Annotated Bibliography." American Literary Realism, 1870-1910 7 (Autumn 1974): 293-378.

Nilles, Mary. "Craddock's Girls: A Look at Some Unliberated Women." Markham Review 3 (October 1972): 74-77.

MUSIL, ROBERT

Titche, Leon, Jr. "The Concept of the Hermaphrodite: Agathe and Ulrich in Musil's Novel Der Mann ohne Eigenschaften." German Life and Letters 23 (1969/70): 160-168.

MUSSET, ALFRED de

Banoun, Merilee. "The Dialectic of Male and Female Principles in the Theatre of Alfred de Musset." Ph. D. Dissertation, The Catholic University of America, 1977.

Fairchild, Sharon L. "Les Personnages de femmes dans huit pièces de Musset." Nineteenth-Century French Studies 4 (Spring 1976): 213-219.

Rees, Margaret A. Alfred de Musset. New York: Twayne, 1971.

- N -

NADEN, CONSTANCE

Smith, Philip E., II and Susan Harris Smith. "Constance Naden: Late Victorian Feminist Poet and Philosopher." Victorian Poetry 15 (Winter 1977): 367-370.

NARAYAN, R. K.

Thwaite, Anthony. New York Times Book Review, 20 June 1976, p. 6. (Review of The Painter of Signs.)

Updike, John. New Yorker, 5 July 1976, p. 81. (Review of The Painter of Signs.)

Zimmerman, P. D. Newsweek, 4 July 1976, p. 99. (Review of The Painter of Signs.)

NEAL, JOHN

Scheick, William J. "Power, Authority, and Revolutionary Impulse in John Neal's Rachel Dyer." Studies in American Fiction 4 (Autumn 1976): 143-155.

NEKROSOV, NIKOLAI

"Nikolai Nekrosov: Poet Who Sang of the Woman's Lot." Soviet Woman no. 1 (January 1972): 32-33.

262 / More Women in Literature

NERVAL, GERARD de

Carroll, Robert C. "Romanesque Seduction in Nerval's
Sylvie. " Nineteenth-Century French Studies 5
(Spring-Summer 1977): 222-235.

Fass, Barbara. La Belle Dame sans Merci and the Aesthetics of Romanticism. Detroit: Wayne State University Press, 1974.

NEWMAN, FRANCES

Seidel, Kathryn Lee. "The Southern Belle: Her Fall
from the Pedestal in Fiction of the Southern Renaissance. " Ph.D. Dissertation, University of Maryland, 1976.

NGUGI, JAMES

Gachukia, Eddah. "A Review of the Role of Women in
James Ngugi's Novels. " Busara (University College,
Nairobe) 3, no. 4 (1972): 30-33.

Larson, Charles R. The Emergence of African Fiction.
Bloomington and London: Indiana University Press,
1971.

Rauch, Erika. "The Central Male-Female Relationships
in The River Between and 'Mission to Kala. ' "
Busara 7 (1975): 42-54.

Rice, Michael. "The River Between--A Discussion. "
English in Africa 2 (September 1975): 11-21.

NIN, ANAÏS

"Anaïs Nin. " North Hollywood: The Center for Cassette Studies, n.d.

Authors in the News, vol. 2. Detroit: Gale Research,
1976, pp. 213-214.

Brians, Paul. "Sexuality and the Opposite Sex: Variations on a Theme by Théophile Gautier and Anaïs
Nin. " Essays in Literature 4 (Spring 1977): 122-
137.

Davidson, Anne Morrissett. "Anaïs Nin vs. Gore Vidal." Village Voice, 17 January 1977, p. 80-82.

Ekbert, Kent. "The Importance of Under a Glass Bell." Under the Sign of Pisces 8 (Spring 1977): 4-18.

Fracchia, Charles A. "Anaïs Nin: Portrait of an Artist as Earth Mother." San Francisco Review of Books 1 (June 1975): 11-17.

Hinz, Evelyn J. "Anaïs Nin: A Reader and the Writer." Canadian Review of American Studies 6 (Spring 1975): 118-127. (Reviews of Anaïs Nin Reader and The Diary of Anaïs Nin: 1947-1955.)

Jason, Philip K. "Anaïs Nin." Deland, Florida: Everett/Edwards, n.d. (Cassette no. 5502.)

Madden, Deanna Kay. "Laboratory of the Soul: The Influence of Psychoanalysis on the Work of Anaïs Nin." Ph.D. Dissertation, University of Miami, 1975.

Morrell, Carol. "Anaïs Nin and the Identity of Women." Women Speaking 3 (January 1973): 18-19.

Spencer, Sharon. "Anaïs Nin: Articulate Dreams." Paper presented at the MLA meeting, San Francisco, December 1975.

_____. "The Art of Collage in Anaïs Nin's Writing." Studies in the Twentieth Century 16 (Fall 1975): 1-11.

Sukenick, Lynn. "Anaïs Nin: The World of Feeling." Paper presented at the MLA meeting, San Francisco, December 1975.

Wakoski, Diane. "The Craft of Plumbers, Carpenters and Mechanics: A Tribute to Anaïs Nin." American Poetry Review, January-February 1973, pp. 46-47.

Walker, Alice. "Anaïs Nin: 1903-1977." Ms. 5 (April 1977): 46.

Zaller, Robert, ed. A Casebook on Anaïs Nin. New York: New American Library, 1974.

NKABINDE, THULANI

Shange, Ntozake. "Black Women Writing/Where Truth
Becomes Hope/Cuz It's Real." Margins no. 17
(February 1975): 50-54, 59-60.

NOGAMI YAEKO

Johnson, Eric W. "Modern Japanese Women Writers."
Literature East and West 8 (March 1974): [90]-102.

NOKAN, CHARLES

Tidjani-Serpos, Nouréini. "L'image de la femme afri-
caine dans le théatre ivoirien: Le cas de Bernard
Dadié et de Charles Nokan." Révue de Litterature
Comparée 48 (1974): 455-461.

NORMAN, JOHN

Lanahan, William. "Slave Girls and Strategies: John
Norman's Gor Series." Algol 12 (November 1974):
22-26.

NORRIS, FRANK

Banta, Martha. "They Shall Have Faces, Minds, and
(One Day) Flesh: Women in Late Nineteenth-century
and Early Twentieth-century American Literature."
In What Manner of Woman: Essays on English and
American Life and Literature, pp. 235-270. Edited
by Marlene Springer. New York: New York University Press, 1977.

McElrath, Joseph R., Jr. "Frank Norris's Vandover
and the Brute: Narrative Technique and the Socio-
Critical Viewpoint." Studies in American Fiction 4
(Spring 1976): 27-43.

NORRIS, KATHLEEN

Maglin, Nan Bauer. "Rebel Women Writers, 1894-
1925." Ph.D. Dissertation, Union Graduate School,
1975.

NOVACK, CAROL

Moorhead, Finola. "Goodbye Prince Hamlet: The New

Australian Women's Poetry." Meanjin Quarterly 34
(Winter 1975): 169-179.

NOVALIS (Friedrich von Hardenberg)

Sheeran, Joan Garner. "Women and the Freedom-to-Be
in Selected Works of Schiller and the Romantics."
Ph.D. Dissertation, University of Minnesota, 1976.

NUKADA, PRINCESS

Ikuko Atsumi. "Modern Japanese Women Poets: After
the Meiji Restoration." Iowa Review 7 (Spring/Sum-
mer 1976): 227-237.

NWAPA, FLORA

Brown, Lloyd W. "The African Woman as Writer."
Canadian Journal of African Studies 9, no. 3 (1975):
493-502.

Emenyonu, Ernest N. "Who Does Flora Nwapa Write
For?" African Literature Today 7 (1975): 28-33.

- O -

OATES, JOYCE CAROL

Allen, Mary. The Necessary Blankness: Women in
Major American Fiction of the Sixties. Urbana:
University of Illinois Press, 1976.

Authors in the News, vol. 1. Detroit: Dale Research,
1976, pp. 365-366.

Avant, J. A. "An Interview with Joyce Carol Oates."
Library Journal, 15 November 1972, pp. 3711-3712.

Barza, Steven. "Joyce Carol Oates: Naturalism and
the Aberrant Response." Paper presented at the
MLA meeting, New York City, December 1976.
(Mimeographed.)

Bender, Eileen Teper. "The Artistic Vision, Theory

and Practice of Joyce Carol Oates." Ph.D. Dissertation, University of Notre Dame, 1977.

_____. "Autonomy and Influence: Joyce Carol Oates' Marriage and Infidelities." Soundings 58 (Fall 1975): 390-406.

Burwell, Rose Marie. "Joyce Carol Oates' First Novel." Canadian Literature no. 73 (Summer 1977): 54-67.

_____. "The Process of Individuation as Narrative Structure: Joyce Carol Oates' Do with Me What You Will." Critique 17 (December 1975): 93-106.

Cooke, Michael G. "Recent Novels: Women Bearing Violence." Yale Review 66 (Autumn 1976): 146-155. (Review of The Assassins.)

Denne, Constance Ayres. "Joyce Carol Oates." Deland, Florida: Everett/Edwards, n.d. (Cassette no. 5511.)

Dike, Donald A. "The Aggressive Victim in the Fiction of Joyce Carol Oates." Greyfriar 15 (1974): 13-29.

Engel, Marian. New York Times Book Review, 24 November 1974, p. 7. (Review of The Goddess and Other Women.)

Fossum, R. H. "Only Control: The Novels of Joyce Carol Oates." Studies in the Novel 7 (Summer 1975): 285-297.

Gibson, Graeme. "Face to Face with Joyce Carol Oates." Maclean's 87 (April 1974): 42-43, 56-60.

Godwin, Gail. "An Oates Scrapbook." North American Review 256 (Winter 1971-1972): 67-70.

Goodman, Charlotte. "Images of American Rural Women in the Novel." University of Michigan Papers in Women's Studies 1 (June 1975): 57-70.

_____. "Women and Madness in the Fiction of Joyce Carol Oates." Women & Literature 5 (Fall 1977): 17-28.

Little, Judy. "Satirizing the Norm: Comedy in Women's Fiction. " Regionalism and the Female Imagination 3 (Fall 1977 and Winter 1977-78): 39-49.

McLaughlin, Marilou Briggs. "The Love Dialectic. " Ph. D. Dissertation, State University of New York at Binghamton, 1976.

Masinton, Martha and Charles G. Masinton. "Second-class Citizenship: The Status of Women in Contemporary American Fiction. " In What Manner of Woman: Essays in English and American Life and Literature, pp. 297-315. Edited by Marlene Springer. New York: New York University Press, 1977.

Mazzaro, Jerome. "Oh Women, Oh Men!" Modern Poetry Studies 1, no. 1 (1970): 39-41. (Review of Anonymous Sins and Other Poems.)

Nichols, Marianna de Vinci. "Women on Women: The Looking Glass Novel. " Denver Quarterly 11 (Autumn 1976): 1-13.

Park, Sue Simpson. "A Study in Counterpoint: Joyce Carol Oates's 'How I Contemplated the World from the Detroit House of Correction and Began My Life Over Again. ' " Modern Fiction Studies 22 (Summer 1976): 213-224.

People, 15 November 1976, pp. 66-68.

Pickering, Samuel F. , Jr. "The Short Stories of Joyce Carol Oates. " Georgia Review 28 (Summer 1974): 218-226.

Pinsker, Sanford. "Suburban Molesters: Joyce Carol Oates' Expensive People. " Midwest Quarterly 19 (October 1977): 89-103.

Shinn, Thelma J. Wardrop. "A Study of Women Characters in Contemporary American Fiction 1940-1970." Ph. D. Dissertation, Purdue University, 1972.

Siegel, Gerald. "Violent Vision: Joyce Carol Oates' Them. " Paper presented at the MLA meeting, New York City, December 1976. (Mimeographed.)

268 / More Women in Literature

Stein, Karen F. "The Lady and the Demon: Some
Models of Self-Definition in Joyce Carol Oates."
Paper presented at the MLA meeting, New York
City, December 1976.

Stevens, Cynthia C. "The Imprisoned Imagination: The
Family in the Fiction of Joyce Carol Oates, 1960-
1970." Ph.D. Dissertation, University of Illinois,
Urbana-Champaign, 1974.

Thurman, Judith. "Joyce Carol Oates: Caviar and a
Big Mac." Ms. (February 1976): 42-43. (Review
of The Assassins.)

Wegs, Joyce M. " 'Don't You Know Who I Am?': The
Grotesque in Oates' 'Where Are You Going, Where
Have You Been?' " Journal of Narrative Technique
5 (January 1975): 64-72.

O'BRIEN, EDNA

Eckley, Grace. Edna O'Brien. Cranbury, N.J.: Bucknell University Press, 1974.

_____. "The Mother in Edna O'Brien's Fiction."
Paper presented at the MLA meeting, New York
City, December 1976. (Mimeographed.)

Kraft, Eugene. Studies in Short Fiction 12 (Summer
1975): 291-292. (Review of A Scandalous Woman and
Other Stories.)

Miles, Rosalind. The Fiction of Sex: Themes and
Functions of Sex Difference in the Modern Novel.
New York: Barnes & Noble, 1974.

O'Brien, Edna. "Night Thoughts on Love." Cosmopolitan 180 (May 1976): 60, 70.

_____. "Three Loves of Childhood--Irish Thoughts
by Edna O'Brien." Listener, 3 June 1976, pp. 701-
702. (Interview of Ludovic Kennedy.)

Scanlon, John. "States of Exile: Alienation and Art in
the Novels of Brian Moore and Edna O'Brien."
Ph.D. Dissertation, The University of Iowa, 1975.

Stephens, Evelyn Delores B. "The Novel of Personal
Relationships: A Study of Three Contemporary
British Women Novelists. " Ph.D. Dissertation,
Emory University, 1976.

West, Rebecca. "And They All Lived Unhappily Ever
After." Times Literary Supplement, 26 July 1974,
p. 779.

O'CASEY, SEAN

Armstrong, W. A. "Integrity of Juno and the Paycock. "
Modern Drama 17 (March 1974): 1-9.

Benstock, Bernard. Paycocks and Others: Sean O'Casey's World. New York: Barnes & Noble, 1976.

Durbach, Errol. "Peacocks and Mothers: Theme and
Dramatic Metaphor in O'Casey's Juno and the Paycock. " Modern Drama 15 (May 1972): 15-25.

O'Donnell, Beatrice. "Synge and O'Casey Women: A
Study in Strong Mindedness. " Ph.D. Dissertation,
Michigan State University, 1976.

O'CONNOR, FLANNERY

Callow, James T. and Robert Reilly. Guide to American Literature from Emily Dickinson to the Present.
New York: Barnes & Noble, 1977.

Gossett, Thomas F. "Flannery O'Connor on Her Fiction." Southwest Review 59, no. 1 (1975): 34-42.

Howell, Elmo. "The Developing Art of Flannery O'Connor." Arizona Quarterly 29 (1975): 266-276.

Hyman, Stanley Edgar. "Flannery O'Connor. " In
American Writers, vol. 3, pp. 337-360. Edited by
Leonard Unger. New York: Charles Scribner's
Sons, 1974.

Maida, Patricia D. "Light and Enlightenment in Flannery O'Connor's Fiction. " Studies in Short Fiction
13 (Winter 1976): 31-36.

Shinn, Thelma J. Wardrop. "A Study of Women

Characters in Contemporary American Fiction 1940-1970. " Ph.D. Dissertation, Purdue University, 1972.

Walker, Alice. "Beyond the Peacock: The Reconstruction of Flannery O'Connor. " Ms. (December 1975): 77-79, 102, 104-106.

OGOT, GRACE

Kilson, Marion. "Women and African Literature. " Journal of African Studies 4 (Summer 1977): 161-166.

OKAMOTO KANOKO

Johnson, Eric W. "Modern Japanese Women Writers. " Literature East and West 8 (March 1974): [90]-102.

Reich, Pauline C. and Atsuko Fukuda, trans. "Japan's Literary Feminists: The Seito Group. " Signs: Journal of Women in Culture and Society 2 (Autumn 1976): 280-287.

OLDENBOURG, ZOE

Bleuzé, Ruth Allen. "Romancières et Critiques: Etude du Prix Fémina, 1904-1968. " Ph.D. Dissertation, University of Colorado at Boulder, 1977.

OLIPHANT, MARGARET

Cunningham, Valentine. Everywhere Spoken Against: Dissent in the Victorian Novel. Oxford: Clarendon Press, 1975.

Reed, John R. Victorian Conventions. Athens: Ohio University Press, 1975.

Showalter, Elaine Cottler. "The Double Standard: Criticism of Women Writers in England, 1845-1880. " Ph.D. Dissertation, California, Davis, 1970.

_____. A Literature of Their Own: British Women Novelists from Brontë to Lessing. Princeton: Princeton University Press, 1977.

OLSEN, TILLIE

McElhiney, Annette Bennington. "Alternative Responses to Life in Tillie Olsen's Work." Frontiers 2 (Spring 1977): [76]-91.

Olsen, Tillie. "Silences: When Writers Don't Write." In Images of Women in Fiction, pp. 97-112. Edited by Susan Koppelman Cornillon. Bowling Green, Ohio: Bowling Green University Press, 1972.

Rose, Ellen Cronan. "Limning: or Why Tillie Writes." Hollins Critic 13 (April 1976): 1-15.

Stimpson, Catharine R. "Three Women Work It Out." Nation, 30 November 1974, pp. 565-568. (Review of Yonnondio: From the Thirties.)

_____. "Tillie Olsen: Witness as Servant." Polit: A Journal for Literature and Politics 1 (Fall 1977): 1-12.

O'NEILL, EUGENE

Bonin, Jane F. Major Themes in Prize-Winning American Drama. Metuchen, N.J.: Scarecrow Press, 1975.

Brown, Susan Rand. "'Mothers' and 'Sons': The Development of Autobiographical Themes in the Plays of Eugene O'Neill." Ph.D. Dissertation, The University of Connecticut, 1975.

Josephs, Lois S. "The Women of Eugene O'Neill: Sex Role Stereotypes." Ball State University Forum 14, no. 3 (1972): 3-8.

ONO NO KOMACHI

Fischer, Felice Renee. "Ono No Komachi--A Ninth Century Poetess of Heian Japan." Ph.D. Dissertation, Columbia University, 1972.

Ikuko Atsumi. "Modern Japanese Women Poets: After the Meiji Restoration." Iowa Review 7 (Spring/Summer 1976): 227-237.

ORZESZKOWA, ELIZA

Kolodziej, Joyce Story. "Eliza Orzeszkowa's Feminist and Jewish Works in Polish and Russian Criticism." Ph.D. Dissertation, Indiana University, 1975.

OSAMU DAZAI

Lyons, Phyllis I. "Women in the Life and Art of Dazai Osamu." Literature East and West 8 (March 1974): [44]-57.

OSBORNE, PAUL

Loudin, Joanne Marie. "The Changing Role of the Comic Heroine in American Drama from 1900 to 1940." Ph.D. Dissertation, University of Washington, 1974.

OSGOOD, FRANCIS SARGENT

Watts, Emily Stipes. The Poetry of American Women from 1632 to 1945. Austin: University of Texas Press, 1977.

OSTENSO, MARTHA

Fulton, E. Margaret. "Out of Our Past: A New Future." Laurentian University Review 9 (November 1976): [87]-102.

OTWAY, THOMAS

Hume, Robert D. "Marital Discord in English Comedy from Dryden to Fielding." Modern Philology 74 (February 1977): 248-272.

OUIDA (Louise De La Ramee)

Garrison, Dee. "Immoral Fiction in the Late Victorian Library." American Quarterly 28 (Spring 1976): 71-89.

OUSMANE, SEMBENE see SEMBENE, OUSMANE

OVID

Atkins, John. Sex in Literature, vol. 2: The Classical

Experience of the Sexual Impulse. London: Calder & Boyars, 1973.

Luck, Georg. "The Woman's Role in Latin Love Poetry." In Perspectives of Roman Poetry, pp. 15-31. Edited by G. Karl Galinsky. Austin and London: University of Texas Press, 1974.

OZICK, CYNTHIA

Wisse, Ruth R. "American Jewish Writing, Act II." Commentary 61 (June 1976): 40-45.

- P -

PADRON, JUAN RODRIQUEZ del

Sims, Edna Niecie. "El antifeminismo en la literatura española hasta 1560." Ph. D. Dissertation, Catholic University, 1970.

PAGE, MYRA

Cook, Sylvia Jenkins. From Tobacco Road to Route 66: The Southern Poor White in Fiction. Chapel Hill: The University of North Carolina Press, 1976.

PALACIOS, LUCILA

Billman, Lynne Lois. "The Political Novels of Lucila Palacios and Marta Lynch." Ph. D. Dissertation, The Catholic University of America, 1976.

PALEY, GRACE

Annan, Gabriele. Times Literary Supplement, 14 February 1975, p. 157. (Review of Enormous Changes at the Last Minute.)

Baumbach, Jonathan. "Life-Size." Partisan Review 42, no. 2 (1975): 303-306.

Crain, J. L. Commentary 58 (July 1974): 92. (Review of Enormous Changes at the Last Minute.)

Harris, Lis. New York Times Book Review, 17 March 1974, p. 3. (Review of Enormous Changes at the Last Minute.)

Kapp, Isa. "Husbands and Heroines." New Leader, 24 June 1974, pp. 17-18.

Little, Judy. "Satirizing the Norm: Comedy in Women's Fiction." Regionalism and the Female Imagination 3 (Fall 1977 and Winter 1977-78): 39-49.

Murray, Michele. New Republic, 16 March 1974, p. 27. (Review of Enormous Changes at the Last Minute.)

Nichols, Marianna de Vinci. "Women on Women: The Looking Glass Novel." Denver Quarterly 11 (Autumn 1976): 1-13.

Novak, William. America, 8 June 1974, pp. 459-460. (Review of Enormous Changes at the Last Minute.)

Packer, Nancy H. Studies in Short Fiction 12 (Winter 1975): 34-35. (Review of Enormous Changes at the Last Minute.)

Roberts, Audrey. "Grace Paley, Love and Death in the Afternoon." Paper presented at the MLA meeting, New York, December 1974.

Sale, Roger. Hudson Review 27 (Winter 1974-75): 629-630. (Review of Enormous Changes at the Last Minute.)

Shinn, Thelma J. Wardrop. "A Study of Women Characters in Contemporary American Fiction 1940-1970." Ph.D. Dissertation, Purdue University, 1972.

Winegarten, Renee. "Paley's Comet." Midstream (December 1974): 65-67.

PARDO BAZAN, EMILIA (Condesa de)

Bieder, Maryellen. "Capitulation: Marriage, Not Freedom--A Study of Emilia Pardo Bazán's Memorias de un solterón and Galdós' Tristana." Symposium 30 (Summer 1976): 93-109.

Cook, Teresa A. "El feminismo en la novelística de
Emilia Pardo Bazán. " Ph. D. Dissertation, University of Virginia, 1974.

PARKER, DOROTHY

Contemporary Authors: Permanent Series, vol. 2.

Douglas, Ann. "Feminist Criticism and Cultural History:
Dorothy Parker and the 1930's. " Paper presented at
the MLA meeting, New York City, December 1976.

Labrie, Ross. "Dorothy Parker Revisited. " Canadian
Review of American Studies 7 (Spring 1976): 48-56.

LaJoy, Maureen. "No Laughing Matter: Women and
Humor. " Women 5, no. 1 (1976): 6-9.

Toth, Emily. "Dorothy Parker, Erica Jong, and New
Feminist Humor. " Regionalism and the Female
Imagination 3 (Fall 1977 and Winter 1977-1978): 70-
85.

PARSONS, ELIZA

Roberts, Bette B. "The Gothic Romance: Its Appeal to
Women Writers and Readers in Late Eighteenth-
Century England. " Ph. D. Dissertation, University
of Massachusetts, 1975.

PARTON, SARA PAYSON WILLIS see FERN, FANNY

PASTERNAK, BORIS

Byek, J. W. Boris Pasternak. New York: Twayne,
1972.

PASTOR, JUAN

Goldman, Rachel Margaret. "The Lucretia Legend from
Livy to Rojas Zorrilla. " Ph. D. Dissertation, City
University of New York, 1976.

PATMORE, COVENTRY

Ball, Patricia M. The Heart's Events: The Victorian
Poetry of Relationships. London: University of
London, The Athlone Press, 1976.

Christ, Carol. "Victorian Masculinity and the Angel in the House." In A Widening Sphere: Changing Roles of Victorian Women, pp. 146-162. Edited by Martha Vicinus. Bloomington: Indiana University Press, 1977.

PAYNE, HENRY NEVILLE

Novak, Maximillian E. "Margery Pinchwife's 'London Disease': Restoration Comedy and the Libertine Offensive in the 1670's." Studies in the Literary Imagination 10 (Spring 1977): 1-24.

PAZ, OCTAVIO

Jaquette, Jane S. "Literary Archetypes and Female Role Alternatives: The Woman and the Novel in Latin America." In Female and Male in Latin America: Essays, pp. 3-28. Edited by Ann Pescatello. Pittsburgh: University of Pittsburgh Press, 1973.

Meyer, Victoria Junco. "The Images of Women in Contemporary Mexican Literature." In Beyond Intellectual Sexism: A New Woman, A New Reality, pp. 210-228. Edited by Joan Roberts. New York: David McKay, 1976.

PEACOCK, THOMAS LOVE

Fass, Barbara. La Belle Dame sans Merci and the Aesthetics of Romanticism. Detroit: Wayne State University Press, 1974.

PEELE, GEORGE

Still, Roger. Love and Death in Renaissance Tragedy. Baton Rouge: Louisiana State University Press, 1976.

PENDARVES, MARY

Dobbs, Jeannine. "The Blue-Stockings: Getting It Together." Frontiers 1 (Winter 1976): 81-93.

PEREIRO, FRANCESCA YETUNDE

Brown, Lloyd W. "The African Woman as Writer."
Canadian Journal of African Studies 9, no. 3 (1975):
493-502.

PERETZ, Y. L.

Adler, Ruth. "The Image of Woman in the Works of
Y. L. Peretz: A Socio-Psychological Study." Ph.D.
Dissertation, New York University, 1974.

PERSE, SAINT-JOHN

Price, John D. "Man, Women and the Problem of Suffering in Saint-John Perse." Modern Language Review 72 (July 1977): 555-564.

PETERKIN, JULIA

Ward, Hazel Mae. "The Black Woman as Character:
Images in the American Novel, 1852-1953." Ph.D.
Dissertation, The University of Texas at Austin,
1977.

PETESCH, NATALIE L. M.

Kaminski, Margaret. "An Odyssey." Margins no. 16
(January 1975): 8, 66. (Review of The Odyssey of
Katinou Kalokovich.)

Sullivan, Walter. "Erewhon and Eros, The Short Story
Again." Sewanee Review 83 (Summer 1975): 537-
546. (Review of After the First Death Is No Other.)

PETRONIUS

Atkins, John. Sex in Literature, vol. 2: The Classical
Experience of the Sexual Impulse. London: Calder
& Boyars, 1973.

Daghistany, Ann. "The Picara Nature." Women's
Studies 5, no. 1 (1977): 51-60.

PETRY, ANN

Brown, Lloyd W. "Mannequins and Mermaids--The

Contemporary Writer and Sexual Images in the Consumer Culture." Women's Studies 5, no. 1 (1977): 1-12.

Davis, Arthur P. From the Dark Tower: Afro-American Writers 1900-1960. Washington, D.C.: Howard University Press, 1974.

Doyle, Sister Mary Ellen. "The Heroine of Black Novels." In Perspectives on Afro-American Women, pp. 112-125. Edited by Willa D. Johnson and Thomas L. Green. Washington, D.C.: ECCA Publications, 1975.

Hill, James Lee. "Bibliography of the Works of Chester Himes, Ann Petry and Frank Yerby." Black Books Bulletin 3 (Fall 1975): 60-72.

Jaskoski, Helen. "Power Unequal to Man: The Significance of Conjure in Works by Five Afro-American Authors." Southern Folklore Quarterly 38 (1974): 91-108.

Lattin, Vernon. "Ann Petry's Fiction: The Rebellion of a Black Intellectual." Paper presented at the MLA meeting, New York City, December 1976.

Madden, David. "Ann Petry: 'The Witness.'" Studies in Black Literature 6 (Fall 1975): 24-26.

Morsberger, Robert E. "The Further Transformation of Tituba." New England Quarterly 47 (1974): 56-58.

O'Brien, John. Interviews with Black Writers. New York: Liveright, 1973.

Peden, William. "The Black Explosion." Studies in Short Fiction 12 (Summer 1975): 231-242.

Royster, Beatrice Horn. "The Ironic Vision of Four Black Women Novelists: A Study of the Novels of Jessie Fauset, Nella Larsen, Zora Neale Hurston, and Ann Petry." Ph.D. Dissertation, Emory University, 1975.

Schraufnagel, Noel. From Apology to Protest: The

Black American Novel. Deland, Florida: Everett/
Edwards, 1973.

Shinn, Thelma J. Wardrop. "A Study of Women Characters in Contemporary American Fiction 1940-1970. "
Ph. D. Dissertation, Purdue University, 1972.

_____. "Women in the Novels of Ann Petry. " In
Contemporary Women Novelists: A Collection of
Critical Essays, pp. 108-117. Edited by Patricia
Meyer Spacks. Englewood Cliffs, N. J. : Prentice-
Hall, 1977.

PHILLIPS, DAVID GRAHAM

Brookner, Anita. "Thoroughly Rotten. " Times Literary
Supplement, 29 April 1977, p. 507. (Review of
Susan Lenox: Her Fall and Rise.)

Janeway, Elizabeth. Afterword to Susan Lenox, Her
Fall and Rise. Carbondale: Southern Illinois University Press, 1977.

PIERCY, MARGE

Brinnin, John Malcolm and Bill Read, eds. Twentieth
Century Poetry: American and British (1900-1970),
2nd ed. New York: McGraw-Hill, 1970.

Casey, Constance. "Interview with Marge Piercy. "
San Francisco Review of Books 2 (November 1976): 5-9.

Chafe, William H. "Sex and Race: The Analogy of
Social Control. " Massachusetts Review 18 (Spring
1977): 147-176.

Contoski, Victor. Margins (January 1975): 10-11, 66.
(Review of To Be of Use.)

Haggerty, Joan. "Going Through Changes. " Room of
One's Own 1 (Spring 1975): 58-63. (Review of
Small Changes.)

Jefferson, Margo. Newsweek, 7 June 1976, p. 94.
(Review of Woman on the Edge of Time.)

Jordan, June. "The Black Poet Speaks of Poetry. "

American Poetry Review 3 (July/August 1974): 62-63.

Kaminski, Margaret. "An Interview with Marge Piercy." Margins no. 16 (January 1975): 9-10, 69.

Masinton, Martha and Charles G. Masinton. "Second-class Citizenship: The Status of Women in Contemporary American Fiction." In What Manner of Woman: Essays in English and American Life and Literature, pp. 297-315. Edited by Marlene Springer. New York: New York University Press, 1977.

Piercy, Marge. "Reading and Thoughts." Deland, Florida: Everett/Edwards, n. d. (Cassette no. 5526.)

Sale, Roger. New York Times Book Review, 20 June 1976, p. 6. (Review of Woman on the Edge of Time.)

Stimpson, Catharine R. "Three Women Work It Out." Nation, 30 November 1974, pp. 565-568. (Review of Small Changes.)

Wallace, Ronald. "Alone with Poems." Colorado Quarterly 23 (1975): 341-353.

PINTER, HAROLD

Baker, William and Stephen Ely Tabachnick. Harold Pinter. New York: Barnes & Noble, 1973.

Clurman, Harold. The Divine Pastime: Theatre Essays. New York: Macmillan, 1974.

Dreyfuss, Cecilia Anne Stiborik. "Femina sapiens in Drama: Aeschylus to Grillparzer." Ph. D. Dissertation, The University of Michigan, 1975.

Fedor, Joan Roberta. "The Importance of the Female in the Plays of Samuel Beckett, Harold Pinter, and Edward Albee." Ph. D. Dissertation, University of Washington, 1976.

Gabbard, Lucina Paquet. The Dream Structure of Pinter's Plays: A Psychoanalytic Approach. Rutherford: Fairleigh Dickinson University Press, 1976.

Gilman, Richard. Common and Uncommon Masks: Writings on Theatre 1961-1970. New York: Random House, 1971.

Henkle, Roger B. "From Pooter to Pinter: Domestic Comedy and Vulnerability. " Critical Quarterly 16 (Summer 1974): 174-189.

Hollis, James R. Harold Pinter: The Poetics of Silence. Carbondale and Edwardsville: Southern Illinois University Press, 1970.

Lamont, Rosette C. "Pinter's The Homecoming: The Contest of the Gods. " Far-Western Forum 1 (February 1974): 47-73.

Osherow, Anita R. "Mother and Whore: The Role of Woman in The Homecoming. " Modern Drama 17 (1974): 413-422.

Quigley, Austin E. The Pinter Problem. Princeton, N.J.: Princeton University Press, 1975.

Sykes, Arlene. Harold Pinter. New York: Humanities Press, 1970.

PIOZZI, HESTER THRALE see THRALE, HESTER

PISAN, CHRISTINE de

Bell, Susan Groag. "Christine de Pizan (1364-1430): Humanism and the Problem of a Studious Woman. " Feminist Studies 3 (Spring-Summer 1976): 173-184.

Bornstein, Diane. "Christine De Pisan. " Deland, Florida: Everett/Edwards, n.d. (Cassette no. 5513.)

Crosland, Margaret. Women of Iron and Velvet: French Women After George Sand. New York: Taplinger, 1976.

Curnow, Maureen Cheney Lois. "The Livre de la Cité des Dames of Christine de Pisan: A Critical Edition. " Ph.D. Dissertation, Vanderbilt University, 1975.

Françon, Marcel. "On the Rondeaux of Christine de Pisan." Harvard Library Bulletin 21 (October 1973): 380-381.

Kelly, Douglas. "Reflections on the Role of Christine de Pisan as a Feminist Writer." Sub-Stance no. 2 (Winter 1972): 63-71.

Margolis, Nadia. "The Poetics of History: An Analysis of Christine de Pizan's Livre de la Mutacion de Fortune." Ph.D. Dissertation, Stanford University, 1977.

Schmitz, Betty Ann. "French Women Writers and Their Critics: An Analysis of the Treatment of Women Writers in Selected Histories of French Literature." Ph.D. Dissertation, The University of Wisconsin-Madison, 1977.

PIX, MARY

Barbour, Paula Louise. "A Critical Edition of Mary Pix's The Spanish Wives (1696), with Introduction and Notes." Ph.D. Dissertation, Yale University, 1975.

Lock, Frederick Peter. "The Dramatic Art of Susanna Centlivre." Ph.D. Dissertation, McMaster University (Canada), 1975.

Suwannabha, Sumitra. "The Feminine Eye: Augustan Society as Seen by Selected Women Dramatists of the Restoration and Early Eighteenth Century." Ph.D. Dissertation, Indiana University, 1973.

PLATH, SYLVIA

Allen, Mary. The Necessary Blankness: Women in Major American Fiction of the Sixties. Urbana: University of Illinois Press, 1976.

Annas, Pamela Jeanne. "A Disturbance in Mirrors: The Poetry of Sylvia Plath." Ph.D. Dissertation, Indiana University, 1977.

Ballif, Gene. "Facing the Worst: A View from Minerva's Buckler." Parnassus: Poetry in Review 5 (Fall/Winter 1976): 231-259.

Blodgett, E. D. "Sylvia Plath: Another View." Modern
Poetry Studies 2, no. 3 (1971): 97-106.

Brinnin, John Malcolm and Bill Read, eds. Twentieth
Century Poetry: American and British (1900-1970),
2nd ed. New York: McGraw-Hill, 1970.

Broe, Mary Lynn. "Persona and Poetic: The Poetry
of Sylvia Plath." Ph.D. Dissertation, The University of Connecticut, 1975.

Buell, Frederick. "Sylvia Plath's Traditionalism."
Boundary 2, 5 (Fall 1976): 195-211.

Butler, Christopher. "Home Journal." Essays in Criticism 27 (January 1977): 77-83. (Review of Letters
Home.)

Butscher, Edward. Sylvia Plath: Method and Madness.
New York: Continuum Books, 1976.

Callow, James T. and Robert Reilly. Guide to American Literature from Emily Dickinson to the Present.
New York: Barnes & Noble, 1977.

Contemporary Authors: Permanent Series, vol. 2.

Davis, William V. "Sylvia Plath's 'Ariel.'" Modern
Poetry Studies 3, no. 4 (1972): 176-184.

Feder, Lillian. "Myths of Madness in Twentieth-Century
Literature: Dionysos, The Maniai, and Hades."
Psychocultural Review 1 (Spring 1977): 131-151.

Gordon, Jan B. "Saint Sylvia." Modern Poetry Studies
2, no. 6 (1972): 282-286. (Review of Winter Trees.)

_____. "'Who Is Sylvia?' The Art of Sylvia Plath."
Modern Poetry Studies 1, no. 1 (1970): 6-34.

Gordon, Lydia Caroline. "'From Stone to Cloud,' A
Critical Study of Sylvia Plath." Ph.D. Dissertation,
University of Pennsylvania, 1975.

Greenberger, Evelyn. "Child of the Fire: Sylvia Plath."
Deland, Florida: Everett/Edwards, n.d. (Cassette
no. 5516.)

Gustafson, Richard. " 'Time Is a Waiting Woman': New Poetic Icons. " Midwest Quarterly 16 (April 1975): 318-327.

Hardwick, Elizabeth. "Sylvia Plath: Poet in Rage (1). " North Hollywood: The Center for Cassette Studies, n. d.

Holbrook, David. Sylvia Plath: Poetry and Existence. London: Athlone Press, 1976.

Holland, Norman N. "Literary Suicide: A Question of Style. " Psychocultural Review 1 (Summer 1977): 285-301.

Juhasz, Suzanne. Naked and Fiery Forms: Modern American Poetry by Women, A New Tradition. New York: Harper & Row, 1976.

Kamel, Rose. " 'A Self to Recover': Sylvia Plath's Bee Cycle Poems. " Modern Poetry Studies 4 (Winter 1973): 304-318.

Kenney, Susan M. "A Room of One's Own Revisited. " University of Michigan Papers in Women's Studies 1 (June 1974): 97-109.

Kinzie, Mary. "A New Life and Other Plath Controversies. " American Poetry Review 5, no. 2 (1976): 5-8. (Reviews of Sylvia Plath: Method and Madness by Edward Butscher and Letters Home, edited by Aurelia Schober Plath.)

Kolodny, Annette. "Some Notes on Defining a 'Feminist Literary Criticism. ' " Critical Inquiry 2 (Autumn 1975): 75-92.

Kroll, Judith. "Chapters in a Mythology: The Poetic Vision of Sylvia Plath. " Ph.D. Dissertation, Yale University, 1976.

Krook, Dorothea. "Recollections of Sylvia Plath. " Critical Quarterly 18 (Winter 1976): 5-14.

Lane, Gary and Maria Stevens. Sylvia Plath: A Bibliography. Metuchen, N.J.: Scarecrow Press, 1978.

Lanser, Susan S. "Beyond The Bell Jar: Women Students in the 1970's. " Radical Teacher (December 1977): 41-44.

Moers, Ellen. Literary Women. Garden City, N. Y. : Doubleday, 1976.

Molesworth, Charles. "Again, Sylvia Plath. " Salmagundi no. 37 (Spring 1977): 140-146.

Northouse, Cameron and Thomas P. Walsh. Sylvia Plath and Anne Sexton: A Reference Guide. Boston: G. K. Hall, 1974.

Olson, Carol Booth. "Madness in the Contemporary American Novel. " Ph. D. Dissertation, University of California, Los Angeles, 1977.

Phillips, Robert. "The Dark Funnel: A Reading of Sylvia Plath. " Modern Poetry Studies 3, no. 2 (1972): 49-74.

Pickard, Linda Kay Haskovec. "A Stylo-Linguistic Analysis of Four American Writers. " Ph. D. Dissertation, Texas Woman's University, 1974.

Plath, Aurelia Schober. Letters Home: Correspondence 1950-1963 by Sylvia Plath. New York: Harper & Row, 1977.

Procopiow, Norma. "Sylvia Plath and the New England Mind. " Thoth 13 (Fall 1973): 3-15.

Reiff, Sandra. "A Conspiracy of Guilt. " San Francisco Review of Books 1 (November 1975): 7-9. (Review of Plath's Letters Home.)

Robinson, Robert, interviewer. "Sylvia Plath's Letters Home--Some Reflections by Her Mother. " Listener, 22 April 1976, pp. 515-516.

Rosenblatt, Jon Michael. "The Poetic Development of Sylvia Plath: A Study of Theme and Image. " Ph. D. Dissertation, The University of North Carolina at Chapel Hill, 1975.

Rosenstein, Harriet. " 'To the Most Wonderful Mummy

... a Girl Ever Had. ' " Ms. 4 (December 1975):
45-49. (Review of Plath's Letters Home.)

Schwartz, Murray M. and Christopher Bollas. "The Ab-
sence of the Center: Sylvia Plath and Suicide. "
Criticism 18 (Spring 1976): 147-172.

Shinn, Thelma J. Wardrop. "A Study of Women Characters in Contemporary American Fiction 1940-
1970. " Ph. D. Dissertation, Purdue University,
1972.

Smith, Stan. "Attitudes Counterfeiting Life: The Irony
of Artifice in Sylvia Plath's The Bell Jar. " Critical
Quarterly 17 (Autumn 1975): 247-260.

Snider, Clifton. "Jung's Psychology of the Conscious
and the Unconscious. " Psychocultural Review 1
(Spring 1977): 216-242.

Snively, Susan Rumble. "The Language of Necessity:
The Poetry of Sylvia Plath. " Ph. D. Dissertation,
Boston University Graduate School, 1976.

Spendal, R. J. "Sylvia Plath's 'Cut. '" Modern Poetry
Studies 6 (Autumn 1975): 128-134.

Stainton, Rita Tomasallo. "The Magician's Girl:
Power and Vulnerability in the Poetry of Sylvia
Plath. " Ph. D. Dissertation, Rutgers University,
The State University of New Jersey, 1975.

Steinbrink, Jeffrey. "Emily Dickinson and Sylvia Plath:
The Values of Mortality. " Women & Literature 4
(Spring 1976): 45-48.

Stone, Carole Barbara. "Sylvia Plath's Spiritual Quest."
Ph. D. Dissertation, Fordham University, 1976.

Talbot, Norman. "Sisterhood Is Powerful: The Moon
in Sylvia Plath's Poetry. " New Poetry (Sydney,
Australia) 21 no. 3 (1973): 23-36.

Uroff, M. D. "Sylvia Plath and Confessional Poetry:
A Reconsideration. " Iowa Review 8 (Winter 1977):
104-115.

Wallace, Ronald. "Alone with Poems." Colorado Quarterly 23 (1975): 341-353.

Whittier, Gayle. "The Divided Woman and Generic Doubleness in The Bell Jar." Women's Studies 3, no. 2 (1976): 127-146.

PLAUTUS

Fantham, Elaine. "Sex, Status, and Survival in Hellenistic Athens: A Study of Women in New Comedy." Phoenix 29 (Spring 1975): 44-74.

POE, EDGAR ALLAN

Baym, Nina. "Portrayal of Women in American Literature, 1790-1870." In What Manner of Woman: Essays on English and American Life and Literature, pp. 211-234. Edited by Marlene Springer. New York: New York University Press, 1977.

Lappit, Noriko Mizuta. "Tanizaki and Poe: The Grotesque and the Quest for Supernal Beauty." Comparative Literature 29 (Summer 1977): 221-240.

POLITE, CARLENE HATCHER

Contemporary Authors, 23/24R.

Schraufnagel, Noel. From Apology to Protest: The Black American Novel. Deland, Florida: Everett/Edwards, 1973.

Schulz, Elizabeth. " 'Free in Fact and at Last': The Image of the Black Woman in Black American Literature." In What Manner of Woman: Essays in English and American Life and Literature, pp. 316-344. Edited by Marlene Springer. New York: New York University Press, 1977.

POLOTAN, KERIMA

Bernard, Miguel A. "The Enemy in Kerima Polotan's Fiction." In Philippine Fiction, pp. 113-131. Edited by Joseph A. Galdon. Quezon City: Ateneo de Manila at the University Press, 1972.

Casper, Leonard. "Desire and Doom in Kerima Polotan." In Philippine Fiction, pp. 133-145. Edited
by Joseph A. Galdon. Quezon City: Ateneo de
Manila at the University Press, 1972.

PONIATOWSKA, ELENA

Miller, Beth. "Interview with Elena Poniatowska."
Latin American Literary Review 4 (Fall-Winter
1975): 73-78.

Young, Rinda Rebeca Stowell. "Six Representative
Women Novelists of Mexico, 1960-1969." Ph.D.
Dissertation, University of Illinois at Urbana-
Champaign, 1975.

POPE, ALEXANDER

Cohen, Ralph. "The Reversal of Gender in 'The Rape
of the Lock.' " South Atlantic Bulletin 37 (November 1972): 54-60.

Delany, Sheila. "Sex and Politics in Pope's Rape of the
Lock." English Studies in Canada 1 (Spring 1975):
[46]-61.

Dubro, James R. "The Third Sex: Lord Hervey and
His Coterie." Eighteenth-Century Life 2 (June
1976): 89-95.

Keogh, J. G. "Pope's 'Epistle to a Lady,' 1-4." Ex-
plication 31 (1973): Item 37.

Kramer, Jerome A. and Judith Kaminsky. " 'These
Contraries Such Unity Do Hold': Structure in The
Rape of Lucrece." Mosaic 10 (Summer 1977): [143]-
155.

Nussbaum, Felicity A. "Pope's 'To a Lady' and the
Eighteenth-Century Woman." Philological Quarterly
54 (Spring 1975): 444-456.

Quivey, James. "Pope's Eloise to Abelard." Studies in
the Humanities 2 (Summer 1971): 14-22.

Richetti, John J. "The Portrayal of Women in Restoration and Eighteenth-Century English Literature." In

What Manner of Woman: Essays on English and American Life and Literature, pp. 65-97. Edited by Marlene Springer. New York: New York University Press, 1977.

Rudat, Wolfgang E. H. "Shakespeare and Virgil Parodied: The Rape of Lucrece in the Light of Pope's Rape of the Lock." Eighteenth-Century Life 2 (June 1976): 98-102.

Trowbridge, Hoyt. From Dryden to Jane Austen: Essays on English Critics and Writers, 1660-1818. Albuquerque: University of New Mexico Press, 1977.

POPE, EDITH EVERETT TAYLOR

Seidel, Kathryn Lee. "The Southern Belle: Her Fall from the Pedestal in Fiction of the Southern Renaissance." Ph.D. Dissertation, University of Maryland, 1976.

PORTER, HENRY

Leggatt, Alexander. Citizen Comedy in the Age of Shakespeare. Toronto: University of Toronto Press, 1973.

PORTER, KATHERINE ANNE

Authors in the News, vol. 2. Detroit: Gale Research, 1976, pp. 226-227.

Callow, James T. and Robert Reilly. Guide to American Literature from Emily Dickinson to the Present. New York: Barnes & Noble, 1977.

Carson, Barbara Harrell. "Winning: Katherine Anne Porter's Women." In The Authority of Experience, pp. [239]-256. Edited by Arlyn Diamond and Lee R. Edwards. Amherst: University of Massachusetts Press, 1977.

Flanders, Jane. "Katherine Anne Porter and the Ordeal of Southern Womanhood." Southern Literary Journal 9 (Fall 1976): 47-60.

Gaston, Edwin W., Jr. "The Mythic South of Katherine Anne Porter." Southwestern American Literature 3 (1973): 81-85.

Givner, Joan. "Katherine Anne Porter, Eudora Welty and Ethan Brand." International Fiction Review 1 (January 1974): 32-37.

Hennessy, Rosemary. "Katherine Anne Porter's Model for Heroines." Colorado Quarterly 25 (Winter 1977): 301-315.

Hosbach, Marguerette. "Porter on Prose." Writer's Digest 57 (November 1977): 6.

McLaughlin, Marilou Briggs. "The Love Dialectic." Ph.D. Dissertation, State University of New York at Binghamton, 1976.

Shinn, Thelma J. Wardrop. "A Study of Women Characters in Contemporary American Fiction 1940-1970." Ph.D. Dissertation, Purdue University, 1972.

Voss, Arthur. The American Short Story: A Critical Survey. Norman: University of Oklahoma, 1973.

Wakoski, Diane. "The Craft of Carpenters, Plumbers, & Mechanics: A Column." American Poetry Review 2 (May/June 1973): 15-16.

West, Ray B., Jr. "Katherine Anne Porter." In American Writers, vol. 3, pp. 433-455. Edited by Leonard Unger. New York: Scribners, 1974.

POWERS, J. F.

Shinn, Thelma J. Wardrop. "A Study of Women Characters in Contemporary American Fiction 1940-1970." Ph.D. Dissertation, Purdue University, 1972.

PRATT, E. J.

Gibbs, Robert. "Poet of Apocalypse." Canadian Literature no. 70 (Autumn 1976): 32-41.

PREVOST D'EXILES, ANTOINE FRANCOIS (L'Abbe Prevost)

Webb, Shawncey Jay. "Aspects of Fidelity and Infidelity

in the Eighteenth-Century French Novel from Chasles to Laclos. " Ph. D. Dissertation, Indiana University, 1977.

PRICE, HANNAH J.

Maglin, Nan Bauer. "Rebel Women Writers, 1894-1925." Ph. D. Dissertation, Union Graduate School, 1975.

PRIYAMVADA, USHA

Poulos, Steven Mark. "Feminine Sense and Sensibility: A Comparative Study of Six Modern Fiction Writers in Hindi and Urdu: Rashid Jahan, Ismat Chughtai, Qurratul-Ain Hyder, Mannu Bhandari, Usha Priyamvada, Vijay Chauhan. " Ph. D. Dissertation, University of Chicago, 1975.

PROPETIUS

Luck, Georg. "The Woman's Role in Latin Love Poetry. " In Perspectives of Roman Poetry, pp. 15-31. Edited by G. Karl Galinsky. Austin: University of Texas Press, 1974.

PROUST, MARCEL

Appignanesi, Lisa. Femininity and the Creative Imagination. New York: Barnes & Noble, 1973.

Robertson, Jane. "The Hero and Françoise in A la recherche du temps perdu. " French Studies 25 (October 1971): 437-441.

Shilts, John A. "To Him She Would Unveil Her Shy Soul's Nakedness: A Study of Sexual Imagery in Joyce and Proust. " Ph. D. Dissertation, The Pennsylvania State University, 1975.

Steiner, Lorraine Florence. "The Role of the Grande Dame in the Milieu of the French Salon, as Represented in Selected Works of Marcel Proust and Jean Anouilh. " Ph. D. Dissertation, University of Minnesota, 1977.

PUIG, MANUEL

Gallagher, David. New York Times Book Review, 16

December 1973, p. 14. (Review of Heartbreak
Tango: A Serial.)

Weiss, Judith A. "Dynamic Correlations in Heartbreak
Tango." Latin American Literary Review 3 (Fall-
Winter 1974): [137]-141.

Wood, Michael. New York Review of Books, 13 December 1973, p. 19. (Review of Heartbreak Tango: A
Serial.)

PURDY, JAMES

Allen, Mary. The Necessary Blankness: Women in Major American Fiction of the Sixties. Urbana: University of Illinois Press, 1976.

PUSHKIN, ALEXANDER

Banerjee, Maria. "The Metamorphosis of an Icon:
Woman in Russian Literature." In Female Studies
IX: Teaching About Women in the Foreign Lan-
guages, pp. 228-235. Edited by Sidonie Cassirer.
Old Westbury, N.Y.: Feminist Press, 1975.

Schwartz, Murray M. and Albert Schwartz. "The Queen
of Spades: A Psychoanalytic Interpretation." Texas
Studies in Literature and Language 17 (Special Russian Issue 1975): 275-288.

PYNCHON, THOMAS

Allen, Mary. The Necessary Blankness: Women in Major American Fiction of the Sixties. Urbana: University of Illinois Press, 1976.

Davidson, Cathy N. "Oedipa as Androgyne in Thomas
Pynchon's The Crying of Lot 49." Contemporary
Literature 18 (Winter 1977): 38-50.

Hendin, Josephine. "What Is Thomas Pynchon Telling
Us?" Harper's (March 1975): 82-92.

Henkle, Roger B. "Pynchon's Tapestries on the Western
Wall." Modern Fiction Studies 17 (Summer 1971):
207-220.

- Q -

QABBANI, NIZAR

Armstrong, Judith. The Novel of Adultery. New York:
Barnes & Noble, 1976.

Loya, Arieh. "Poetry as a Social Document: The Social Position of the Arab Woman as Reflected in the
Poetry of Nizâr Qabbânî. " Muslim World 53 (January 1973): 39-52; also published in International
Journal of Middle East Studies 6 (October 1975):
481-494.

QUEIROZ, RACHEL de

Coutinho, Afrânio, ed. A literatura no Brasil. Rio de
Janeiro: Editorial Sul Americana, 1970.

Martins, Wilson. Encyclopedia of World Literature in
the 20th Century, vol. 3. New York: Ungar, 1971.

QUIROGA, ELENA

Hadjopoulos, Theresa Mary. "Four Women Novelists of
Postwar Spain: Matute, Lafôret, Quiroga, and Medio. " Ph.D. Dissertation, Columbia University,
1974.

- R -

RABELAIS, FRANÇOIS

Lerner, Julianna Kitty. "Rabelais and Woman. " Ph.D.
Dissertation, City University of New York, 1976.

RACINE, JEAN

Cloonan, William. "Love and Gloire in Bérénice: A
Freudian Perspective. " Kentucky Romance Quarterly 22, no. 4 (1975): 517-525.

Dainard, J. A. "The Power of the Spoken Word in
Bérénice. " Romanic Review 67 (May 1976): 157-171.

Dreyfuss, Cecilia Anne Stiborik. "Femina sapiens in Drama: Aeschylus to Grillparzer." Ph.D. Dissertation, The University of Michigan, 1975.

Herrera, Bertilia. "Racine, Alfieri, and Schiller: A Comparative Study of Heroines." Ph.D. Dissertation, University of California, Riverside, 1977.

Méron, Evelyne. "De l'Hippolyte d'Euripide à la Phèdre de Racine: deux conceptions du tragique." XVII Siècle 100 (1973): 35-54.

Miles, John Edward. "Athalie: A Study in the Eternal Triangle." Sub-Stance no. 3 (Spring 1972): 85-99.

Sussman, Ruth. "Bérénice and the Tragic Moment." L'Esprit Créateur 15 (Spring-Summer 1975): 241-251.

RADCLIFFE, ANN

Bauska, Kathy Anderson. "The Feminine Dream of Happiness: A Study of the Woman's Search for Intelligent Love and Recognition in Selected English Novels from Clarissa to Emma." Ph.D. Dissertation, University of Washington, 1977.

Durant, David S., Jr. "Ann Radcliffe's Novels: Experiments in Setting." Ph.D. Dissertation, University of North Carolina, 1972.

Epstein, Lynne. "Ann Radcliffe's Gothic Landscape of Fiction and the Various Influences Upon It." Ph.D. Dissertation, New York University, 1972.

Frank, Frederick S. "A Bibliography of Writings About Ann Radcliffe." Extrapolation 17 (December 1975): 54-62.

Moers, Ellen. Literary Women. Garden City, N.Y.: Doubleday, 1976.

Roberts, Bette B. "The Gothic Romance: Its Appeal to Women Writers and Readers in Late Eighteenth-Century England." Ph.D. Dissertation, University of Massachusetts, 1975.

Sherman, Leona F. "Ann Radcliffe and the Gothic

Romance: A Psychoanalytic Approach. " Ph. D. Dissertation, State University of New York at Buffalo, 1975.

Stoler, John A. "Ann Radcliffe: The Novel of Suspense and Terror. " Ph. D. Dissertation, University of Arizona, 1972.

RADEMACHER, HANNA

Novak, Sigrid Scholtz. "The Invisible Woman: The Case of the Female Playwright in German Literature. " Journal of Social Issues 28, no. 2 (1972): 47-57.

RAJA RAO

Larson, Charles R. The Novel in the Third World. Washington, D. C. : Inscape, 1976.

Sharma, Som P. "Raja Rao's Search for the Feminine. " Journal of South Asian Literature 12 (Spring-Summer 1977): 95-101.

RAMESAY, WILLIAM

Novak, Maximillian E. "Margery Pinchwife's 'London Disease': Restoration Comedy and the Libertine Offensive in the 1670's. " Studies in the Literary Imagination 10 (Spring 1977): 1-24.

READ, HARRIETTE FANNING

Watts, Emily Stipes. The Poetry of American Women from 1632 to 1945. Austin: University of Texas Press, 1977.

REAGE, PAULINE

Crosland, Margaret. Women of Iron and Velvet: French Women After George Sand. New York: Taplinger, 1976.

May, Charles E. "Sex, Submission, and the Story of O. " Carleton Miscellany 16 (1976-77): 22-32.

Mickelsen, David. "X-Rated O. " Western Humanities Review 31 (Spring 1977): 165-173.

Perkins, Michael. The Secret Record: Modern Erotic
Literature. New York: William Morrow, 1976.

REED, MARK

Loudin, Joanne Marie. "The Changing Role of the Comic
Heroine in American Drama from 1900 to 1940. "
Ph. D. Dissertation, University of Washington, 1974.

REESE, LIZETTE WOODWORTH

Dietrich, Mae. "Lizette Woodworth Reese. " Emily
Dickinson Bulletin 15 (1970): 114-122.

Walker, Cheryl Lawson. "The Women's Tradition in
American Poetry. " Ph. D. Dissertation, Brandeis
University, 1973.

Watts, Emily Stipes. The Poetry of American Women
from 1632 to 1945. Austin: University of Texas
Press, 1977.

REEVE, CLARA

Portner, Ruth Lee. "A Study of Marriage in the English
Novel. " Ph. D. Dissertation, City University of New
York, 1977.

Roberts, Bette B. "The Gothic Romance: Its Appeal to
Women Writers and Readers in Late Eighteenth-
Century England. " Ph. D. Dissertation, University
of Massachusetts, 1975.

REGIO, PAOLO

Goldman, Rachel Margaret. "The Lucretia Legend from
Livy to Rojas Zorrilla. " Ph. D. Dissertation, City
University of New York, 1976.

RENAULT, MARY

Heilbrun, Carolyn G. "Axiothea's Grief: The Disability
of the Female Imagination. " In From Parnassus:
Essays in Honor of Jacques Barzun, pp. 227-236.
Edited by Dora B. Weiner and William R. Keylor.
New York: Harper & Row, 1976.

REYNOLDS, GEORGE W. M.

Garrison, Dee. "Immoral Fiction in the Late Victorian Library." American Quarterly 28 (Spring 1976): 71-89.

REYNOLDS, GERTRUDE

Gibson, Susan Monteith. "Love and the Vote: Fiction of the Suffrage Movement in Edwardian England." Ph.D. Dissertation, University of Massachusetts, 1975.

RHYS, JEAN

Babakhanian, Grace Schneck. "Expatriation and Exile as Themes in the Fiction of Jean Rhys." Ph.D. Dissertation, University of Illinois at Urbana-Champaign, 1976.

Baybrooke, Neville. "The Return of Jean Rhys." Caribbean Quarterly 16 (December 1970): 43-46.

Cantwell, M. "I'm a Person at a Masked Ball Without a Mask: Interview." Mademoiselle (October 1974): 170-171.

James, Louis. "Sun Fire--Painted Fire: Jean Rhys as a Caribbean Novelist." Ariel: A Review of International English Literature 8 (July 1977): 111-127.

Johnson, Diane. Book World (Washington Post), 3 November 1974, pp. 1-2. (Review of Tigers Are Better Looking.)

Leiter, Robert. New Republic, 7 December 1974, p. 22. (Review of Tigers Are Better Looking.)

Mellown, Elgin W. "Character and Themes in the Novels of Jean Rhys." In Contemporary Women Novelists: A Collection of Critical Essays, pp. 118-136. Edited by Patricia Meyer Spacks. Englewood Cliffs, N.J.: Prentice-Hall, 1977.

_____. "Jean Rhys's Sleep It Off, Lady." World Literature Written in English 16 (November 1977): 473-474.

Miles, Rosalind. The Fiction of Sex: Themes and Functions of Sex Difference in the Modern Novel. New York: Barnes & Noble, 1974.

Moss, Howard. New Yorker, 16 December 1974, pp. 161-166.

Nichols, Marianna de Vinci. "Women on Women: The Looking Glass Novel." Denver Quarterly 11 (Autumn 1976): 1-13.

Stade, George. New York Times Book Review, 20 October 1974, p. 5. (Review of Tigers Are Better Looking.)

Sullivan, Walter. "Erewhon and Eros, The Short Story Again." Sewanee Review 83 (Summer 1975): 537-546. (Review of Tigers Are Better Looking.)

Thorpe, Michael. " 'The Other Side': Wide Sargasso Sea and Jane Eyre." Ariel: A Review of International English Literature 8 (July 1977): 99-100.

Thurman, Judith. "The Mistress and the Mask." Ms. 41 (January 1976): 50-52, 81.

Tyler, Ralph. "Luckless Heroines, Swinish Men." Atlantic Monthly 235 (January 1975): 81-84.

Wahlstrom, Ruth Margaret. "The Fiction of Jean Rhys." Ph. D. Dissertation, University of Kentucky, 1977.

RICH, ADRIENNE

Chenoy, Polly Naoshir. "Dives and Descents: Thematic Strategies in the Poetry of Adrienne Rich and Ann Stanford." Ph. D. Dissertation, University of Utah, 1975.

Clemons, Walter. New York Times Book Review, 27 April 1975, p. 5. (Review of Poems: Selected and New.)

Dahlen, Beverly. "The Poetry of Adrienne Rich." San Francisco Review of Books 2 (September 1976): 19-21.

DuPlessis, Rachel Blau. "The Critique of Consciousness and Myth in Levertov, Rich, and Rukeyser. "
Feminist Studies 3 (Fall 1975): [199]-221.

Farwell, Marilyn R. "Adrienne Rich and an Organic
Feminist Criticism. " College English 39 (October
1977): 191-203.

Flynn, Gale. "The Radicalization of Adrienne Rich. "
Hollins Critic 11 (October 1974): [1]-15.

Goldstein, Laurence. "The Evolution of Adrienne Rich. "
Michigan Quarterly Review 15 (Summer 1976): 360-
366.

Grimstad, Kirsten and Susan Rennie, interviewers.
"Adrienne Rich and Robin Morgan Talk About Poe-
try and Women's Culture. " In The New Woman's
Survival Sourcebook, pp. 106-111. Edited by Kir-
sten Grimstad and Susan Rennie. New York: Alfred
A. Knopf, 1975.

Gustafson, Richard. " 'Time Is a Waiting Woman': New
Poetic Icons. " Midwest Quarterly 16 (April 1975):
318-327.

Juhasz, Suzanne. Naked and Fiery Forms: Modern
American Poetry by Women, A New Tradition.
New York: Harper & Row, 1976.

Lazarre, Jane. "Adrienne Rich Comes to Terms with
the Woman in the Mirror. " Village Voice, 8 November 1976, pp. 81-82.

Lefcowitz, Barbara. "The Search Motif in Some Contemporary Female Poets. " University of Michigan
Papers in Women's Studies 2, no. 3 (1977): 84-89.

Miner, Valerie. "An Interview with Adrienne Rich and
Mary Daly. " San Francisco Review of Books 3
(October 1977): 8-14.

Morrison, Margaret. "Adrienne Rich: Poetry of 'Re-
Vision. ' " Ph. D. Dissertation, The George Washington University, 1977.

Plumly, Stanley, Wayne Dodd, and Walter Trevis.

"Talking with Adrienne Rich. " Ohio Review 13 (Spring 1971): 28-46.

Poss, Stanley. "A Gathering of Poets. " Western Humanities Review 29 (Autumn 1975): 388-391. (Review of Poems: Selected and New, 1950-1974.)

Pritchard, William H. "Despairing at Styles. " Poetry 127 (February 1976): 292-302.

Rich, Adrienne. "Caryatid: A Column. " American Poetry Review 2 (May/June 1973): 10-11.

_____. "It Is the Lesbian in Us.... " Sinister Wisdom no. 3 (Spring 1977): 6-9.

Savery, Pancho. "Conversations With the Self. " Epoch 23 (Fall 1973): 120-123.

Schulman, Grace. American Poetry Review 2 (September/October 1973): 11. (Review of Diving into the Wreck.)

Spiegelman, Willard. "Voice of the Survivor: The Poetry of Adrienne Rich. " Southwest Review 60 (Autumn 1975): 370-388.

Stanley, Julia. "The Rhetoric of Denial. " Sinister Wisdom no. 3 (Spring 1977): 80-98.

Stender, Fay. San Francisco Review of Books 2 (March 1977): 6-7. (Review of Of Woman Born.)

Tenenhaus, Beverly. "Adrienne Rich's Poetry: Feminism as a Moral Response. " Paper presented at the MLA meeting, New York City, December 1976.

Van Dyne, Susan R. "The Mirrored Vision of Adrienne Rich. " Modern Poetry Studies 8 (Autumn 1977): 140-173.

Wagner, Linda. "Levertov and Rich: The Later Poems. " Paper presented at the MLA meeting, San Francisco, December 1975.

Walker, Cheryl. "Welcome Eumenides: Contemporary Feminist Poets. " Feminist Art Journal 2 (Winter 1973-74): 6-7.

Wallace, Ronald. "Alone with Poems." Colorado Quarterly 23 (1975): 341-353.

RICHARDSON, DOROTHY

Bangs, Carol June. "The Open Circle: A Critical Study of Dorothy Richardson's Pilgrimage." Ph. D. Dissertation, University of Oregon, 1977.

Bell, Millicent. "The Single Self." New Republic, 20 October 1973, pp. 23-27.

Craig, Patricia. "Dorothy Richardson--'The Damned Egotistical Self.'" Books and Bookmen 18 (September 1973): 43-45.

Fromm, Gloria G. Dorothy Richardson: A Bibliography. Urbana: University of Illinois Press, 1977.

_____. "Dorothy M. Richardson." English Literature in Transition 18 (1975): 70-72.

_____. "The Misfortunes of Dorothy Richardson: A Review Essay." Modernist Studies: Literature and Culture 1920-1940 1, no. 3 (1974-75): 59-64.

Gilbert, Sandra M. "A Painful Case." Nation, 20 September 1975, pp. 246-247.

Kaplan, Sydney Janet. Feminine Consciousness in the British Novel. Urbana: University of Illinois Press, 1975.

Rose, Shirley. "Dorothy Richardson: The First Hundred Years, a Retrospective View." Dalhousie Review 53 (1973): 92-96.

_____. "Dorothy Richardson's Focus on Time." English Literature in Transition 17 (1974): 163-172.

Showalter, Elaine. A Literature of Their Own: British Women Novelists from Brontë to Lessing. Princeton: Princeton University Press, 1977.

Taylor, Nancy McKeon. "Conscious Construction: The Concept of Plot in Five Novels by Women." Ph. D. Dissertation, Loyola University of Chicago, 1977.

Tudor, Kathleen R. "The Androgynous Mind in W. B. Yeats, D. H. Lawrence, Virginia Woolf and Dorothy Richardson." Ph. D. Dissertation, University of Toronto, 1974.

RICHARDSON, SAMUEL

Albert, Theodore Gibbs. "The Law vs. Clarissa Harlowe." Ph. D. Dissertation, Rutgers University, The State University of New Jersey, 1976.

Bauska, Kathy Anderson. "The Feminine Dream of Happiness: A Study of the Woman's Search for Intelligent Love and Recognition in Selected English Novels from Clarissa to Emma." Ph. D. Dissertation, University of Washington, 1977.

Bedick, David B. "The Changing Role of Anxiety in the Novel." Ph. D. Dissertation, New York University, 1975.

Brownstein, Rachel Mayer. " 'An Examplar to Her Sex': Richardson's Clarissa." Yale Review 67 (Autumn 1977): [30]-47.

Byrd, Max. "The Madhouse, the Whorehouse, and the Convent." Partisan Review 44, no. 2 (1977): 268-278.

Doody, Margaret Anne. A Natural Passion: A Study of the Novels of Samuel Richardson. New York and London: Oxford University Press, 1974.

Eaves, T. C. Duncan and Ben D. Kimpel. Samuel Richardson: A Biography. Oxford University Press, 1971.

Frank, Frederick S. "From Boudoir to Castle Crypt: Richardson and the Gothic Novel." Revue des Langues Vivantes 41, no. 1 (1975): 49-59.

Henry, Rolanne. Women & Literature 3 (Spring 1975): 44-56. (Review of Eaves and Kimpel's Samuel Richardson: A Biography.)

Klotman, Phyllis R. "Sin and Sublimation in the Novels of Samuel Richardson." CLA Journal 20 (March 1977): 365-373.

LeGates, Marlene. "The Cult of Womanhood in Eighteenth-Century Thought. " Eighteenth-Century Studies 10
(Fall 1976): 21-39.

Litwack, David Michael. "Clarissa and La Nouvelle
Héloïse: A Comparative Study. " Ph. D. Dissertation, Boston University Graduate School, 1977.

Longerbeam, Larry Simpson. "Seduction as Symbolic
Action: A Study of the Seduction Motif in Six Victorian Novels. " Ph. D. Dissertation, George Peabody College for Teachers, 1975.

McAlexander, Patricia Jewell. "The Creation of the
American Eve: The Cultural Dialogue on the Nature
and Role of Women in Late-Eighteenth-Century
America. " Early American Literature 9 (Winter
1975): 252-266.

Moers, Ellen. Literary Women, Garden City, N. Y. :
Doubleday, 1976.

Moynihan, R. D. "Clarissa and the Enlightened Woman
as Literary Heroine. " Journal of the History of
Ideas 36 (January 1975): 159-166.

Portner, Ruth Lee. "A Study of Marriage in the English Novel. " Ph. D. Dissertation, City University
of New York, 1977.

Richetti, John J. "The Portrayal of Women in Restoration and Eighteenth-Century English Literature. " In
What Manner of Woman: Essays on English and
American Life and Literature, pp. 65-97. Edited
by Marlene Springer. New York: New York University Press, 1977.

Rogers, Katherine. "Richardson's Empathy with Women. " In The Authority of Experience, pp. [118]-
136. Edited by Arlyn Diamond and Lee R. Edwards.
Amherst: University of Massachusetts Press, 1977.
Also published as "Sensitive Feminism vs. Conven-
tional Sympathy: Richardson and Fielding on Women. " Novel 9 (Spring 1976): 256-270.

Smidt, Kristian. "Character and Plot in the Novels of
Samuel Richardson. " Critical Quarterly 17 (Summer
1975): 155-166.

Spacks, Patricia Meyer. Imagining a Self: Autobiography and Novel in Eighteenth-Century England. Cambridge: Harvard University Press, 1976.

Spector, Judith Ann. "Sexual Dialectic in Four Novels: The Mythos of the Masculine Aesthetic." Ph.D. Dissertation, Indiana University, 1977.

RICHLER, MORDECAI

Fulton, E. Margaret. "Out of Our Past: A New Future." Laurentian University Review 9 (November 1976): [87]-102.

Gibson, Graeme, interviewer. Eleven Canadian Novelists. Toronto: Anansi, n.d.

RIDGE, LOLA

Juhasz, Suzanne. "Lola Ridge: Poetry and Protest." Paper presented at the MLA meeting, New York City, December 1976.

RIDING, LAURA

Atlas, James. Poetry 125 (February 1975): 295. (Review of Selected Poems.)

Auster, Paul. "The Return of Laura Riding." New York Review of Books, 7 August 1975, pp. 36-38. (Review of Selected Poems.)

Thurman, Judith. "Forgeries of Ourselves." Nation, 30 November 1974, pp. 570-571. (Review of Selected Poems.)

Watts, Emily Stipes. The Poetry of American Women from 1632 to 1945. Austin: University of Texas Press, 1977.

RILEY, ELIZABETH

Bellamy, Sue. " 'Fucking Men Is for Saints.' " Refractory Girl: A Journal of Feminist Thought no. 11 (June 1976): 32-35. (Review of All That False Instruction.)

Higgins, Sue. "Breaking the Rules: New Fiction by Australian Women. " Meanjin Quarterly 34 (December 1975): 415-420.

RILKE, RAINER MARIA

Dominquez, Maria Alicia. "La mujer en la poesia de Rilke. " Histonium 32 (December 1971): 30-31.

Segal, Charles. "Eurydice: Rilke's Transformation of a Classical Myth. " Bucknell Review 21 (Spring 1973): 137-144.

Tucker, Cynthia G. "Rilke's Eternal Woman and the Translation of Louise Labé. " Modern Language Notes 89 (October 1974): 829-839.

Webb, Karl. "Themes in Transition: Girls and Love in Rilke's Buch der Bilder. " German Quarterly 43 (1970): 406-417.

RIMBAUD, ARTHUR

De Lutri, Joseph R. "Rimbaud and Fournier: The End of the Quest. " Romance Notes 18 (Winter 1977): 153-156.

Mathieu, Bertrand. "Seven Paragraphs on Rimbaud and Illuminations. " American Poetry Review 2 (July/August 1973): 26-27.

RITCHIE, LADY ANNE THACKERAY

Boyd, Elizabeth French. Bloomsbury Heritage: Their Mothers and Their Aunts. London: Hamish Hamilton, 1976.

Callow, Steven D. "A Biographical Sketch of Lady Anne Thackeray Ritchie. " Virginia Woolf Quarterly 2 (Summer & Fall 1976): 285-293. (Includes bibliography.)

RIUZ, JUAN

Sims, Edna Niecie. "El antifeminismo en la literatura española hasta 1560. " Ph. D. Dissertation, Catholic University, 1970.

ROBBINS, TOM

> Cameron, Ann. Nation, 28 August 1976, p. 152. (Review of Even Cowgirls Get the Blues.)
>
> LeClair, Thomas. New York Times Book Review, 23 May 1976, p. 5. (Review of Even Cowgirls Get the Blues.)

ROBERTS, ELIZABETH MADOX

> Cook, Sylvia Jenkins. From Tobacco Road to Route 66: The Southern Poor White in Fiction. Chapel Hill: The University of North Carolina Press, 1976.
>
> Tyree, Wade. "Time's Own River: The Three Major Novels of Elizabeth Madox Roberts." Michigan Quarterly Review 16 (Winter 1977): 33-46.

ROBINS, ELIZABETH

> Gibson, Susan Monteith. "Love and the Vote: Fiction of the Suffrage Movement in Edwardian England." Ph.D. Dissertation, University of Massachusetts, 1975.
>
> Maglin, Nan Bauer. "Rebel Women Writers, 1894-1925." Ph.D. Dissertation, Union Graduate School, 1975.
>
> Marcus, Jane C. "Elizabeth Robins." Ph.D. Dissertation, Northwestern University, 1973.
>
> Showalter, Elaine. A Literature of Their Own: British Women Novelists from Brontë to Lessing. Princeton: Princeton University Press, 1977.

ROBINSON, EDWIN ARLINGTON

> Vincent, Sybil Korff. "Flat Breasted Miracles: Realistic Treatment of the Woman's Problem in the Poetry of Edwin Arlington Robinson." Markham Review 6 (Fall 1976): 14-15.

ROCHE, REGINA MARIA

> Roberts, Bette B. "The Gothic Romance: Its Appeal to Women Writers and Readers in Late Eighteenth-

Century England." Ph. D. Dissertation, University
of Massachusetts, 1975.

ROCHEFORT, CHRISTIANE

Steckel, Ailsa. "Narration and Metaphor as Ideology in
the Novels of Christiane Rochefort." Ph. D. Dissertation, The University of Wisconsin-Madison, 1975.

Wenzel, Helen V. "Feminist Criticism: Theory and
Application to Christiane Rochefort." Paper presented
at the MLA meeting, San Francisco, December 1975.

ROE, MARY ABIGAIL

Gasser, Larry Winston. "Social Reform in the Late
Nineteenth-Century American Strike Novel." Ph. D.
Dissertation, University of Denver, 1975.

ROJAS, FERNANDO de

Sims, Edna Niecie. "El antifeminismo en la literatura
española hasta 1560." Ph. D. Dissertation, Catholic
University, 1970.

Trisler, Barbara Jean. "A Comparative Study of the
Character Portrayal of 'Celestina' and Other Golden
Age Celestinesque Protagonists." Ph. D. Disserta-
tion, The University of Oklahoma, 1977.

ROLIN, DOMINIQUE

Bleuzé, Ruth Allen. "Romancières et Critiques: Etude
du Prix Fémina, 1904-1968." Ph. D. Dissertation,
University of Colorado at Boulder, 1977.

ROLVAAG, O. E.

Goodman, Charlotte. "Images of American Rural Women in the Novel." University of Michigan Papers
in Women's Studies 1 (June 1975): 57-70.

Meldrum, Barbara. "Images of Women in Western
American Literature." Midwest Quarterly 17 (April
1976): 252-267.

ROSSETTI, CHRISTINA

Dombrowski, Theo. "Dualism in the Poetry of Christina Rossetti." Victorian Poetry 14 (Spring 1976): 70-76.

Fass, Barbara. "Christina Rossetti." Deland, Florida: Everett/Edwards, n.d. (Cassette no. 5501.)

_____. "Christina Rossetti and St. Agnes' Eve." Victorian Poetry 14 (Spring 1976): 33-46.

Golub, Ellen. "Untying Goblin Apron Strings: A Psycho-analytic Reading of 'Goblin Market.'" Literature and Psychology 25, no. 4 (1975): 158-165.

Quill, Katherine Mayberry. "The Poetry of Christina Rossetti: A Study in the Creative Imagination." Ph.D. Dissertation, The University of Rochester, 1977.

Wion, Ann Holt. "'Give Me the Lowest Place': The Poetry of Christina Rossetti." Ph.D. Dissertation, Cornell University, 1976.

ROSSETTI, DANTE GABRIEL

Bentley, D. M. R. "Light, Architecture, and Awe in Rossetti's Early Annunciations." Ariel 7 (April 1976): 22-30.

Goff, Barbara Munson. "Artists and Models: Rossetti's Images of Women." Ph.D. Dissertation, Rutgers University, The State University of New Jersey, 1976.

Hardesty, William H., III. "Rossetti's Lusty Women." Cimarron Review no. 35 (April 1976): 20-24.

Johnson, Wendell Stacy. Sex and Marriage in Victorian Poetry. Ithaca: Cornell University Press, 1975.

Keane, Robert N. "Rossetti's 'Jenny': Moral Ambiguity and the 'Inner Standing Point.'" Papers on Language and Literature 9 (Summer 1973): 271-280.

Pittman, Philip McM. "The Strumpet and the Snake: Rossetti's Treatment of Sex as Original Sin." Victorian Poetry 12 (Spring 1974): 45-54.

ROSSNER, JUDITH

Authors in the News, vol. 2. Detroit: Gale Research, 1976, p. 235.

Blackwood, Caroline. "Getting It All Over With." Times Literary Supplement, 12 September 1975, p. 1012. (Review of Looking for Mr. Goodbar.)

Cameron, Julia. "Candy from Strangers." Book World-- The Washington Post, 1 June 1975, p. 1. (Review of Looking for Mr. Goodbar.)

Dickstein, Lore. "The Deadly Pickup." Ms. 3 (June 1975): 86-87. (Review of Looking for Mr. Goodbar.)

Duffy, Martha. Time, 7 July 1975, p. 60. (Review of Looking for Mr. Goodbar.)

Nichols, Marianna de Vinci. "Women on Women: The Looking Glass Novel." Denver Quarterly 11 (Autumn 1976): 1-13.

Rinzler, C. E. New York Times Book Review, 9 June 1975, p. [24]. (Review of Looking for Mr. Goodbar.)

Turner, Alice K. "Of Housewives and Siamese Twins." Ms. 6 (October 1977): 36-37. (Review of Attachments.)

ROTH, PHILIP

Allen, Mary. The Necessary Blankness: Women in Major American Fiction of the Sixties. Urbana: University of Illinois Press, 1976.

Cohen, Sarah Blacker. "Philip Roth's Would-Be Patriarchs and Their Shikses and Shrews." Studies in American Jewish Literature 1 (Spring 1975): 16-22.

Dervin, Daniel A. "Breast Fantasy in Barthelme, Swift, and Philip Roth: Creativity and Psychoanalytic Structure." American Imago 33 (Spring 1976): 102-122.

Grossman, Joel. " 'Happy as Kings': Philip Roth's Men and Women." Judaism 26 (Winter 1977): 7-17.

310 / More Women in Literature

Koltun, Elizabeth. The Jewish Woman: New Perspectives. New York: Schocken, 1976.

Miles, Rosalind. The Fiction of Sex: Themes and Functions of Sex Difference in the Modern Novel. New York: Barnes & Noble, 1974.

"Philip Roth in Conversation with Joyce Carol Oates." New Review 2 (May 1975): 3-7.

Shinn, Thelma J. Wardrop. "A Study of Women Characters in Contemporary American Fiction 1940-1970." Ph.D. Dissertation, Purdue University, 1972.

Weinberg, Helen A. "Philip Roth: A Feminist Appraisal." Paper presented at the MLA meeting, New York City, December 1976.

ROUSSEAU, JEAN-JACQUES

Brooks, Richard A. "Rousseau's Antifeminism in the Lettre à d'Alembert and Emile." In Literature and History of the Age of Ideas, pp. 209-227. Edited by Charles G. S. Williams, Columbus: Ohio State University Press, 1975.

De Magnin, Peggy Kamuf. "The Cast of Helen: Metaphorical Woman in the Text of Rousseau." Ph.D. Dissertation, Cornell University, 1975.

LeGates, Marlene. "The Cult of Womanhood in Eighteenth-Century Thought." Eighteenth-Century Studies 10 (Fall 1976): 21-39.

Litwack, David Michael. "Clarissa and La Nouvelle Héloïse: A Comparative Study." Ph.D. Dissertation, Boston University Graduate School, 1977.

McAlexander, Patricia Jewell. "The Creation of the American Eve: The Cultural Dialogue on the Nature and Role of Women in Late-Eighteenth-Century America." Early American Literature 9 (Winter 1975): 252-266.

Miller, Nancy K. "Female Sexuality and Narrative Structure in La Nouvelle Héloïse and Les Liaisons dangereuses. " Signs: Journal of Women in Culture and Society 1 (Spring 1976): 609-638.

Moers, Ellen. Literary Women. Garden City, N.Y.: Doubleday, 1976.

Scanlon, Timothy M. "The Notion of 'Paradis sun la terre' in Rousseau's La Nouvelle Héloïse. " Nottingham French Studies 13 (May 1974): 12-22.

Senior, Nancy. "Les Solitaires as a Test for Emile and Sophie. " French Review 49 (March 1976): 528-535.

Stock, Phyllis. "The Theory and Practice of Women's Education in Eighteenth-Century France. " Eighteenth-Century Studies 2 (June 1976): 79-82.

Tanner, Tony. "Julie and 'La Maison Paternelle': Another Look at Rousseau's La Nouvelle Héloïse. " Daedalus 105 (Winter 1976): 23-45.

ROWLEY, WILLIAM

Duffy, Joseph M. "Madhouse Optics: The Changeling. " Comparative Drama 8 (Summer 1974): 184-198.

ROWSON, SUSANNA

Franklin, H. Bruce. " 'A' Is for Afro-American: A Primer on the Study of American Literature. " Minnesota Review NS 5 (Fall 1975): 53-65.

Giffen, J. C. "Susanna Rowson and Her Academy. " Antiques 98 (September 1970): 436-440.

Hornstein, Jacqueline. "Comic Vision in the Literature of New England Women Before 1800. " Regionalism and the Female Imagination 3 (Fall 1977/Winter 1977-78): 11-19.

Parker, Patricia L. "Charlotte Temple: America's First Best Seller. " Studies in Short Fiction 13 (Fall 1976): 518-520.

Watts, Emily Stipes. The Poetry of American Women from 1632 to 1945. Austin: University of Texas Press, 1977.

Weil, Dorothy. In Defence of Women: Susanna Rowson (1762-1824). University Park: Pennsylvania State University Press, 1976.

ROXLO, NALE

Tull, John F. , Jr. "Shifting Dramatic Perspectives in Nalé Roxlo's 'Judith y las Rosas.' " Hispania 55 (March 1972): 55-59.

ROY, GABRIELLE

Bleuzé, Ruth Allen. "Romancières et Critiques: Etude du Prix Fémina, 1904-1968. " Ph. D. Dissertation, University of Colorado at Boulder, 1977.

Atwood, Margaret. Survival: A Thematic Guide to Canadian Literature. Toronto: Anansi, 1972.

RUBIN DE CELIS, CARMEN

Young, Rinda Rebeca Stowell. "Six Representative Women Novelists of Mexico, 1960-1969. " Ph. D. Dissertation, University of Illinois at Urbana-Champaign, 1975.

RUKEYSER, MURIEL

Adkins, Joan F. "The Esthetics of Science: Muriel Rukeyser's Waterlily Fire. " Contemporary Poetry 1 (Winter 1973): 23-27.

Bernikow, Louise. " 'Rare Battered She-Poet. ' " Ms. (April 1974): 35-36.

Brinnin, John Malcolm and Bill Read, eds. Twentieth Century Poetry: American and British (1900-1970), 2nd ed. New York: McGraw-Hill, 1970.

DuPlessis, Rachel Blau. "The Critique of Consciousness and Myth in Levertov, Rich, and Rukeyser. " Feminist Studies 3 (Fall 1975): [199]-221.

Lefcowitz, Barbara. "The Search Motif in Some Contemporary Female Poets. " University of Michigan Papers in Women's Studies 2, no. 3 (1977): 84-89.

Terris, Virginia. "Muriel Rukeyser." Deland, Florida: Everett/Edwards, n.d. (Cassette no. 5520.)

RULE, JANE

Glassco, John. "Her Goodness, Our Grimace." Books in Canada 6 (March 1977): 3-4. (Review of The Young in One Another's Arms.)

Hofsess, John. "Calumnity Jane." Books in Canada 5 (October 1976): 3-6.

Martin, Sandra. Canadian Literature no. 72 (Spring 1977): 87-89. (Review of Theme for Diverse Instruments.)

RULFO, JUAN

Bastos, Maria Luisa and Sylvia Molloy. "La estrella junto a la luna: Variantes de la figura materna en Pedro Páramo." MLN 92 (March 1977): 246-268.

Meyer, Victoria Junco. "The Images of Women in Contemporary Mexican Literature." In Beyond Intellectual Sexism: A New Woman, A New Reality, pp. 210-228. Edited by Joan Roberts. New York: David McKay, 1976.

RUSS, JOANNA

Lynn, Elizabeth. San Francisco Review of Books 1 (December 1975): 17. (Review of The Female Man.)

Russ, Joanna. "Reflections on Science Fiction." Quest 2 (Summer 1975): 40-49.

Piercy, Marge. "From Where I Work: A Column." American Poetry Review 6, no. 3 (1977): 37-39.

Zimmerman, Bonnie. "Sex Roles and Science Fiction." Lavender Woman 4 (April 1975): 13.

- S -

SACHS, HANS

> Belka, Robert W. "A Functional Definition of Satire
> Applied to Women in the Fastnachtspiele of Hans
> Sachs. " Ph. D. Dissertation, Brigham Young Uni-
> versity, 1975.

SACHS, NELLY

> Bosmajian, Hamida. " 'Landschaft aus Schreien': The
> Shackled Leaps of Nelly Sachs. " Bucknell Review
> 21 (Spring 1973): 43-62.

> Contemporary Authors: Permanent Series, vol. 2.

SACKVILLE-WEST, VICTORIA

> Edwards, Mary Irene. "Inheritance in the Fiction of
> Victoria Sackville-West. " Ph. D. Dissertation, The
> University of Michigan, 1976.

> Klaich, Dolores. Woman + Woman: Attitudes Toward
> Lesbianism. New York: Simon & Schuster, 1974.

> Miles, Rosalind. The Fiction of Sex: Themes and
> Functions of Sex Difference in the Modern Novel.
> New York: Barnes & Noble, 1974.

> Rule, Jane. Lesbian Images. Garden City, N. Y. :
> Doubleday, 1975.

> Stimpson, Catharine R. "Three Women Work It Out. "
> Nation, 30 November 1974, pp. 565-568.

SADE, MARQUIS de

> Byrd, Max. "The Madhouse, the Whorehouse, and the
> Convent. " Partisan Review 44, no. 2 (1977): 268-
> 278.

> Carter, Angela. The Sadeian Woman. London: Virago,
> 3 Cheyne Place, n. d.

> Josephs, Herbert. "Sade and Woman: Exorcising the

Awe of the Sacred." Studies in Burke and His Time 18 (Spring 1977): 99-113.

Miller, Nancy Kipnis. "Gender and Genre: An Analysis of Literary Femininity in the Eighteenth-Century Novel." Ph.D. Dissertation, Columbia University, 1974.

Miller, Nancy K. "Juliette and the Posterity of Prosperity." L'Esprit Créateur 15 (Winter 1975): 413-424.

SAGAN, FRANÇOIS

Crosland, Margaret. Women of Iron and Velvet: French Women After George Sand. New York: Taplinger, 1976.

SAKS, KATIA

Jaquette, Jane S. "Literary Archetypes and Female Role Alternatives: The Woman and the Novel in Latin America." In Female and Male in Latin America: Essays, pp. 3-28. Edited by Ann Pescatello. Pittsburgh: University of Pittsburgh Press, 1973.

SALAS BARBADILLO, ALONSO J. de

Sánchez-Díez, Francisco Javier. "La novela picaresca de protagonista femenino en España durante el siglo XVII." Ph.D. Dissertation, University of North Carolina, Chapel Hill, 1972.

SALINGER, J. D.

Shinn, Thelma J. Wardrop. "A Study of Women Characters in Contemporary American Fiction 1940-1970." Ph.D. Dissertation, Purdue University, 1972.

SALTUS, EDGAR

Evans, Sarah Ann. "Decadence and Love in the American Novel: Edgar Saltus and His Contemporaries." Ph.D. Dissertation, University of Kansas, 1975.

SAN PEDRO, DIEGO de

Sims, Edna Niecie. "El antifeminismo en la literatura
española hasta 1560." Ph.D. Dissertation, Catholic
University, 1970.

SANCHEZ, LOIS RAPHAEL

Ben-Ur, Lorraine Elena. "Myth Montage in a Con-
temporary Puerto Rican Tragedy: La pasión según
Antígona Pérez [The Passion According to Antigone
Pérez]." Latin American Literary Review 4 (Fall-
Winter 1975): [15]-21.

SANCHEZ, SONIA

Arata, Esther S. and Nicholas J. Rotoli. Black American Playwrights 1800 to the Present: A Bibliography. Metuchen, N.J.: Scarecrow Press, 1976.

Barnes, Clive. "Theatre: 'Black Visions.'" New
York Times, 5 April 1972, p. 37.

Clarke, Sebastian. "Sonia Sanchez and Her Work."
Black World 20 (June 1971): 44-48, 96-98.

Kerr, Walter. "Gloria Is the Glory." New York Times,
26 March 1972, II, p. 3. (Review of Sister Son/Ji.)

Riach, W. A. D. "Telling It Like It Is: An Examination of Black Theatre as Rhetoric." Quarterly
Journal of Speech 46 (April 1970): 183.

SAND, GEORGE (Mme Dudevant)

Barry, Joseph A. Infamous Woman: The Life of
George Sand. Garden City, N.Y.: Doubleday,
1976.

Bochenek-Franczakowa, Regina. "Quelques aspects du
'féminisme' dans les premiers romans de Sand
(1832-1834)." Romanica wratislaviensia 10 (1975):
77-90.

Bonsirven-Fontana, Marie-Louise. Dans l'ombre de
George Sand. Monte Carlo: Pastorelly, 1976.

Carson, Katharine. "George Sand." Deland, Florida: Everett/Edwards, n.d. (Cassette no. 5510.)

Cate, Curtis. George Sand: A Biography. Boston: Houghton Mifflin, 1975.

Crosland, Margaret. Women of Iron and Velvet: French Women After George Sand. New York: Taplinger, 1976.

Davis, Mary Byrd. "George Sand and the Poetry of Matthew Arnold." Texas Studies in Literature and Language 19 (Summer 1977): [204]-226.

Maurin, Mario. "Un modèle d'Indiana?" French Review 50 (1976-77): 317-320.

Maurois, André. Lélia: The Life of George Sand. New York: Penguin Books, 1977.

Mercier, Michel. Le roman féminin. Paris: P.U.F., 1976.

Moers, Ellen. Literary Women. Garden City, N.Y.: Doubleday, 1976.

Rabine, Leslie. "George Sand and the Myth of Femininity." Women & Literature 4 (Fall 1976): 2-17.

Ruhe, Deborah. "George Sand's Consuelo--La Comtesse de Rudolstadt: A Novel of Initiation." Ph.D. Dissertation, The University of Iowa, 1977.

Schmitz, Betty Ann. "French Women Writers and Their Critics: An Analysis of the Treatment of Women Writers in Selected Histories of French Literature." Ph.D. Dissertation, The University of Wisconsin-Madison, 1977.

Thomson, Patricia. George Sand and the Victorians: Her Influence and Reputation in 19th Century England. Irvington: Columbia University Press, 1976.

Toth, Emily. "The Independent Woman and 'Free' Love." Massachusetts Review 16 (Autumn 1975): 647-664.

SANDOZ, MARI

Greenwell, Scott L. "Fascists in Fiction: Two Early Novels of Mari Sandoz." Western American Literature 12 (August 1977): 133-143.

SANTAYANA, GEORGE

Bromberger, Eric Aldridge. "An Odour of Old Maid Boston as Literary Symbol." Ph. D. Dissertation, University of California, Los Angeles, 1976.

SANTILLANA, MARQUES de

Kuzma, Mary Kathryn. "The Feminine Literary Figures in the Works of the Marqués de Santillana." Ph. D. Dissertation, Case Western Reserve, 1977.

SAPPHO

Atkins, John. Sex in Literature, vol. 2. The Classical Experience of the Sexual Impulse. London: Calder & Boyars, 1973.

Klaich, Dolores. Woman + Woman: Attitudes Toward Lesbianism. New York: Simon & Schuster, 1974.

Pomeroy, Sarah B. Goddesses, Whores, Wives, and Slaves: Women in Classical Antiquity. New York: Schocken Books, 1975.

Segal, Charles. "Eros and Incantation: Sappho and Oral Poetry." Arethusa 7 (Fall 1974): 139-150.

Toth, Emily. "The Independent Woman and 'Free' Love." Massachusetts Review 16 (Autumn 1975): 647-664.

SARRAUTE, NATHALIE

Cornwell, Ethel F. "Virginia Woolf, Nathalie Sarraute, and Mary McCarthy: Three Approaches to Character in Modern Fiction." International Fiction Review 4 (January 1977): 3-10.

Crosland, Margaret. Women of Iron and Velvet: French Women After George Sand. New York: Taplinger, 1976.

Mercier, Michel. Le roman féminin. Paris: P.U.F.,
1976.

Otten, Anna. "Perpetual Motion in Nathalie Sarraute's
Novels." Paper presented at the MLA meeting,
New York City, December 1976.

Racevskis, Karlis. "Social Satire of Nathalie Sarraute."
Paper presented at the MLA meeting, New York
City, December 1976.

Shaw, Elizabeth Baird. "The Comic Novels of Ivy Compton-Burnett and Nathalie Sarraute." Ph.D. Dissertation, University of Colorado, 1974.

SARTON, MAY

Bakerman, Jane S. "A Conversation with May Sarton:
Interview." Paper presented at the MLA meeting,
New York City, December 1976.

Blouin, Lenora P. May Sarton: A Bibliography. Metuchen, N.J.: Scarecrow Press, 1978.

Brown, Rosellen. Parnassus, Spring/Summer 1973,
pp. 49-50. (Review of A Durable Fire.)

Chasin, Helen. Village Voice, 13 June 1974, pp. 36-38.
(Review of Mrs. Stevens Hears the Mermaids Singing.)

Cleveland, Carol L. "Outclassed in America." Paper
presented at the MLA meeting, San Francisco,
December 1975.

Connelly, Maureen. "Death and Love: The Eternal
Equation: The Sonnets of May Sarton." Paper
presented at the MLA meeting, San Francisco, December 1975.

Grumbach, Doris. "The Long Solitude of May Sarton."
New Republic, 8 June 1974, pp. 31-32.

Klein, Kathleen Gregory. "To Grow Old and Die."
Paper presented at the MLA meeting, San Francisco, December 1975.

Knies, Elizabeth. Commonweal 102, no. 8 (1975): 250-252. (Review of Collected Poems, 1930-1973.)

Lydon, Mary. "A French Scholar's Feminist View of May Sarton." Paper presented at the MLA meeting, San Francisco, December 1975.

Martin, James. "Questions of Style." Poetry 126 (May 1975): 103-115. (Review of Collected Poems, 1930-1973.)

Nichols, Marianna de Vinci. "Women on Women: The Looking Glass Novel." Denver Quarterly 11 (Autumn 1976): 1-13.

Rule, Jane. Lesbian Images. Garden City, N.Y.: Doubleday, 1975.

Shulman, Bonnie. "Exemplary Encounters: An Airplane's View of American Life." Third Press Review 1 (September/October 1975): 49. (Review of Crucial Conversations.)

Taylor, Henry. "Home to a Place Beyond Exile: The Collected Poems of May Sarton." Hollins Critic 11 (June 1974): 1-16.

Wortham, Thomas. "'Teach Me to Heare Mermaides Singing': Sacred and Profane Love in the Novels of May Sarton." Paper presented at the MLA meeting, San Francisco, December 1975.

SAYERS, DOROTHY L.

Auerbach, Nina. "Dorothy Sayers and the Amazons." Feminist Studies 3 (Fall 1975): 54-62.

Hitchman, Janet. Such a Strange Lady: A Biography of Dorothy L. Sayers, 1893-1957. New York: Harper & Row, 1975.

Wölcken, Fritz. "Dorothy Sayers." In Englische Dichter du Moderne: Ihr Leben und Werk, pp. 393-398. Edited by Rudolf Suhnel and Dieter Riesner. Berlin: Schmidt, 1971.

SCHAEFFER, SUSAN FROMBERG

Alexander, Edward. "The Holocaust in American-Jewish Fiction: A Slow Awakening." Judaism 25 (Summer 1976): 320-330.

Brown, Linda. "Books in Short." Ms. 4 (November 1975): 59. (Review of Granite Lady.)

Haverkamp, Larry. Chicago Review 27 (Summer 1975): 192-196. (Review of Granite Lady.)

Koltun, Elizabeth. The Jewish Woman: New Perspectives. New York: Schocken, 1976.

Parisi, Joseph. "Personae, Personalities." Poetry 126 (July 1975): 239-241. (Review of Granite Lady.)

SCHILLER, FRIEDRICH

Borchardt, Frank L. "Goethe, Schiller, Sphinx, Centaur, and Sex." Monatschefte 64 (February 1972): 247-255.

Dreyfuss, Cecilia Anne Stiborik. "Femina sapiens in Drama: Aeschylus to Grillparzer." Ph.D. Dissertation, The University of Michigan, 1975.

Herrera, Bertilia. "Racine, Alfieri, and Schiller: A Comparative Study of Heroines." Ph.D. Dissertation, University of California, Riverside, 1977.

Ross, Carol Jean. "Schiller and Hebbel: Characters and Ideas and the Portrayal of Women." Ph.D. Dissertation, University of Toronto, 1974.

Sheeran, Joan Garner. "Women and the Freedom-to-Be in Selected Works of Schiller and the Romantics." Ph.D. Dissertation, University of Minnesota, 1976.

SCHLEGEL, FRIEDRICH von

Flavell, M. Kay. "Women and Individualism: A Reexamination of Schlegel's Lucinde and Gutzkow's Wally die Zweiflerin." Modern Language Review 70 (July 1975): 550-566.

Littlejohns, Richard. "The 'Bekenntnisse eines unge-
schickten': A Re-Examination of Emancipatory
Ideas in Friedrich Schlegel's Lucinde." Modern
Language Review 72 (July 1977): 605-614.

Sheeran, Joan Garner. "Women and the Freedom-to-Be
in Selected Works of Schiller and the Romantics."
Ph. D. Dissertation, University of Minnesota, 1976.

SCHLEGEL, JOHANN ELIAS

Sanders, Ruth Hetmanski. "The Virtuous Woman in the
Comedies of the Early German Enlightenment."
Ph. D. Dissertation, State University of New York at
Stony Brook, 1975.

SCHNITZLER, ARTHUR

Driver, B. R. "Arthur Schnitzler's Frau Berta Garlan:
A Study in Form." Germanic Review 46 (November
1971): 285-298.

Rose, Ingrid Barbara. "Social Stereotypes and Female
Actualities: A Dimension of the Social Criticism in
Selected Works by Fontane, Hauptmann, Wedekind,
and Schnitzler." Ph. D. Dissertation, Princeton University, 1976.

SCHOR, LYNDA

Schwartz, Lynne Sharon. "The Courage to Go Too Far."
Ms. 4 (January 1976): 30, 37-38.

SCHREINER, OLIVE

Bastian, Carol Emery. "A First Generation of Autobio-
graphical Novelists: Olive Schreiner, William Hale
White ('Mark Rutherford') and Samuel Butler."
Ph. D. Dissertation, Indiana University, 1975.

Fernando, Lloyd. "New Women" in the Late Victorian
Novel. University Park: Pennsylvania State University Press, 1977.

Fox, Marcia Rose. "The Woman Question in Selected
Victorian Fiction, 1883-1900." Ph. D. Dissertation,
The City University of New York, 1975.

Gray, Stephen. "Schreiner's Trooper at the Hanging Tree." English in Africa 2 (September 1975): 23-37.

Heywood, Christopher. "Olive Schreiner's The Story of an African Farm: Prototype of Lawrence's Early Novels." English Language Notes 14 (September 1976): 44-50.

Higgins, Sue. "Olive Schreiner: A Free Human Being." Refractory Girl 6 (1974): 18-22.

Kmetz, Gail Kessler. "Lost Women: Olive Schreiner-- Woman of the Karroo." Ms. 6 (August 1977): 90-94.

Scanlon, Leone. "The New Woman in the Literature of 1883-1909." University of Michigan Papers in Women's Studies 2, no. 2 (1976): 133-159.

Showalter, Elaine. A Literature of Their Own: British Women Novelists from Brontë to Lessing. Princeton: Princeton University Press, 1977.

Speegle, Katherine Sloan. "God's Newer Will: Four Examples of Victorian Angst Resolved by Humanitarianism." Ph.D. Dissertation, North Texas State University, 1975.

Toth, Emily. "The Independent Woman and 'Free' Love." Massachusetts Review 16 (Autumn 1975): 647-664.

SCHWARZ-BART, SIMONE

Danielson, J. David. " 'Télumée Miracle' and the Creole Experience." International Fiction Review 3 (January 1976): 35-46.

Larson, C. R. New Republic, 6 April 1974, p. 28. (Review of The Bridge of Beyond.)

Updike, John. New Yorker, 12 August 1974, p. 96-97. (Review of The Bridge of Beyond.)

SCOTT, EVELYN

Seidel, Kathryn Lee. "The Southern Belle: Her Fall from the Pedestal in Fiction of the Southern

Renaissance. " Ph. D. Dissertation, University of
Maryland, 1976.

SCOTT, SIR WALTER

Bedick, David B.   "The Changing Role of Anxiety in the
Novel. "   Ph. D. Dissertation, New York University,
1975.

Hoffeld, Laura Diamond.   "The Servant Heroine in 18th
and 19th Century British Fiction: The Social Reality
and Its Image in the Novel. "   Ph. D. Dissertation,
New York University, 1975.

SCUDDER, VIDA

Maglin, Nan Bauer.   "Rebel Women Writers, 1894-1925."
Ph. D. Dissertation, Union Graduate School, 1975.

SCUDERY, MADELEINE de

Crosland, Margaret.   Women of Iron and Velvet: French
Women After George Sand.   New York: Taplinger,
1976.

MacLean, Ian.   Woman Triumphant: Feminism in
French Literature 1610-1652.   New York: Oxford
University Press, 1977.

SECOND MAIDEN'S TRAGEDY

Lancashire, Anne.   "The Second Maiden's Tragedy: A
Jacobean Saint's Life. "   Review of English Studies
25 (1974): 267-279.

SEDGWICK, CATHARINE MARIE

Doubleday, Neal Frank.   Variety of Attempt: British
and American Fiction in the Early Nineteenth Century.   Lincoln: University of Nebraska Press,
1976.

Douglas, Ann.   The Feminization of American Culture.
New York: Alfred A. Knopf, 1977.

Foster, Edward Halsey.   The Civilized Wilderness:
Backgrounds to American Romantic Literature,
1817-1860.   New York: Free Press, 1975.

SEGAL, ERICH

Yurick, Sol. " 'Oliver's Story' Means Never Having to Say You're ... Poor. " <u>Ms.</u> 5 (May 1977): 74-76, 101-102.

SEMBENE, OUSMANE

Lanthiez-Schweitzer, Marie-Alice Louise Simone. "Ousmane Sembène: Romancier de l'Afrique Emergente. " Ph. D. Dissertation, The University of British Columbia, 1976.

Lee, Sonia. "The Awakening of the Self in the Heroines of Sembene Ousmane. " <u>Critique</u> 17 (December 1975): 17-25.

_____. "Women in the Novels of Ousmane Sembène. " Paper presented at the MLA meeting, San Francisco, December 1975.

SEMONIDES

Badian, E. <u>New York Review of Books</u>, 30 October 1975, p. 28. (Review of Lloyd-Jones' <u>Females of the Species: Semonides on Women.</u>)

Lloyd-Jones, Hugh. "Females of the Species: On 118 Lines of Semonides. " <u>Encounter</u> 44 (May 1975): 42-55.

SENDER, RAMON J.

Alvarez, Elsa Delia. "La obra de Ramón J. Sender (estudio de sus personajes femeninos). " Ph. D. Dissertation, Michigan State University, 1971.

SENECA

Fantham, Elaine. "Virgil's Dido and Seneca's Tragic Heroines. " <u>Greece & Rome</u> 22 (April 1975): 1-9.

Motto, Anna Lydia. "Seneca on Women's Liberation. " <u>Classical World</u> 65 (January 1972): 155-157.

SENGHOR, LEOPOLD SEDAR

Brown, Lloyd W. "The African Woman as Writer. "

Canadian Journal of African Studies 9, no. 3 (1975): 493-502.

_____ . "Mannequins and Mermaids--The Contemporary Writer and Sexual Images in the Consumer Culture." Women's Studies 5, no. 1 (1977): 1-12.

SERAO, MATILDE

Howard, J. J. "The Feminine Vision of Matilde Serao." Italian Quarterly 18 (Winter 1975): 55-77.

SERRANA, ELISA

Welles, Marcia L. " 'El casamiento engañoso': Marriage in the Novels of María Luisa Bombal, Silvina Bullrich, and Elisa Serrana." In Female Studies IX: Teaching About Women in the Foreign Languages, pp. 121-128. Edited by Sidonie Cassirer. Old Westbury, N.Y.: Feminist Press, 1975.

SETOUCHI HARUMI

Johnson, Eric W. "Modern Japanese Women Writers." Literature East and West 8 (March 1974): [90]-102.

SEWARD, ANNA

Mahl, Mary R. and Helene Koon, eds. The Female Spectator: English Women Writers Before 1800. Bloomington and Old Westbury, N.Y.: Indiana University Press and The Feminist Press, 1977.

SEWELL, ELIZABETH MISSING

Frerichs, Sarah Cutts. "Elizabeth Missing Sewell: A Minor Novelist's Search for the Via Media in the Education of Women in the Victorian Era." Ph.D. Dissertation, Brown University, 1974.

Showalter, Elaine. A Literature of Their Own: British Women Novelists from Brontë to Lessing. Princeton: Princeton University Press, 1977.

SEXTON, ANNE

Anne Sexton. San Francisco: San Francisco State University/The Poetry Center, n.d. (Video cassette.)

Armstrong, Roberta R. "Sexton's Transformations: Beyond Confessionalism." Iowa English Bulletin Yearbook 24 (Fall 1974): 57-66.

Axelrod, Steven G. Modern Poetry Studies 6, no. 2 (1975): 187-189. (Review of The Awful Rowing Toward God.)

Brinnin, John Malcolm and Bill Read, eds. Twentieth Century Poetry: American and British (1900-1970), 2nd ed. New York: McGraw-Hill, 1970.

Dash, Irene. "The Literature of Birth and Abortion." Regionalism and the Female Imagination 3 (Spring 1977): 8-13.

Feder, Lillian. "Myths of Madness in Twentieth-Century Literature: Dionysos, the Maniai, and Hades." Psychocultural Review 1 (Spring 1977): 131-151.

Heyen, William. "Holy Whispers Beside the Grave." Newsday, 23 March 1975, pp. 16, 20.

Howard, Ben. "Shattered Glass." Poetry 127 (February 1976): 286-292.

Juhasz, Suzanne. Naked and Fiery Forms: Modern American Poetry by Women, A New Tradition. New York: Harper & Row, 1976.

Mazzocco, Robert. New York Review of Books, 3 April 1975, p. 20. (Review of The Awful Rowing Toward God.)

Meinke, Peter. "Poet as Loser." New Republic, 22 June 1974, pp. 27-28.

Northouse, Cameron and Thomas P. Walsh. Sylvia Plath and Anne Sexton: A Reference Guide. Boston: G. K. Hall, 1974.

Oates, Joyce Carol. New York Times Book Review, 23 March 1975, p. 3. (Review of The Awful Rowing Toward God.)

Phillips, Robert. "The Bleeding Rose and the Blooming Mouth." Modern Poetry Studies 1, no. 1 (1970): 41-47.

Showalter, Elaine and Carol Smith. "A Nurturing Relationship: A Conversation with Anne Sexton and
Maxine Kumin, April 15, 1974." Women's Studies
4, no. 1 (1976): 115-135.

Tarozzi, Bianca. "Poesia e regressione: Anne Sexton."
Annali de Ca' Foscari (Venezia) 12 (1973): 355-365.

Whitman, Ruth. Harvard Magazine (July/August 1975):
66. (Review of The Awful Rowing Toward God.)

SHADWELL, THOMAS

Hume, Robert D. "The Myth of the Rake in 'Restoration' Comedy." Studies in the Literary Imagination
10 (Spring 1977): 25-55.

Novak, Maximillian E. "Margery Pinchwife's 'London
Disease': Restoration Comedy and the Libertine Of-
fensive in the 1670's." Studies in the Literary
Imagination 10 (Spring 1977): 1-24.

SHAKESPEARE, WILLIAM

Asals, Heather. "Venus and Adonis: The Education of
a Goddess." Studies in English Literature 3 (Winter
1973): 31-51.

Bamber, Linda Vigderman. "Comic Women, Tragic
Men: Genre and Sexuality in Shakespeare's Plays."
Ph.D. Dissertation, Tufts University, 1974.

Bean, John C. "Passion Versus Friendship in the Tudor Matrimonial Handbooks and Some Shakespearean
Implications." Wascana Review 9 (Spring 1974): 231-
240.

Boose, Lynda E. "Othello's Handkerchief: 'The Recog-
nizance and Pledge of Love.'" English Literary
Renaissance 5 (Autumn 1975): 360-374.

Brown, Gillian Fansler. "The Disguised Heroines in
Shakespeare's Comedies." Ph.D. Dissertation, Tulane University, 1975.

Browne, Marlene Consuela. "Shakespeare's Lady Mac-
Beth and Cleopatra: Women in a Political Context."
Ph.D. Dissertation, Brown University, 1976.

Byars, John A. "Taming of the Shrew and Who's Afraid of Virginia Woolf?" Cimarron Review 21 (1972): 41-48.

Cox, Marjorie Kolb. "Adolescent Processes in Romeo and Juliet." Psychoanalytic Review 63 (Autumn 1976): 379-392.

Doran, Madeleine. "The Idea of Excellence in Shakespeare." Shakespeare Quarterly 27 (Spring 1976): 133-149.

Dreyfuss, Cecilia Anne Stiborik. "Femina sapiens in Drama: Aeschylus to Grillparzer." Ph.D. Dissertation, The University of Michigan, 1975.

Dunn, Catherine M. "The Changing Image of Woman in Renaissance Society and Literature." In What Manner of Woman: Essays on English and American Life and Literature, pp. 15-38. Edited by Marlene Springer. New York: New York University Press, 1977.

Dusinberre, Juliet. Shakespeare and the Nature of Women. New York: Barnes & Noble, 1975.

Everett, Barbara. "Romeo and Juliet: The Nurse's Story." Critical Quarterly 14 (Summer 1972): 129-139.

Fineman, Joel. "Fratricide and Cuckoldry: Shakespeare's Doubles." Psychoanalytic Review 64 (Fall 1977): [409]-453.

Fitz, L. T. "Egyptian Queens and Male Reviewers: Sexist Attitudes in Antony and Cleopatra criticism." Shakespeare Quarterly 28 (Summer 1977): 297-316.

Ford, Jane M. "The Father/Daughter/Suitor Triangle in Shakespeare, Dickens, James, Conrad, and Joyce." Ph.D. Dissertation, State University of New York at Buffalo, 1975.

Gira, Catherine Russell. "Shakespeare's Venus Figures and Renaissance Tradition." Ph.D. Dissertation, The American University, 1975.

Goldman, Rachel Margaret. "The Lucretia Legend from Livy to Rojas Zorrilla." Ph.D. Dissertation, City University of New York, 1976.

Gourlay, Patricia Southard. " 'O my most sacred lady': Female Metaphor in The Winter's Tale." English Literary Renaissance 5 (Autumn 1975): 375-395.

Gross, George C. "Mary Cowden Clarke, 'The Girlhood of Shakespeare's Heroines,' and the Sex Education of Victorian Women." Victorian Studies 16 (September 1972): 37-58.

Hill, W. Speed. "Marriage as Destiny: An Essay on All's Well That Ends Well." English Literary Renaissance 5 (Autumn 1975): 344-359.

Hodgson, John A. "Desdemona's Handkerchief as an Emblem of Her Reputation." Texas Studies in Literature and Language 19 (Fall 1977): 313-322.

Jiji, Vera M. "Portia Revisited: The Influence of Unconscious Factors upon Theme and Characterization in The Merchant of Venice." Literature and Psychology 26, no. 1 (1976): 5-15.

Kahn, Coppélia. "Self and Eros in Venus and Adonis." Centennial Review 20 (Fall 1976): 351-371.

_____. "The Taming of the Shrew: Shakespeare's Mirror of Marriage." In The Authority of Experience. Edited by Arlyn Diamond and Lee R. Edwards. Amherst: University of Massachusetts Press, 1977.

Knight, W. Nicholas. "Patrimony and Shakespeare's Daughters." Hartford Studies in Literature 9, nos. 2-3 (1977): 175-186.

Labriola, Albert C. "Renaissance Neoplatonism and Shakespeare's Characterization of Cleopatra." Hebrew University Studies in Literature 3 (Spring 1975): 20-36.

Leggatt, Alexander. Citizen Comedy in the Age of Shakespeare. Toronto: University of Toronto Press, 1973.

McDonald, Margaret Lamb. "The Independent Woman in the Restoration Comedy of Manners." Ph. D. Dissertation, University of Colorado, 1975.

McKewin, Carole. "Shakespeare Liberata: Shakespeare, the Nature of Women, and the New Feminist Criticism." Mosaic 10 (Spring 1977): [157]-164.

Marquit, Doris Grieser. " 'Be Suddenly Revenged': A Shakespearian Way from the Bedroom to the Barricades." University of Michigan Papers in Women Studies 2 (September 1975): 103-111. (Presented under the title "Sex and Politics in Shakespeare's Rape of Lucrece," Midwest Modern Language Association, St. Louis, 1 November 1974.)

Marsh, Derick R. C. Passion Lends Them Power: A Study of Shakespeare's Love Tragedies. New York: Barnes & Noble, 1976.

Miles, Rosalind. The Fiction of Sex: Themes and Functions of Sex Difference in the Modern Novel. New York: Barnes & Noble, 1974.

Novy, Marianne. "Games and Male-Female Relationships in Shakespearean Comedy." Paper presented at the MLA meeting, San Francisco, December 1975.

Peter, Lilian Augustine. "Women as Educative Guardians in Shakespeare's Comedies." Ph. D. Dissertation, Indiana University, 1975.

Rackin, Phyllis. "Coriolanus: Shakespeare's Anatomy of Virtus." Paper presented at the MLA meeting, New York City, December 1976. (Mimeographed.)

Ranald, Margaret. "Gold, Power, and Sex: Shakespeare and the Themes of Citizen Comedy." Paper presented at the MLA meeting, New York City, December 1976.

_____. "Women in Shakespeare: Classical Figures." Deland, Florida: Everett/Edwards, n. d. (Cassette no. 5305.)

_____. "Women in Shakespeare's Comedies." Deland, Florida: Everett/Edwards, n. d. (Cassette no. 5302.)

_____. "Women in Shakespeare's Histories." De-
land, Florida: Everett/Edwards, n. d. (Cassette
no. 5303.)

_____. "Women in Shakespeare's Last Plays." De-
land, Florida: Everett/Edwards, n. d. (Cassette
no. 5306.)

_____. "Women in Shakespeare's Tragedies." De-
land, Florida: Everett/Edwards, n. d. (Cassette
no. 5304.)

Rice, Nancy Hall. "Beauty and the Beast and the Little
Boy: Clues About the Origins of Sexism and Racism
from Folklore and Literature: Chaucer's 'The
Prioress's Tale', Sir Gawain and the Green Knight,
Webster's The Duchess of Malfi, Shakespeare's
Othello, Hawthorne's 'Rappaccini's Daughter', Mel-
ville's 'Benito Cereno.'" Ph.D. Dissertation, Uni-
versity of Massachusetts, 1975.

Rinehart, Keith. "Shakespeare's Cleopatra and England's
Elizabeth." Shakespeare Quarterly 23 (Winter 1972):
81-86.

Rockas, Leo. "'Lechery eats itself': Troilus and
Cressida." Ariel: A Review of International English Literature 8 (January 1977): [17]-32.

Rothchild, Herbert B., Jr. "The Oblique Encounter:
Shakespeare's Confrontation of Plutarch with Special
Reference to Antony and Cleopatra." English Lite-
rary Renaissance 6 (Autumn 1976): 404-429.

Rothenberg, Alan B. "Infantile Fantasies in Shakespearean Metaphor: III. Photophobia, Love of Darkness,
and 'Black' Complexions." Psychoanalytic Review
64 (Summer 1977): 173-202.

Rowse, A. L. Sex and Society in Shakespeare's Age:
Simon Forman the Astrologer. New York: Charles
Scribner's Sons, 1974.

Rudat, Wolfgang E. H. "Shakespeare and Virgil Parodied: The Rape of Lucrece in the Light of Pope's
Rape of the Lock." Eighteenth-Century Life 2 (June
1976): 98-102.

Sadler, Lynn Veach. "The Three Guises of Lady Macbeth." CLA Journal 19 (September 1975): 10-19.

Salter, Nancy Kay Clark. "Masks and Roles: A Study of Women in Shakespeare's Drama." Ph.D. Dissertation, The University of Connecticut, 1975.

Schwartz, Murray M. "The Winter's Tale: Loss and Transformation." American Imago 32 (Summer 1975): 145-199.

Shapiro, Michael. "Pathetic Heroines and the Rival Traditions: Shakespeare's Antony and Cleopatra in Relation to Plays of the Children's Companies." Paper presented at the MLA meeting, New York City, December 1976.

Smith, Karen Diane. "Women of Nobility in Shakespeare's English History Plays." Ph.D. Dissertation, Northwestern University, 1975.

Sproat, Kezia Bradford Vanmeter. "A Reappraisal of Shakespeare's View of Women." Ph.D. Dissertation, The Ohio State University, 1975.

Still, Roger. Love and Death in Renaissance Tragedy. Baton Rouge: Louisiana State University Press, 1976.

Trombetta, James. "Versions of Dying in Measure for Measure." English Literary Renaissance 6 (Winter 1976): 60-76.

Zimmerman, Eugenia Noik. "The Proud Princess Gets Her Comeuppance: Structures of Patriarchal Order." Canadian Review of Comparative Literature 3 (Fall 1976): [252]-268.

SHANGE, NTOZAKE

Bambara, Toni Cade. " 'For Colored Girls'--And White Girls, Too." Ms. 5 (September 1976): 36-38. (Review of For Colored Girls Who Have Considered Suicide/When the Rainbow Is Enuf.)

Bond, Jean Carey. Freedomways 16 (Third Quarter 1976): 187-191. (Review of For Colored Girls Who Have Considered Suicide/When the Rainbow is Enuf.)

Gussow, Mel. 'Stage: 'Colored Girls' on Broadway.''
New York Times, 16 September 1976, p. 53.

Harris, Jessica. '' 'For Colored Girls Who Have Considered Suicide/When the Rainbow Is Enuf'--The
Women Who Are the Rainbow.'' Essence 7 (November 1976): 87-89, 102-104, 120-122, 147.

Hughes, Catherine. ''Two Black Plays.'' America, 9
October 1976, p. 214. (Review of For Colored
Girls Who Have Considered Suicide/When the Rain-
bow Is Enuf.)

''An Interview with Ntozake Shange.'' New Yorker, 2
August 1976, pp. 17-19.

Latour, M. ''Ntozake Shange: Driven Poet/Playwright
(An Interview).'' Mademoiselle (September 1976):
182+.

Lewis, Barbara. ''The Poet.'' Essence 7 (November
1976): 86, 119-120. (Interview.)

''Ntozake Shange Interviews Herself.'' Ms. 6 (December
1977): 35, 70, 72.

People, 5 July 1976, pp. 68-69.

Players 3 (December 1976): 24-25. (Review of For
Colored Girls Who Have Considered Suicide/When
the Rainbow Is Enuf.)

Ribowsky, Mark. ''A Poetess Scores a Hit with Play on
What's Wrong with Black Men.'' Sepia 25 (December 1976): 42-48.

Wallace, Michele. ''For Colored Girls the Rainbow Is
Not Enough.'' Village Voice, 16 August 1976,
pp. 108-109.

SHARP, EVELYN

Gibson, Susan Monteith. ''Love and the Vote: Fiction
of the Suffrage Movement in Edwardian England.''
Ph.D. Dissertation, University of Massachusetts,
1975.

SHAW, GEORGE BERNARD

Brown, Barbara Browning. "Qualities of Bernard Shaw's 'Unreasonable Man.' " Ph.D. Dissertation, Ohio University, 1976.

Dolis, John J., Jr. "Bernard Shaw's Saint Joan: Language Is Not Enough." Massachusetts Studies in English 4 (Autumn 1974-Winter 1975): 17-25.

Henderson, Lucile Kelling. "Shaw and Woman: A Bibliographical Checklist." Shaw Review 17 (January 1974): 60-66.

Knight, Eunice Edna. "The Role of Women in the Don Juan and Faust Literature." Ph.D. Dissertation, Florida State University, 1973.

Meyers, Jeffrey. Married to Genius. New York: Barnes & Noble, 1977.

Potter, Roseanne Guiditta. "The Rhetoric of Seduction: The Structure and Meaning of Shaw's Major Barbara." Ph.D. Dissertation, The University of Texas at Austin, 1975.

Scanlon, Leone. "The New Woman in the Literature of 1883-1909." University of Michigan Papers in Women's Studies 2, no. 2 (1976): 133-159.

Stockholder, Fred E. "A Schopenhauerian Reading of Heartbreak House." Shaw Review 19 (January 1976): 22-43.

Turco, Alfred, Jr. Shaw's Moral Vision: The Self and Salvation. Ithaca: Cornell University Press, 1976.

Watson, Barbara Bellow. "On Power and the Literary Text." Signs: Journal of Women in Culture and Society 1 (Autumn 1975): 111-118.

Weintraub, Rodelle, ed. Fabian Feminist: Bernard Shaw and Woman. University Park: The Pennsylvania State University Press, 1977.

SHELLEY, MARY WOLLSTONECRAFT

Gardner, Joseph H. "Mary Shelley's Divine Tragedy." Essays in Literature 4 (Fall 1977): 182-197.

Hill, J. M. "Frankenstein and the Physiognomy of Desire." American Imago 32 (1975): 335-358.

Hirsch, Gordon D. "The Monster Was a Lady: On the Psychology of Mary Shelley's Frankenstein." Hartford Studies in Literature 7, no. 2 (1975): 116-153.

Joseph, Gerhard. "Frankenstein's Dream: The Child as Father of the Monster." Hartford Studies in Literature 7, no. 2 (1975): 97-115.

Moers, Ellen. Literary Women. Garden City, N.Y.: Doubleday, 1976.

Rubenstein, Marc A. " 'My accursed Origin': The Search for the Mother in Frankenstein." Studies in Romanticism 15 (1976): 165-194.

Smith, Susan Harris. "Frankenstein: Mary Shelley's Psychic Divisiveness." Women & Literature 5 (Fall 1977): 42-53.

Taylor, Irene and Gina Luria. "Gender and Genre: Women in British Romantic Literature." In What Manner of Woman: Essays on English and American Life and Literature, pp. 98-124. Edited by Marlene Springer. New York: New York University Press, 1977.

Todd, Janet M. "Frankenstein's Daughter: Mary Shelley and Mary Wollstonecraft." Women & Literature 4 (Fall 1976): 18-27.

Weissman, Judith. "A Reading of Frankenstein as the Complaint of a Political Wife." Colby Library Quarterly 12 (December 1976): 171-180.

SHELLEY, PERCY BYSSHE

Martinez, Alicia. "The Hero and Heroine of Shelley's The Revolt of Islam." Ph.D. Dissertation, Columbia University, 1974.

Norton, Henry Raymond, II. "The Archetypal Feminine in the Poetry of Percy Bysshe Shelley." Ph. D. Dissertation, Syracuse University, 1976.

Taylor, Irene and Gina Luria. "Gender and Genre: Women in British Romantic Literature." In What Manner of Woman: Essays on English and American Life and Literature, pp. 98-124. Edited by Marlene Springer. New York: New York University Press, 1977.

SHERIDAN, RICHARD BRINSLEY

Durant, Jack D. "Sheridan's 'Royal Sanctuary': A Key to The Rivals." Ball State University Forum 14, no. 1 (1973): 23-30.

SHIH MIN

Eber, Irene. "Images of Women in Recent Chinese Fiction: Do Women Hold Up Half the Sky?" Signs: Journal of Women in Culture and Society 2 (Autumn 1976): 24-34.

SHIPMAN, SAMUEL

Shafer, Y. B. "Liberated Women in American Plays of the Past." Players Magazine 49 (Spring 1974): 95-100.

SHIRAISHI KAZUKO

Ikuko Atsumi. "Five Modern Women Poets on Love." Literature East and West 8 (March 1974): [58]-75.

_____. "Modern Japanese Women Poets: After the Meiji Restoration." Iowa Review 7 (Spring/Summer 1976): 227-237.

SHIRLEY, JAMES

Hume, Robert D. "Marital Discord in English Comedy from Dryden to Fielding." Modern Philology 74 (February 1977): 248-272.

McDonald, Margaret Lamb. "The Independent Woman in the Restoration Comedy of Manners." Ph. D. Dissertation, University of Colorado, 1975.

SHUDRAKA

Hagman, Lorri. "Two Famous Courtesans: Vasantesena and Miss Tu." Journal of South Asian Literature 12 (Spring-Summer 1977): 31-36.

SHULMAN, ALIX KATES

Kolodny, Annette. "Some Notes on Defining a 'Feminist Literary Criticism.'" Critical Inquiry 2 (Autumn 1975): 75-92.

Masinton, Martha and Charles G. Masinton. "Second-class Citizenship: The Status of Women in Contemporary American Fiction." In What Manner of Woman: Essays in English and American Life and Literature, pp. 297-315. Edited by Marlene Springer. New York: New York University Press, 1977.

SICILIANO, ENZO

Barrett, Joanna. International P.E.N. 25, no. 4 (1976): 89-90. (Review of La notte matrigna.)

SIGOURNEY, MRS. LYDIA HUNTLEY

Douglas, Ann. The Feminization of American Culture. New York: Alfred A. Knopf, 1977.

Riley, Glenda Gates. "The Subtle Subversion: Changes in the Traditionalist Image of the American Woman." Historian 32 (February 1970): 210-227.

Watts, Emily Stipes. The Poetry of American Women from 1632 to 1945. Austin: University of Texas Press, 1977.

Wood, Ann Douglas. "Mrs. Sigourney and the Sensibility of the Inner Space." New England Quarterly 45 (June 1972): 163-181.

_____. "The 'Scribbling Women' and Fanny Fern: Why Women Wrote." American Quarterly 23 (Spring 1971): 3-24.

SILKO, LESLIE

Blicksilver, Edith. "Leslie Silko and the American

Indian Woman: Traditionalism versus Modernity."
Paper presented at the MLA meeting, New York
City, December 1976.

Ruoff, LaVonne. "Keres Sources for Leslie Silko's
'Yellow Woman.'" Paper presented at the MLA
meeting, New York City, December 1976.

SILVA, FELICIANO de

Trisler, Barbara Jean. "A Comparative Study of the
Character Portrayal of 'Celestina' and Other Golden
Age Celestinesque Protagonists." Ph.D. Disserta-
tion, The University of Oklahoma, 1977.

SILVER, JOAN MICKLIN

Rosen, Marjorie. "Three Films in Search of a Dis-
tributor." Ms. 4 (July 1975): 30-33. (Review of
Hester Street.)

SIMMS, WILLIAM GILMORE

Kolodny, Annette. The Lay of the Land: Metaphor as
Experience and History in American Life and Letters.
Chapel Hill: University of North Carolina Press,
1975.

SIMON, CLAUDE

DuVerlie, Claud. "Amor Interruptus: The Question of
Eroticism or, Eroticism in Question in the Works of
Claude Simon." Sub-Stance no. 8 (Winter 1974): 21-
33.

Loubère, J. A. E. The Novels of Claude Simon. Ithaca: Cornell University Press, 1975.

Makward, Christiane. "Claude Simon: Earth, Death
and Eros." Sub-Stance no. 8 (Winter 1974): 35-43.

SINCLAIR, MAY

Gibson, Susan Monteith. "Love and the Vote: Fiction
of the Suffrage Movement in Edwardian England."
Ph.D. Dissertation, University of Massachusetts,
1975.

Kaplan, Sydney Janet. "May Sinclair." In The Feminine Consciousness and the British Novel. Urbana: University of Illinois Press, 1975.

Kinnamon, Rebeccah Ann. "May Sinclair's Fiction of the Supernatural." Ph. D. Dissertation, Duke University, 1974.

SINGER, ISAAC BASHEVIS

Penn, Joyce Paula. "Some Major Themes in the Short Fiction of Isaac Bashevis Singer." Ph. D. Dissertation, Stanford University, 1975.

SITWELL, EDITH

Brinnin, John Malcolm and Bill Read, eds. Twentieth Century Poetry: American and British (1900-1970), 2nd ed. New York: McGraw-Hill, 1970.

Ehrstine, John and Douglas Rich. "Edith Sitwell." Bulletin of Bibliography 31, no. 3 (1975): 111-116.

Ower, John B. "Cosmic Aristocracy and Cosmic Democracy in Edith Sitwell." Contemporary Literature 12 (Autumn 1971): 527-553.

_____. "A Golden Labyrinth: Edith Sitwell and the Theme of Time." Renascence 26 (1974): 207-217.

SLESSINGER, TESS

Baum, Charlotte, Paula Hyman and Sonya Michel. The Jewish Woman in America. New York: Dial Press, 1975.

SMEDLEY, AGNES

Hesford, Walter. "Literary Contexts of 'Life in the Iron-Mills.'" American Literature 49 (March 1977): 70-85.

Kahn, Coppelia. "Lost and Found." Ms. 2 (April 1974): 36, 117-118. (Review of Life in the Iron Mills.)

Lander, Dawn. "Women and the Wilderness: Tabus in American Literature." University of Michigan Papers in Women's Studies 2, no. 3 (1977): 62-83.

Lauter, Paul. Afterword to Daughter of Earth by Agnes Smedley. Old Westbury, N.Y.: Feminist Press, 1974.

MacKinnon, Jan and Steve. "Agnes Smedley: A Working Introduction." Bulletin of Concerned Asian Scholars 7 (January-March 1975): 6-11.

Olsen, Tillie. Biographical Interpretation to Life in the Iron Mills. Old Westbury, N.Y.: Feminist Press, 1974.

Piercy, Marge. "Writer's Choice." Partisan Review 22, no. 1 (1975): 157. (Review of Daughters of Earth.)

SMEDLEY, CONSTANCE

Gibson, Susan Monteith. "Love and the Vote: Fiction of the Suffrage Movement in Edwardian England." Ph.D. Dissertation, University of Massachusetts, 1975.

SMITH, CHARLOTTE

Ellis, Katherine. "Charlotte Smith's Subversive Gothic." Feminist Studies 3 (Spring-Summer 1976): 51-55.

Roberts, Bette B. "The Gothic Romance: Its Appeal to Women Writers and Readers in Late Eighteenth-Century England." Ph.D. Dissertation, University of Massachusetts, 1975.

Rogers, Katharine M. "Inhibitions on Eighteenth-Century Women Novelists: Elizabeth Inchbald and Charlotte Smith." Eighteenth-Century Studies 11 (Fall 1977): 63-78.

SMITH, CORDWAINER

Wymer, Thomas L. "Cordwainer Smith: Satirist or Male Chauvinist?" Extrapolation 14 (May 1973): 157-162.

SMITH, ELIZABETH OAKES

> Douglas, Ann. The Feminization of American Culture.
> New York: Alfred A. Knopf, 1977.

> Watts, Emily Stipes. The Poetry of American Women
> from 1632 to 1945. Austin: University of Texas
> Press, 1977.

SMITH, HARRY JANES

> Loudin, Joanne Marie. "The Changing Role of the
> Comic Heroine in American Drama from 1900 to
> 1940." Ph. D. Dissertation, University of Washing-
> ton, 1974.

SMITH, LILLIAN

> Contemporary Authors: Permanent Series, vol. 2.

SMITH, SEBA

> Curry, Jane Anne. "Women as Subjects and Writers of
> Nineteenth-Century American Humor." Ph. D. Dis-
> sertation, The University of Michigan, 1975.

SMOLLETT, TOBIAS

> Flanders, W. Austin. "The Significance of Smollett's
> Memoirs of a Lady of Quality." Genre 8 (June
> 1975): 146-164.

SOLZHENITSYN, ALEKSANDR

> Gasiorowska, X. "Solzhenitsyn's Women." In Aleksandr
> Solzhenitsyn: Critical Essays and Documentary Ma-
> terials. Edited by J. B. Dunlop, R. Haugh, and
> A. Klimoff. Nordland, 1973.

> Jackson, Robert Louis. "'Matryona's Home': The Mak-
> ing of a Russian Icon." In Solzhenitsyn: A Collec-
> tion of Critical Essays, pp. 60-70. Edited by
> Kathryn Feuer. Englewood Cliffs, N. J.: Prentice-
> Hall, 1976.

> Rothberg, Abraham. Aleksandr Solzhenitsyn: The Ma-
> jor Novels. Ithaca: Cornell University Press, 1971.

Spitz, Sheryl A. "The Impact of Structure in Solzhenitsyn's 'Matryona's Home.' " Russian Review 36
(April 1977): 167-183.

SOMERSET, LADY HENRY

Gibson, Susan Monteith. "Love and the Vote: Fiction
of the Suffrage Movement in Edwardian England. "
Ph. D. Dissertation, University of Massachusetts,
1975.

SONO AYAKO

Johnson, Eric W. "Modern Japanese Women Writers. "
Literature East and West 8 (March 1974): [90]-102.

SONTAG, SUSAN

Shinn, Thelma J. Wardrop. "A Study of Women Characters in Contemporary American Fiction 1940-
1970. " Ph. D. Dissertation, Purdue University,
1972.

SOPHOCLES

Dreyfuss, Cecilia Anne Stiborik. "Femina sapiens in
Drama: Aeschylus to Grillparzer. " Ph. D. Dissertation, The University of Michigan, 1975.

Gelderman, Carol W. "The Male Nature of Tragedy. "
Prairie Schooner 49 (Fall 1975): 220-227.

Pomeroy, Sarah B. Goddesses, Whores, Wives, and
Slaves: Women in Classical Antiquity. New York:
Schocken Books, 1975.

Wiltshire, Susan Ford. "Antigone's Disobedience. "
Arethusa 9 (Spring 1976): 29-36.

Yim, Chol Kyu. "Mythological Figures in Ancient Greek
and Modern Drama: Orestes and Antigone. " Ph. D.
Dissertation, Indiana University, 1975.

SORENSEN, VIRGINIA

Geary, Edward A. "Women Regionalists of Mormon
Country. " Paper presented at the MLA meeting,
New York City, December 1976. (Mimeographed.)

SOSEKI NATSUME

Ueda, Makoto. Modern Japanese Writers and the Nature of Literature. Stanford: Stanford University Press, 1976.

SOUTHERNE, THOMAS

Greenberg, Joseph Lawrence. "English Marriage and Restoration Comedy, 1688-1710." Ph.D. Dissertation, Princeton University, 1976.

Hume, Robert D. "Marital Discord in English Comedy from Dryden to Fielding." Modern Philology 74 (February 1977): 248-272.

_____. "The Myth of the Rake in 'Restoration' Comedy." Studies in the Literary Imagination 10 (Spring 1977): 25-55.

Kaufman, Anthony. "This Hard Condition of a Woman's Fate: Southerne's The Wives' Excuse." Modern Language Quarterly 34 (March 1973): 36-47.

SOUTHWORTH, MRS. E. D. E. N.

Foster, Edward Halsey. The Civilized Wilderness: Backgrounds to American Romantic Literature, 1817-1860. New York: Free Press, 1975.

Garrison, Dee. "Immoral Fiction in the Late Victorian Library." American Quarterly 28 (Spring 1976): 71-89.

SOUZA, MME de

Schwartz, Lucy McCallum. "The Image of Women in the Novels of Mme de Souza." University of Michigan Papers in Women's Studies 1 (June 1974): 142-148.

SOYINKA, WOLE

Staudt, Kathleen. "The Characterization of Women by Soyinka and Armah." Afras Review (Sussex) 1, no. 1 (1975): 40-43.

SOYSU, NOEMIA de

Brown, Lloyd W. "The African Woman as Writer."
Canadian Journal of African Studies 9, no. 3 (1975):
493-502.

SPARK, MURIEL

Blodgett, Harriet. "Desegregated Art by Muriel Spark."
International Fiction Review 3 (January 1976): 25-29.

Bradbury, Malcolm. "Muriel Spark's Fingernails." In
Contemporary Women Novelists: A Collection of
Critical Essays, pp. 137-149. Edited by Patricia
Meyer Spacks. Englewood Cliffs, N.J.: Prentice-
Hall, 1977.

Harrison, Bernard. "Muriel Spark and Jane Austen."
In The Modern English Novel: The Reader, The
Writer, and The Work, pp. 225-251. Edited by
Gabriel Josipovici. New York: Barnes & Noble,
1976.

Kemp, Peter. Muriel Spark. New York: Barnes &
Noble, 1975.

Kmetz, Gail Kessler. " 'Come Let Us Mock at the
Great....' " Ms. 4 (May 1976): 22-24, 27. (Re-
view of The Abbess of Crewe: A Modern Morality
Tale.)

Laffin, Gerry Starr. "Unresolved Dualities in the
Novels of Muriel Spark." Ph.D. Dissertation, University of Wisconsin, 1973.

Mongeon, Joanne Catherine Parnell. "A Theology of
Juxtaposition: Muriel Spark as a Catholic Comic
Novelist." Ph.D. Dissertation, University of Rhode
Island, 1977.

Schneider, Mary W. "The Double Life in Muriel
Spark's The Prime of Miss Jean Brodie." Midwest
Quarterly 18 (July 1977): 418-431.

Tominaga, Thomas T. and Wilma Schneidermeyer. Iris
Murdoch and Muriel Spark: A Bibliography. Metuchen, N.J.: Scarecrow Press, 1976.

SPENCE, CATHERINE HELEN

Ramson, W. S., ed. The Australian Experience. Canberra: Australian National, 1974.

SPENCER, ANNE

Greene, J. Lee. Time's Unfading Garden: Anne Spencer's Life and Poetry. Baton Rouge: Louisiana State University Press, 1977.

Greene, Johnny Lee. "Anne Spencer: A Study of Her Life and Poetry." Ph.D. Dissertation, The University of North Carolina at Chapel Hill, 1974.

SPENSER, EDMUND

Baxter, Charles. "Spider Lady: Images of Domination in Book II of The Faerie Queene." Paunch 35 (1972): 67-99.

Bledsoe, Audrey Shaw. "Spenser's Use of the Myth of Isis in The Faerie Queene." Ph.D. Dissertation, Emory University, 1975.

Blitch, Alice Fox. "Proserpina Preserved: Book VI of The Faerie Queene." Studies in English Literature 3 (Winter 1973): 15-30.

Brill, Lesley W. "Battles That Need Not Be Fought: The Faerie Queene, III.i." English Literary Renaissance 5 (Spring 1975): 198-211.

Dunn, Catherine M. "The Changing Image of Woman in Renaissance Society and Literature." In What Manner of Woman: Essays on English and American Life and Literature, pp. 15-38. Edited by Marlene Springer. New York: New York University Press, 1977.

Geller, Lila. "The Acidalian Vision: Spenser's Graces in Book VI of The Faerie Queene." Review of English Studies 23 (August 1972): 267-277.

Gerenday, Lynnde. "The Problem of Self-Reflective Love in Book III of The Faerie Queene." Literature and Psychology 26, no. 1 (1976): 37-48.

Holahan, Michael. "Imaque opus exegi: Ovid's Changes and Spenser's Brief Epic of Mutability." English Literary Renaissance 6 (Spring 1976): 244-270.

Hutchinson, Mary Anne. "The Devil's Gateway: The Evil Enchantress in Ariosto, Tasso, Spenser, and Milton." Ph. D. Dissertation, Syracuse University, 1975.

Sims, Dwight J. "The Syncretic Myth of Venus in Spenser's Legend of Chastity." Studies in Philology 71 (October 1974): 427-450.

SPIVACK, KATHLEEN

Gilbert, Sandra M. Poetry 127 (October 1975): 44. (Review of The Jane Poems.)

Klappert, Peter. "Knowing It." Parnassus 3 (Fall/ Winter 1974): 93-96. (Review of Flying Inland.)

Ostroff, Anthony. Western Humanities Review 28 (Summer 1974): 305-306. (Review of Flying Inland.)

Pritchard, William H. New York Times Book Review, 18 May 1975, pp. 36, 38. (Review of The Jane Poems.)

STAËL, MME de

Crosland, Margaret. Women of Iron and Velvet: French Women After George Sand. New York: Taplinger, 1976.

Gutwirth, Madelyn. Madame de Staël, Novelist: The Emergence of the Artist as Woman. Urbana: University of Illinois Press, 1978.

Harmon, Danuté Staknis. "The Antithetical World View of Madame de Staël: Ideology, Structure, and Style in Delphine and Corinne." Ph. D. Dissertation, The George Washington University, 1975.

Johnson, Danielle Paulette Cousin. "Origines et developpement du cosmopolitisme de Madame de Staël à travers son theatre." Ph. D. Dissertation, University of Illinois at Urbana-Champaign, 1977.

Michaels, Marianne Spalding. "Feminist Tendencies in
the Works of Mme de Staël. " Ph. D. Dissertation,
The University of Connecticut, 1977.

Moers, Ellen. Literary Women. Garden City, N. Y. :
Doubleday, 1976.

Schmitz, Betty Ann. "French Women Writers and Their
Critics: An Analysis of the Treatment of Women
Writers in Selected Histories of French Literature. "
Ph. D. Dissertation, The University of Wisconsin-
Madison, 1977.

Tenebaum, Susan. "Mme DeStaël. " Deland, Florida:
Everett/Edwards, n. d. (Cassette no. 5522.)

STAFFORD, JEAN

Galfant, Blanche H. New Republic, 10 May 1975,
pp. 22-25. (Review of The Mountain Lion.)

Mann, Jeanette W. "Toward New Archetypal Forms:
Boston Adventure. " Studies in the Novel 8 (Fall
1976): 291-303.

_____. "Toward New Archetypal Forms: Jean Staf-
ford's The Catherine Wheel. " Critique 17 (December 1975): 77-92.

Shinn, Thelma J. Wardrop. "A Study of Women Characters in Contemporary American Fiction 1940-1970. "
Ph. D. Dissertation, Purdue University, 1972.

STANFORD, ANN

Chenoy, Polly Naoshir. "Dives and Descents: Thematic
Strategies in the Poetry of Adrienne Rich and Ann
Stanford. " Ph. D. Dissertation, University of Utah,
1975.

STEAD, CHRISTINA

"Christina Stead: An Interview. " Australian Literary
Studies 6 (May 1974): 230-248.

Gardiner, Judith Kegan. "Christina Stead: Dark Places
of the Heart. " North American Review 262 (Spring
1977): 67-71.

Koch, Stephen. Saturday Review, 10 July 1976, p. 50.
(Review of Miss Herbert.)

Lidoff, Joan. "Christina Stead: An Interview." Aphra
6 (Spring-Summer 1976): 39-64.

Lipsett, Suzanne. "Discovering Christina Stead." San
Francisco Review of Books 2 (September 1976): 15-
16.

McLaughlin, Marilou Briggs. "The Love Dialectic."
Ph.D. Dissertation, State University of New York at
Binghamton, 1976.

Nestor, Pauline. "An Impulse to Self-Expression: The
Man Who Loved Children." Critical Review no. 18
(1976): 61-78.

Updike, John. New Yorker, 9 August 1976, p. 74. (Review of Miss Herbert.)

Yglesias, Helen. New York Times Book Review, 13
June 1976, p. 4. (Review of Miss Herbert.)

STEELE, RICHARD

Hume, Robert D. "Marital Discord in English Comedy
from Dryden to Fielding." Modern Philology 74
(February 1977): 248-272.

McDonald, Margaret Lamb. "The Independent Woman in
the Restoration Comedy of Manners." Ph.D. Dissertation, University of Colorado, 1975.

STEGNER, WALLACE

Ahearn, Kerry. "Heroes vs. Women: Conflict and Du-
plicity in Stegner." Western Humanities Review 31
(Spring 1977): 125-141.

STEIN, GERTRUDE

Cooper, Janet and Cynthia Secor. "The Lesbian in
Literature." Los Angeles, Calif.: Pacifica Tape
Library, 1974.

Copeland, Carolyn Faunce. Language and Time and Gertrude Stein. Iowa City: University of Iowa Press, 1975.

Denne, Constance Ayres. "Gertrude Stein." Deland, Florida: Everett/Edwards, n.d. (Cassette no. 5512.)

Farber, Lawren. "Fading: A Way. Gertrude Stein's Sources for Three Lives." Journal of Modern Literature 5 (September 1976): 463-480.

Fifer, Elizabeth. "Put the Language in the Waist: Stein's Critique of Women in Geography and Plays." University of Michigan Papers in Women's Studies 2 (September 1975): 96-102.

Hoffman, Frederick J. "Gertrude Stein." In American Writers, vol. 4, pp. 25-48. Edited by Leonard Unger. New York: Charles Scribner's Sons, 1974.

Hoffman, Michael J. Gertrude Stein. New York: Twayne, 1976.

Katz, Leon. "Introduction" to Fernhurst, Q. E. D., and Other Early Writings by Gertrude Stein. New York: Liveright, 1971.

Klaich, Dolores. Woman + Woman: Attitudes Toward Lesbianism. New York: Simon & Schuster, 1974.

Kostelanetz, Richard. "Gertrude Stein: The New Literature." Hollins Critic 12 (June 1975): [1]-15.

LaJoy, Maureen. "No Laughing Matter: Women and Humor." Women 5, no. 1 (1976): 6-9.

Mellow, James R. Charmed Circle: Gertrude Stein and Company. New York: Avon Books, 1975.

Moers, Ellen. Literary Women. Garden City, N.Y.: Doubleday, 1976.

Rose, Marilyn Gaddis. "Gertrude Stein and Cubist Narrative." Modern Fiction Studies 22 (Winter 1976-77): 543-555.

Rule, Jane. Lesbian Images. Garden City, N.Y.: Doubleday, 1975.

Simm, Linda, ed. Gertrude Stein: A Composite Portrait. New York: Avon, 1974.

Sorell, Walter. Three Women: Lives of Sex and Genius. New York: Bobbs-Merrill, 1975.

Steiner, Wendy Lois. "Gertrude Stein's Portrait Form." Ph.D. Dissertation, Yale University, 1974.

Stimpson, Catharine R. "The Mind, the Body, and Gertrude Stein." Critical Inquiry 3 (Spring 1977): 489-506.

Thurman, J. "Gertrude Stein." Ms. 2 (February 1974): 54-57.

Ward, Hazel Mae. "The Black Woman as Character: Images in the American Novel, 1852-1953." Ph.D. Dissertation, The University of Texas at Austin, 1977.

Watts, Emily Stipes. The Poetry of American Women from 1632 to 1945. Austin: University of Texas Press, 1977.

Wilson, Ellen. They Named Me Gertrude Stein. New York: Farrar, Straus & Giroux, 1973.

Wilson, Robert A. Gertrude Stein: A Bibliography. New York: Phoenix Bookshop, 1974.

STEINBECK, JOHN

Cook, Sylvia Jenkins. From Tobacco Road to Route 66: The Southern Poor White in Fiction. Chapel Hill: The University of North Carolina Press, 1976.

Ditsky, John M. "The Ending of The Grapes of Wrath: A Further Commentary." Agora: A Journal in the Humanities and Social Sciences 2, no. 2 (1973): 41-50.

_____. "Words and Deeds in Viva Zapata!" Dalhousie Review 56 (Spring 1976): [125]-131.

Goodman, Charlotte. "Images of American Rural Women in the Novel." University of Michigan Papers in Women's Studies 1 (June 1975): 57-70.

Mitchell, Marilyn L. "Steinbeck's Strong Women:

Feminine Identity in the Short Stories." Southwest Review 61 (Summer 1976): 304-315.

Morita, Shoji. "Steinbeck's View of Womanhood: The Meaning of 'the time of waiting' in The Long Valley." Studies in American Literature 8 (1972): 39-52.

Spilka, Mark. "Of George and Lennie and Curley's Wife: Sweet Violence in Steinbeck's Eden." Modern Fiction Studies 20 (Summer 1974): 169-180.

Sweet, Charles A., Jr. "Ms. Elisa Allen and Stein-beck's 'The Chrysanthemums.' " Modern Fiction Studies 20 (Summer 1974): 210-214.

Tuttleton, James W. " 'Combat in the Erogenous Zone': Women in the American Novel Between the Two World Wars." In What Manner of Woman: Essays in English and American Life and Literature, pp. 271-296. Edited by Marlene Springer. New York: New York University Press, 1977.

STENDHAL (Marie Henri Beyle)

Bolster, Richard. Stendhal, Balzac, et le féminisme romantique. Paris: Lettres modernes, 1970.

Davidson, Joan Marie. "The Heroines in the Novels of Stendhal." Ph.D. Dissertation, The City University of New York, 1976.

Yalom, Marilyn K. "Triangles and Prisons: A Psycho-logical Study of Stendhalian Love." Hartford Studies in Literature 8, no. 2 (1976): 82-97.

STEPHENS, ANN SOPHIA

Garrison, Dee. "Immoral Fiction in the Late Victorian Library." American Quarterly 28 (Spring 1976): 71-89.

STERN, DANIEL

Crosland, Margaret. Women of Iron and Velvet: French Women After George Sand. New York: Taplinger, 1976.

Rabine, Leslie Ruth. "The Other Side of the Ideal: Women Writers of Mid-Nineteenth-Century France (George Sand, Daniel Stern, Hortense Allart, and Flora Tristan)." Ph.D. Dissertation, Stanford University, 1973.

STERNE, LAURENCE

Baker, Van R. "Whatever Happened to Lydia Sterne?" Eighteenth-Century Life 2 (September 1975): 6-11.

Spacks, Patricia Meyer. Imagining a Self: Autobiography and Novel in Eighteenth-Century England. Cambridge: Harvard University Press, 1976.

STEVENS, WALLACE

Flake, Carol Ann. "Demoiselles and Paramours: Wallace Stevens' ad hoc Muses." Ph.D. Dissertation, Tulane University, 1973.

Gustafson, Richard. "'Time Is a Waiting Woman': New Poetic Icons." Midwest Quarterly 16 (April 1975): 318-327.

Mizejewski, Linda. "Images of Woman in Wallace Stevens." Thoth 14, no. 1 (1973-74): 13-21.

Watsky, Paul Norman. "The Human Figures in Wallace Stevens' Poetry." Ph.D. Dissertation, State University of New York at Buffalo, 1974.

STEVENSON, ANNE

Conn, Stewart. Listener, 28 November 1974. (Review of Travelling Behind Glass.)

Dunn, Douglas. Encounter 43 (December 1974): 72. (Review of Correspondences.)

Matthias, John. Poetry 127 (November 1975): 98. (Review of Correspondences.)

STODDARD, ELIZABETH DREW

Weir, Sybil. "The Morgesons: A Neglected Feminist Bildungsroman." New England Quarterly 49 (September 1976): 427-439.

STOKER, BRAM

Weissman, Judith. "Women as Vampires: Dracula as a
Victorian Novel." Midwest Quarterly 18 (July 1977):
392-405.

STORMI, ALFORSINA

Wolf, Donna M. "Women in Latin American Literature."
Room of One's Own 1 (Fall 1975): 73-83.

STOWE, HARRIET BEECHER

Adams, John R. "Structure and Theme in the Novels of
Harriet Beecher Stowe." American Transcendental
Quarterly 24, part 1 (1974): 50-55A.

Ammons, Elizabeth. "Heroines in Uncle Tom's Cabin."
American Literature 49 (May 1977): 161-179.

Douglas, Ann. The Feminization of American Culture.
New York: Alfred A. Knopf, 1977.

Eakin, Paul John. The New England Girl: Cultural
Ideals in Hawthorne, Stowe, Howells, and James.
Athens: University of Georgia Press, 1976.

Foster, Edward Halsey. The Civilized Wilderness:
Backgrounds to American Romantic Literature, 1817-
1860. New York: Free Press, 1975.

Lebedun, Jean. "Harriet Beecher Stowe's Interest in
Sojourner Truth, Black Feminist." American Literature 46 (1974): 359-363.

Marotta, Kenny Ralph. "The Literary Relationship of
George Eliot and Harriet Beecher Stowe." Ph.D.
Dissertation, Johns Hopkins University, 1974.

Moers, Ellen. Literary Women. Garden City, N.Y.:
Doubleday, 1976.

Rotundo, Barbara. "Harriet Beecher Stowe and the
Mythmakers." American Notes and Queries 12
(May/June 1974): 131-133.

Ruoff, John C. "Frivolity to Consumption: Or,

Southern Womanhood in Antebellum Literature."
Civil War History 181 (September 1972): 213-229.

Seidel, Kathryn Lee. "The Southern Belle: Her Fall
from the Pedestal in Fiction of the Southern Renaissance." Ph.D. Dissertation, University of Maryland, 1976.

Ward, Hazel Mae. "The Black Woman as Character:
Images in the American Novel, 1852-1953." Ph.D.
Dissertation, The University of Texas at Austin, 1977.

STRATTON-PORTER, GENE

Ifkovic, Edward. "The Garden of the Lord: Gene
Stratton-Porter and the Death of Evil in Eden."
Journal of Popular Culture 8 (Spring 1975): 757-766.

STRINDBERG, AUGUST

Stenberg, Peter. "Strindberg and Grillparzer: Contrasting Approaches to the War of the Sexes." Canadian
Review of Comparative Literature 1 (1974): 65-75.

STYRON, WILLIAM

Shinn, Thelma J. Wardrop. "A Study of Women Characters in Contemporary American Fiction 1940-
1970." Ph.D. Dissertation, Purdue University, 1972.

SUCKLING, JOHN

Latt, David J. "Praising Virtuous Ladies: The Literary Image and Historical Reality in Seventeenth-
Century England." In What Manner of Woman: Essays on English and American Life and Literature,
pp. 39-64. Edited by Marlene Springer. New York:
New York University Press, 1977.

Markel, Michael H. "John Suckling's Semi-serious
Love Poetry." Essays in Literature 4 (Fall 1977):
152-158.

SUCKOW, RUTH

Goodman, Charlotte. "Images of American Rural Women in the Novel." University of Michigan Papers
in Women's Studies 1 (June 1975): 57-70.

Omreanin, Margaret Steward. <u>Ruth Suckow</u>. Philadelphia: Dorrance, 1972.

SUGITA HISAJO

Ikuko Atsumi. "Modern Japanese Women Poets: After the Meiji Restoration." <u>Iowa Review</u> 7 (Spring/ Summer 1976): 227-237.

SUTHERLAND, EFUA T.

Brown, Lloyd W. "The African Woman as Writer." <u>Canadian Journal of African Studies</u> 9, no. 3 (1975): 493-502.

SUYIN, HAN

Rule, Jane. <u>Lesbian Images</u>. Garden City, N.Y.: Doubleday, 1975.

SVEVO, ITALO

Robison, Paula. "Senileta: The Secret of Svevo's Weeping Madonna." <u>Italian Quarterly</u> 14 (Winter 1972): 61-84.

SWENSON, MAY

Brinnin, John Malcolm and Bill Read, eds. <u>Twentieth Century Poetry: American and British (1900-1970)</u>, 2nd ed. New York: McGraw-Hill, 1970.

<u>Poetry Is Alive and Well and Living in America</u>. Pleasantville, N.Y.: Educational Audio Visual Inc., n.d. (LP recordings and filmstrips.)

Wallace, Ronald. "Alone with Poems." <u>Colorado Quarterly</u> 23 (1975): 341-353.

SWIFT, JONATHAN

Byrd, Max. "The Madhouse, the Whorehouse, and the Convent." <u>Partisan Review</u> 44, no. 2 (1977): 268-278.

Dervin, Daniel A. "Breast Fantasy in Barthelme, Swift, and Philip Roth: Creativity and Psychoanalytic

Structure. " American Imago 33 (Spring 1976): 102-
122.

Jaffe, Nora Crow. "Swift and the Agreeable Young
Lady, but Extremely Thin. " Paper presented at
the MLA meeting, New York City, December 1976.

Richetti, John J. "The Portrayal of Women in Restoration and Eighteenth-Century English Literature. "
In What Manner of Woman: Essays on English and
American Life and Literature, pp. 65-97. Edited
by Marlene Springer. New York: New York University Press, 1977.

Schakel, Peter J. "Swift's Remedy for Love: The
'Scatological' Poems. " Paper presented at the
MLA meeting, New York City, December 1976.
(Mimeographed.)

Tyne, James L. , S. J. "Vanessa and the Houghnhnms:
A Reading of 'Cadenus and Vanessa. ' " Studies in
English Literature, 1500-1900 11 (Summer 1971):
517-534.

SWINBURNE, ALGERNON CHARLES

Fass, Barbara. La Belle Dame sans Merci and the
Aesthetics of Romanticism. Detroit: Wayne State
University Press, 1974.

Fricke, Douglas C. "The Proserpine Figure in Swinburne's Poems and Ballads I. " In Aeolian Harps,
pp. 191-206. Edited by Donna G. Fricke and Douglas C. Fricke. Bowling Green: Bowling Green University Press, 1976.

Johnson, Wendell Stacy. Sex and Marriage in Victorian
Poetry. Ithaca: Cornell University Press, 1975.

Snider, Clifton. "The Archetypal Self in Swinburne's
'Tristram of Lyonesse. ' " Psychocultural Review
1 (Summer 1977): 371-390.

Workman, Gillian. "La Soeur de la Reine and Related
'Victorian Romances' by Swinburne. " Harvard Library Bulletin 21 (October 1973): 356-364.

SYDNEY, SIR PHILIP

Lanham, Richard A. "Astrophil and Stella: Pure and
Impure Persuasion." English Literary Renaissance
2 (Winter 1972): 100-115.

SYMONDS, EMILY

Gibson, Susan Monteith. "Love and the Vote: Fiction
of the Suffrage Movement in Edwardian England."
Ph.D. Dissertation, University of Massachusetts,
1975.

SYNGE, JOHN MILLINGTON

O'Donnell, Beatrice. "Synge and O'Casey Women: A
Study in Strong Mindedness." Ph.D. Dissertation,
Michigan State University, 1976.

Solomen, Albert J. "The Bird Girls of Ireland." Colby
College Quarterly 10 (March 1974): 259-269.

- T -

TABASSUM, BEGUM

Agrawakm, Chandra P. "Dreams, Schemes and Rebellion in the Fiction of Begum Tabassum." Journal
of South Asian Literature 12 (Spring-Summer 1977):
45-54.

TADA CHIMAKO

Ikuko Atsumi. "Five Modern Women Poets on Love."
Literature East and West 8 (March 1976): [58]-75.

TAGORE, RABINDRANATH

Lago, Mary M. "Tagore's Liberated Women." Journal
of South Asian Literature 12 (Spring-Summer 1977):
103-107.

TANAZAKI JUN'ICHIRO

Flood, Cynthia. "Images of Women in Modern

Japanese Fiction." Room of One's Own 1 (Spring 1975): 18-25.

Lippit, Noriko Mizuta. "Tanizaki and Poe: The Grotesque and the Quest for Supernal Beauty." Comparative Literature 29 (Summer 1977): 221-240.

Makoto Ueda. Modern Japanese Writers and the Nature of Literature. Stanford: Stanford University Press, 1976.

TARKINGTON, BOOTH

Sorkin, Adam J. " 'She Doesn't Last, Apparently': A Reconsideration of Booth Tarkington's Alice Adams." American Literature 46 (May 1974): 182-199.

TASSO, TORQUATO

Cooper, Henry Ronald Jr. "Tasso's Women: The Slavic Literary Epic." Ph.D. Dissertation, Columbia University, 1974.

Hutchinson, Mary Anne. "The Devil's Gateway: The Evil Enchantress in Ariosto, Tasso, Spenser, and Milton." Ph.D. Dissertation, Syracuse University, 1975.

MacLean, Ian. Woman Triumphant: Feminism in French Literature 1610-1652. New York: Oxford University Press, 1977.

Musumeci, Antonino. "Tasso, Zola and the Vicissitudes of Pastoralism." Nineteenth-Century French Studies 4 (Spring 1976): 344-360.

TATE, ALLEN

Seidel, Kathryn Lee. "The Southern Belle: Her Fall from the Pedestal in Fiction of the Southern Renaissance." Ph.D. Dissertation, University of Maryland, 1976.

TAYLOR, ELEANOR ROSS

Jong, Erica. "Three Sisters." Parnassus no. 1 (Fall-Winter 1972): 77-78. (Review essay.)

Walker, Cheryl. "Welcome Eumenides: Contemporary
Feminist Poets." Feminist Art Journal 2 (Winter
1973-74): 6-7.

TAYLOR, ELIZABETH

Maddox, Brenda. Who's Afraid of Elizabeth Taylor?
New York: M. Evans, 1977.

TENCIN, CLAUDINE-ALEXANDRINE de

Kavaliunas, Jolita Elijana Jurate. "Passions and the
Search for Happiness: The Concepts of Passions
and Guilts in Their Relationship to Happiness, as
Manifested in Certain French Novels of the Eighteenth
Century." Ph.D. Dissertation, Case Western Re-
serve, 1972.

Vachon, Marie-Françoise. "Les Romans de Madame de
Tencin." Ph.D. Dissertation, Columbia University,
1975. (French text.)

TENNYSON, ALFRED

Ball, Patricia M. The Heart's Events: The Victorian
Poetry of Relationships. London: University of
London, The Athlone Press, 1976.

Behnken, Eloise. "Love, Desire, and Victorian Poets."
Occasional Review Issue 6 (Summer 1977): [149]-157.

Bonner, Arnold Frank. "Tennyson's Treatment of Married Love." Ph.D. Dissertation, The University of
North Carolina at Chapel Hill, 1977.

Christ, Carol. "Victorian Masculinity and the Angel in
the House." In A Widening Sphere: Changing Roles
of Victorian Women, pp. 146-162. Edited by Martha
Vicinus. Bloomington: Indiana University Press,
1977.

Gallant, Christine. "Tennyson's Use of the Nature Goddess in 'The Hesperides,' 'Tithonus,' and 'Demeter
and Persephone.'" Victorian Poetry 14 (Summer
1976): 155-160.

Johnson, Wendell Stacy. Sex and Marriage in Victorian
Poetry. Ithaca: Cornell University Press, 1975.

Kissane, James D. Alfred Tennyson. New York: Twayne, 1970.

Kozicki, Henry. "The 'Medieval Ideal' in Tennyson's 'The Princess.'" Criticism 17 (Spring 1975): 121-130.

Reed, John R. Victorian Conventions. Athens: Ohio University Press, 1975.

Sait, James E. "Tennyson's The Princess and Queen Mary: Two Examinations of Sex and Politics." Durham University Journal 37 (December 1975): 70-78.

Springer, Marlene. "Angels and Other Women in Victorian Literature." In What Manner of Woman: Essays on English and American Life and Literature, pp. 124-159. Edited by Marlene Springer. New York: New York University Press, 1977.

Story, Kenneth E. "Theme and Image in The Princess." In Tennessee Studies in Literature, pp. 50-59. Knoxville: The University of Tennessee Press, 1975.

Trudgill, Eric. Madonnas and Magdalens: The Origins and Development of Victorian Sexual Attitudes. New York: Holmes & Meier, 1976.

Twitchell, James. "Desire with Loathing Strangely Mixed: The Dream Work of Christobel." Psychoanalytic Review 61 (Spring 1974): 33-44.

Ward, Arthur Douglas. "Death and Eroticism in the Poetry of Keats and Tennyson." Ph.D. Dissertation, University of California, Berkeley, 1975.

TERENCE

Fantham, Elaine. "Sex, Status, and Survival in Hellenistic Athens: A Study of Women in New Comedy." Phoenix 29 (Spring 1975): 44-74.

TERRIS, VIRGINIA R.

Faery, Rebecca B. Hollins Critic 14 (February 1977): 16-17. (Review of Tracking.)

THACKERAY, WILLIAM MAKEPEACE

Allen, Richard O. "If You Have Tears: Sentimentalism as Soft Romanticism." Genre 8 (June 1975): 119-145.

Calder, Jenni. Women and Marriage in Victorian Fiction. London: Thames & Hudson, 1976.

Ferris, Ina. "The Breakdown of Thackeray's Narrator: Lovel the Widower." Nineteenth-Century Fiction 32 (June 1977): 36-53.

Hoffeld, Laura Diamond. "The Servant Heroine in 18th and 19th Century British Fiction: The Social Reality and Its Image in the Novel." Ph.D. Dissertation, New York University, 1975.

Lerner, Laurence. "Thackeray and Marriage." Essays in Criticism 25 (July 1975): 279-303.

McMaster, Juliet. "Thackeray's Things: Time's Local Habitation." In The Victorian Experience: The Novelists, pp. 49-86. Edited by Richard A. Levine. Athens: Ohio University Press, 1976.

Natov, Roni L. "The Strong-Minded Heroine in Mid-Victorian Fiction." Ph.D. Dissertation, New York University, 1975.

Parker, David. "Thackeray's Barry Lyndon." Ariel 6 (October 1975): 68-80.

Rawlins, Jack P. Thackeray's Novels: A Fiction That Is True. Berkeley: University of California Press, 1974.

Reed, John R. Victorian Conventions. Athens: Ohio University Press, 1975.

Roussel, Roy. "Reflections on the Letter: The Reconciliation of Distance and Presence in Pamela." ELH 41 (Fall 1974): 375-399.

Sullivan, Karen Lever. "The Muse of Fiction: Fatal Women in the Novels of W. M. Thackeray, Thomas Hardy, and John Fowles." Ph.D. Dissertation, The Johns Hopkins University, 1973.

Trudgill, Eric. Madonnas and Magdalens: The Origins and Development of Victorian Sexual Attitudes. New York: Holmes & Meier, 1976.

Williams, Kristi Fayle. "The Idealized Heroine in Victorian Fiction." Ph.D. Dissertation, Brown University, 1975.

THEOCRITUS

Swigart, Rob. "Theocritus' Pastoral Response to City Women." Bucknell Review 21 (Spring 1973): 145-174.

THOMAS, AUDREY

Atwood, Margaret. New York Times Book Review, 1 February 1976, p. 8. (Review of Blown Figures.)

Wachtel, Eleanor. "The Image of Africa in the Fiction of Audrey Thomas." Room of One's Own 2, no. 4 (1977): 21-28.

THOMAS, AUGUSTUA

Kolb, Deborah S. "The Rise and Fall of the New Woman in American Drama." Educational Theater Journal 27 (1975): 149-160.

THOREAU, HENRY

Moller, Mary Elkins. "Thoreau, Womankind, and Sexuality." ESQ: A Journal of the American Renaissance 22 (Third Quarter 1976): 123-148.

THRALE, MRS (Hester Thrale Piozzi)

Bell, A. S. "A Late View of Mrs. Piozzi." Notes and Queries 18 (September 1971): 337-338.

Bodek, Evelyn Gordon. "Salonières and Bluestockings: Educated Obsolescence and Germinating Feminism." Feminist Studies 3 (Spring-Summer 1976): 183-199.

Corrigan, Beatrice. "Three Englishwomen in Italy." Queen's Quarterly 79 (1972): 147-158.

Dobbs, Jeannine. "The Blue-Stockings: Getting It Together." Frontiers 1 (Winter 1976): 81-93.

Fritz, Paul and Richard Morton, eds. Woman in the Eighteenth Century and Other Essays. Toronto: Samuel Stevens Hakkert, 1976.

Hyde, Mary. The Thrales of Streatham Park. Cambridge: Harvard University Press, 1977.

Lustig, Irma S. "Boswell at Work: The 'Animadversions' on Mrs. Piozzi." Modern Language Review 67 (January 1972): 11-30.

Myers, Sylvia H. "The Ironies of Education." Aphra 4 (Spring 1973): 61-72.

Riely, John C. "Bozzy and Piozzi: The History of Literary Friendship and Rivalry." Ph.D. Dissertation, University of Pennsylvania, 1972.

_____. "Johnson's Last Years with Mrs. Thrale: Facts and Problems." Bulletin of the John Rylands Library 57 (Autumn 1974): 196-212.

_____. "Lady Knight's Role in the Boswell-Piozzi Rivalry." Philological Quarterly 51 (October 1972): 961-965.

Spacks, Patricia Meyer. Imagining a Self: Autobiography and Novel in Eighteenth-Century England. Cambridge: Harvard University Press, 1976.

_____. "Scrapbook of a Self: Mrs. Piozzi's Late Journals." Harvard Library Bulletin 18 (1970): 221-247.

THURMAN, WALLACE

Brown, Martha Hursey. "Images of Black Women: Family Roles in Harlem Renaissance Literature." D. A. Dissertation, Carnegie-Mellon University, 1976.

Doyle, Sister Mary Ellen. "The Heroine of Black Novels." In Perspectives on Afro-American Women, pp. 112-125. Edited by Willa D. Johnson and

Thomas L. Green.   Washington, D.C.: ECCA Publications, 1975.

Gayle, Addison, Jr. The Way of the New World: The Black Novel in America. Garden City, N.Y.: Anchor Press/Doubleday, 1975.

Schulz, Elizabeth. " 'Free in Fact and at Last': The Image of the Black Woman in Black American Literature. " In What Manner of Woman: Essays in English and American Life and Literature, pp. 316-344. Edited by Marlene Springer. New York: New York University Press, 1977.

Ward, Hazel Mae. "The Black Woman as Character: Images in the American Novel, 1852-1953. " Ph.D. Dissertation, The University of Texas at Austin, 1977.

TIBULLUS

Luck, Georg. "The Woman's Role in Latin Love Poetry. " In Perspectives in Roman Poetry, pp. 15-31. Edited by G. Karl Galinsky. Austin: University of Texas Press, 1974.

TIECK, LUDWIG

Fass, Barbara. La Belle Dame sans Merci and the Aesthetics of Romanticism. Detroit: Wayne State University Press, 1974.

Sherran, Joan Garner. "Women and the Freedom-to-Be in Selected Works of Schiller and the Romantics. " Ph.D. Dissertation, University of Minnesota, 1976.

TIRSO DE MOLINA

Knight, Eunice Edna. "The Role of Women in the Don Juan and Faust Literature. " Ph.D. Dissertation, Florida State University, 1973.

TOLSTOY, COUNT LEO

Armstrong, Judith. The Novel of Adultery. New York: Barnes & Noble, 1976.

Banerjee, Marie. "The Metamorphosis of an Icon: Woman in Russian Literature." In Female Studies IX: Teaching About Women in the Foreign Languages, pp. 228-235. Edited by Sidonie Cassirer. Old Westbury, N.Y.: Feminist Press, 1975.

Calder, Jenni. Women and Marriage in Victorian Fiction. London: Thames & Hudson, 1976.

Greene, Gayle. "Women, Character, and Society in Tolstoy's Anna Karenina." Frontiers 2 (Spring 1977): [106]-125.

Grossman, J. D. Slavic Review 33 (December 1974): 833. (Review of Benson's Women in Tolstoy: The Ideal and the Erotic.)

Greenwood, E. B. Tolstoy: The Comprehensive Vision. New York: St. Martin's Press, 1975.

Grossman, Joan. "Tolstoy's Portrait of Anna: Keystone in the Arch." Criticism 18 (Winter 1976): 1-14.

Hamblin, Ellen N. "Adulterous Heroines in Nineteenth Century Literature: A Comparative Literature Study." Ph.D. Dissertation, The Florida State University, 1977.

Kumar, Prem. "Four Figures in Love: Anna Karenin, Emma Bovary, Constance Chatterly [sic], and Chitralekha." Journal of South Asian Literature 12 (Spring-Summer 1977): 73-80.

Meyers, Jeffrey. Married to Genius. New York: Barnes & Noble, 1977.

Nevo, Natan. "Anna Karénine et Thérèse Desqueyroux: Parallèles." Comparative Literature Studies 14 (September 1977): 214-222.

TOMIOKA TAEKO

Ikuko Atsumi. "Five Modern Women Poets on Love." Literature East and West 8 (March 1974): [58]-75.

_____. "Modern Japanese Women Poets: After the Meiji Restoration." Iowa Review 7 (Spring/Summer 1976): 227-237.

TONNA, CHARLOTTE ELIZABETH

Kovacevic, Ivanka and Barbara S. Kanna. "Blue Book into Novel: The Forgotten Industrial Fiction of Charlotte Elizabeth Tonna." Nineteenth Century Fiction 25 (September 1970): 152-173.

Moers, Ellen. Literary Women. Garden City, N.Y.: Doubleday, 1976.

Skilton, David. The English Novel: Defoe to the Victorians. New York: Barnes & Noble, 1977.

TOOMER, JEAN

Brown, Martha Hursey. "Images of Black Women: Family Roles in Harlem Renaissance Literature." D.A. Dissertation, Carnegie-Mellon University, 1976.

Edwards, Sister Ann. "Three Views on Blacks: The Black Woman in American Literature." CEA Critic 37 (May 1975): 14-16.

Faulkner, Howard. "The Buried Life: Jean Toomer's Cane." Studies in Black Literature 7 (Winter 1976): 1-5.

Larson, Charles R. The Novel in the Third World. Washington, D.C.: Inscape, 1976.

Martin, Odette C. "Cane: Method and Myth." Obsidian 2 (Spring 1976): 5-20.

TORRES, DON JULIO ROMERO de

Rodeiro, Joseph Manuel. "A Comparative Study of English 'Pre-Raphaelitism' and Italian 'Preraphaelitism's' Influence on the 'Modernismo' Art of Don Julio Romero de Torres and the Literature of Don Ramón del Valle-Inclán in Their Use of the Feminine Mystique." Ph.D. Dissertation, Ohio University, 1976.

TOURNEUR, CYRIL

Arnold, Peter A. "The Revenger's Tragedy: The

Dramatic Significance of Sex." North Dakota Quarterly 45 (Summer 1977): 70-81.

McDonald, Margaret Lamb. "The Independent Woman in the Restoration Comedy of Manners." Ph. D. Dissertation, University of Colorado, 1975.

Mirenda, Angela Marie. "The Noble Lie: Selfhood and Tragedy in the Renaissance." Ph. D. Dissertation, The Pennsylvania State University, 1977.

Shaw, Sharon K. "Medea on Pegasus: Some Speculations on the Parallel Rise of Women and Melodrama on the Jacobean Stage." Ball State University Forum 14, no. 4 (1973): 13-21.

Still, Roger. Love and Death in Renaissance Tragedy. Baton Rouge: Louisiana State University Press, 1976.

TOURVILLE, ANNE de

Bleuzé, Ruth Allen. "Romancières et Critiques: Etude du Prix Fémina, 1904-1968." Ph. D. Dissertation, University of Colorado at Boulder, 1977.

TOWNSEND, CHRISTINE

Higgins, Sue. "Breaking the Rules: New Fiction by Australian Women." Meanjin Quarterly 34 (December 1975): 415-420.

TRAMBLEY, ESTELA PORTILLO de

Castellano, Ilivia. "Of Clarity and the Moon: A Study of Two Women in Rebellion." La Cosecha: Literatura y la Mujer Chicana 3, no. 3 (1977): 25-29.

TREADWELL, SOPHIE

Hays, Janice. "Themes and Modes of Women's Drama in the Twentieth Century." Paper presented at the MLA meeting, New York City, December 1976. (Mimeographed.)

Heck-Rabi, Louise Evelyn. "Sophie Treadwell: Subjects and Structures in 20th Century American Drama." Ph. D. Dissertation, Wayne State University, 1976.

Shafer, Y. B. "Liberated Women in American Plays of the Past." Players Magazine 49 (Spring 1974): 95-100.

TRISTAN, FLORA

De Santi, Dominique. Excerpt from Flora Tristan. Virginia Woolf Quarterly 2 (Summer & Fall 1976): 219-228.

_____, trans. Elizabeth Zelvin. A Woman in Revolt: A Biography of Flora Tristan. New York: Crown, 1976.

Moers, Ellen. Literary Women. Garden City, N.Y.: Doubleday, 1976.

Pincetl, Giselle. "An Introduction to Flora Tristan." Harvest Quarterly no. 6 (Summer 1977): 3-5.

Rabine, Leslie Ruth. "The Other Side of the Ideal: Women Writers of Mid-Nineteenth Century France (George Sand, Daniel Stern, Hortense Allart, and Flora Tristan)." Ph.D. Dissertation, Stanford University, 1973.

TROLLOPE, ANTHONY

ApRoberts, Ruth. "Emily and Nora and Dorothy and Priscilla and Jemima and Carry." In The Victorian Experience: The Novelists, pp. 87-120. Edited by Richard A. Levine. Athens: Ohio University Press, 1976.

Bartrum, Barry A. "The Parliament Within: A Study of Anthony Trollope's Palliser Novels." Ph.D. Dissertation, Princeton University, 1976.

Eliasberg, Ann Pringle. "The Victorian Anti-Heroine: Her Role in Selected Novels of the 1860's and 1870's." Ph.D. Dissertation, The City University of New York, 1975.

Kennedy, John Dorrance. "Trollope's Widows: Beyond the Stereotypes of Maiden and Wife." Ph.D. Dissertation, The University of Florida, 1975.

Lawson, Mary Sterner. "Class Structure and the Female Character in Anthony Trollope's The Way We Live Now." Ph.D. Dissertation, Bowling Green State University, 1975.

Rinehart, Nana Merete. "Anthony Trollope's Treatment of Women, Marriage, and Sexual Morality Seen in the Context of Contemporary Debate." Ph.D. Dissertation, University of Maryland, 1975.

Weissman, Judith. " 'Old Maids Have Friends': The Unmarried Heroine of Trollope's Barsetshire Novels." Women & Literature 5 (Spring 1977): 15-25.

Williams, Kristi Fayle. "The Idealized Heroine in Victorian Fiction." Ph.D. Dissertation, Brown University, 1975.

TROLLOPE, FRANCES

Heineman, Helen. "Frances Trollope's Jessie Phillips: Sexual Politics and the New Poor Law." International Journal of Women's Studies 1 (January/February 1978): 96-106.

Mitchell, Sally. "Lost Women: Feminist Implications of the Fallen in Works by Forgotten Women Writers of the 1840's." University of Michigan Papers in Women's Studies 1 (June 1974): 110-124.

Skilton, David. The English Novel: Defoe to the Victorians. New York: Barnes & Noble, 1977.

Wallins, Roger P. "Mrs. Trollope's Artistic Dilemma in Michael Armstrong." Ariel: A Review of International English Literature 8 (April 1977): [5]-15.

TROTTER, CATHERINE

Lock, Frederick Peter. "The Dramatic Art of Susanna Centlivre." Ph.D. Dissertation, McMaster University (Canada), 1975.

Reed, John R. Victorian Conventions. Athens: Ohio University Press, 1975.

TSUNG CHING

>Eber, Irene. "Images of Women in Recent Chinese Fiction: Do Women Hold Up Half the Sky?" Signs: Journal of Women in Culture and Society 2 (Autumn 1976): 24-34.

TSVETAEVA, MARINA

>Gove, Antonina Filonov. "The Feminine Stereotype and Beyond: Role Conflict and Resolution in the Poetics of Marina Tsvetaeva." Slavic Review 36 (June 1977): 231-255.

>Taubman, Jane. "Between Letter and Lyric: The Epistolary. Poetic Friendships of Marina Tsvetaeva." Ph.D. Dissertation, Yale University, 1972.

TURGENEV, IVAN SERGEYEVICH

>Banerjee, Marie. "The Metamorphosis of an Icon: Woman in Russian Literature." In Female Studies IX: Teaching About Women in Foreign Languages, pp. 228-235. Edited by Sidonie Cassirer. Old Westbury, N.Y.: Feminist Press, 1975.

TURPIN, WATERS

>Ford, Nick Aaron. "Waters Turpin: I Knew Him Well." CLA Journal 21 (September 1977): 1-18.

TURRELL, JANE COLMAN

>Watts, Emily Stipes. The Poetry of American Women from 1632 to 1945. Austin: University of Texas Press, 1977.

TUTUOLO, AMOS

>Ogunyemi, Chikwenye Okonjo. "The Africanness of The Conjure Woman and Feather Woman of the Jungle." Ariel: A Review of International English Literature 8 (April 1977): [17]-30.

TWAIN, MARK

>Banta, Martha. "They Shall Have Faces, Minds, and

(One Day) Flesh: Women in Late Nineteenth-century
and Early Twentieth-century American Literature. "
In What Manner of Woman: Essays on English and
American Life and Literature, pp. 235-270. Edited
by Marlene Springer. New York: New York University Press, 1977.

Beauchamp, Virginia Walcott. "A Feminist Looks at
Tom and Huck. " Maryland English Journal 12 (Fall
1973): 28-33.

Karpowitz, Stephen. "Tom Sawyer and Mark Twain:
Fictional Women and Real in the Play of Conscience
with the Imagination. " Literature and Psychology
33, no. 1 (1973): 5-12.

TYLER, ANNE

Bouton, Katherine. "Earthly Possessions. " Ms. 6
(August 1977): 35-36. (Review of Earthly Possessions.)

- U -

UNAMUNO, MIGUEL de

Lahr-Well, Almeda Marie. "The Don Juan and Feminist
Myths in Unamuno: A Struggle Toward Consciousness. " Ph. D. Dissertation, Saint Louis University,
1975.

Morales Galán, Carmen. "El tema maternal en la con-
cepción Unamunesca de la mujer. " Ph. D. Dissertation, Louisiana State University, 1971.

Wood, Cynthia Nunnally. "The Mother Image in Selected
Works of Miguel de Unamuno. " Ph. D. Dissertation,
University of Virginia, 1975.

UNO CHIYO

Johnson, Eric W. "Modern Japanese Women Writers. "
Literature East and West 8 (March 1974): [90]-102.

UPDIKE, JOHN

Allen, Mary. The Necessary Blankness: Women in Major American Fiction of the Sixties. Urbana: University of Illinois Press, 1976.

Henden, Josephine. Nation, 30 October 1976, p. 437. (Review of Marry Me.)

Howard, Maureen. New York Times Book Review, 31 October 1976, p. 2. (Review of Marry Me.)

Hunt, G. W. America, 8 January 1977, p. 18. (Review of Marry Me.)

LeClair, Thomas. Commonweal, 4 February 1977, p. 89. (Review of Marry Me.)

Masinton, Martha and Charles G. Masinton. "Second-class Citizenship: The Status of Women in Contemporary American Fiction." In What Manner of Woman: Essays in English and American Life and Literature, pp. 297-315. Edited by Marlene Springer. New York: New York University Press, 1977.

Miller, Karl. New York Review of Books, 3 February 1977, p. 38. (Review of Marry Me.)

Plagman, Linda Marie. "The Modern Pilgrims: Marriage and the Self in the Work of John Updike." Ph.D. Dissertation, Marquette University, 1974.

Schopen, Bernard Anthony. "The Aesthetics of Ambiguity: The Novels of John Updike." Ph.D. Dissertation, University of Nevada, Reno, 1975.

Shinn, Thelma J. Wardrop. "A Study of Women Characters in Contemporary American Fiction 1940-1970." Ph.D. Dissertation, Purdue University, 1972.

Todd, Richard. Atlantic 238 (November 1976): 115. (Review of Marry Me.)

Uphaus, Suzanne Henning. "The Unified Vision of A Month of Sundays." University of Windsor Review 12 (Spring-Summer 1977): 5-16.

- V -

VALENQUELA, LUISA

Cooke, Michael G. "Recent Novels: Women Bearing
Violence." Yale Review 66 (Autumn 1976): 146-155.
(Review of Clara.)

VALERY, PAUL

Knight, Eunice Edna. "The Role of Women in the Don
Juan and Faust Literature." Ph.D. Dissertation,
Florida State University, 1973.

VALLE-INCLAN, RAMON del

Ledesma, Enrique. "Isabel II: Semblanza historica y
creacion literaria." Ph.D. Dissertation, New York
University, 1976.

Ling, D. "Valle-Inclán's Compromise with the Spanish
Stage: El Marqués de Bradomín and Sonatas."
Revue des Langues Vivantes 39, no. 1 (1973): 46-
58.

Rodeiro, Joseph Manuel. "A Comparative Study of English 'Pre-Raphaelitism' and Italian 'Preraphaelitism's' Influence on the 'Modernismo' Art of Don
Julio Romero de Torres and the Literature of Don
Ramón del Valle-Inclán in Their Use of the Feminine
Mystique." Ph.D. Dissertation, Ohio University,
1976.

VANBRUGH, SIR JOHN

Greenburg, Joseph Lawrence. "English Marriage and
Restoration Comedy, 1688-1710." Ph.D. Dissertation, Princeton University, 1976.

Hume, Robert D. "Marital Discord in English Comedy
from Dryden to Fielding." Modern Philology 74
(February 1977): 248-272.

_____. "The Myth of the Rake in 'Restoration'
Comedy." Studies in the Literary Imagination 10
(Spring 1977): 25-55.

VAN DRUTEN, JOHN

>Shafer, Y. B. "Liberated Women in American Plays of the Past." Players Magazine 49 (Spring 1974): 95-100.

VAN DUYN, MONA

>Howard, Richard. "Cutting at the Joints: A Column." American Poetry Review 2 (November/December 1973): 9.

>Wallace, Ronald. "Alone with Poems." Colorado Quarterly 23 (1975): 341-353.

VAN VORST, MARIE

>Maglin, Nan Bauer. "Rebel Women Writers, 1894-1925." Ph.D. Dissertation, Union Graduate School, 1975.

VARGAS LLOSA, MARIO

>Jaquette, Jane S. "Literary Archetypes and Female Role Alternatives: The Woman and the Novel in Latin America." In Female and Male in Latin America: Essays, pp. 3-28. Edited by Ann Pescatello. Pittsburgh: University of Pittsburgh Press, 1973.

VEGA CARPIO, F. LOPE DE see LOPE DE VEGA CARPIO, FELIX

VELASCO, VELASQUEZ de

>Trisler, Barbara Jean. "A Comparative Study of the Character Portrayal of 'Celestina' and Other Golden Age Celestinesque Protagonists." Ph.D. Dissertation, The University of Oklahoma, 1977.

VERGA, GIOVANNI

>Patruno, Nicholas. "An Interpretation of Verga's Eva." Romance Notes 17 (Fall 1976): 57-65.

VERGIL

>Fantham, Elaine. "Virgil's Dido and Seneca's Tragic

Heroines. " Greece & Rome 22 (April 1975): 1-9.

Rudat, Wolfgang E. H. "Shakespeare and Virgil Parodied: The Rape of Lucrece in the Light of Pope's Rape of the Lock. " Eighteenth-Century Life 2 (June 1976): 98-102.

West, Grace Starry. "Women in Vergil's Aeneid. " Ph. D. Dissertation, University of California, Los Angeles, 1975.

VERLAINE, PAUL

Reff, Theodore. "The Influence of Flaubert's Queen of Sheba on Later Nineteenth-Century Literature. " Romanic Review 65 (November 1974): 249-265.

VERMA, BHAGWATI CHARAN

Kumar, Prem. "Four Figures in Love: Anna Karenin, Emma Bovary, Constance Chatterly [sic], and Chitralekha. " Journal of South Asian Literature 12 (Spring-Summer 1977): 73-80.

VESEY, ELIZABETH

Dobbs, Jeannine. "The Blue-Stockings: Getting It Together. " Frontiers 1 (Winter 1976): 81-93.

VICTOR, FRANCES

Sklar, Kathryn Kish. "American Female Historians in Context, 1770-1930. " Feminist Studies 3, nos. 1 and 2 (1975): 171-184.

VIGANO, RENATA

Klopp, Charles D. "Nature and Human Nature in Renata Vigano's L'Agnese va a morjre. " Italian Quarterly 19 (Summer-Fall 1975): 35-52.

VIIDIKAS, VICKI

Higgins, Sue. "Breaking the Rules: New Fiction by Australian Women. " Meanjin Quarterly 34 (December 1975): 415-420.

Moorhead, Finola. "Goodbye Prince Hamlet: The New

Australian Women's Poetry. '' <u>Meanjin Quarterly</u> 34 (Winter 1975): 169-179.

VIK, BJØRG

Lange-Nielson, Sissel. <u>International P. E. N.</u> 21, no. 2 (1970): 150-151. (Review of <u>Weep Beloved Man.</u>)

Waal, Carla. ''The Norwegian Short Story: Bjørg Vik. '' <u>Scandinavian Studies</u> 49 (Spring 1977): 217-223.

VILLALON, CRISTOBAL de

Sims, Edna Niecie. ''El Antifeminismo en la literatura española hasta 1560. '' Ph. D. Dissertation, Catholic University, 1970.

VINCENT, RAYMONDE

Bleuzé, Ruth Allen. ''Romancières et Critiques: Etude du Prix Fémina, 1904-1968. '' Ph. D. Dissertation, University of Colorado at Boulder, 1977.

VIRGIL see VERGIL

VIVES, JUAN LUIS

Schomner, Judith Hughes. ''Juan Luis Vives and Women's Liberation. '' Ph. D. Dissertation, Florida State University, 1975.

Sims, Edna N. ''El antifeminismo en la literatura española hasta 1560. '' Ph. D. Dissertation, Catholic University, 1970.

_____ . ''The Antifeminist Element in the Works of Alfonso Martínez and Juan Luis Vives. '' <u>CLA Journal</u> 18 (September 1974): 52-68.

VIVIEN, RENEE

Brée, Germaine. <u>Women Writers in France: Variations on a Theme.</u> New Brunswick, N. J. : Rutgers University Press, 1973.

Crosland, Margaret. <u>Women of Iron and Velvet: French Women After George Sand.</u> New York: Taplinger, 1976.

Klaich, Dolores. Woman + Woman: Attitudes Toward Lesbianism. New York: Simon & Schuster, 1974.

VOLTAIRE

Gain, Philippe de. "Voltaire et les femmes." Ph.D. Dissertation, Indiana University, 1973.

VONNEGUT, KURT, JR.

Crump, G. B. "D. H. Lawrence and the Immediate Present: Kurt Vonnegut, Jr., Ken Kesey, and Wright Morris." D. H. Lawrence Review 10 (Summer 1977): 103-141.

- W -

WADDINGTON, MIRIAM

Wachtel, Eleanor. "Miriam Waddington in Vancouver." Room of One's Own 3, no. 1 (1977): 2-7.

Zitner, S. P. Canadian Forum 49 (March 1970): 299. (Review of Say Yes.)

WAGMAN, FREDRICA

Berman, Susan K. "You Are What You Eat & Eat & Eat & Eat & Eat." Ms. 3 (May 1975): 94-96. (Review of Magic Man, Magic Man.)

Levin, Martin. New York Times Book Review, 2 February 1975, p. 10. (Review of Magic Man, Magic Man.)

Roth, Philip. Reading Myself and Others. New York: Farrar, Straus, 1975.

WAKOSKI, DIANE

Beis, Patricia Sharon. "Cold Fire: Some Contemporary American Women Poets." Ph.D. Dissertation, St. Louis University, 1972.

Brown, Rosellen. Parnassus (Spring/Summer 1973): 52-59.

Gerber, Philip L. and Robert J. Gemmett, eds. "A Terrible War: A Conversation with Diane Wakowski." Far Point 4 (Spring-Summer 1970): 44-54.

Gustafson, Richard. " 'Time Is a Waiting Woman': New Poetic Icons." Midwest Quarterly 16 (April 1975): 318-327.

Healey, Claire. "An Interview with Diane Wakoski." Contemporary Literature 18 (Winter 1977): 1-19.

Hulbert, Debra. "True Poems." Prairie Schooner 47 (Spring 1973): 81-83.

Ives, Dan and Rick Smith. "Death on the Nile: An Interview with Diane Wakoski." Stonecloud no. 5 (1975): 23-28.

Judy Grahn/Diane Wakoski. San Francisco: San Francisco State University/The Poetry Center, n. d. (Videocassette.)

Kolodny, Annette. "Some Notes on Defining a 'Feminist Literary Criticism.' " Critical Inquiry 2 (Autumn 1975): 75-92.

McClatchy, J. D. Yale Review 65 (Autumn 1975): 95. (Review of Virtuoso Literature for Two and Four Hands.)

Mottram, Eric. Parnassus (Fall/Winter 1972): 160-162.

Olson, Toby, ed. "A Symposium on Diane Wakoski." Margins nos. 28/29/30 (1976): 90-129. (Includes essays by Toby Olson, David R. Smith, Gloria Bowles, Michael Rossman, Theodore Enslin, Rochelle Owens, William E. Thompson, Andrea Musher, Carole Ferrier, Armand Schwerner, David Ignatow, George Economou, Louis Rowan, James F. Mersmann; Poem by Clayton Eshleman.)

Pritchard, William H. "Despairing at Styles." Poetry 127 (February 1976): 292-302.

Raeschild, Sheila. "Awakened: Sexuality in the New Women's Poetry (Judy Grahn, Alta, Diane Wakoski)." Paper presented at the MLA meeting, San Francisco, December 1975.

Smith, Larry. "A Conversation with Diane Wakoski. "
Chicago Review 29 (Summer 1977): 115-125.

Sukenick, Lynn. "Diane Wakoski Dreams Our Dream
for Us. " Village Voice, 17 May 1976, pp. 55-56.

Vendler, Helen. New York Times Book Review, 6 April
1975, p. 4. (Review of Virtuoso Literature for Two
and Four Hands.)

Wakoski, Diane. "The Craft of Carpenters, Plumbers,
& Mechanics: A Column. " American Poetry Review 2 (May/June 1973): 15-16.

Walker, Cheryl Lawson. "The Women's Tradition in
American Poetry. " Ph.D. Dissertation, Brandeis
University, 1973.

Wallace, Ronald. "Alone with Poems. " Colorado Quarterly 23 (1975): 341-353.

Weller, Sheila. "The Mercy of Ironies of Memory: The
Poetry of Wakoski. " Ms. 4 (March 1976): 82-3. (Review of Virtuoso Literature for Two and Four Hands.)

Young, Vernon. Hudson Review 26 (Winter 1973-74): 724-5.

Zweig, Paul. New York Times Book Review, 12 December 1971, pp. 5, 18, 20. (Review of The Motor-
cycle Betrayal Poems.)

WALKER, ALICE

Alice Walker/Al Young. San Francisco: San Francisco
State Univ. /The Poetry Center, n.d. (Videocassette.)

Coles, Robert. "To Try Men's Souls. " New Yorker,
27 February 1971, pp. 104-106. (Review of The
Third Life of Grange Copeland.)

Cooke, Michael G. "Recent Novels: Women Bearing
Violence. " Yale Review 66 (Autumn 1976): 146-155.
(Review of Meridian.)

Doyle, Sister Mary Ellen. "The Heroine of Black Novels."
In Perspectives on Afro-American Women, pp. 112-
25. Edited by Willa D. Johnson and Thomas L.
Green. Washington, D.C. : ECCA Publications, 1975.

Emanuel, James A. In Contemporary Novelists. Edited by James Vinson. New York: St. Martin's Press, 1976.

Fowler, Carolyn. "Solid at the Core." Freedomways 14 (1974): 59-62. (Review of In Love and Trouble.)

Harris, Jessica. "An Interview with Alice Walker." Essence 7 (July 1976): 33.

Kraus, Willis Keith. "A Critical Survey of the Contemporary Adolescent-Girl Problem Novel." Ph.D. Dissertation, University of Southern Illinois, 1974.

Marcus, Greil. New Yorker, 7 June 1976, pp. 133-136. (Review of Meridian.)

Mueller, Lisel. Poetry 117 (February 1971): 328-329. (Review of Once.)

Nyabongo, V. S. Books Abroad 48 (Autumn 1974): 787. (Review of In Love and Trouble: Stories of Black Women.)

Piercy, Marge. New York Times Book Review, 23 May 1976, pp. 5, 12.

Rogers, Norma. Freedomways 16 (Second Quarter 1976): 120-122. (Review of Meridian.)

Schorer, Mark. "Novels and Nothingness." American Scholar 40 (Winter 1970-1971): 168-174. (Review of The Third Life of Grange Copeland.)

Schulz, Elizabeth. " 'Free in Fact and at Last': The Image of the Black Woman in Black American Literature." In What Manner of Woman: Essays in English and American Life and Literature, pp. 316-344. Edited by Marlene Springer. New York: New York University Press, 1977.

Shapiro, Paula Meinetz. "Pygmalion Revised." New Leader, 25 January 1971, pp. 19-20. (Review of The Third Life of Grange Copeland.)

Smith, Cynthia J. "Black Fiction by Black Females." Cross Currents 26 (Fall 1976): 340-343. (Review of Meridian.)

Ward, Jerry. CLA Journal 17 (September 1973): 127-129. (Review of Revolutionary Petunias.)

WALKER, MARGARET

Love, Theresa R. "The Black Woman Afro-American Literature." Paper presented at the Midwest Modern Language Association meeting, Chicago, November 1975. (Mimeographed.)

Rowell, Charles H. "An Interview with Margaret Walker." Black World 25 (December 1975): 4-17.

WALTER, EUGENE

Gottlieb, Lois C. "The Perils of Freedom: The New Woman in Three American Plays of the 1900's." Canadian Review of American Studies 6 (Spring 1975): 84-98.

WARD, ELIZABETH

Gasser, Larry Winston. "Social Reform in the Late Nineteenth-Century American Strike Novel." Ph.D. Dissertation, University of Denver, 1975.

Welter, Barbara. Dimity Convictions: The American Woman in the Nineteenth Century. Athens: Ohio University Press, 1976.

WARD, MRS HUMPHREY

Higgins, Susan. "The Suffragettes in Fiction." Hecate 2 (July 1976): 31-47.

Miles, Rosalind. The Fiction of Sex: Themes and Functions of Sex Difference in the Modern Novel. New York: Barnes & Noble, 1974.

Showalter, Elaine. A Literature of Their Own: British Women Novelists from Brontë to Lessing. Princeton: Princeton University Press, 1977.

Speegle, Katherine Sloan. "God's Newer Will: Four Examples of Victorian Angst Resolved by Humanitarianism." Ph.D. Dissertation, North Texas State University, 1975.

Williams, Kenneth E. "Faith, Intention, and Fulfillment:
The Religious Novels of Mrs. Humphrey Ward."
Ph.D. Dissertation, Temple University, 1970.

WARNER, SUSAN

Douglas, Ann. The Feminization of American Culture.
New York: Alfred A. Knopf, 1977.

Foster, Edward Halsey. The Civilized Wilderness:
Backgrounds to American Romantic Literature, 1817-
1860. New York: Free Press, 1975.

Wood, Ann D. "The 'Scribbling Women' and Fanny
Fern: Why Women Wrote." American Quarterly
23 (Spring 1971): 3-24.

WARREN, MERCY OTIS

Watts, Emily Stipes. The Poetry of American Women
from 1632 to 1945. Austin: University of Texas
Press, 1977.

WARREN, ROBERT PENN

Ilacqua, Alma A. "Amanda Starr: Victim of Her Own
False Assumptions." Hartford Studies in Literature
8, no. 3 (1976): 178-189.

Shinn, Thelma J. Wardrop. "A Study of Women Characters in Contemporary American Fiction 1940-1970."
Ph.D. Dissertation, Purdue University, 1972.

WATERS, CLARA

Sklar, Kathryn Kish. "American Female Historians in
Context, 1770-1930." Feminist Studies 3, nos. 1 and
2 (1975): 171-184.

WATSON, SHEILA

Atwood, Margaret. Survival: A Thematic Guide to
Canadian Literature. Toronto: Anansi, 1972.

Corbett, Nancy J. "Closed Circle." Canadian Literature no. 61 (Summer 1974): 46-53. (Review of The
Double Hook.)

Lennox, John Watt. "The Past: Themes and Symbols of Confrontation in The Double Hook and Le Torretin." Journal of Canadian Fiction 2 (1973): 70-72.

Livesey, Dorothy. "Two Women Novelists of Canada's West." Review of National Literature 7 (1976): 127-32.

Mitchell, Beverly. "Association and Allusion in The Double Hook." Journal of Canadian Fiction 2 (1973): 63-69.

Morriss, Margaret. "The Elements Transcended." Canadian Literature no. 42 (Autumn 1969): 56-71.

WEBSTER, JOHN

Benston, Kimberly W. "The Duchess of Malfi: Webster's Tragic Vision." Gypsy Scholar 3 (Fall 1975): 20-36.

Forker, Charles R. "Love, Death, and Fame: The Grotesque Tragedy of John Webster." Anglia 91, no. 2 (1973): 194-218.

Hawkins, Harriett. "The Victim's Side: Chaucer's Clerk's Tale and Webster's Duchess of Malfi." Signs: Journal of Women in Culture and Society 1 (Winter 1975): 339-361.

Holdsworth, R. V., ed. Webster, "The White Devil" and "The Duchess of Malfi": A Casebook. Toronto: Macmillan of Canada, 1975.

Kaye, Melanie. "The Sword Philippan: Woman as Hero in Stuart Tragedy." Ph. D. Dissertation, University of California, Berkeley, 1976.

Leggatt, Alexander. Citizen Comedy in the Age of Shakespeare. Toronto: University of Toronto Press, 1973.

McDonald, Margaret Lamb. "The Independent Woman in the Restoration Comedy of Manners." Ph. D. Dissertation, University of Colorado, 1975.

Mirenda, Angela Marie. "The Noble Lie: Selfhood and Tragedy in the Renaissance." Ph. D. Dissertation, The Pennsylvania State University, 1977.

Mitchell, Giles and Eugene Wright. "Duke Ferdinand's

Lycanthropy as a Disguise Motive in Webster's The Duchess of Malfi. " Literature and Psychology 25, no. 3 (1975): 117-123.

Moody, JoAnn. "Britomart, Imogen, Perdita, The Duchess of Malfi: A Study of Women in English Renaissance Literature. " Ph. D. Dissertation, University of Minnesota, 1971.

Rice, Nancy Hall. "Beauty and the Beast and the Little Boy: Clues about the Origins of Sexism and Racism from Folklore and Literature: Chaucer's 'The Prioress's Tale, ' Sir Gawain and the Green Knight, the Alliterative Morte Arthure, Webster's The Duchess of Malfi, Shakespeare's Othello, Hawthorne's 'Rappaccini's Daughter, ' Melville's 'Benito Cereno. ' " Ph. D. Dissertation, University of Massachusetts, 1975.

Shaw, Sharon K. "Medea on Pegasus: Some Speculations on the Parallel Rise of Women and Melodrama on the Jacobean Stage. " Ball State University Forum 14, no. 4 (1973): 13-21.

Still, Roger. Love and Death in Renaissance Tragedy. Baton Rouge: Louisiana State University Press, 1976.

WEDEKIND, FRANK

Harris, E. P. "Liberation of Flesh from Stone: Pygmalion in Frank Wedekind's Erdgeist. " Germanic Review 52 (January 1977): 44-56.

Place, Mary Elizabeth. "The Characterization of Women in the Plays of Frank Wedekind. " Ph. D. Dissertation, Vanderbilt University, 1977.

Rose, Ingrid Barbara. "Social Stereotypes and Female Actualities: A Dimension of the Social Criticism in Selected Works by Fontane, Hauptmann, Wedekind, and Schnitzler. " Ph. D. Dissertation, Princeton University, 1976.

WELDON, FAYE

Blackburn, Sara. New York Times Book Review, 10 November 1974, p. 18. (Review of Female Friends.)

Glendinning, Victoria. Times Literary Supplement, 24 September 1976, p. 1199. (Review of Remember Me.)

Gray, Paul. "Among the Ruins." Time, 28 October 1974, pp. 101-102. (Review of Female Friends.)

Jones, D. A. N. Times Literary Supplement, 28 February 1975, p. 213. (Review of Female Friends.)

Mortimer, Penelope. "Ephemeral Triangle." Book World--The Washington Post, 3 November 1974, p. 2. (Review of Female Friends.)

Oates, Joyce Carol. New York Times Book Review, 21 November 1976, p. 7. (Review of Remember Me.)

Sissman, L. E. New Yorker, 10 March 1975, p. 96. (Review of Female Friends.)

WELLS, H. G.

Braendlin, Bonnie Hoover. "The 'New Woman' in the Bildungsromane of Somerset Maugham, H. G. Wells, and D. H. Lawrence." Paper presented at the MLA meeting, New York City, December 1976.

Calder, Jenni. Women and Marriage in Victorian Fiction. London: Thames & Hudson, 1976.

Higgins, Susan. "The Suffragettes in Fiction." Hecate 2 (July 1976): 31-47.

Scanlon, Leone. "The New Woman in the Literature of 1883-1909." University of Michigan Papers in Women's Studies 2, no. 2 (1976): 133-159.

Strauss, Sylvia. "Women in 'Utopia.'" South Atlantic Quarterly 75 (Winter 1976): 115-131.

WELTY, EUDORA

Armes, Nancy Ruth. "The Feeder: A Study of the Fiction of Eudora Welty and Carson McCullers." Ph.D. Dissertation, University of Illinois, 1975.

Arnold, St. George Tucker, Jr. "Consciousness and
the Unconscious in the Fiction of Eudora Welty."
Ph.D. Dissertation, Stanford University, 1975.

Bartel, Roland. "Life and Death in Eudora Welty's 'A
Worn Path.'" Studies in Short Fiction 14 (Summer
1977): 288-290.

Bryant, J. A., Jr. "Eudora Welty." In American
Writers, vol. 4, pp. 260-284. Edited by Leonard
Unger. New York: Charles Scribner's Sons, 1974.

Callow, James T. and Robert Reilly. Guide to American Literature from Emily Dickinson to the Present.
New York: Barnes & Noble, 1977.

Fullinwider, Carol Manning. "Eudora Welty's Fiction:
Its Unconventional Relationship to the Southern Literary Tradition." Ph.D. Dissertation, State University of New York at Albany, 1975.

Gray, R. J. "Eudora Welty: A Dance to the Music of
Order." Canadian Review of American Studies 7
(Spring 1976): 57-65.

Hardy, John Edward. "Delta Wedding as Region and
Symbol." In Contemporary Women Novelists: A
Collection of Critical Essays, pp. 150-166. Edited
by Patricia Meyer Spacks. Englewood Cliffs, N.J.:
Prentice-Hall, 1977.

Herlong, Ruby Padgette. "A Study of Human Relationships in the Novels of Eudora Welty." Ph.D. Dissertation, University of South Carolina, 1975.

Kieft, Ruth Vande. "Eudora Welty." Deland, Florida:
Everett/Edwards, n.d. (Cassette no. 5517.)

Kreyling, Michael. "Life with People: Virginia Woolf,
Eudora Welty and The Optimist's Daughter."
Southern Review 13 (Spring 1977): 250-271.

_____. "The Novels of Eudora Welty." Ph.D. Dis-
sertation, Cornell University, 1975.

LaJoy, Maureen. "No Laughing Matter: Women and
Humor." Women 5, no. 1 (1976): 6-9.

Landess, Thomas H. "More Trouble in Mississippi: Family v. Antifamily in Miss Welty's Losing Battles." Sewanee Review 79 (Autumn 1971): 626-634.

McGowan, Marcia Phillips. "Patterns of Female Experience in Eudora Welty's Fiction." Ph.D. Dissertation, Rutgers University, The State University of New Jersey (New Brunswick), 1977.

Nash, Chas. Crawford. "The Theme of Human Isolation in the Works of Eudora Welty." Ph.D. Dissertation, University of Minnesota, 1975.

Oates, Joyce Carol. "Eudora's Web." In Contemporary Women Novelists: A Collection of Critical Essays, pp. 167-172. Edited by Patricia Meyer Spacks. Englewood Cliffs, N.J.: Prentice-Hall, 1977.

Polk, Noel. "A Eudora Welty Checklist." Mississippi Quarterly 26 (Fall 1973): 662-693.

Shinn, Thelma J. Wardrop. "A Study of Women Characters in Contemporary American Fiction 1940-1970." Ph.D. Dissertation, Purdue University, 1972.

Stuckey, William J. "The Use of Marriage in Welty's The Optimist's Daughter." Critique 17 (December 1975): 36-46.

Tarbox, Raymond. "Eudora Welty's Fiction: The Salvation Theme." American Imago 29 (Spring 1972): 70-91.

WEST, REBECCA

"Communing with Reality." Times Literary Supplement, 21 December 1973, pp. 1553-1554.

Kobler, Turner S. "The Eclecticism of Rebecca West." Critique 13, no. 2 (1971): 30-49.

Redd, Tony N. "Rebecca West: Master of Reality." Ph.D. Dissertation, University of South Carolina, 1973.

WHARTON, EDITH

Anderson, Hilton. "Edith Wharton as Fictional Hero-ine." South Atlantic Quarterly 69 (Winter 1970): 118-123.

Auchincloss, Louis. "Edith Wharton." In American Writers, vol. 4, pp. 308-330. Edited by Leonard Unger. New York: Scribners, 1974.

Beauchamp, Andrea Louise Roberts. "The Heroine of Our Common Scene: Portrayals of American Women in Four Novels by Edith Wharton and Henry James." Ph.D. Dissertation, The University of Michigan, 1976.

Bloom, Lillian D. "On Daring to Look Back with Wharton and Cather." Novel 10 (Winter 1977): [167]-178. (Review essay.)

Callow, James T. and Robert Reilly. Guide to American Literature from Emily Dickinson to the Present. New York: Barnes & Noble, 1977.

Clarke, G. Time, 1 September 1975, pp. 60-61. (Review of Lewis' Edith Wharton.)

Dahl, Curtis. "Edith Wharton's The House of Mirth: Sermon on a Text." Modern Fiction Studies 21 (Winter 1975-76): 572-576.

Davidson, Colleen Tighe. "Beyond the Sentimental Hero-ine: The Feminist Character in American Novels, 1899-1937." Ph.D. Dissertation, University of Minnesota, 1975.

Gargano, James W. "Edith Wharton's The Reef: The Genteel Woman's Quest for Knowledge." Novel 10 (Fall 1976): 40-48.

Lawson, Richard H. Edith Wharton. New York: Frederick Ungar, 1977.

L'Enfant, Julia Chandler. "Edith Wharton and Virginia Woolf: Tradition and Experiment in the Modern Novel." Ph.D. Dissertation, Louisiana State University, 1975.

Lewis, R. W. B. Edith Wharton: A Biography. New York: Harper & Row, 1977.

_____. "Edith Wharton: The Beckoning Quarry." American Heritage 26 (October 1975): 53-56, 73.

McDowell, Margaret B. Edith Wharton. New York: Twayne, 1976.

"On Writing and Writers." Los Angeles, Calif.: Pacifica Tape Library, 1975.

Parker, Jeri. Uneasy Survivors: Five Women Writers. Salt Lake City: Peregrine Smith, 1975.

Potter, Rosemary. "The Mistakes of Lily in The House of Mirth." Taius 4, no. 1 (1975): 89-93.

Price, Richard Alan. "The Culture of Despair: Characters and Society in the Novels of Edith Wharton and Theodore Dreiser." Ph.D. Dissertation, The University of Rochester, 1976.

Robinson, James A. "Psychological Determinism in The Age of Innocence." Markham Review 5 (Fall 1975): 1-5.

Rooke, Constance. "Beauty in Distress: Daniel Deronda and The House of Mirth." Women & Literature 4 (Fall 1976): 28-39.

Rose, Alan Henry. " 'Such Depths of Sad Initiation': Edith Wharton and New England." New England Quarterly 50 (September 1977): 423-439.

Saunders, Judith P. "Ironic Reversal in Edith Wharton's Bunner Sisters." Studies in Short Fiction 14 (Summer 1977): 241-245.

Turner, Jean. "The Ideology of Women in the Fiction of Edith Wharton, 1899-1920." Ph.D. Dissertation, University of Wisconsin, 1975.

Tuttleton, James W. " 'Combat in the Erogenous Zone': Women in the American Novel Between the Two World Wars." In What Manner of Woman: Essays in English and American Life and Literature, pp. 271-

296. Edited by Marlene Springer. New York:
New York University Press, 1977.

_____. "Edith Wharton: An Essay in Bibliography."
Resources for American Literary Studies 3 (1973):
163-202.

Vella, Michael Wayne. "Technique and Theme in The
House of Mirth." Markham Review 2 (May 1970):
no pp.

Watts, Emily Stipes. The Poetry of American Women
from 1632 to 1945. Austin: University of Texas
Press, 1977.

Widmer, Eleanor. "Edith Wharton: The Nostalgia for
Innocence." In The Twenties: Fiction, Poetry,
Drama, pp. 27-38. Edited by Warren French. De-
land, Florida: Everett/Edwards, 1975.

Wolff, Cynthia Griffin. "The Age of Innocence: Wharton's 'Portrait of a Gentleman.' " Southern Review
12 (Summer 1976): 640-658.

_____. A Feast of Words: The Triumph of Edith
Wharton. New York: Oxford University Press, 1977.

WHEATLEY, PHILLIS

Applegate, Anne. "Phillis Wheatley: Her Critics and
Her Contribution." Negro American Literature
Forum 9 (Winter 1975): 123-126.

Burroughs, Margaret G. "Do Birds of a Feather Flock
Together?" Jackson State Review 6 (1974): 61-73.

Collins, Terence. "Phillis Wheatley; The Dark Side of
the Poetry." Phylon 36 (March 1975): 78-88.

Giddings, Paula. "Critical Evaluation of Phillis Wheatley." Jackson State Review 6 (1974): 74-81.

Holder, Kenneth R. 'Some Linguistic Aspects of the
Heroic Couplet in the Poetry of Phillis Wheatley."
Ph.D. Dissertation, North Texas State University,
1974.

Huddleston, Eugene L.   "Matilda's 'On Reading the Poems of Phillis Wheatley, The African Poetess.'" Early American Literature 5 (Winter 1970-1971): 57-67.

Kuncio, Robert C.   "Some Unpublished Poems of Phillis Wheatley." New England Quarterly 43 (June 1970): 287-297.

Parks, Carole A.   "Phillis Wheatley Comes Home." Black World 23 (February 1974): 92-97.

Porter, Dorothy B.   "Historical and Bibliographical Data of Phillis Wheatley's Publications." Jackson State Review 6 (1974): 54-60.

Richmond, Merle.   Bid the Vassal Soar: Interpretive Essays on the Life and Poetry of Phillis Wheatley and George Moses Horton. Washington: Howard University Press, 1974.

Watts, Emily Stipes.   The Poetry of American Women from 1632 to 1945. Austin: University of Texas Press, 1977.

WHEELER, EDWARD L.

Gartner, Carol B.   "Three Ednas." Kate Chopin Newsletter 1 (Winter 1975-76): 11-20.

WHIPPLE, MAURINE

Geary, Edward A.   "Women Regionalists of Mormon Country." Paper presented at the MLA meeting, New York City, December 1976. (Mimeographed.)

WHITCHER, FRANCES

Curry, Jane Anne.   "Women as Subjects and Writers of Nineteenth Century Humor." Ph.D. Dissertation, The University of Michigan, 1975.

WHITE, PATRICK

Garebian, Keith.   "The Desert and the Garden: The Theme of Completeness in Voss." Modern Fiction Studies 22 (Winter 1976): 557-569.

Ward, Jill. "Patrick White's A Fringe of Leaves."
Critical Quarterly 19 (Autumn 1977): 77-81.

WHITEHEAD, SARAH R.

Mitchell, Sally. "Lost Women: Feminist Implications
of the Fallen in Works by Forgotten Women Writers
of the 1840's." University of Michigan Papers in
Women's Studies 1 (June 1974): 110-124.

WHITMAN, WALT

Baym, Nina. "Portrayal of Women in American Literature, 1790-1870." In What Manner of Woman: Essays on English and American Life and Literature,
pp. 211-234. Edited by Marlene Springer. New
York: New York University Press, 1977.

Wrobel, Arthur. " 'The Towering Feminine': Whitman,
Perfect Women, and America's Future." Paper presented at the MLA meeting, New York City, December 1976.

WILCOX, ELLA WHEELER

Pittock, Malcolm. "In Defense of Ella Wheeler Wilcox."
Durham University Journal 65 (December 1972): 86-
89.

Watts, Emily Stipes. The Poetry of American Women
from 1632 to 1945. Austin: University of Texas
Press, 1977.

WILDE, OSCAR

Horowitz, Grace. "Convention and Moral Ambiguity in
the Dramas of Oscar Wilde." Paper presented at
the MLA meeting, New York City, December 1976.

Kellogg, Patricia Rossworm. "The Myth of Salome in
Symbolist Literature and Art." Ph.D. Dissertation,
New York University, 1975.

McCoy, Cathleen. "The Happy Fall of the Restoration
Heroine." Paper presented at the MLA meeting,
New York City, December 1976.

Marcus, Jane Connor. "Salome: The Jewish Princess Was a New Woman." Bulletin of the New York Public Library 78 (Fall 1974): 95-113.

Stein, Joseph. "The New Woman and the Decadent Dandy." Dalhousie Review 55 (Spring 1975): 54-62.

WILFORD, FLORENCE

Showalter, Elaine. A Literature of Their Own: British Women Novelists from Brontë to Lessing. Princeton: Princeton University Press, 1977.

WILHELM, GALE

Rule, Jane. Lesbian Images. Garden City, N.Y.: Doubleday, 1975.

WILHELM, KATE

Charyn, Jerome. New York Times Book Review, 22 February 1976, pp. 36-37. (Review of The Clewiston Test.)

Russ, Joanna. Magazine of Fantasy and Science Fiction (November 1971): 19-21. (Review of Abyss.)

Tarvis, Carol. Psychology Today (October 1975): 101. (Review of The Infinity Box.)

WILKINS, GEORGE

Hume, Robert D. "Marital Discord in English Comedy from Dryden to Fielding." Modern Philology 74 (February 1977): 248-272.

WILLARD, NANCY

Poss, Stanley. "A Gathering of Poets." Western Humanities Review 29 (Autumn 1975): 391-393. (Review of Carpenter of the Sun.)

WILLIAMS, CHARLES

Bolling, Douglass. "The Journey into Self: Charles Williams's The Place of the Lyon." Cresset 37 (April 1974): 14-18.

WILLIAMS, JESSE LYNCH

Bonin, Jane. Major Themes in Prize-Winning American Drama. Metuchen, N.J.: Scarecrow Press, 1975.

Loudin, Joanne Marie. "The Changing Role of the Comic Heroine in American Drama from 1900 to 1940." Ph.D. Dissertation, University of Washington, 1974.

Shafer, Y. B. "Liberated Women in American Plays of the Past." Players Magazine 49 (Spring 1974): 95-100.

WILLIAMS, MARIA

Taylor, Irene and Gina Luria. "Gender and Genre: Women in British Romantic Literature." In What Manner of Woman: Essays on English and American Life and Literature, pp. 98-124. Edited by Marlene Springer. New York: New York University Press, 1977.

WILLIAMS, TENNESSEE

Adler, Jacob H. "Williams' Eight Ladies." Southern Literary Journal 8 (Fall 1975): 165-169. (Review of Eight Mortal Ladies Possessed.)

Bonin, Jane F. Major Themes in Prize-Winning American Drama. Metuchen, N.J.: Scarecrow Press, 1975.

Draya, Ren. "The Frightened Heart: A Study of Character and Theme in the Fiction, Poetry, Short Plays, and Recent Drama of Tennessee Williams." Ph.D. Dissertation, University of Colorado at Boulder, 1977.

Embrey, Glenn Thomas. "Sexual Confusion in the Major Plays of Tennessee Williams." Ph.D. Dissertation, University of California, Los Angeles, 1975.

Kolb, Deborah S. "The Rise and Fall of the New Woman in American Drama." Educational Theater Journal 27 (1975): 149-160.

Malin, Irving. New Republic, 14 September 1974, p. 27. (Review of Eight Mortal Ladies Possessed.)

Rorem, Ned. Saturday Review/World, 21 September 1974, p. 24. (Review of Eight Mortal Ladies Possessed.)

White, Edmund. New York Times Book Review, 6 October 1974, p. 14. (Review of Eight Mortal Ladies Possessed.)

WILLIAMS, WILLIAM CARLOS

Ashton, Diane Ward. "The Virgin-Whore Motif in William Carlos Williams' Paterson. " Modern Poetry Studies 4 (Autumn 1973): 193-209.

Doyle, Charles. "A Reading of 'Paterson III. ' " Modern Poetry Studies 1, no. 3 (1970): 141+ .

Mazzaro, Jerome. "The Descent Once More: 'Paterson V' and 'Pictures from Brueghel. ' " Modern Poetry Studies 1, no. 6 (1970): 278-300.

WILLIS, SARA P. see FERN, FANNY

WILSON, ANGUS

Faulkner, Peter. Humanism in the English Novel. New York: Barnes & Noble, 1976.

WILSON, AUGUSTA EVANS

Garrison, Dee. "Immoral Fiction in the Late Victorian Library. " American Quarterly 28 (Spring 1976): 71-89.

Welter, Barbara. Dimity Convictions: The American Woman in the Nineteenth Century. Athens: Ohio University Press, 1976.

WILSON, ETHEL

Gottlieb, Lois and Wendy Keitner. "Mothers and Daughters in Four Recent Canadian Novels. " Sphinx 4 (1975): 21-34.

Livesay, Dorothy. "Two Women Novelists of Canada's West. " Review of National Literature 7 (1976): 127-132.

New, W. H. Articulating West: Essays on Purpose and
Form in Modern Canadian Literature. Toronto:
New Press, 1972.

Stouck, David. "Ethel Wilson's Novels." Canadian Literature no. 74 (Autumn 1977): 74-88.

Woodcock, George. "Ethel Wilson." Canadian Fiction
Magazine 15 (1975): 44-49.

WINSLOW, THYRA

Baum, Charlotte, Paula Hyman and Sonya Michel. The
Jewish Women in America. New York: Dial Press,
1975.

Koltun, Elizabeth. The Jewish Woman: New Perspectives. New York: Schocken, 1976.

WINTERS, NANCY

Weller, Sheila. Ms. 5 (April 1977): 44. (Review of
The Girl on the Coca-Cola Tray.)

WINTHER, SOPHUS KEITH

Meldrum, Barbara. "Images of Women in Western
American Literature." Midwest Quarterly 17 (April
1976): 252-267.

WISTER, OWEN

Meldrum, Barbara. "Images of Women in Western
American Literature." Midwest Quarterly 17 (April
1976): 252-267.

WITTIG, MONIQUE

Arnold, June, et al. "Lesbians and Literature." Sinister Wisdom 1 (Fall 1976): 20-33.

Crosland, Margaret. Women of Iron and Velvet:
French Women After George Sand. New York:
Taplinger, 1976.

Higgins, Lynn. "Nouvelle Nouvelle Autobiographie:
Monique Wittig's Le Corps lesbien." sub-stance 8
(1976): 160-166.

Spraggins, Mary. "Myth and Ms. : Entrapment and Liberation in Monique Wittig's Les Guérillères." International Fiction Review 3 (January 1976): 47-51.

Wenzel, Helen. "Monique Wittig: Form and Feminism." Paper presented at the MLA meeting, New York City, December 1976.

WOLLSTONECRAFT, MARY

Bouten, Jacob. Mary Wollstonecraft and the Beginnings of Female Emancipation in France and England. New York: Porcupine Press, 1975.

Kelly, Gary. "Mary Wollstonecraft Texts and Contexts." Eighteenth-Century Life 2 (December 1975): 38-40.

McGarron, Margaret Ross. "Mary and Margaret: The Triumph of Woman." Ph. D. Dissertation, Cornell University, 1973.

Moers, Ellen. Literary Women. Garden City, N.Y.: Doubleday, 1976.

Portner, Ruth Lee. "A Study of Marriage in the English Novel." Ph. D. Dissertation, City University of New York, 1977.

Spacks, Patricia Meyer. Imagining a Self: Autobiography and Novel in Eighteenth-Century England. Cambridge: Harvard University Press, 1976.

Sunstein, Emily W. A Different Face: The Life of Mary Wollstonecraft. New York: Harper & Row, 1975.

Taylor, Irene and Gina Luria. "Gender and Genre: Women in British Romantic Literature." In What Manner of Woman: Essays on English and American Life and Literature, pp. 98-124. Edited by Marlene Springer. New York: New York University Press, 1977.

Todd, Janet M. "Frankenstein's Daughter: Mary Shelley and Mary Wollstonecraft." Women & Literature 4 (Fall 1976): 18-27.

_____. Mary Wollstonecraft: An Annotated Bibliography of Her Works and Criticism. New York: Garland, 1976.

Tyson, G. P. "A Found Woman: Some Recent Biographies of Mary Wollstonecraft." Eighteenth-Century Studies 9, no. 2 (1975): 262-269. (Review essay.)

WOOD, ELLEN PRICE

Garrison, Dee. "Immoral Fiction in the Late Victorian Library." American Quarterly 28 (Spring 1976): 71-89.

WOOD, MRS HENRY

Detter, Howard Montgomery. "The Female Sexual Outlaw in the Victorian Novel: A Study of the Conventions of Fiction." Ph.D. Dissertation, Indiana University, 1971.

Elliott, Jeanne B. "A Lady to the End: The Case of Isabel Vane." Victorian Studies 19 (March 1976): 329-334.

Showalter, Elaine. "Desperate Remedies: Sensation Novels of the 1860's." Victorian Newsletter no. 49 (Spring 1976): [1]-5.

_____. A Literature of Their Own: British Women Novelists from Brontë to Lessing. Princeton: Princeton University Press, 1977.

WOODBRIDGE, MERCY DUDLEY

Watts, Emily Stipes. The Poetry of American Women from 1632 to 1945. Austin: University of Texas Press, 1977.

WOODS, MARGARET

Gibson, Susan Monteith. "Love and the Vote: Fiction of the Suffrage Movement in Edwardian England." Ph.D. Dissertation, University of Massachusetts, 1975.

WOOLF, VIRGINIA

Alexander, Sally Jeanette. "Outsiders and Educated Men's Daughters: The Feminist as Heroine in Six Novels of Virginia Woolf." Ph.D. Dissertation, The Florida State University, 1975.

Ariail, Jacqueline Ann. "An Elegy for Androgyny." Iowa English Bulletin Yearbook 24 (Fall 1974): 13-20.

Bell, Barbara Currier and Carol Ollman. "Virginia Woolf's Criticism: A Polemical Preface." In Feminist Literary Criticism, pp. 48-60. Edited by Josephine Donovan. Lexington: University of Kentucky Press, 1975; reprinted from Critical Inquiry 1 (1974): 361-371.

Bollas, Sara Flanders. "The Narrow Bridge of Art: A Psychoanalytic Study of Virginia Woolf's First Four Novels." Ph.D. Dissertation, State University of New York at Buffalo, 1976.

Bolstad, Robert Montelle. "The Passionate Self in George Eliot, Adam Bede, The Mill on the Floss, and Daniel Deronda." Ph.D. Dissertation, University of Washington, 1975.

Brown, Dorothy Ann Duff. "The Aesthetics of Feminism in Virginia Woolf's Fiction." Ph.D. Dissertation, University of California, Berkeley, 1976.

Comstock, Margaret. " 'The Current Answers Don't Do': The Comic Form of Night and Day." Women's Studies 4, nos. 2/3 (1977): 153-171.

_____. "The Loudspeaker and the Human Voice: Politics and the Form of The Years." Bulletin of the New York Public Library 80 (Winter 1977): 252-275.

Comstock, Margaret von Szeliski. "George Meredith, Virginia Woolf, and Their Feminist Comedy." Ph.D. Dissertation, Stanford University, 1975.

Cornwell, Ethel F. "Virginia Woolf, Nathalie Sarraute, and Mary McCarthy: Three Approaches to Character

in Modern Fiction. " International Fiction Review 4
(January 1977): 3-10.

Curtin, James F. " 'Colour Burning on a Framework
of Steel': Form and Identity in the Novels of Virginia Woolf. " Ph. D. Dissertation, University of
Virginia, 1975.

Cwiakala-Piatkowska, Jadwigz. "The Feminist Pam-
· phlets of Virginia Woolf. " Kwartalnik Neofilologiczny
19 (1972): 271-279.

Daziel, Bradford Dudley. " 'The Sentence in Itself
Beautiful': A Study of Virginia Woolf's Mannerist
Fiction. " Ph. D. Dissertation, Boston University
Graduate School, 1975.

Delbaere-Garant, Jeanne. " 'The Mark on the Wall':
Virginia Woolf's World in a Snailshell. " Revue des
Langues Vivantes 40, no. 5 (1974): 457-465.

Dietche, Julia Phelps. "Virginia Woolf's The Waves:
Portrait of the Author. " Ph. D. Dissertation, The
University of North Carolina at Chapel Hill, 1977.

Eder, Doris. "Review of Virginia Woolf and Her World
by John Lehmann and Forster's Women: Eternal
Differences by Bonnie B. Finkelstein. " Virginia
Woolf Quarterly 2 (Summer & Fall 1976): 383-386.

Edwards, Lee R. 'War and Roses: The Politics of
Mrs. Dalloway. " In The Authority of Experience,
pp. [160]-177. Edited by Arlyn Diamond and Lee R.
Edwards. Amherst: University of Massachusetts
Press, 1977.

Farwell, Marilyn R. "Virginia Woolf and Androgyny. "
Contemporary Literature 16 (Autumn 1975): 433-451.

Faulkner, Peter. Humanism in the English Novel.
New York: Barnes & Noble, 1976.

Flaherty, Luke. 'Woman as Peacemaker in Virginia
Woolf's Novels. " Ph. D. Dissertation, The University of Iowa, 1977.

Freeman, Alma Susan. "The Androgynous Ideal: A

Study of Selected Novels by D. H. Lawrence, James Joyce, and Virginia Wolf." Ed. D. Dissertation, Rutgers University, The State University of New Jersey, 1974.

Garber, Lawrence. "Bloomsbury Biography." Ph. D. Dissertation, University of Toronto, 1974.

Gibson, Susan Monteith. "Our Part Is to Be the Audience: Virginia Woolf's Between the Arts." Gypsy Scholar 2 (Fall 1974): 5-12.

Gillen, Francis. " 'I Am This, I Am That': Shifting Distance and Movement in Mrs. Dalloway." Studies in the Novel 4 (Fall 1972): 484-493.

Gillespie, Diane Filby. "Virginia Woolf's Miss LaTrobe: The Artist's Last Struggle Against Masculine Values." Women & Literature 5 (Spring 1977): 38-46.

Gish, Robert. "Mr. Forster and Mrs. Woolf: Aspects of the Novelist as Critic." Virginia Woolf Quarterly 2 (Summer and Fall 1976): 255-269.

Hafley, James. "Virginia Woolf and the Art of Lying." Paper presented at the MLA meeting, New York City, December 1976. (Mimeographed.)

Hawthorn, Jeremy. Virginia Woolf's Mrs. Dalloway: A Study of Alienation. Atlantic Highlands, N.J.: Humanities Press, 1977.

Heilbrun, Carolyn G. "Virginia Woolf and Feminist Thought." Paper presented at the MLA meeting, New York City, December 1976.

Henke, Suzette. "Virginia Woolf's To the Lighthouse: In Defense of the Woman Artist." Virginia Woolf Quarterly 2 (Winter & Spring 1976): 39-47.

Higgins, Susan. "The Suffragettes in Fiction." Hecate 2 (July 1976): 31-47.

Hulcoop, John. " 'The Only Way I Keep Afloat': Work as Virginia Woolf's Raison D'Etre." Women's Studies 4, nos. 2/3 (1977): 223-245.

Hummel, Madeline M. "From the Common Reader to the Uncommon Critic: Three Guineas and the Epistolary Form." Bulletin of the New York Public Library 80 (Winter 1977): 151-157.

Hunter, Dianne. "Between Death and Art: The Mother-Daughter Conflict in Virginia Woolf." Paper presented at the MLA meeting, New York City, December 1976.

Kaplan, Sydney Janet. The Feminine Consciousness and the British Novel. Chicago: University of Illinois Press, 1975.

Kenney, Susan M. "Two Endings: Virginia Woolf's Suicide and Between the Acts." University of Toronto Quarterly 44 (Summer 1975): 265-289.

Klaich, Dolores. Woman + Woman: Attitudes Toward Lesbianism. New York: Simon & Schuster, 1974.

Kreyling, Michael. "Life with People: Virginia Woolf, Eudora Welty and The Optimist's Daughter." Southern Review 13 (Spring 1977): 250-271.

Lakshmi, Vjay. "The Solid and the Intangible: Virginia Woolf's Theory of the Androgynous Mind." Literary Criticism 1 (1971): 28-34.

Leaska, Mitchell A. The Novels of Virginia Woolf: From Beginning to End. New York: John Jay Press, 1977.

_____. "Virginia Woolf: Seeker of Voices." North Hollywood: The Center for Cassette Studies, n. d.

_____. "Virginia Woolf, the Pargeter: A Reading of The Years." Bulletin of the New York Public Library 80 (Winter 1977): 172-210.

Lilienfeld, C. Jane. "The Necessary Journey: Virginia Woolf's Voyage to the Lighthouse." Ph. D. Dissertation, Brandeis University, 1975.

Lipking, Joanna. "Looking at the Monuments: Woolf's Satiric Eye." Bulletin of the New York Public Library 80 (Winter 1977): 141-145.

Little, Judy. "Festive Comedy in Woolf's Between the Acts." Women & Literature 5 (Spring 1977): 26-37.

_____. "Satirizing the Norm: Comedy in Women's Fiction." Regionalism and the Female Imagination 3 (Fall 1977 and Winter 1977-78): 39-49.

Lyons, Richard S. "The Intellectual Structure of Virginia Woolf's Between the Acts." Modern Language Quarterly 38 (June 1977): 149-166.

Marcus, Jane. " 'No More Horses': Virginia Woolf on Art and Propaganda." Women's Studies 4, nos. 2/3 (1977): 265-290.

Matro, Thomas Gaetano. "Life as Creative Activity in the Early Novels of Virginia Woolf." Ph.D. Dissertation, Rutgers University, The State University of New Jersey, 1975.

Mepham, John. "Figures of Desire: Narration and Fiction in To the Lighthouse." In The Modern English Novel: The Reader, The Writer, and The Work, pp. 149-185. Edited by Gabriel Josipovici. New York: Barnes & Noble, 1976.

Meyerowitz, Selma S. "Class Perspectives and the Works of Virginia Woolf." Ph.D. Dissertation, Wayne State University, 1975.

Meyers, Jeffrey. Married to Genius. New York: Barnes & Noble, 1977.

Middleton, Victoria S. "The Years: 'A Deliberate Failure.' " Bulletin of the New York Public Library 80 (Winter 1977): 158-171.

Miles, Rosalind. The Fiction of Sex: Themes and Functions of Sex Difference in the Modern Novel. New York: Barnes & Noble, 1974.

Moers, Ellen. Literary Women. Garden City, N.Y.: Doubleday, 1976.

Moore, Madeline. "Introduction: Another Version of Virginia Woolf." Women's Studies 4, nos. 2/3 (1977): 149-152.

_____. "Virginia Woolf's The Years and Years of Adverse Male Reviewers." Women's Studies 4, nos. 2/3 (1977): 247-263.

Nicolson, Nigel, and Joanne Trautmann, eds. The Letters of Virginia Woolf: 1888-1912, vol. 1. New York: Harcourt Brace Jovanovich, 1975.

_____. The Letters of Virginia Woolf: 1912-1922, vol. 2. New York: Harcourt Brace Jovanovich, 1976.

Ohmann, Carol. "Culture and Anarchy in Jacob's Room." Contemporary Literature 18 (Spring 1977): 160-172.

"On Writing and Writers." Los Angeles, Calif.: Pacifica Tape Library, 1975.

Perazzini, Randolph. "Mrs. Dalloway: 'Buds on the Tree of Life.'" Midwest Quarterly 18 (July 1977): 406-417.

Philipson, Morris. "Virginia Woolf's Orlando: Biography as a Work of Fiction." In From Parnassus: Essays in Honor of Jacques Barzun, pp. 237-248. Edited by Dora B. Weiner and William R. Keylor. New York: Harper & Row, 1976.

Poresky, Louise Ann. "The Elusive Self: Psyche and Spirit in Virginia Woolf's Novels." Ph.D. Dissertation, Drew University, 1977.

Quick, Jonathan R. "The Shattered Moment: Form and Crisis in Mrs. Dalloway and Between the Acts." Mosaic 7 (1974): 127-136.

Radin, Grace. "'I Am Not a Hero': Virginia Woolf and the First Version of The Years." Massachusetts Review 16 (Winter 1975): 195-208.

_____. "'Two enormous chunks': Episodes Excluded During the Final Revisions of The Years." Bulletin of the New York Public Library 80 (Winter 1977): 221-251.

Rigney, Barbara. Madness and Sexual Politics in the

Feminist Novel: Studies of Charlotte Brontë, Virginia Woolf, Doris Lessing, and Margaret Atwood. Madison: University of Wisconsin Press, forthcoming.

Rogat, Ellen H. "The Virgin in the Bell Biography." Twentieth Century Literature 20 (April 1974): 96-113.

Ruddick, Sara. "Learning to Live with the Angel in the House." Women's Studies 4, nos. 2/3 (1977): 181-200.

Rudman, Carol. "Minuet and Military March: Divergent Choreographic Patterns for Women and Men in The Years and Three Guineas." Paper presented at the MLA meeting, San Francisco, December 1975.

Ruotolo, Lucio. "Mrs. Dalloway: The Journey Out of Subjectivity." Women's Studies 4, nos. 2/3 (1977): 173-178.

Sakamoto, Tadanobu. "Virginia Woolf: 'Mrs. Dalloway in Bond Street' and Mrs. Dalloway." Studies in English Literature, English Number (1974): 75-88.

Schaefer, Josephine O'Brien. "Moments of Vision in Virginia Woolf's Biographies." Virginia Woolf Quarterly 2 (Summer & Fall 1976): 294-303.

_____. "Sterne's A Sentimental Journey and Woolf's Jacob's Room." Modern Fiction Studies 23 (Summer 1977): 189-198.

Schlack, Beverly Ann. "Virginia Woolf's Strategy of Scorn in The Years and Three Guineas." Bulletin of the New York Public Library 80 (Winter 1977): 146-150.

Sears, Salie. "Notes on Sexuality: The Years and Three Guineas." Bulletin of the New York Public Library 80 (Winter 1977): 211-220.

Sharma, O. P. "Feminism as Aesthetic Vision: A Study of Virginia Woolf's Mrs. Dalloway." Women's Studies 3 (1975): 61-74.

Showalter, Elaine. A Literature of Their Own: British Women Novelists from Brontë to Lessing. Princeton: Princeton University Press, 1977.

Silver, Brenda. "Virginia Woolf and the Concept of Community: The Elizabethan Playhouse." Women's Studies 4, nos. 2/3 (1977): 291-298.

Snow, Lotus. "The Heat of the Sun: The Double in Mrs. Dalloway." Research Studies 41 (1973): 75-83.

Swartz, Mary Ann. "Making the Waves Heard." Virginia Woolf Quarterly 2 (Summer & Fall 1976): 304-312.

Taylor, Nancy McKeon. "Conscious Construction: The Concept of Plot in Five Novels by Women." Ph.D. Dissertation, Loyola University of Chicago, 1977.

Throne, Sara R. "Virginia Woolf's Feminist Identity and the Parthenogenesis of Female Culture." University of Michigan Papers in Women's Studies 2 (September 1975): 146-161.

Tudor, Kathleen. "The Androgynous Mind in W. B. Yeats, D. H. Lawrence, Virginia Woolf and Dorothy Richardson." Ph.D. Dissertation, University of Toronto, 1975.

Watson, Barbara Bellow. "On Power and the Literary Text." Signs: Journal of Women in Culture and Society 1 (Autumn 1975): 111-118.

Wilson, J. J. "A Comparison of Parties, with Discussion of Their Function in Woolf's Fiction." Women's Studies 4, nos. 2/3 (1977): 201-217.

WOOLSON, CONSTANA FENIMORE

Weir, Sybil B. 'Southern Womanhood in the Novels of Constana Fenimore Woolson." Mississippi Quarterly 29 (Fall 1976): 559-568.

WORDSWORTH, WILLIAM

Ball, Patricia M. The Heart's Events: The Victorian Poetry of Relationships. London: University of London, The Athlone Press, 1976.

Finch, Geoffrey J. "Wordsworth's Solitary Song: The Substance of 'true art' in 'The Solitary Reaper.' " Ariel 6 (July 1975): 91-100.

Radner, John B. "The Youthful Harlot's Curse: The Prostitute as Symbol of the City in 18th-Century English Literature." Eighteenth-Century Life 2 (March 1976): 59-64.

Taylor, Irene and Gina Luria. "Gender and Genre: Women in British Romantic Literature." In What Manner of Woman: Essays on English and American Life and Literature, pp. 98-124. Edited by Marlene Springer. New York: New York University Press, 1977.

Watson, J. R. "Lucy and the Earth-Mother." Essays in Criticism 27 (July 1977): [187]-202.

WRIGHT, RICHARD

Keady, Sylvia H. "Richard Wright's Women Characters and Inequality." Negro American Literature Forum 10 (Winter 1976): 124-128.

Mebane, Mary Elizabeth. "The Family in the Works of Charles W. Chesnutt and Selected Works of Richard Wright." Ph. D. Dissertation, University of North Carolina at Chapel Hill, 1973.

Smith, Barbara. "Sexual Politics in the Fiction of Richard Wright." Paper presented at the MLA meeting, New York City, December 1976.

Timmerman, John. "Trust and Mistrust: The Role of Black Women in Three Works by Richard Wright." Studies in the Twentieth Century 10 (Fall 1972): 33-45.

Ward, Hazel Mae. "The Black Woman as Character: Images in the American Novel, 1852-1953." Ph. D. Dissertation, The University of Texas at Austin, 1977.

WRIGHT, RICHARD B.

Fulton, E. Margaret. "Out of Our Past: A New

Future. " Laurentian University Review 9 (November 1976): [87]-102.

WRIGHT, THOMAS

Hume, Robert D. "Marital Discord in English Comedy from Dryden to Fielding." Modern Philology 74 (February 1977): 248-272.

WYCHERLEY, WILLIAM

Beless, Rosemary June. "Reflections of the Law in the Comedies of Etherege, Wycherley, and Congreve." Ph. D. Dissertation, University of Utah, 1977.

Bratton, Clinton Woodrow. "The Use of Marriage in the Comedies of Etherege, Wycherley, Dryden and Congreve." Ph. D. Dissertation, University of Colorado, 1975.

Chadwick, W. R. The Four Plays of William Wycherley: A Study in the Development of a Dramatist. The Hague: Mouton, 1975.

Fraustino, Daniel V. "The Country Wife Comes to The End of the Road: Wycherley Bewitches Barth." Arizona Quarterly 33 (Spring 1977): 76-85.

Hume, Robert D. "Marital Discord in English Comedy from Dryden to Fielding." Modern Philology 74 (February 1977): 248-272.

Kaufman, Anthony. "Wycherley's The Country Wife and the Don Juan Character." Eighteenth-Century Studies 9 (Winter 1975-76): 216-231.

Morris, David B. "Language and Honor in The Country Wife." South Atlantic Bulletin 37 (November 1972): 3-10.

Novak, Maximillian E. "Margery Pinchwife's 'London Disease': Restoration Comedy and the Libertine Offensive in the 1670's." Studies in the Literary Imagination 10 (Spring 1977): 1-24.

Roper, Alan. "Sir Harbottle Grimstone and the Country Wife." Studies in the Literary Imagination 10 (Spring 1977): 109-123.

WYLIE, ELINOR

> Walker, Cheryl. "Sorcery and Sarcastic Sigil: The
> Self-Portrait of Elinor Wylie. " Paper presented at
> the MLA meeting, New York City, December 1976.

> Watts, Emily Stipes. The Poetry of American Women
> from 1632 to 1945. Austin: University of Texas
> Press, 1977.

- Y -

YAGI MIKAJO

> Ikuko Atsumi. "Modern Japanese Women Poets: After
> the Meiji Restoration. " Iowa Review 7 (Spring/Sum-
> mer 1976): 227-237.

YAMAKAWA TOMIKO

> Ikuko Atsumi. "Modern Japanese Women Poets: After
> the Meiji Restoration. " Iowa Review 7 (Spring/Sum-
> mer 1976): 227-237.

YEATS, WILLIAM BUTLER

> Bessai, Diane E. "Who Was Cathleen ni Houlihan. "
> Malahat Review no. 42 (April 1977): 114-129.

> Fass, Barbara. La Belle Dame sans Merci and the
> Aesthetics of Romanticism. Detroit: Wayne State
> University Press, 1974.

> Smith, Carol. "Women in Yeats and Eliot. " Deland,
> Florida: Everett/Edwards, n. d. (Cassette no.
> 5321.)

> Tudor, Kathleen. "The Androgynous Mind in W. B.
> Yeats, D. H. Lawrence, Virginia Woolf, and Doro-
> thy Richardson. " Ph. D. Dissertation, University
> of Toronto, 1975.

> Wedwick, Catherine. "The Treatment of Women in the
> Plays of William Butler Yeats. " Ph. D. Disserta-
> tion, Bowling Green State University, 1975.

YEZIERSKA, ANZIA

Baum, Charlotte, Paula Hyman and Sonya Michel. The Jewish Woman in America. New York: Dial Press, 1975.

Inglehart, Babbette. "Daughters of Loneliness: Anzia Yezierska and the Immigrant Woman Writer." Studies in American Jewish Literature 1 (Winter 1975): 1-10.

Maglin, Nan Bauer. "Rebel Women Writers, 1894-1925." Ph.D. Dissertation, Union Graduate School, 1975.

Rivlin, Lilly. "In Short: Bread Givers." Ms. 4 (May 1976): 36-37. (Review of Bread Givers.)

YONGE, CHARLOTTE

O'Flaherty, Gerald. "In Search of the Self: The Quest for Spiritual Identity in Five Nineteenth Century Religious Novels." Ph.D. Dissertation, University of Pennsylvania, 1973.

Showalter, Elaine. A Literature of Their Own: British Women Novelists from Brontë to Lessing. Princeton: Princeton University Press, 1977.

Springer, Marlene. "Angels and Other Women in Victorian Literature." In What Manner of Woman: Essays on English and American Life and Literature, pp. 124-159. Edited by Marlene Springer. New York: New York University Press, 1977.

Stark, Myra C. "The Clever Woman of the Family-- And What Happened to Her." Mary Wollstonecraft Journal 2 (May 1974): 13-20.

YOSANO AKIKO

Cranston, Edwin A. "Young Akiko: The Literary Debut of Yosano Akiko (1878-1942)." Literature East and West 8 (March 1974): [19]-43.

Ikuko Atsumi. "Modern Japanese Women Poets: After the Meiji Restoration." Iowa Review 7 (Spring/Summer 1976): 227-237.

Reich, Pauline C. and Atsuko Fukuda, trans. "Japan's Literary Feminists: The Seito Group. " Signs: Journal of Women in Culture and Society 2 (Autumn 1976): 280-287.

YOSHIHARA SACHIKO

Ikuko Atsumi. "Five Modern Women Poets on Love. " Literature East and West 8 (March 1974): [58]-75.

_____. "Modern Japanese Women Poets: After the Meiji Restoration. " Iowa Review 7 (Spring/Summer 1976): 227-237.

YOUNG, STARK

Seidel, Kathryn Lee. "The Southern Belle: Her Fall from the Pedestal in Fiction of the Southern Renaissance. " Ph. D. Dissertation, University of Maryland, 1976.

YOURCENAR, MARGUERITE

Crosland, Margaret. Women of Iron and Velvet: French Women After George Sand. New York: Taplinger, 1976.

- Z -

ZÄUNEMANN, SIDONIA HEDWIG

De Berdt, August Joseph Julien. "Sidonia Hedwig Zäunemann: Poet Laureate and Emancipated Woman 1714-1740. " Ph. D. Dissertation, The University of Tennessee, 1977.

ZAYAS, MARIA DE (María de Zayas y Sotomayor)

Charrón, Germán. "María Zayas de Sotomayor: Novelista Española del Siglo XVII. " Ph. D. Dissertation, University of California, Los Angeles, 1975.

Foa, Sandra Margherita. "Feminismo y forma narrativa: Estudio del tema y las técnicas de María de

Zayas y Sotomayor. " Ph. D. Dissertation, Princeton University, 1975.

Griswold, Susan Cass. "The Fictional Art of María de Zayas. " Ph. D. Dissertation, Vanderbilt University, 1975.

Karr, Nancy Rees. "Creation and Tradition in the Novels of María de Zayas. " Ph. D. Dissertation, University of California, Riverside, 1977.

Pérez-Erdélyi, Mireya. "La imagen de las mujeres en las novelas picaresco-cortesanas de Maria de Zayas y Sotomayor y Alonso de Castillo Solórzano. " Ph. D. Dissertation, Rutgers University, The State University of New Jersey (New Brunswick), 1977.

ZEAMI

Brazell, Karen. "Zeami and Women in Love. " Literature East and West 8 (March 1974): [8]-18.

ZOLA, EMILE

Alcorn, Clayton, Jr. "Zola's Forgotten Spokesman: Veronique in La Joie de Vivre. " French Review 49 (October 1975): 76-80.

Armstrong, Judith. The Novel of Adultery. New York: Barnes & Noble, 1976.

Crane, Robert Arthur. "The Courtisane Character in the Nineteenth Century French Novel from Balzac to Zola. " Ph. D. Dissertation, The University of North Carolina at Chapel Hill, 1976.

Dezaley, Auguste. "La 'nouvelle Phèdre' de Zola ou les mésaventures d'un personnage tragique. " Travaux de Linguistique et de Litterature 9, no. 2 (1971): 121-134.

Fernando, Lloyd. "New Women" In the Late Victorian Novel. University Park: Pennsylvania State University Press, 1977.

Maguire, Karen. "Venus Dethroned: Zola's Nana. " Paper presented at the MLA meeting, New York City, December 1976.

414 / More Women in Literature

Michot-Dietrick, Hela. "Blindness to 'Goodness': The Critics' Chauvinism? An Analysis of Four Novels by Zola and the Goncourts." Modern Fiction Studies 21 (Summer 1975): 215-222.

Musumeci, Antonino. "Tasso, Zola and the Vicissitudes of Pastoralism." Nineteenth-Century French Studies 4 (Spring 1976): 344-360.

Reff, Theodore. "The Influence of Flaubert's Queen of Sheba on Later Nineteenth-Century Literature." Romanic Review 65 (November 1974): 249-265.

Smith, Elyzabeth Marie-Pierre Richer. "Nana, Santa, et Nacha Regules: trois courtisanes modernes." Ph.D. Dissertation, University of Georgia, 1974.

ZORRILLA, JOSE

Knight, Eunice Edna. "The Role of Women in the Don Juan and Faust Literature." Ph.D. Dissertation, Florida State University, 1973.

GENERAL BIBLIOGRAPHY

Abrahams, Roger D. "Negotiating Respect: Patterns of Presentation Among Black Women." Journal of American Folklore 88 (January-March 1975): 58-80.

Agress, Lynne Joy. "The Feminine Irony: Treatments of Women by Women in Early Nineteenth-Century Literature." Ph.D. Dissertation, University of Massachusetts, 1975.

Allen, Carolyn. "The Tensions of Language in Modern Women Writers." Paper presented at the MLA meeting, New York City, December 1976.

Allen, Mary. The Necessary Blankness: Women in Major American Fiction of the Sixties. Urbana: University of Illinois Press, 1976.

Allen, Richard O. "If You Have Tears: Sentimentalism as Soft Romanticism." Genre 8 (June 1975): 119-145.

Alta. "Like It Is." Small Press Review 3, no. 3 (1972): 1-6.

"... and the New Science Fiction." In The New Woman's Survival Sourcebook, pp. 131-132. Edited by Kirsten Grimstad and Susan Rennie. New York: Alfred A. Knopf, 1975.

Andersen, Margret. "Feminist Criticism." In Mother Was Not a Person, pp. 87-90. Edited by Margret Andersen. Montreal: Content Publishing Limited and Black Rose Books, 1972.

Anderson, Carleton D. "The Evolution of the Inés de Castro Story in Drama." Ph.D. Dissertation, Brigham Young University, 1970.

Angress, Ruth K. "Inculcating a Slave Mentality: Women in German Popular Fiction of the Early Twentieth Century." In Female Studies IX: Teaching About Women in Foreign Languages, pp. 189-199. Edited by Sidonie Cassirer. Old Westbury, N.Y.: Feminist Press, 1975.

Ardinger, Barbara R. "Cleopatra on Stage: An Examination of the Persona of the Queen in English Drama, 1592-1898." Ph.D. Dissertation, Southern Illinois University, 1976.

Armstrong, Judith. The Novel of Adultery. New York: Barnes & Noble, 1976.

Arnold, June, et al. "Lesbians and Literature." Sinister Wisdom 1 (Fall 1976): 20-33.

_____ and Bertha Harris. "Lesbian Fiction: A Dialogue." Sinister Wisdom 1 (Fall 1976): 42-51.

Ashby, Warren Delaplane, Jr. "The Lady of the Fountain: A Study of a Medieval Myth." Ph.D. Dissertation, University of Miami, 1976.

Atkins, John. Sex in Literature, vol. 2: The Classical Experience of the Sexual Impulse. London: Calder & Boyars, 1973.

Auerbach, Nina. Communities of Women: An Idea in Fiction. Cambridge: Harvard University Press, forthcoming.

Austin, Annemarie. " 'Under the Steam.' " Hecate 3 (February 1977): 72-76.

Awsienko. "The Burdens of 'Superfluous' Talent: Russian Women Writers in the Eighteenth and Nineteenth Century." Journal of Russian Studies 29 (1975): 11-19.

Bacchiega, Franca. "Femminismo e letteratura." Paragone 23 (February 1972): 110-126.

Backscheider, Paula R. and Felicity A. Nussbaum. An Annotated Bibliography of 20th Century Critical Studies of Women and Literature, 1660-1800. New York: Garland, 1977.

Badami, Mary Kenny. "A Checklist of SF Novels with Female Protagonists." Extrapolation 18 (December 1976): 6-19.

Bailliet, Theresia Sauter. "She Warriors in Literature." Paper presented at the MLA meeting, New York City, December 1976.

Ball, Patricia M. The Heart's Events: The Victorian Poetry of Relationships. London: University of London, The Athlone Press, 1976.

Banta, Martha. "They Shall Have Faces, Minds, and (One Day) Flesh: Women in Late Nineteenth-Century and Early Twentieth-Century American Literature." In What Manner of Woman: Essays on English and American Life and Literature, pp. 235-270. Edited by Marlene Springer. New York: New York University Press, 1977.

Barnes, Annette. "Female Criticism: A Prologue." In The Authority of Experience, pp. 1-15. Edited by Arlyn Diamond and Lee R. Edwards. Amherst: University of Massachusetts Press, 1977.

Barr, Marleen. "Idols and Manipulators: Some Women Characters in SF." Witch and Chameleon 5/6 (1976): 20-22. (Published by Amanda Bankier, Apt. 6, 2 Paisley Ave. S., Hamilton, Ontario.)

Bass, Alan. "Time and the Witch: Femininity, Metapsychology and the Temporality of the Unconscious." MLN 91 (October 1976): 871-912.

Baum, Charlotte, Paula Hyman and Sonya Michel. The Jewish Woman in America. New York: Dial Press, 1975.

Bauska, Kathy Anderson. "The Feminine Dream of Happiness: A Study of the Woman's Search for Intelligent Love and Recognition in Selected English Novels from Clarissa to Emma." Ph.D. Dissertation, University of Washington, 1977.

Baym, Nina. "Portrayal of Women in American Literature, 1790-1870." In What Manner of Woman: Essays on English and American Life and Literature, pp. 211-234.

Edited by Marlene Springer. New York: New York University Press, 1977.

Beck, Evelyn Torton. "Sexism, Racism and Class Bias in German Utopias of the Twentieth Century." Soundings 58 (Spring 1975): 112-129.

Beebe, Sandra. "Women in American Literature." English Journal 64 (September 1975): 32-35.

Behnken, Eloise. "Love, Desire, and Victorian Poets." Occasional Review Issue 6 (Summer 1977): 149-157.

Bell, Carmine Jane. "The Role of Monastic Women in the Life and Letters of Early Medieval England and Ireland." Ph.D. Dissertation, University of Virginia, 1975.

Bernikow, Louise. Introduction to The World Split Open: Four Centuries of Women Poets in England and America, 1552-1950. New York: Random House, 1974.

Blackwell, Fritz. "Mysogyny and Philogyny: The Bifurcation and Ambivalence of the Stereotypes of the Courtesan and the Mother in Literary Tradition." Journal of South Asian Literature 12 (Spring-Summer 1977): 37-43.

Bleuzé, Ruth Allen. "Romancières et Critiques: Etude du Prix Fémina, 1904-1968." Ph.D. Dissertation, University of Colorado at Boulder, 1977.

Blicksilver, Edith. "Literature as Social Criticism: The Ethnic Woman Writer." Modern Language Studies 5, no. 2 (1975): 46-54.

Blodgett, E. D. Canadian Review of Comparative Literature 3 (Spring 1976): 215-222. (Review of Woman as Image in Medieval Literature by Joan M. Ferrante.)

Bloom, Lynn Z. "Two Genres, One Gender: Definitions of Feminist and Sexist Biographies of Women." Paper presented at the MLA meeting, New York City, December 1976.

Bougard, Roger Gilbert. "Erotisme et amour physique dans la litterature française du XVIIe siècle." Ph.D. Dissertation, The University of North Carolina at Chapel Hill, 1974.

Bowers, Myra Ellen. "The Liber Manualis of Dhuoda: Advice of a Ninth-Century Mother for Her Sons." Edited with an Introduction and Translation. Ph.D. Dissertation, The Catholic University of America, 1977.

Bowles, Gloria. "Poetry as Popular Form: Women's Writing Circles in Berkeley." Paper presented at the MLA meeting, San Francisco, December 1975.

_____. "That Generation Before Ours: An Overview." Paper presented at the MLA meeting, New York City, December 1976.

Boyers, Robert and Maxine Bernstein. "Women, the Arts, and the Politics of Culture: An Interview with Susan Sontag." Salmagundi no. 31-32 (Fall 1975-Winter 1976): 29-48.

Bragger, Jeannette. "Women in Contemporary French Society: A Brief Annotated Bibliography of Materials Suitable for a Civilization Course." In Female Studies IX: Teaching about Women in the Foreign Languages, pp. 37-44. Edited by Sidonie Cassirer. Old Westbury, N.Y.: Feminist Press, 1975.

Brée, Germaine. "French Women Writers: A Problematic Perspective." In Beyond Intellectual Sexism: A New Woman, A New Reality, pp. 196-209. Edited by Joan Roberts. New York: David McKay, 1976.

Bremer, Sidney H. "The Fiction of Femininity: American Literature and Battered Women." Wisconsin Ideas 2 (December 1977): 3.

Brewer, June. "A Comparative Study of the Autobiographies of Three Black Women." Paper presented at the MLA meeting, New York City, December 1976.

Brinkley, Robert A. "The Unfaithful Text: Harold Bloom, A map of misreading." Massachusetts Studies in English 5 (Fall 1975): 31-39.

Bronfman, Judith. "The Griselda Legend in English Literature." Ph.D. Dissertation, New York University, 1977.

Brown, Lloyd W. "The African Woman as Writer." Canadian Journal of African Studies 9, no. 3 (1975): 493-502.

Burroway, Janet and Cynthia Ozick. "Does Genius Have a Gender?" Ms. 6 (December 1977): 56, 79-81, 83-84.

Byrd, Max. "The Madhouse, the Whorehouse, and the Convent." Partisan Review 44, no. 2 (1977): 268-278.

Cain, Joan. "Three Peninsular Novelists Comment on the Spanish Woman." In Female Studies IX: Teaching About Women in the Foreign Languages, pp. 136-137. Edited by Sidonie Cassirer. Old Westbury, N.Y.: Feminist Press, 1975.

Caine, Barbara. "Woman's 'Natural' State: Marriage and the 19th Century Feminists." Hecate 3 (February 1977): 84-102.

Calamawy, Sahair el. "The Impact of Tradition on Modern Arabic Literature." Mundus Artium 10, no. 1 (1977): 100-105.

Calder, Jenni. Women and Marriage in Victorian Fiction. London: Thames & Hudson, 1976.

Calvert, Brian. "Plato and the Equality of Women." Phoenix 29 (Autumn 1975): 231-243.

Capozzi, Frank. "The Evolution and Transformation of the Judith and Holofernes Theme in Italian Drama and Art Before 1627." Ph.D. Dissertation, University of Wisconsin-Madison, 1975.

Carré, Marie-Rose. "Arnolphe, Chrysale et Chrysalde aux conférences de Theophraste Renaudot." French Review 48 (1975): 548-556.

Cassirer, Sidonie, ed. Female Studies IX: Teaching About Women in the Foreign Languages. Old Westbury, N.Y.: Feminist Press, 1975.

Catron, David Lloyd. "Saint Mary Magdalene in Spanish and Portuguese Literature of the Sixteenth and Seventeenth Centuries." Ph.D. Dissertation, University of Michigan, 1972.

Chafe, William H. "Sex and Race: The Analogy of Social Control." Massachusetts Review 18 (Spring 1977): 147-176.

Chatfield, Jean. "Some Women in Modern Tamil Short Stories: A Study in Irony." Journal of South Asian Literature 12 (Spring-Summer 1977): 19-24.

Christ, Carol P. "Spiritual Quest and Women's Experience." Anima: An Experimental Journal (Spring 1974): 4-14.

_____. "Victorian Masculinity and the Angel in the House." In A Widening Sphere: Changing Roles of Victorian Women, pp. 146-162. Edited by Martha Vicinus. Bloomington: Indiana University Press, 1977.

Clancy-Hepburn, Ken. "Sexism and Sci Fi." Human Ecology Forum 4 (Autumn 1973): 28-30.

Coffin, Tristram Potter. The Female Hero in Folklore and Legend. New York: Seabury Press, 1975.

Cohen, Sarah Blacher. "The Humor of Jewish-American Women Writers." Paper presented at the MLA meeting, San Francisco, December 1975.

Conrad, Cinthia. "What Can Brain Research Tell Us About Feminine Consciousness and Modes of Expression?" Paper presented at the MLA meeting, New York City, December 1976.

Conroy, Anne Rosemarie. "The Isle of Ladies: A Fifteenth Century English Chaucerian Poem." Ph.D. Dissertation, Yale University, 1976.

Cook, Sylvia Jenkins. From Tobacco Road to Route 66: The Southern Poor White in Fiction. Chapel Hill: The University of North Carolina Press, 1976.

Cooke, Michael G. "Recent Novels: Women Bearing Violence." Yale Review 66 (Autumn 1976): 146-155.

Cooper, Janet. "Female Crushes, Affections, and Friendships in Children's Literature." Paper presented at the MLA meeting, New York City, December 1976.

_____ and Cynthia Secor. "The Lesbian in Literature." Los Angeles, Calif.: Pacifica Tape Library, 1974.

Crane, Robert Arthur. "The Courtisane Character in the Nineteenth Century French Novel from Balzac to Zola."

Ph.D. Dissertation, The University of North Carolina at Chapel Hill, 1976.

Crosland, Margaret. Women of Iron and Velvet: French Women After George Sand. New York: Taplinger, 1976.

Cuddon, J. A. "Exotic Women." Twentieth Century 179, no. 1049 (1972): 12-14.

Cunningham, Valentine. Everywhere Spoken Against: Dissent in the Victorian Novel. Oxford: Clarendon Press, 1975.

Curry, Jane Anne. "Women as Subjects and Writers of Nineteenth Century American Humor." Ph.D. Dissertation, The University of Michigan, 1975.

Curtis, Bruce. "Victorians Abed: William Graham Sumner on the Family, Women and Sex." American Studies 18 (Spring 1977): 101-122.

Daghistany, Ann. "The Picara Nature." Women's Studies 5, no. 1 (1977): 51-60.

Damon, Gene. Lesbiana: Book Reviews from "The Ladder 1966-1972." Reno: Naiad Press, 1976.

_____, Jan Watson and Robin Jordan. The Lesbian in Literature: A Bibliography, 2nd ed. Reno: Ladder, 1975.

Danahy, Michael. "Le roman est-il chose femme?" Poetique 25 (1976): 85-106.

Dash, Irene. "The Literature of Birth and Abortion." Regionalism and the Female Imagination 3 (Spring 1977): 8-13.

Davidson, Colleen Tighe. "Beyond the Sentimental Heroine: The Feminist Character in American Novels, 1899-1937." Ph.D. Dissertation, University of Minnesota, 1975.

Dean, Nancy. "Feminist Short Fiction: New Forms and Styles." Paper presented at the MLA meeting, New York City, December 1976.

Déjeux, Jean. "Le thème de l'étrangère dans le roman

maghrébin de langue française. " Présence Francophone
11 (1975): 15-36.

Delaney, Marshall. "The Case of the Missing Woman:
Notes on the Female Image in Films. " Saturday Night,
May 1975, p. 77.

Delcourt, Maria. "Deux interpretations romanesques du
mythe de l'androgyne: Mignon and Seraphite. " Revue
des langues vivantes 38, no. 3 (1972): 228-240; 38, no.
4 (1972): 340-347.

Dell, David. "The Sati Theme. " Journal of South Asian
Literature 12 (Spring-Summer 1977): 55-65.

Denne, Constance Ayers and Katherine M. Rogers. "On
Women Writers: Discussion at the Modern Language
Association meeting. " Nation, 30 August 1975, pp. 151-
153.

_____. "Women Novelists: A Distinct Group?" Women's
Studies 3 (1975): 5-28.

Dersofi, Nancy. "Feminism in Italy: A Prospectus. " Mary
Wollstonecraft Journal 2 (May 1974): 20-26.

Dickison, S. K. "Forum. " Arethusa 9 (Spring 1976): 119-
120. (Response to C. G. Thomas' "Matriarchy in Early
Greece: The Bronze and Dark Ages. ") Arethusa 6
(1973).

Dinnage, Rosemary. "Men, Women and Books: The Rule
of Heroism. " Times Literary Supplement, 29 November
1974, p. 1333.

Dobbs, Jeannine. "The Blue-Stockings: Getting It Together."
Frontiers 1 (Winter 1976): 81-93.

Donovan, Josephine. "Afterword: Critical Re-Vision. "
Feminist Literary Criticism. Lexington: University of
Kentucky Press, 1975.

_____. "Feminism and Aesthetics. " Critical Inquiry 3
(Spring 1977): 605-608.

Doubleday, Neal Frank. Variety of Attempt: British and
American Fiction in the Early Nineteenth Century. Lincoln: University of Nebraska Press, 1976.

Douglas, Ann. The Feminization of American Culture. New York: Alfred A. Knopf, 1977.

Drake, Sandra. "Aspects of the Image of Black Women in Some Modern Caribbean Fiction." Paper presented at the MLA meeting, New York City, December 1976.

Dreyfuss, Cecilia Ann Stiborik. "Femina sapiens in Drama: Aeschylus to Grillparzer." Ph.D. Dissertation, The University of Michigan, 1975.

Duncan, Erika. "Portrait of the Artist as a Young Woman 3. Choral Voices of Contemporary Women Writers." Book Forum 3, no. 1 (1977): 59-80.

Dunn, Catherine M. "The Changing Image of Woman in Renaissance Society and Literature." In What Manner of Woman: Essays on English and American Life and Literature, pp. 15-38. Edited by Marilyn Springer. New York: New York University Press, 1977.

Eber, Irene. "Images of Women in Recent Chinese Fiction: Do Women Hold Up Half the Sky?" Signs: Journal of Women in Culture and Society 2 (Autumn 1976): 24-34.

Edmunds, Lynne. "Why Aren't There More Women Writing for the Stage?" Daily Telegraph, 12 June 1974, p. 17.

Edward, Sister Ann. "Three Views on Blacks: The Black Woman in American Literature." CEA Critic 37 (May 1975): 14-16.

Elsom, John. Erotic Theatre. New York: Delta, 1974.

Erickson, Carolly and Kathleen Casey. "Women in the Middle Ages: A Working Bibliography." Medieval Studies 37 (1975): 340-359.

Fantham, Elaine. Phoenix 30 (Spring 1976): 80-84. (Review of Sarah B. Pomeroy's Goddesses, Whores, and Slaves.)

_____. "Sex, Status, and Survival in Hellenistic Athens: A Study of Women in New Comedy." Phoenix 29 (Spring 1975): 44-74.

Farber, Ada. "Segmentation of the Mother: Women in Greek Myth." Psychoanalytic Review 62 (Spring 1975): 29-47.

Fass, Barbara. La Belle Dame sans Merci & the Aesthetics of Romanticism. Detroit: Wayne State University Press, 1974.

"Feminist Fiction...." In The New Woman's Survival Sourcebook, pp. 128-129. Edited by Kirsten Grimstad and Susan Rennie. New York: Alfred A. Knopf, 1975.

"Feminist Movement Reflected in Plays." Flint (Michigan) Journal, 10 October 1975. (Newsbank 68 C2 C3.)

Fergus, George. "Checklist of SF Novels with Female Protagonists." Extrapolation 18 (December 1976): 20-27.

Ferguson, Mary Anne. "Sexist Images of Women in Literature." In Female Studies V, pp. 77-83. Edited by Rae Lee Siporin. Pittsburgh: KNOW, Inc., 1972.

Fernando, Lloyd. "New Women" in the Late Victorian Novel. University Park: Pennsylvania State University Press, 1977.

Ferrante, Joan M. Woman as Image in Medieval Literature from the Twelfth Century to Dante. New York: Columbia University Press, 1975.

_____. "Women in Medieval Literature." Deland, Florida: Everett/Edwards, n.d. (Cassette.)

Ferrier, Carole. "Notes Towards a Feminist Criticism." Hecate 2 (January 1976): 92-96.

Fetterley, Judith. "Feminist Criticism and New Criticism." Paper presented at the MLA meeting, New York City, December 1976.

Fiedler, Leslie A. "Eros and Thanatos: Or, The Mythic Aetiology of the Dirty Old Man." Salmagundi no. 38-39 (Summer-Fall 1977): 3-19.

Fine, David M. The City, The Immigrant and American Fiction, 1880-1920. Metuchen, N.J.: Scarecrow Press, 1977.

Finnegan, Robert Emmett. "Eve and 'Vincible Ignorance' in Genesis B." Texas Studies in Literature and Language 18 (Summer 1976): 329-339.

Flemming, Leslie A. "Courtesans, Prostitutes, and Wives: Varieties of Love in Recent Urdu Fiction." Paper presented at the MLA meeting, San Francisco, December 1975.

Flora, Cornelia Butler. "The Passive Female and Social Change: A Cross-Cultural Comparison of Women's Magazine Fiction." In Female and Male in Latin America: Essays, pp. 59-86. Edited by Ann Pescatello. Pittsburgh Press, 1973.

Foster, Edward Halsey. The Civilized Wilderness: Backgrounds to American Romantic Literature, 1817-1860. New York: Free Press, 1975.

Fox, Marcia Rose. "The Woman Question in Selected Victorian Fiction, 1883-1900." Ph. D. Dissertation, The City University of New York, 1975.

Frankel, Hans. The Flowering Plum and the Palace Lady: Interpretations of Chinese Poetry. New Haven: Yale University Press, 1976.

Frankel, Judith and Norman Mirsky. "Changing Stereotype of Jewish Women in Popular Culture." (ERIC 108 242.)

Franzwa, Helen H. "Working Women in Fact and Fiction." Journal of Communication 24 (Spring 1974): 104-109.

Fraser, Kathleen. "On Being a West Coast/Woman Poet." Paper presented at the MLA meeting, San Francisco, December 1975.

French, W. "Women in Our Literary Life." Imperial Oil Review 59, no. 1 (1975): 2-7.

Friend, B. "Virgin Territory: The Bonds and Boundaries of Women in Science Fiction." In Many Futures, Many Worlds, pp. 140-163. Edited by T. D. Clareson. Kent, Ohio: Kent State University Press, 1977.

Frym, Gloria. "Women's Poetry." San Francisco Review of Books 2 (March 1977): 28-30. (Review essay.)

Fullard, Joyce. "Some Remarks on the Representation of Eighteenth Century Women Poets in Anthologies." Mary Wollstonecraft Journal 2 (May 1974): 44-46.

_____ and Rhoda Walgren Schueller. "Eighteenth Century Poets: A Bibliography of Women Not Listed in the CBEL." Mary Wollstonecraft Journal 2 (May 1974): 40-43.

Fulton, E. Margaret. "Out of Our Past: A New Future." Laurentian University Review 9 (November 1976): 87-102.

Gaitan, Marcella Trujillo. "The Dilemma of the Modern Chicana Artist and Critic." La Cosecha: Literatura y la Mujer Chicana 3, no. 3 (1977): 38-48.

Garrison, Dee. "Immoral Fiction in the Late Victorian Library." American Quarterly 28 (Spring 1976): 71-89.

Gasiorowska, Xenia. "Portrait of a Lady in Polish Positivist Fiction." Slavanic and East European Review 20 (Fall 1976): 261-272.

Gasser, Larry Winston. "Social Reform in the Late Nineteenth-Century American Strike Novel." Ph.D. Dissertation, University of Denver, 1975.

Geary, Edward A. "Women Regionalists of Mormon Country." Paper presented at the MLA meeting, New York City, December 1976.

Gelderman, Carol W. "The Male Nature of Tragedy." Prairie Schooner 49 (Fall 1975): 220-227.

Gherman, Dawn Lander. "From Parlour to Tepee: The White Squaw on the American Frontier." Ph.D. Dissertation, University of Massachusetts, 1975.

Gibaldi, Joseph. "Petrarch and the Baroque Magdalene Tradition." Hebrew University Studies in Literature 3 (Spring 1975): 1-19.

Gibson, Susan Monteith. "Love and the Vote: Fiction of the Suffrage Movement in Edwardian England." Ph.D. Dissertation, University of Massachusetts, 1975.

Gilbert, Sandra and Susan Gubar. "A Revisionary Company." Novel 10 (Winter 1977): 158-166. (Review essay.)

Gilbert, Sandra M. "Out of the Women's Museum." Poetry 127 (October 1975): 44-45. (Review essay.)

Gillespie, Diane F. "The Female Artist in British and American Literature: Overview and Checklist. " Modernist Studies 1 (1974-1975): 39-50.

Goldfarb, Russell M. Sexual Repression and Victorian Literature. Lewisburg: Bucknell University Press, 1970.

Goldman, Maureen. "American Women and the Puritan Heritage: Anne Hutchinson to Harriet Beecher Stowe. " Ph.D. Dissertation, Boston University Graduate School, 1975.

Goldman, Rachel Margaret. "The Lucretia Legend from Livy to Rojas Zorrilla. " Ph.D. Dissertation, City University of New York, 1976.

Gontier, Fernande. "Nouvelles 'écrivaines' françaises: L'Esthétique au féminin ou l'esthétique de l'éclatement. " Paper presented at the MLA meeting, New York City, December 1976.

Goodman, Charlotte. "Images of American Rural Women in the Novel. " University of Michigan Papers in Women's Studies 1 (June 1975): 57-70.

Gornick, Vivian. "Feminist Writers: Hanging Ourselves on a Party Line?" Ms. 4 (July 1975): 104-107.

_____. "Why Do These Men Hate Women?" Village Voice, 6 December 1976, 12-15.

Gower, Kathy. "Science Fiction and Women. " In Mother Was Not a Person, pp. 98-101. Edited by Margret Anderson. Montreal: Content Publishing Limited and Black Rose Books, 1972.

Gray, Nigel. The Silent Majority: A Study of the Working Class in Post-War British Fiction. New York: Barnes & Noble, 1973.

Greco, Norma and Ronaele Novotny. "Bibliography of Women in the English Renaissance. " University of Michigan Papers in Women's Studies 1 (June 1974): 30-57.

Green, Rayna. "Magnolias Grow in Dirt: The Bawdy Lore of Southern Women. " Radical Teacher (December 1977): 26-30.

_____. "The Pocahontas Perplex: The Image of Indian Women in American Culture." Massachusetts Review 16 (Autumn 1975): 698-714.

Greenberg, Joseph Lawrence. "English and Marriage and Restoration Comedy, 1688-1710." Ph. D. Dissertation, Princeton University, 1976.

Greer, Germaine. "Women and Literature: Flying Pigs and Double Standards." Times Literary Supplement, 26 July 1974, pp. 784-785.

Gross, Amy. "Women as Sex Object: 'I'm Fragile, I'm Female, I Confess!' Life as It's Lived (More or Less) in the Confession Magazine." Mademoiselle (July 1972): 128.

Hagstrum, Jean H. "Eros and Psyche: Some Versions of Romantic Love and Delicacy." Critical Inquiry 3 (Spring 1977): 521-542.

Hahn, Emily. Once Upon a Pedestal: An Informal History of Women's Lib. New York: T. Y. Crowell, 1974.

Haimsath, Charles H. "Shakti: The Female Component of Indian Culture." Illustrated Weekly of India, 4 June 1972, pp. 26-29.

Hall, Margaret Miller. "Victorian Questions." Novel 10 (Spring 1977): 272-275. (Review of Jenni Calder's Women and Marriage in Victorian Fiction.)

Hallett, Judith P. "Women in Roman Elegy. A Reply." Arethusa 7 (1974): 211-219.

Hammond, Thomas Napolis. "The Image of Women in Senegalese Fiction." Ph. D. Dissertation, State University of New York at Buffalo, 1976.

Harris, Bertha. "Rescued from Moral Smugness." Ms. 5 (September 1976): 106, 110. (Review of Lesbian Images.)

Harris, Janice H. "Our Mute, Inglorious Mothers." Midwest Quarterly 16 (April 1975): 244-254.

Hart, George L., III. "Women and the Sacred in Ancient Tamiland." Journal of Asian Studies 32 (February 1973): 233-250.

Hartman, Mary S. "Murder for Respectability: The Case of Madeleine Smith. " Victorian Studies 16 (June 1973): 381-400.

Hawkes, David. "The Quest for the Goddess. " In Studies in Chinese Literary Genres, pp. 42-68. Edited by Cyril Birch. Berkeley: University of California Press, 1974.

Hawkes, Ellen G. "Private Female Resentments. " Ms. 5 (July 1976): 44, 104. (Review of Ellen Moers' Literary Women.)

Haworth, H. E. "Romantic Female Writers and the Critics. " Texas Studies in Literature and Language 17 (Winter 1976): 725-736.

Haymes, Howard J. "Postwar Writing and the Literature of Women's Liberation. " Psychiatry 38 (November 1975): 318-327.

Hays, Janice. "Themes and Modes of Women's Drama in the Twentieth Century." Paper presented at the MLA meeting, New York City, December 1976.

Heilbrun, Carolyn G. "Axiothea's Grief: The Disability of the Female Imagination. " In From Parnassus: Essays in Honor of Jacques Barzun, pp. 227-236. Edited by Dora B. Weiner and William R. Keylor. New York: Harper & Row, 1976.

_____. "Female Sleuths and Others. " Hecate 2 (July 1976): 74-79.

_____. "Marriage Perceived: English Literature 1873-1941. " In What Manner of Woman: Essays on English and American Life and Literature, pp. 160-184. Edited by Marlene Springer. New York: New York University Press, 1977.

_____ and Catherine Stimpson. "Theories of Feminist Criticism: A Dialogue. " In Feminist Literary Criticism, pp. 61-73. Edited by Josephine Donovan. Lexington: University of Kentucky Press, 1975.

Heisch, Allison. "Political Aesthetics and Woman's Fiction. " Paper presented at the MLA meeting, New York City, December 1976.

Heiserman, Arthur. The Novel Before the Novel: Essays
and Discussions About the Beginnings of Prose Fiction
in the West. Chicago: University of Chicago Press,
1977.

Helbig, Althea K. "Women in Ireland: Three Heroic Figures. " University of Michigan Papers in Women's
Studies 1 (June 1974): 73-88.

Heller, Sondra Roslyn. "The Characterization of the Virgin
Mary in Four Thirteenth-Century Narrative Collections
of Miracles: Jacobus de Voragine's Legenda Aurea,
Gonzalo de Berceo's Milagros de nuestra Señora, Gautier de Coinci's Miracles de nostre Dame, and Alfonso
el Sabio's Cantigas de Santa María. " Ph. D. Dissertation, New York University, 1975.

Henderson, Katherine. "Images of Women in the Modern
Novel: Male and Female Views. " Deland, Florida:
Everett/Edwards, n. d.   (Cassette no. 5312.)

Hetric, Willard Deane. "The Eulogy of the Lady in the
Early Poetry of the Cancionero de Baena. " Ph. D. Dissertation, Case Western Reserve University, 1971.

Hiatt, Mary P. "Stylistics and Feminist Criticism. " Paper
presented at the MLA meeting, New York City, December 1976.

_____. The Way Women Write: Sex and Style in Con-
temporary Prose. New York: Teachers College Press,
1978.

Higgins, Jean M. "The Myth of Eve: The Temptress. "
Journal of the American Academy of Religion 44 (December 1976): 639-647.

Higgins, Sue. "Breaking the Rules: New Fiction by Australian Women. " Meanjin Quarterly 34 (December 1975):
415-420.

Higgins, Susan. "The Suffragettes in Fiction. " Hecate 2
(July 1976): 31-47.

Holly, Marcia. "Consciousness and Authenticity: Toward a
Feminist Aesthetic. " In Feminist Literary Criticism,
pp. 38-47. Edited by Josephine Donovan. Lexington:
University of Kentucky Press, 1975.

Homosexuality in Literature: Fiction, Non-fiction, Biography, Autobiography. Elmhurst, N.Y.: Elysian Fields... Booksellers, n. d.

Honey, Maureen. "Images of Women in The Saturday Evening Post 1931-1936." Journal of Popular Culture 10 (Fall 1976): 3 52-3 58.

Horsley, Ritta Jo. "Women and German Literature: A Bibliography." In Female Studies IX: Teaching About Women in Foreign Languages, pp. 202-211. Edited by Sidonie Cassirer. Old Westbury, N.Y.: Feminist Press, 1975.

Hovet, Grace O'Neill. "The American Eve Misunderstood." North American Review 260 (Summer 1975): 87-88. (Review of Earnest's The American Eve in Fact and Fiction, 1775-1914.)

Howard, Maureen. "Vive la difference!" Hudson Review 28 (Autumn 1975): 441-445. (Review of Spacks' The Female Imagination.)

Huddleston, Eugene L. "Early American Verse Satire on Women." University of Michigan Papers in Women's Studies 1 (June 1975): 85-94.

_____. "Feminist Satire in America: A Checklist, 1700-1800." Bulletin of Bibliography 32 (July-September 1975): 115-121, 132.

Hull, Gloria T. "Black Women Poets from Wheatley to Walker." Negro American Literature Forum 9 (1975): 91-96.

_____. "Rewriting Afro-American Literature: A Case for Black Women Writers." Radical Teacher (December 1977): 10-13.

Hull, Raymona E. "'Scribbling' Females and Serious Males: Hawthorne's Comments from Abroad on Some American Authors." Nathaniel Hawthorne Journal (1975): 35-58.

Hume, Robert D. "Marital Discord in English Comedy from Dryden to Fielding." Modern Philology 74 (February 1977): 248-272.

_____. "The Myth of the Rake in 'Restoration' Comedy. " Studies in the Literary Imagination 10 (Spring 1977): 25-55.

Ikuko Atsumi. "Five Modern Women Poets on Love. " Literature East and West 8 (March 1974): 58-75.

_____. "Modern Japanese Women Poets: After the Meiji Restoration. " Iowa Review 7 (Spring/Summer 1976): 227-237.

Irvine, Lorna Marie. "Hostility and Reconciliation: The Mother in English Canadian Fiction. " Ph.D. Dissertation, The American University, 1977.

Jaquette, Jane S. "Literary Archetypes and Female Role Alternatives: The Woman and the Novel in Latin America. " In Female and Male in Latin America: Essays, pp. 3-28. Edited by Ann Pescatello. Pittsburgh: University of Pittsburgh Press, 1973.

Jay, Carla. "Carol Grosberg on Lesbian Theater. " WIN (New York), 26 June 1975, pp. 15-17.

Jelinek, Estelle C. "Differences Between Women's and Men's Autobiographies. " Paper presented at the MLA meeting, New York City, December 1976.

_____. "Teaching Women's Autobiographies. " College English 38 (September 1976): 32-45.

Johnson, Eric W. "Modern Japanese Women Writers. " Literature East and West 8 (March 1974): 90-102.

Johnson, Gloria C. "Black Women and the Search for the Promised Land. " Paper presented at the 1976 Popular Culture Association in the South meeting. (Available from author, English Department, University of Tennessee, Knoxville, TN 37916.)

Johnson, Wendell Stacy. Sex and Marriage in Victorian Poetry. Ithaca: Cornell University Press, 1975.

Jones, Betty H. and Alberta Arthurs. "The American Eve: A New Look at American Heroines and Their Critics. " International Journal of Women's Studies 1 (January/February 1978): 1-12.

Joseph, Gerhard. "Review of Sex and Marriage in Victorian Poetry by Wendell Stacy Johnson. " Victorian Poetry 14 (Summer 1976): 165-168.

Journal of American Folklore 88 (January-March 1975): Special Issue on Women and Folklore.

Juhasz, Suzanne. " 'But Is It Poetry?' Critical Forms and Criteria for Recent Poetry by Women. " Paper presented at the MLA meeting, San Francisco, December 1975.

_____. "Form and Women's Autobiography. " Paper presented at the MLA meeting, New York City, December 1976.

_____. Naked and Fiery Forms: Modern American Poetry by Women, A New Tradition. New York: Harper & Row, 1976.

Justin, Dena. "From Mother Goddess to Dishwasher. " Natural History 82 (February 1973): 40-45.

Karlinsky, Simon. "Sexual Liberation Themes in Post-1905 Drama. " Paper presented at the MLA meeting, San Francisco, December 1975.

Katz, Phyllis B. "The Myth of Psyche: A Definition of the Nature of the Feminine?" Arethusa 9 (Spring 1976): 111-118.

Kedesdy, Deidre Ann Ling. "Images of Women in the American Best Seller: 1870-1900. " Ph.D. Dissertation, Tufts University, 1976.

Kellogg, Patricia Rossworm. "The Myth of Salome in Symbolist Literature and Art. " Ph.D. Dissertation, New York University, 1975.

Kenevan, Phyllis. "The Jungian Interpretation of the Feminine. " Frontiers: A Journal of Women Studies 1 (Fall 1975): 122-127.

Kennard, Jean E. "Victims of Convention. " Pacific Coast Philology 8 (1973): 23-27.

Kenney, Susan M. "A Room of One's Own Revisited. " University of Michigan Papers in Women's Studies 1 (June 1974): 97-109.

Kenzel, Elaine and Jean Williams. "Women in Literature, English, World Literature." ERIC, 1972.

Kerber, Linda. "The Republican Mother: Women and the Enlightenment--An American Perspective." American Quarterly 28 (Summer 1976): 187-205.

Kilson, Marion. "Women and African Literature." Journal of African Studies 4 (Summer 1977): 161-166.

Kishi, Masaki. "Images of Americans in Japanese Popular Literature." Journal of Popular Culture 9 (Summer 1975): 1-13.

Klaich, Dolores. Woman + Woman: Attitudes Toward Lesbianism. New York: Simon & Schuster, 1974.

Klinck, Anne Lingard. "Female Characterisation in Old English Poetry." Ph.D. Dissertation, The University of British Columbia, 1976.

Klinkowitz, Jerome. "Ideology or Art: Women Novelists in the 1970s." North American Review 260 (Summer 1975): 88-90.

Kolodny, Annette. "The Feminist as Literary Critic." Critical Inquiry 2 (Summer 1976): 821-832.

_____. The Lay of the Land: Metaphor as Experience and History in American Life and Letters. Chapel Hill: University of North Carolina Press, 1975.

_____. "Some Notes on Defining a 'Feminist Literary Criticism.'" Critical Inquiry 2 (Autumn 1975): 75-92.

Koltun, Elizabeth. The Jewish Woman: New Perspectives. New York: Schocken, 1976.

Konig, F. H., trans. "The Woman's Voice in Modern Norwegian Poetry." North American Review 257 (Spring 1972): 58-69.

Kraus, Willis Keith. "A Critical Survey of the Contemporary Adolescent-Girl Problem Novel." Ph.D. Dissertation, Southern Illinois University, 1974.

Kriegel, Harriet, ed. Introduction to Women in Drama. New York: New American Library, 1975.

Kuda, Marie J. Women Loving Women: A Select and Annotated Bibliography of Women Loving Women in Literature. Chicago: Lavender Press, n. d.

LaJoy, Maureen. "No Laughing Matter: Women and Humor. " Women 5, no. 1 (1976): 6-9.

Lander, Dawn. "Eve Among the Indians. " In The Authority of Experience, pp. 194-211. Edited by Arlyn Diamond and Lee R. Edwards. Amherst: University of Massachusetts Press, 1977; also published as "Women in the Wilderness: Tabus in American Literature. " University of Michigan Papers in Women's Studies 2, no. 3 (1977): 62-83.

Landy, Marcia. "The Silent Woman: Towards a Feminist Critique. " In The Authority of Experience, pp. 16-27. Edited by Arlyn Diamond and Lee R. Edwards. Amherst: University of Massachusetts Press, 1977.

Latt, David J. "Praising Virtuous Ladies: The Literary Image and Historical Reality in Seventeenth-Century England. " In What Manner of Woman: Essays on English and American Life and Literature, pp. 39-64. Edited by Marlene Springer. New York: New York University Press, 1977.

Lau, Joseph S. M. "Types of Friendship in Traditional Chinese Fiction. " Paper presented at the MLA meeting, San Francisco, December 1975.

Lee, Sonia. "The Image of the Woman in the African Folktale from the Sub-Sahara Francophone Area. " Yale French Studies 53 (1976): 19-28.

LeGates, Marlene. "The Cult of Womanhood in Eighteenth-Century Thought. " Eighteenth-Century Studies 10 (Fall 1976): 21-39.

Leggatt, Alexander. Citizen Comedy in the Age of Shakespeare. Toronto: University of Toronto Press, 1973.

Lesage, Julia. "Feminist Film Criticism: Theory and Practice. " Women and Film 1, nos. 5/6 (1974): 12-19.

Levin, Susan M. "The Great Spousal Verse: The Marriage Metaphor in English Romantic Poetry. " South Carolina Review 8 (November 1975): 5-12.

Levine, Richard A., ed. <u>The Victorian Experience: The Novelists</u>. Athens: Ohio University Press, 1976.

Lewandowski, Marylou. "Feminism and the Emerging Woman Poet: Four Bay Area Poets." Paper presented at the MLA meeting, San Francisco, December 1975.

Little, Judy. "Satirizing the Norm: Comedy in Women's Fiction." <u>Regionalism and the Female Imagination</u> 3 (Fall 1977 and Winter 1977-78): 39-49.

Livesay, Dorothy. "Women as Poets." <u>Room of One's Own</u> 1 (Spring 1975): 12-13.

Löb, Ladislaus. "Domestic Tragedy--Realism and the Middle Classes." In <u>The German Theatre: A Symposium</u>, pp. 59-86. Edited by Ronald Hayman. New York: Barnes & Noble, 1975.

Longerbeam, Larry Simpson. "Seduction as Symbolic Action: A Study of the Seduction Motif in Six Victorian Novels." Ph.D. Dissertation, George Peabody College for Teachers, 1975.

Loudin, Joanne Marie. "The Changing Role of the Comic Heroine in American Drama from 1900 to 1940." Ph.D. Dissertation, University of Washington, 1974.

Lovenheim, Barbara. "Female as Subject and Object in Literature: From Austen to Jong." Deland, Florida: Everett/Edwards, n.d. (Cassette no. 5315.)

Loya, A. "Poetry as a Social Document: The Social Position of the Arab Woman." <u>International Journal of Middle East Studies</u> 6 (October 1975): 481-494.

Lozar, Paula Marie. "The Virgin Mary in the Medieval Drama of England: A Psychoanalytic Study." Ph.D. Dissertation, University of California, Berkeley, 1974.

Lurie, Alison. "Fairy Tales for a Liberated Age." <u>Horizon</u> 19 (July 1977): 80-85.

McAlexander, Patricia Jewell. "The Creation of the American Eve: The Cultural Dialogue on the Nature and Role of Women in Late Eighteenth-Century America." <u>Early American Literature</u> 9 (Winter 1975): 252-266.

McCaffrey, Anne. "Hitch Your Dragon to a Star: Romance and Glamour in Science Fiction. " In Science Fiction, Today and Tomorrow, pp. 278-292. Edited by Reginald Bretnor. New York: Harper & Row, 1974.

McDonald, Margaret Lamb. "The Independent Woman in the Restoration Comedy of Manners. " Ph. D. Dissertation, University of Colorado, 1975.

McDowell, Margaret B. "The Children's Feature: A Guide to the Editors' Perceptions of Adult Readers of Women's Magazines. " Midwest Quarterly 19 (October 1977): 36-50.

MacEachern, Barbara. "Imperfect Chrysolites in Elizabethan Drama. " Paper presented at the MLA meeting, New York City, December 1976.

Machwe, Prabhakar. "Prominent Women Writers in Indian Literature after Independence. " Journal of South Asian Literature 12 (Spring-Summer 1977): 145-149.

Mackey, Mary. "Women's Poetry: Almost Subversive. " Small Press Review 3, no. 3 (1972): 17.

MacLean, Ian. Woman Triumphant: Feminism in French Literature 1610-1652. New York: Oxford University Press, 1977.

Maglin, Nan Bauer. "Discovering Women's Activist Fiction." University of Michigan Papers in Women's Studies 2, no. 2 (1976): 96-104.

_____. "Rebel Women Writers, 1894-1925. " Ph. D. Dissertation, Union Graduate School, 1975.

Malkin, Michael R. "The Dramatic Function of Matricide in the Greek Electra Plays. " Studies in the Humanities 3 (October 1972): 22-24.

Malmsheimer, Lonna M. "Daughters of Zion: New England Roots of American Feminism. " New England Quarterly 50 (September 1977): 484-504.

Malone, P. "Learning About Women in Junior High. " Chatelaine 48 (October 1975): 32.

Manning, Olivia. "Olivia Manning on the Perils of the Female Writer." Spectator, 7 December 1974, pp. 734-735.

Marcus, Steven. The Other Victorians: A Study of Sexuality and Pornography in Mid-Nineteenth-Century England. New York: Basic Books, 1974.

Mariah, Paul. "From Lesbos with Love." Margins no. 8 (October-November 1973): 8-14.

Marks, Elaine. " 'I Am My Own Heroine': Some Thoughts About Women and Autobiography in France." In Female Studies IX: Teaching About Women in the Foreign Languages, pp. 1-10. Edited by Sidonie Cassirer. Old Westbury, N.Y.: Feminist Press, 1975.

Marriner, Gerald L. "A Victorian in the Modern World: The 'Liberated' Male's Adjustment to the New Woman and the New Morality." South Atlantic Quarterly 76 (Spring 1977): 190-203.

Martin, Wendy. "Seduced and Abandoned in American Literature." Deland, Florida: Everett/Edwards, n.d. (Cassette no. 5301.)

Masinton, Martha and Charles G. Masinton. "Second-class Citizenship: The Status of Women in Contemporary American Fiction." In What Manner of Woman: Essays in English and American Life and Literature, pp. 297-315. Edited by Marlene Springer. New York: New York University Press, 1977.

Mason, Bobbie Ann. The Girl Sleuth: A Feminist Guide. Old Westbury, N.Y.: Feminist Press, 1975.

Mathews, Robin. "Le roman engagé: The Social/Political Novel in English Canada." Laurentian University Review 9 (November 1976): 15-31.

Matossian, Mary Kilbourne. "In the Beginning, God Was a Woman." Journal of Social History 6 (Spring 1973): 325-343.

Meagher, John Henry, III. "The Castle and the Virgin in Medieval and Early Renaissance Drama." Ph.D. Dissertation, Bowling Green State University, 1976.

Meldrum, Barbara. "Images of Women in Western American Literature. " Midwest Quarterly 17 (April 1976): 252-267.

Mercier, Michel. Le roman féminin. Paris: P. U. F. , 1976.

Merriam, Eve. "Poems They Never Let Us Read in School." Ms. (July 1975): 36-39. (Review of Bernikow's The World Split Open: Four Centuries of Women Poets in England and America, 1552-1950.)

Meyersohn, Mary Lea. "The Secret Garden: Infantilization of the Woman Writer. " Paper presented at the MLA meeting, New York City, December 1976.

Micheline, Hugues. "Le sommeil d'Adam et la création d'Eve dans la littérature hexamérale des XVIe siècles. " Revue de Litterature Comparée 49 (April-June 1975): 179-203.

Miles, Rosalind. The Fiction of Sex: Themes and Functions of Sex Difference in the Modern Novel. New York: Barnes & Noble, 1974.

Miller, James E. , Jr. "The Creation of Women: Confessions of a Shaken Liberal. " Centennial Review 18 (Summer 1974): 231-247.

Miller, Jeanne-Marie A. "Images of Black Women in Plays by Black Playwrights. " CLA Journal 20 (June 1977): 494-507.

Miller, Nancy K. "The Exquisite Cadavers: Women in Eighteenth-Century Fiction. " Diacritics 5 (Winter 1975): 37-43. (Review of Pierre Fauchery's La Destinée Féminine dans le Roman European du Dix-Huitienne Siècle 1713-1807: Essai de Gynecomythie Romanesque.)

Millstone, Amy Blythe. "Feminist Theatre in France: 1870-1914. " Ph. D. Dissertation, The University of Wisconsin-Madison, 1977.

Mitchell, Sally. "Implications of Realism: Four Stories from The London Journal. " Studies in Short Fiction 12 (Spring 1975): 145-154.

_____. "Sentiment and Suffering: Women's Recreational Reading in the 1860s." Victorian Studies 21 (Autumn 1977): 29-45.

Moore, Honor. Introduction to The New Women's Theatre: Ten Plays by Contemporary American Women. New York: Vintage Books, 1977.

Moorhead, Finola. "Goodbye Prince Hamlet: The New Australian Women's Poetry." Meanjin Quarterly 34 (June 1975): 169-179.

Mora, Gabriela. "Hispanic American Fiction and Drama Written by Women: Suggested Readings." In Female Studies IX: Teaching About Women in the Foreign Languages, pp. 138-144. Edited by Sidonie Cassirer. Old Westbury, N.Y.: Feminist Press, 1975.

Morgan, William W. "Feminism and Literary Study: A Reply to Annette Kolodny." Critical Inquiry 2 (Summer 1976): 807-816.

Morrison, Gayle. "A Look at Antifeminist Literature." World Order 9 (Spring 1975): 40-59.

Mosley, Mary Krehbiel. "Women in Fifteenth Century Cancioneros." Ph.D. Dissertation, University of Missouri-Columbia, 1976.

Moynihan, R. D. "Clarissa and the Enlightened Woman as Literary Heroine." Journal of the History of Ideas 36 (January 1975): 159-166.

Murray, Robert. "Mary, the Second Eve in the Early Suriac Fathers." Eastern Churches Review 3 (August 1971): 372-384.

Mussell, Kay J. "Beautiful and Damned: The Sexual Woman in Gothic Fiction." Journal of Popular Culture 9 (Summer 1975): 84-89.

Myers, Carol Fairbanks. Women in Literature: Criticism of the Seventies. Metuchen, N.J.: Scarecrow Press, 1976.

Myers, Mitzi. "Women in Eighteenth Century Fiction." Mary Wollstonecraft Journal 2, no. 1 (1974): 39.

Natov, Roni L. "The Strong-Minded Heroine in Mid-Victorian Fiction." Ph.D. Dissertation, New York University, 1975.

Nemes, Palau de. "El machismo en la literatura." Americas 26 (April 1974): 2-7.

Newton, Sarah Emily. "An Ornament to Her Sex: Rhetorics of Persuasion in Early American Conduct Literature for Women and the Eighteenth-Century American Seduction Novel." Ph.D. Dissertation, University of California, Davis, 1976.

Nichols, Marianna de Vinci. "Women on Women: The Looking Glass Novel." Denver Quarterly 11 (Autumn 1976): 1-13.

Niera, David. "The Treatment of Women in the Modern Portuguese Theater: A Rebel-Lion Against Traditionalism." Paper presented at the Kentucky Foreign Language meeting, April 1976. (Paper available from the author, SUNY Geneseo, Geneseo, New York 14454.)

_____. "The Widow and Second Marriage as a Theme in Classical Hispanic Letters." Paper presented at the Mountain Interstate meeting, October 1974. (Paper available from the author, SUNY Geneseo, Geneseo, New York 14454.)

Nilsson, Usha Saksena. "A Woman's Experience: Three Novels of Hindi." Journal of South Asian Literature 12 (Spring-Summer 1977): 11-18.

Novak, Maximillian E. "Margery Pinchwife's 'London Disease': Restoration Comedy and the Libertine Offensive in the 1670's." Studies in the Literary Imagination 10 (Spring 1977): 1-24.

Novak, Sigrid Scholtz. "The Invisible Woman: The Case of the Female Playwright in German Literature." Journal of Social Issues 28, no. 2 (1972): 47-57.

Nowak, Marion. " 'How to Be a Woman': Theories of Female Education in the 1950's." Journal of Popular Culture 9 (Summer 1975): 77-83.

Nye, Russel B. "The Novel as Dream and Weapon:

Women's Popular Novels in the Nineteenth Century. "
Historical Society of Michigan Chronicle 11 (Fourth
Quarter 1975): 14-16.

Oaks, Priscilla. "Don't You Cry for Me: Women in American Folk Song. " Paper presented at the MLA meeting,
New York City, December 1976.

Oates, Joyce Carol. "Black-Eyed Susans Pledge No Alle-
giance. " Ms. 4 (March 1976): 46, 79-80. (Review of
Washington's Black-Eyed Susans: Classic Stories By and
About Black Women.)

O'Brien, James A. "Expressions of Love in Japanese Poetry. " Paper presented at the MLA meeting, San Francisco, December 1975.

Okonkwo, Juliet I. "Adam and Eve: Igbo Marriages in the
Nigerian Novel. " Conch 3 (September 1971): 137-151.

"On Writing and Writers. " Los Angeles, California: Pacifica Tape Library, 1975.

O'Neill, John H. "Sexuality, Deviance, and Moral Character in the Personal Satire of the Restoration. " Eighteenth-Century Life 2 (September 1975): 16-19.

Orenstein, Gloria F. "Art History and the Case of the Women for Surrealism. " Journal of General Education 27
(Spring 1975): 31-54.

Overbury, Bertha Van Riper. "Collecting American Women
Authors. " Barnard Alumnae 62 (Spring 1973): 4-5.

Paden, William D. , Jr. , et al. "The Troubadour's Lady:
Her Marital Status and Social Rank. " Studies in Philology 72 (1975): 28-50.

Paglia, Camille Anna. "Sexual Personae: The Androgyne
in Literature and Art. " Ph.D. Dissertation, Yale University, 1974.

Palacio, Jean de. "La quête de l'Eden: Mary Wollstonecraft entre Milton et Rousseau. " Révue de Littérature
Comparée 49 (April-June 1975): 217-234.

Palmegiano, E. M. "Women and British Periodicals 1832-

1867: A Bibliography. " Victorian Periodicals Newsletter 9 (March 1976): entire issue.

Pannill, Linda Susanne. "The Artist-Heroine in American Fiction, 1890-1920. " Ph. D. Dissertation, The University of North Carolina at Chapel Hill, 1975.

Pappas, John J. "Women and Men in the Fiction of the New World: A Community of Sufferers. " CEA Critic 37 (May 1975): 28-29.

Parish, Margaret Holt. "Women at Work: Housewives and Paid Workers as Mothers in Contemporary Realistic Fiction for Children. " Ph. D. Dissertation, Michigan State University, 1976.

Payne, Alma J. "Woman Militant in The Arena of Benjamin Orange Flower. " In Popular Literature in America: A Symposium in Honor of Lyon N. Richardson, pp. 171-183. Edited by James C. Austin. Bowling Green: Bowling Green University Popular Press, 1972.

Pearson, Carol. "Loose and Baggy Monsters: Feminism in Novelistic Form?" Paper presented at the MLA meeting, New York City, December 1976.

_____ and Katherine Pope. "Toward a Typology of Female Portraits in Literature. " CEA Critic 37 (May 1975): 9-13.

Peckenpaugh, Angela. Margins no. 9 (December 1973-January 1974): 39-41, 64. (Review of Mountain Moving Day: Poems by Women.)

Pelckmans, Paul. "Salomé, une figure de l'Anima. " Revue des Langues Vivantes 42, no. 1 (1976): 25-36.

Perkins, Michael. The Secret Record: Modern Erotic Literature. New York: William Morrow, 1976.

Perloff, Marjorie. "Beyond The Bell Jar: Women Poets in Transition. " Paper presented at the MLA meeting, San Francisco, December 1975.

Perry, Ruth. "Women, Letters, and the Origins of English Fiction: A Study of the Early Epistolary Novel. " Ph. D. Dissertation, University of California, Santa Cruz, 1974.

Petschauer, Peter. "Femme et Philosophe." Eighteenth-Century Studies 9 (Winter 1975-76): 257-261.

Polukhina, Liana. "The Theme of Work in Literature." Soviet Literature no. 8 (1975): 129-141.

Pomerleau, Cynthia Stodola. "British Women Autobiographers Before 1800." Paper presented at the MLA meeting, New York City, December 1976.

Pomeroy, Sarah R. "Feminism in Book V of Plato's Republic." Apeiron 8 (May 1974): 33-35.

_____. Goddesses, Whores, Wives, and Slaves: Women in Classical Antiquity. New York: Schocken Books, 1975.

Portner, Ruth Lee. "A Study of Marriage in the English Novel." Ph.D. Dissertation, City University of New York, 1977.

Poulos, Steven Mark. "Feminine Sense and Sensibility: A Comparative Study of Six Modern Short Fiction Writers in Hindi and Urdu: Rashid Jahan, Ismat Chughtai, Qurratul-Ain Hyder, Mannu Bhandari, Usha Priyamvada, Vijay Chauhan." Ph.D. Dissertation, University of Chicago, 1975.

Pratt, Annis V. "The New Feminist Criticisms: Exploring the History of the New Space." In Beyond Intellectual Sexism: A New Woman, A New Reality, pp. 175-195. Edited by Joan Roberts. New York: David McKay, 1976.

Purdy, Strother B. "On the Psychology of Erotic Literature." Literature and Psychology 20 (1970): 23-29.

Radner, John B. "The Youthful Harlot's Curse: The Prostitute as Symbol of the City in 18th-Century English Literature." Eighteenth-Century Life 2 (March 1976): 59-64.

Rea, Charlotte. "Women for Women." Drama Review 18 (December 1974): 77-87.

_____. "Women's Theatre Groups." Drama Review 16 (June 1972): 79-89.

Redding (Karosi), Sherry. "Touching the Muse: The Politics of Lesbian Poetry." Paper presented at the MLA
meeting, New York City, December 1976.

Reed, John R. Victorian Conventions. Athens: Ohio University Press, 1975.

Reff, Theodore. "The Influence of Flaubert's Queen of Sheba
on Later Nineteenth-Century Literature." Romanic Review 65 (November 1974): 249-265.

Register, Cheri. "American Feminist Literary Criticism:
A Bibliographic Introduction." In Feminist Literary
Criticism, pp. 1-28. Edited by Josephine Donovan.
Lexington: University Press of Kentucky, 1975.

Reich, Pauline C. and Atsuko Fukuda, trans. "Japan's
Literary Feminists: The Seito Group." Signs: Journal
of Women in Culture and Society 2 (Autumn 1976): 280-
287.

Rexroth, Kenneth and Ikuko Atsumi. "The Women Poets of
Japan--A Brief Summary." In The Burning Heart:
Women Poets of Japan. New York: Seabury Press,
1977.

Reynolds, C. Russell. "The Santa Maria Egipciaca Motif
in Modern Brazilian Letters." Romance Notes 13 (1972):
71-76.

Rice, Nancy Hall. "Beauty and the Beast and the Little
Boy: Clues about the Origins of Sexism and Racism
from Folklore and Literature: Chaucer's 'The Prioress's
Tale,' Sir Gawain and the Green Knight, the Alliterative
Morte Arthure, Webster's The Duchess of Malfi, Shake-
speare's Othello, Hawthorne's 'Rappaccini's Daughter,'
Melville's 'Benito Cereno.' Ph.D. Dissertation, Univer-
sity of Massachusetts, 1975.

_____. "Women and Other Monsters: The Sin of Sexuali-
ty." Paper presented at the South Central MLA meeting, December 1975.

Rich, Adrienne. "Caryatid: A Column." American Poetry
Review 2 (May/June 1973): 10-11.

Richetti, John J. "The Portrayal of Women in Restoration

and Eighteenth-century English Literature. " In What Manner of Woman: Essays on English and American Life and Literature, pp. 65-97. Edited by Marlene Springer. New York: New York University Press, 1977.

Richmond, Velma Bourgeois. "Women as Critics: A Look to the Future. " CEA Critic 37 (May 1975): 20-22.

Richter, Donald C. "The Position of Women in Classical Athens. " Classical Journal 67 (October-November 1971): 1-8.

Richter, Linda K. "Roles of Women in Indian Magazine Fiction. " Journal of South Asian Literature 12 (Spring-Summer 1977): 81-93.

Robinson, Lillian S. Sex, Class and Culture. Bloomington: Indiana University Press, forthcoming.

Rodriguez-Luis, Julio. "An Interpretation of the Picaresque Novel from the Perspective of the Picara. " Paper presented at the MLA meeting, San Francisco, December 1975.

Rogers, Katherine M. "The Antifeminist Bias in Traditional Criticism. " ERIC, ED 101 362.

_____. "Misogyny in Literature. " Deland, Florida: Everett/Edwards, n. d. (Cassette no. 5328.)

Rogers, Pat. The Augustan Vision. London: Weidenfeld & Nicholson, 1974.

Rooke, Constance. "Feminist Literary Criticism: A Brief Polemic. " Room of One's Own 2, no. 4 (1977): 40-43.

Ross, Margaret Clunies. "Women in Early Scandinavian Myth and Literature. " Refractory Girl: Journal of Radical Feminist Thought nos. 13-14 (March 1977): 29-37.

Rossi, Lee D. "The Whore vs. the Girl-Next-Door: Stereotypes of Woman in Playboy, Penthouse and Oui. " Journal of Popular Culture 9 (Summer 1975): 90-94.

Rovira, Rosalina R. "La funcion de la mujer en la

literatura contemporánea española. " Explicación de textos literios 20 (1974): 21-24.

Rowse, A. L. Sex and Society in Shakespeare's Age: Simon Forman the Astrologer. New York: Scribners, 1974.

Rubaii, Sandra. "Women's Studies at the Community College. " College English 37 (January 1976): 510-517.

Ruby, Kathryn. "Chants, Parables, Sagas: New Books by Women Poets. " Ms. 5 (September 1976): 103-105.

Rudick, Michael. Western Humanities Review 30 (Winter 1976): 66-69. (Review of Kelly's Love and Marriage in the Age of Chaucer.)

Rudikoff, Sonya. "Psychoanalysis and Feminism. " Hudson Review 28 (Autumn 1975): 433-440.

Rule, Jane. Lesbian Images. Garden City, N.Y.: Doubleday, 1975.

Rupprecht, Carol Schreier. "The Martial Maid: Androgyny in Epic from Virgil to the Poets of the Italian Renaissance. " Ph.D. Dissertation, Yale University, 1977.

Rushing, Andrea. "The Image of Black Women in African Poetry. " Paper presented at the MLA meeting, New York City, December 1976.

_____. "Images of Black Women in Afro-American Poetry." Black World 24 (September 1975): 18-30.

Russ, Joanna. "Outta Space: Women Write Science Fiction." Ms. (January 1976): 109-111.

Ruthchild, Nancy M. "Lesbian Books: A Long and Painful Search. " Mother Jones 1 (April 1976): 63-65.

Sadoff, Dianne F. "Forms of Female Contrition: The Heroine in Women's Nineteenth-Century English Novels. " Paper presented at the MLA meeting, New York City, December 1976.

Sage, Lorna. "Women and Literature: The Case of the Active Victim. " Times Literary Supplement, 26 July 1974, pp. 803-804.

Sanchez, Rita. "Chicana Writer: Breaking Out of the Silence." La Cosecha: Literatura y la Mujer Chicana 3, no. 3 (1977): 31-37.

Santos, Nelly E. "La poesía hispanica del '900's escrita por mujeres (La problemática de la trascendencia historica de la mujer y su expresión poética en los dos ultimos cuartos de siglo). " Ph.D. Dissertation, University of Connecticut, 1973.

Sargent, Lyman Tower. "An Ambiguous Legacy: The Role and Position of Women in the English Eutopia." Extrapolation 19 (December 1977): 39-49.

Sargent, Pamela. Introduction to More Women of Wonder. New York: Random House, 1976.

_____ . "Women in Science Fiction." Futures 7 (October 1975): 433-441.

Scanlon, Leone. "The New Woman in the Literature of 1883-1909." University of Michigan Papers in Women's Studies 2, no. 2 (1976): 133-159.

Schafer, Edward H. "Dragon Ladies, Water Fairies, Fish Maidens, Rain Mothers, and Other Hybrid Creatures." Horizon 25 (Summer 1973): 104-109.

Schiff, Ellen Frankfurt. "From Stereotype to Metaphor: The Role and Image of the Jew in French, English and American Dramatic Literature, 1945-1974." Ph.D. Dissertation, University of Massachusetts, 1976.

Schlissel, Lillian. "Women's Diaries on the Western Frontier." American Studies 18 (Spring 1977): 87-100.

Schmitz, Betty. "Feminine Form(lessness): Phallic and Feminist Views of Female Creativity." Paper presented at the MLA meeting, New York City, December 1976.

Schmitz, Betty Ann. "French Women Writers and Their Critics: An Analysis of the Treatment of Women Writers in Selected Histories of French Literature." Ph.D. Dissertation, The University of Wisconsin-Madison, 1977.

Schneider, Suzanne. "The Heroine in Women's Cinema."

Paper presented at the MLA meeting, New York City, December 1976.

Schnorrenberg, Barbara Brandon. "Toward a Bibliography of Eighteenth-Century Englishwomen." Eighteenth-Century Life 1 (March 1975): 50-52.

Schulz, Elizabeth. " 'Free in Fact and at Last': The Image of the Black Woman in Black American Literature." In What Manner of Woman: Essays in English and American Life and Literature, pp. 316-344. Edited by Marlene Springer. New York: New York University Press, 1977.

Schulz, Joan. "Teaching Lesbian Literature: Will the Perfect Reader Please Stand Up?" Paper presented at the MLA meeting, New York City, December 1976.

Schumacher, Dorin. "Subjectivities: A Theory of the Critical Process." In Feminist Literary Criticism, pp. 29-37. Edited by Josephine Donovan. Lexington: University of Kentucky Press, 1975.

Schwartz, Narda L. Articles on Women Writers, 1960-1975: A Bibliography. Santa Barbara: American Bibliographical Center-Clio Press, 1977.

Seidel, Kathryn L. "The Southern Belle as an Antebellum Ideal." Southern Quarterly 15 (July 1977): 387-401.

_____. "The Southern Belle: Her Fall from the Pedestal in Fiction of the Southern Renaissance." Ph. D. Dissertation, University of Maryland, 1976.

Serlen, Ellen. "The Rage of Caliban: Realism and Romance in the Nineteenth-Century Novel." Ph. D. Dissertation, State University of New York at Stony Brook, 1975.

Shafer, Y. B. "Liberated Women in American Plays of the Past." Players Magazine 49 (Spring 1974): 95-100.

Shain, Merle. "Some of Our Best Poets Are Women." Chatelaine (October 1972): 48+.

Shainess, Natalie. "The Social Images of Women in Film." Deland, Florida: Everett/Edwards, n. d. (Cassette no. 5309.)

Shange, Ntozake. "Black Women Writing/Where Truth Becomes Hope/Cuz It's Real. " Margins no. 17 (February 1975): 50-54, 59-60.

Shapiro, Charles. "Women in Modern Jewish American Fiction. " Deland, Florida: Everett/Edwards, n. d. (Cassette no. 5320.)

Shaw, Sharon K. "Medea on Pegasus: Some Speculations on the Parallel Rise of Women and Melodrama on the Jacobean Stage. " Ball State University Forum 14, no. 4 (1973): 13-21.

Shaw, V. "Sisterly Sensibilities. " Times Literary Supplement, 4 March 1977, p. 234.

Sheeran, Joan Garner. "Women and the Freedom-to-Be in Selected Works of Schiller and the Romantics. " Ph. D. Dissertation, University of Minnesota, 1976.

Shinn, Thelma J. Wardrop. "A Study of Women Characters in Contemporary American Fiction 1940-1970. " Ph. D. Dissertation, Purdue University, 1972.

Showalter, Elaine. "Desperate Remedies: Sensation Novels of the 1860s. " Victorian Newsletter no. 49 (Spring 1976): 1-5.

_____. A Literature of Their Own: British Women Novelists from Brontë to Lessing. Princeton: Princeton University Press, 1977.

_____. "Review Essay: Literary Criticism. " Signs: Journal of Women in Culture and Society 1 (Winter 1975): 435-460.

Siefert, Susan Elizabeth. "The Dilemma of the Talented Woman: A Study in Nineteenth-Century Fiction. " Ph. D. Dissertation, Marquette University, 1974.

Skillman, Betty Lou. "The Characterization of American Women in Twentieth Century American Literature for Children. " Ph. D. Dissertation, Ohio University, 1975.

Skilton, David. The English Novel: Defoe to the Victorians. New York: Barnes & Noble, 1977.

Skinner, Veronica Mary Lowe. "Guenevere: A Study of Arthurian Legend." Ph.D. Dissertation, University of Massachusetts, 1976.

Slater, Philip E. "The Greek Family in History and Myth." Arethusa 2 (Spring 1974): 9-44.

Slung, Michele B. Introduction to Crime on Her Mind: Fifteen Stories of Female Sleuths from the Victorian Era to the Forties. New York: Pantheon Books, 1975.

Smith, Barbara. "Invisible Woman Teaches Invisible Literature: How It Feels to Teach Black Women Writers." Paper presented at the MLA meeting, New York City, December 1976.

Smith, M. Dwayne and Marc Matre. "Social Norms and Sex Roles in Romance and Adventure Magazines." Journalism Quarterly 52 (Summer 1975): 309-315.

Snider, Clifton. "Jung's Psychology of the Conscious and the Unconscious." Psychocultural Review 1 (Spring 1977): 216-242.

Somerville, Rose M. "The Future of Family Relationships in the Middle and Older Years: Clues in Fiction." Family Coordinator 21 (October 1972): 487-498.

Spacks, Patricia Meyer. Contemporary Women Novelists: A Collection of Critical Essays. Englewood Cliffs, N.J.: Prentice-Hall, 1977.

_____. Imagining a Self: Autobiography and Novel in Eighteenth-Century England. Cambridge: Harvard University Press, 1976.

_____. "Women's Stories, Women's Selves." Hudson Review 30 (Spring 1977): 29-46.

Sponsler, Lucy A. "Women in Spain: Medieval Law Versus Epic Literature." Revista de Estudios Hispánicos 7 (1973): 427-448.

Springer, Marlene. "Angels and Other Women in Victorian Literature." In What Manner of Woman: Essays on English and American Life and Literature, pp. 124-159. Edited by Marlene Springer. New York: New York University Press, 1977.

_____, ed. What Manner of Woman: Essays on English and American Life and Literature. New York: New York University Press, 1977.

Staib, Mary Pauline. "The Academic Woman in the American College Novel." Ph.D. Dissertation, Arizona State University, 1975.

Stamm, Therese Dolan. "The Grisette and the Lorette: Romantic Imagery of the Courtesan in Nineteenth-Century French Caricature." Paper presented at the MLA meeting, New York City, December 1976.

Stanford, Ann. "Images of Women in Early American Literature." In What Manner of Woman: Essays on English and American Life and Literature, pp. 185-210. Edited by Marlene Springer. New York: New York University Press, 1977.

Stanley, Julia P. "Uninhabited Angels: Metaphors for Love." Margins no. 23 (August 1975): 7-10.

Stanley, Margaret P. "The 'Protesta femenina' in Latin America." In Female Studies IX: Teaching about Women in the Foreign Languages, pp. 131-135. Edited by Sidonie Cassirer. Old Westbury, N.Y.: Feminist Press, 1975.

Steeves, Edna L. "The Girl that I Marry: Feminine Stereotypes in Literature." CEA Critic 37 (May 1975): 22-24.

Stepto, Robert. "I Thought I Knew These People: Richard Wright and the Afro-American Literary Tradition." Massachusetts Review 18 (Autumn 1977): 525-541.

Stilling, Roger. Love and Death in Renaissance Tragedy. Baton Rouge: Louisiana State University Press, 1976.

Stimpson, Catharine. "Women as Scapegoats." In Female Studies V, pp. 7-16. Edited by Rae Lee Siporin. Pittsburgh: KNOW, Inc., 1972.

Stock, Phyllis. "The Theory and Practice of Women's Education in Eighteenth-Century France." Eighteenth-Century Studies 2 (June 1976): 79-82.

Strauss, Sylvia. "Women in 'Utopia.'" South Atlantic Quarterly 75 (Winter 1976): 115-131.

Sukenick, Lynn. "On Women and Fiction. " In The Authority of Experience, pp. 28-44. Edited by Arlyn Diamond and Lee R. Edwards. Amherst: University of Massachusetts, 1977.

Sullerot, Evelyne. The History and Mythology of Love: Eight Centuries of Feminine Writing. Garden City, N.Y.: Doubleday, forthcoming.

"Symposium: Women and Tragedy. " Prairie Schooner 49 (Fall 1975): 227-236. (Participants include Lorraine M. Keilstrup, Betty Jochmans, JoAnna Lathrop.)

Taylor, Irene and Gina Luria. "Gender and Genre: Women in British Romantic Literature. " In What Manner of Woman: Essays on English and American Life and Literature, pp. 98-124. Edited by Marlene Springer. New York: New York University Press, 1977.

Temple, Joanne. "Women's Theatre Finds a Stage of Its Own. " Village Voice, 27 October 1975, p. 84.

Tilton, Helga. "Virgins and Other Victims: Aspects of German Middle-Class Theatre. " In Female Studies IX: Teaching About Women in Foreign Languages, pp. 180-186. Edited by Sidonie Cassirer. Old Westbury, N.Y.: Feminist Press, 1975.

Toth, Emily. "Dorothy Parker, Erica Jong, and New Feminist Humor. " Regionalism and the Female Imagination 3 (Fall 1977 and Winter 1977-78): 70-85.

_____. "The Independent Woman and 'Free' Love. " Massachusetts Review 16 (Autumn 1975): 647-664.

_____. "Myth and the Curse. " Paper presented at the South Central MLA meeting, December 1975.

_____. "Some Introductory Notes on Women Regionalists. " Paper presented at the MLA meeting, New York City, December 1976.

Toth, Susan Allen. " 'The Rarest and Most Peculiar Grape': Versions of the New England Woman in Nineteenth-Century Local Color Literature. " Paper presented at the MLA meeting, New York City, December 1976.

Trachy, Carole Law. "The Mythology of Artemis and Her Role in Greek Popular Religion." Ph.D. Dissertation, The Florida State University, 1977.

Trible, Phyllis. "Two Women in a Man's World: A Reading of the Book of Ruth." Soundings 59 (Fall 1976): 251-279.

Trudgill, Eric. Madonnas and Magdalens: The Origins and Development of Victorian Sexual Attitudes. New York: Holmes & Meier, 1976.

Tugusheva, Maya. "Diary of a Young Girl." Soviet Literature no. 3 (1975): 155-157.

Tuttleton, James W. " 'Combat in the Erogenous Zone': Women in the American Novel Between the Two World Wars." In What Manner of Woman: Essays in English and American Life and Literature, pp. 271-296. Edited by Marlene Springer. New York: New York University Press, 1977.

Ulrich, Laurel Thatcher. "Vertuous Women Found: New England Ministerial Literature, 1668-1735." American Quarterly 28 (Spring 1976): 20-40.

Vance, Birgitta. "The Great Clash: Feminist Criticism Meets Up with Spanish Reality." Journal of Spanish Studies: Twentieth Century 2 (1974): 109-114.

Vipond, Mary. "The Image of Women in Canadian Mass Circulation Magazines in the 1920's." Modernist Studies 1 (1974-1975): 5-14.

Voloshin, Beverly. "A Historical Note on Women's Fiction: A Reply to Annette Kolodny." Critical Inquiry 2 (Summer 1976): 817-820.

_____. "The Rise of the Common Woman: Domestic Novels with Orphan Heroines, 1847-1867." Paper presented at the MLA meeting, New York City, December 1976.

Wade, Gerald E. "The Spanish Woman and the Don Juan Figure." Reflexión 2 (1973): 97-100.

Walker, Cheryl. "Welcom Eumenides: Contemporary

Feminist Poets." Feminist Art Journal 2 (Winter 1973-74): 6-7.

Wallace, Ronald. "Alone with Poems." Colorado Quarterly 23 (1975): 341-353.

Waller, Claudia Joan. "The Opaque Labyrinth: Chiaroscuro and the Evolution of the Spanish American Novel." Ph.D. Dissertation, University of Miami, 1975.

Ward, Hazel Mae. "The Black Woman as Character: Images in the American Novel, 1852-1953." Ph.D. Dissertation, The University of Texas at Austin, 1977.

Washington, Mary Helen. "The Black Woman as Suppressed Artist in Fiction." Paper presented at the MLA meeting, New York City, December 1976.

Watson, Barbara Bellow. "On Power and the Literary Text." Signs: Journal of Women in Culture and Society 1 (Autumn 1975): 111-118.

Watts, Emily Stipes. The Poetry of American Women from 1632 to 1945. Austin: University of Texas Press, 1977.

Webb, Shawncey Jay. "Aspects of Fidelity and Infidelity in the Eighteenth-Century French Novel from Chasles to Laclos." Ph.D. Dissertation, Indiana University, 1977.

Welter, Barbara. Dimity Convictions: The American Woman in the Nineteenth Century. Athens: Ohio University Press, 1976.

West, Rebecca. "Women and Literature: And They All Lived Unhappily Ever After." Times Literary Supplement, 26 July 1974, p. 779.

Williams, Kristi Fayle. "The Idealized Heroine in Victorian Fiction." Ph.D. Dissertation, Brown University, 1975.

Williams, William Corey. "An Examination of the Relationship Between Solidarity and Adultery in Ancient Israel." Ph.D. Dissertation, New York University, 1975.

Wolf, Donna M. "Women in Latin American Literature." Room of One's Own 1 (Fall 1975): 73-83.

Women and Literature: An Annotated Bibliography, 3rd ed. Cambridge, Mass.: Women and Literature Collective, December 1976.

Women in Literature. Pleasantville, N.Y.: Education Audio Visual, 1976. (Filmstrip with sound.)

"Women in Modern Drama." Intellect 105 (May 1977): 388.

Young, Ann Venture. "The Black Woman in Afro-Caribbean Poetry." In Blacks in Hispanic Literature: Critical Essays, pp. 137-142. Port Washington, N.Y.: Kennikat Press, 1977.

Zahler, Leah. "Matriarchy and Myth." Aphra 4 (Summer 1973): 25-32.

Zamora, Bernice. "The Chicana as a Literary Critic." La Cosecha: Literatura y la Mujer Chicana 3, no. 3 (1977): 16-19.

Zapata, Celia de. "One Hundred Years of Women Writers in Latin America." Latin American Literary Review 3 (Spring-Summer 1975): 7-16.

Zastrow, Sylvia Verginia Horning. "The Structure of Selected Plays by American Women Playwrights: 1920-1970." Ph.D. Dissertation, Northwestern University, 1975.

Zimmerman, Bonnie. "The New Tradition." Sinister Wisdom 1 (Fall 1976): 34-41.